Foundations for African Theological Ethics offers an accessible and thoughtful guide to thinking about ethics in Africa. The approach is both biblical and practical and deals with many of the current challenges for Christianity in Africa. I can't imagine a more timely topic and James Nkansah-Obrempong is just the person to write it. This is an ideal text for theological students, pastors, and especially for lay Christians who wrestle with God's calling in contemporary Africa. Readers will be impressed both by the range of topics covered, from ecology and economics, to work and poverty, and by the clear and readable presentation of the method and biblical foundation for thinking and acting ethically.

William A. Dyrness
Dean Emeritus and Professor of Theology and Culture
Fuller Theological Seminary, Pasadena, California, USA

One of the greatest enemies of the modern African society is that it has tended to let her good things die out while it borrows from elsewhere wholesale. A more balanced approach to life in Africa would be "to maintain what is good in her, borrow the valuable from elsewhere and subject it all to the authority of Scripture".

This work passionately points us to some fundamental African values we must cherish, alerts us to some possible pitfalls if we borrow from the West wholesale, and establishes the Biblical foundation for establishing a truly African Christian ethics for the continent.

The work is not just left at the general principles of acceptable African Christian ethics but moves on to show how those principles apply to some concrete matters as we serve the African society, noting that such things as peaceful families and communities, strong economies and good governance will bring the change needed in the Africa of today.

With so many things going wrong in Africa while there is so much good to build on for much greater Africa, I can only wish that many will take time to read this work. Our inter-personal, inter-tribal and inter-ethnic conflicts contradict what the African society is traditionally, what it should be in view of Christian influence based on Scripture, and the good to emulate from elsewhere, especially the West. It is not enough to pray for better Africa. We must work at it. Reading this piece will stimulate the reader to that end. God bless Africa and help all of us to promote a culture of love and community and not one of self-interest and endless conflicts!

Samuel M. Ngewa
Professor of New Testament
Africa International University, Karen, Kenya

The book, *Foundations for African Theological Ethics* by Reverend Professor James Nkansah of Africa International University (AIU), Karen, Kenya is a master piece in current African theological ethical discourse. The author started off with a great burden which states: *I have come to the painful reality of lack of materials on ethics that integrates the African social, religious, cultural, and moral values with biblical and theological values.* He succeeded in integrating the cultural, moral, and social values from three contexts—Africa, Western and Biblical.

This book is well researched, well thought through, systematically organized and beautifully written. Though small in comparison, it contains all that is necessary for an African Christian, and indeed, any African to have a solid foundation in African Theological Ethics. As a theologian and social ethicist myself, this very author fascinates me with his style and approach which has effectively laid a solid foundation in theological ethics for African Christians. As I read this book through, I found it refreshing, informative, creative, innovative and yet critical of the products of theological ethics in Africa. The author synthesized and systematized his theological ethical reflection by drawing a lot from three very important traditions and sources, namely, African, Western and Biblical. The author demonstrated vast knowledge of these three great traditions. He also demonstrated his scholarship and skills in constructing a theological ethical foundation for use by Africans. With this synthesized, systematized and constructed theological ethical base, he then turned to use it to address, evaluate, analyze and critique the social ethical issues emanating from the pairs of select social factors as applied in Africa, the pairs of: politics and governance; economics and poverty; work and unemployment; righteousness/justice and morality; ethnicity and reconciliation; ecology and care of creation; culture and family and Biblical law and African Legal systems.

The significance of this book lies in its theological ethical methodology. The author rooted his synthesis, systematization and construction of theological ethics from the three traditions in the Triune God. The nature, attributes and the moral character of God are the primary foundation of theological ethics. This is what makes morality and ethics of character superior to all ethics at the level of outer acts and deeds.

I recommend this book to university and theological students, pastors, and all those who are interested in theological ethics discourse in Africa.

Yusufu Turaki
Professor of Theology and Social Ethics
Director of the Centre for the Study of Religion, Church and Society
Jos ECWA Theological Seminary, Jos, Nigeria

Foundations for African Theological Ethics

James Nkansah-Obrempong

MONOGRAPHS

© 2013 by James Nkansah-Obrempong

Published 2013 by Langham Monographs
an imprint of Langham Creative Projects

Langham Partnership
PO Box 296, Carlisle, Cumbria CA3 9WZ, UK
www.langham.org

ISBNs:
978-1-907713-16-3 Print
978-1-907713-85-9 Mobi
978-1-907713-84-2 ePub

James Nkansah-Obrempong has asserted his right under the Copyright, Designs and Patents Act, 1988 to be identified as the Author of this work.

All rights reserved. No part of this publication may be reproduced, stored in a retrieval system or transmitted, in any form or by any means, electronic, mechanical, photocopying, recording or otherwise, without the prior written permission of the publisher or the Copyright Licensing Agency.

Scripture quotations are taken from the Holy Bible, New Living Translation, copyright ©1996, 2004, 2007 by Tyndale House Foundation. Used by permission of Tyndale House Publishers, Inc., Carol Stream, Illinois 60188. All rights reserved.

British Library Cataloguing in Publication Data
James Nkansah-Obrempong.
    Foundations for African Theological Ethics
    1. Christian ethics--Africa.
    2. Africa--Religious life and customs.
    I. Title
    241-dc23
    ISBN-13: 9781907713163

Cover & Book Design: projectluz.com

Langham Partnership actively supports theological dialogue and a scholars right to publish but does not necessarily endorse the views and opinions set forth, and works referenced within this publication or guarantee its technical and grammatical correctness. Langham Partnership does not accept any responsibility or liability to persons or property as a consequence of the reading, use or interpretation of its published content.

Contents

Introduction 1
    Defining some key Terms 4
        Morality and ethics 4
        Principles and values 5
        Social ethics 5
        Character and virtues 6

PART 1

FOUNDATIONS FOR AFRICAN THEOLOGICAL ETHICS

Chapter 1 11
The Anthropological, Social, and Religious Foundations of African Ethics and Morality
    Introduction 11
    The nature of African morality and ethics 12
        Anthropological nature of African ethical values 12
        Social and humanistic nature of African ethical values 16
        Religious nature of African ethical values 19
    African moral values as bases for character development 22
    How character is developed 24
    The significance and implications of African ethical and moral values for Christian ethical reflection 28
    Conclusion 30

Chapter 2 31
Foundations of Western Morality/Ethics
    Introduction 31
    Religious and philosophical traditions and western morality .. 31
    The legacy of Protestantism and enlightenment 32
        Protestantism: its influence on Western morality/ ethics .. 32
        The enlightenment: its influence on Western ethics 33
    The nature of western ethical and moral values 36
    The influence of philosophical thought on western ethical theories 38
    Deontological or non-consequential approaches to morality .. 39
    Teleological or consequential approaches to morality 41
    Utilitarian theories of moral reasoning 42

  Character and virtue ethical theories/approaches................................45
  The relationship between the foundations of African and
   western ethics...46
  Significance and implications of the findings for Christian ethical
   reflection in Africa...48
  Conclusion 48

Chapter 3...51
 Human Nature and the Moral Life
  Introduction 51
  African views of human nature and its impact on morality................52
  Western views of human nature: the idealist and humanistic views
   of human nature and their impact on morality........................54
   The idealists view of human nature and its impact on morality....55
   The humanistic view of human beings and its impact
    on morality..59
  The Biblical views of human nature 62
   Old Testament view of human nature 62
   New Testament views on human nature....................................62
   The impact of Adam's sin on human nature 63
  Human beings possess corrupt and sinful nature............................64
  The implications of biblical view of humanity for morality 65
  The corruption of sin in the "inward being" makes the
   moral life impossible 67
  The indwelling sin in the human body makes the
   moral life impossible 69
  Conclusion 71

Chapter 4...73
 Foundations for Biblical and Theological Ethics: Old Testament
  Introduction 73
  The foundations of biblical and theological ethics 73
  The nature and character of Old Testament ethics and morality..........74
   The theological nature and character of Old Testament ethics.......75
  Biblical ethics was grounded on the authority of God's laws/word
   not in human reason 80
  The social nature of Old Testament ethics/morality............................83
  The relational nature of Old Testament moral laws and ethics............85
  The eschatological nature of Old Testament ethics 88
  Conclusion 89

Chapter 5 91
The Nature and Character of New Testament Ethics and Morality

- Introduction 91
- The nature and character of New Testament ethics...............................91
  - The nature and character of Jesus' ethics 91
- Theological themes that form the foundation for Jesus' ethics 93
  - Jesus' ethics as kingdom ethics 93
  - Jesus' ethics as family ethics...95
  - Jesus' ethics as the ethics of imitation 96
- Theological themes that shaped Paul's Ethics.......................................97
  - The Christological ground for Paul's moral indicative 97
  - The Christian's union with Christ and the moral Life 98
  - The theological and Christological grounds for Paul's moral imperatives 101
  - God's mercies as foundation for Paul's ethical imperative in Romans 12:1–2 103
  - The Spirit as foundation of Paul's ethics 106
- The indicative and imperative relations to eschatology and the Spirit... 107
- The community of God as a moral community................................110
- Nurturing and cultivating virtues as the critical component of New Testament ethics..112
- Character transformation as goal for biblical ethics 113
- Conclusion 113

Chapter 6 115
Integrating African, Western, and Biblical Ethical Norms/Values for African Theological and Social Ethics

- Introduction 115
- Methodological implications of the indicative and imperative for African theological social ethics/morality...118
- Triune God: Model source and power for the Christian's moral life...119
- The Spirit as Power for the Ethical Life 120
- Indicative and imperative: Having a Proper Balance.........................123
  - Dangers in emphasizing only the indicative 123
  - Dangers in emphasizing only the imperative...............................124
- The indicative and imperative framework: Hermeneutical implications for morality and ethics...126
  - The primacy of a Christian counter-community and discipleship 126

Character as the moral engine for both African, western and
biblical ethics..130
Theological Ethics: African, Western and Biblical Principles
and Values 132
Conclusion 134

PART 2
CONTEMPORARY SOCIAL AND ETHICAL ISSUES

Chapter 7 137
Politics and Governance
Introduction 137
Defining politics and governance 139
Understanding politics and governance in contemporary African
societies..141
Human nature and its influence on politics and governance 141
The African colonial legacy: its cultural, social, and moral values
that shaped African political morality and governance..................144
African legacy: the religious and cultural values that shaped the
African's perception of power...147
The moral roles, character, and responsibility of leaders/kings in
African societies..149
The moral role and responsibility of kings/governments in the Bible... 151
The moral character of the model king and his responsibilities...151
The moral implications of the ideal king for political practice
and governance 155
Governance as stewardship, empowerment and partnership
with God..160
Conclusion 164

Chapter 8 165
Economics and Poverty
Introduction 165
Modern economic systems and its values..166
God the Economist...171
God is the source of all economic resources......................................173
Jesus and economics..174
Defining poverty...178
Causes of poverty..179
Dealing with poverty in contemporary western and African societies... 182
Welfare systems in the west..182

  Caring for the poor in African societies—community and
  human solidarity..183
 The Biblical mandate to care for the poor..184
  The role and the responsibilities of the rich in society towards
  the poor..184
   The proper use of wealth and treatment of the poor in society ...185
 Biblical models for just economic relationships, poverty alleviation,
  and economic empowerment..188
 Responding to economic injustice and poverty in Africa 191
  Empowering the poor to create wealth through dignified
  hard work 191
  Developing just economic policies to aid poverty reduction........195
 Conclusion 196

Chapter 9 197
Work and Unemployment
 Introduction 197
 Defining work..198
 Some contemporary misconceptions about work 199
 Work is important 202
 God: the moral and theological foundation for human
  engagement in work..205
 The tediousness and ambiguity of work..207
 The value and dignity of work..211
 The rights and responsibilities of employers 213
  Provide right and just conditions for work..................................213
  Just and timely payment for services rendered............................214
  Give adequate rest to workers 214
  The rights and duties of employees 215
 Work creation is our human responsibility as co-creators with God ...216
  The role of governments to provide work for citizens 216
  The place of educational institutions to train citizens to be
  entrepreneurs...217
  The place and role of the Church: creating opportunities for
  its youth and its advocacy role 217
  The place and role of a labor organization to ensure job
  security for citizens 218
 Conclusion 219

Chapter 10 221
Righteousness, Justice, and Morality
 Introduction 221

    African understanding of righteousness and justice 222
    Modern Western definitions and understandings of righteousness
        and justice 224
    Biblical understanding of righteousness and justice 226
        Righteousness in the Old Testament 227
        A summary of the meaning of righteousness in the
        Old Testament 232
    Righteousness in the New Testament 233
        Righteousness in early Christianity: its Jewish and Greek
        influence..233
        Righteousness in Paul 234
    Biblical understanding of justice 235
        Jesus and justice in the New Testament.......................................237
        Who's justice, God's or human justice? 238
    The mandate to reflect God's character in our behavior in society 240
    God demands righteousness and justice from all human beings
        especially leaders..241
    The theological and biblical notions of righteousness and justice:
        implications for Christian social moral vision..............................243
    Conclusion 245

Chapter 11 247
Ethnicity and Reconciliation
    Introduction 247
    Defining ethnicity...248
    The reality of ethnicity in Africa..251
    Ethnic diversity: A blessing or a curse? 253
    Theological and biblical foundation for ethnic diversity 256
    The Cross is God's remedy for ethnocentrism....................................258
    Triune God as model for equality and respect for humanity 260
    Reconciliation and forgiveness: God's solution to ethnocentrism
        and exclusion..261
        Reconciliation and forgiveness as the grounds for embracing
        and accepting one another 261
    Our mandate: Humanity is given the ministry of reconciliation
        and forgiveness...264
    Some practical suggestions for dealing with ethnocentrism 268
    Dealing with ethnicity and ethnocentrism in Africa: some biblical
        values and principles..270
    Conclusion 271

Chapter 12 273
  Ecology and Care of Creation
    Introduction 273
    Defining ecology and environment 274
    The moral dilemma: the ecological crisis in Africa 275
      Human values and the ecological crisis 275
      Religious beliefs and the ecological crisis......................278
      Responding to the ecological and environmental crises 281
    African cultural, religious, and moral values shaped their ethics for
      creation care 282
      The solidarity of all life with creation 282
      Creation and all life are sacred 283
    Western ethical approaches to creation care.........................285
      Eco-justice approaches to environmental ethics...........285
    Creation care: theological and biblical grounds 289
      Theological grounds...289
      Biblical grounds for the theological affirmation..........293
    Humans and creation restored and reconciled 296
    Creation care: Some practical principles..............................298
      The individual level..298
      The community level 299
      The national level..299
      Church and pastoral level 301
    Conclusion 302

Chapter 13 303
  Culture and Family
    Introduction 303
    Culture and its role in creating values and shaping morality 304
    Evaluating our cultural values 308
    The place and role of family in African cultures.................310
    African family values under attack by western ideological,
      cultural, and moral values...313
    Family as the primary place for building strong relationships
      and moral values...316
    Biblical foundations for family and its role in shaping the moral life ... 318
    Creating godly and responsible families for society............321
    Modeling the Fatherhood of God in the family...................324
    Some practical suggestions and principles we need to apply to curb
      the incipient ideologies threatening family life in Africa 325
    Conclusion 327

Chapter 14 329
    Biblical Law and African Legal Systems
        Introduction 329
        The nature of law and order: Some definitions 330
            The rule of law..331
            The relationship between law and religion 332
            The relationship between law and morality/ethics 334
            The role, function of law and order in traditional
            African societies 336
        Restoration and reconciliation as a goal of the African
            justice systems 337
        The African modern legal systems: Its problems 339
        The role, function, and purpose of the biblical law in society 341
            The role of biblical laws in society..............................341
            The functions and purposes of biblical laws 343
        The scope and extent of biblical laws..................................345
        The administration of justice and the moral character of its officers...347
            The need for local/traditional courts 347
            The character of law enforcement agents....................348
        Creating just and righteous legal systems............................350
        The necessity to uphold law and order in society...............353
        Some basic biblical principles and values we need to apply to
            improve our African legal systems...............................355
        Conclusion 360

Bibliography...361

Introduction

Morality is central to the life of every community or society. Any society that ignores this important issue as central to its life will crumble and destroy itself. It is very important for us to discuss this important topic to ensure we have a stable and vibrant society that is making a difference to the wellbeing of its people.

Every community or society has beliefs and moral values that govern its life and ethos. These beliefs and values explain the moral behavior of that society. Our ethical decisions and choices are made based on our convictions about how we perceive God, the world, and ourselves. At the core of these convictions are our biblical, religious, social, moral, and cultural values that shape our character and behavior. What shape the African moral life are its culture, social, religious beliefs, and moral values. Any ethics we envisage as African Christians must take into consideration the moral values that have shaped the African moral life.

As a lecturer teaching Ethics in Africa for the last nine years, I have come to the painful reality of lack of materials on ethics that integrate the African social, religious, cultural, and moral values with biblical and theological values. A survey in the discipline grossly ignores the rich moral and ethical heritage from the African socio-cultural context. Although most of the people who have written on morality in Africa mention the critical place African cultural, social, and moral values play in shaping the moral stance of African ethics, yet, none of the writers has consciously used these materials in their writings. There is also lack of solid theological grounding for morality and ethics in Africa.

This book has integrated the cultural, moral, and social values from three contexts—African, western, and biblical. I have argued these values are very important foundations for dealing with the contemporary moral and social issues facing the church in Africa and African societies.

The lack of solid theological and biblical foundation for ethical reflection has left the books on African ethics weak. Most ethical reflections have focused on decision-making rather than the moral agent. More importantly, the book shifts emphasis from ethics as a discipline of decision making to one of character formation. Recent ethicists are moving in this direction. Most of the current books written by Africans have not taken the issue of character in ethical discourse seriously. I believe there are theological and biblical grounds for this move.

Though the book addresses different social issues, it has one central thesis. The triune God is the model and source for the moral life. Theological and biblical ethics have its focus on radical discipleship that focuses on character formation. Biblical ethics has its grounding on God's relationship with humanity through his decisive act of redemption of humanity and creation. Humanity must therefore respond in loving obedience to his laws and reflect his character and being in all areas of its life and activities. Therefore, reflecting God's character is primal for Christian ethics.

This single thesis runs through the entire book, especially they are the foundations for our ethical response to the moral and social issues I address in part 2 of the book. There I apply the model of our identity as God's people to reflect his character and nature by drawing on the biblical and moral values that reflect God's character and nature as foundation to respond to specific contemporary social issues facing Africa. I have attempted to integrate the cultural wisdom—enshrined in African proverbs, values, ethical concepts, western ethical theories, and values, with biblical values and principles to address these ethical issues.

Part 1 of the book lays the theoretical, biblical, and theological foundations for Theological Ethics. This section explores three contexts. Chapter 1 deals with the cultural, religious, social, and moral values that shape African morality. Chapter 2 deals with those cultural, social, and moral values that shaped western morality. Chapter 3 addresses the critical issue of human nature and its effect on morality. This is a biblical and theological critique of both African and western views of human nature and its role in morality. Chapters 4 and 5 deal with biblical and theological foundations for Christian social ethics. Chapter 4 deals with the Old Testament and chapter 5 deals with the New Testament. Chapter 6 affirms the indicative and imperative framework as theoretical foundation for Christian social ethics. The triune God's character and being is the basis for biblical ethics and it is based on God's relationship to his people as Creator and King. Humanity's ethical response to God's acts in redeeming humanity is to reflect his nature and character. Building on this theoretical foundation, I draw some critical principles and values from these contexts as important values that are essential for our ethical reflections on the issues I address in part 2 of the book.

Jesus' teaching that Christians are salt and light in the world is a metaphor that speaks of our identity as people who are expected to reflect the values and ideals of God to influence the moral life of society. The notion to influence society with godly and biblical values is based on who we are, as salt and light. Therefore, who we are is very essential to our moral life. We contest the notion that undermines character as essential vehicle for moral life. In addition, we reject the assumption by some that one can live the moral life by sheer human efforts. I have argued humanity's sinful nature makes such a moral life impossible.

Part 2 addresses some contemporary ethical issues facing the continent of Africa generally, but specifically to the Church in Africa. These issues are different from the normal ethical issues like abortion, corruption, euthanasia, etc, that we find in most ethics books in Africa. The issues addressed in this book deal with broader social moral issues that affect the socio-political and economic life of African people and the church. I will address these issues drawing from the principles and values developed in part 1 of the book. Before I delve into our discussion, I need to define some key terms in this book.

Defining some key Terms

Morality and ethics

Ethicists tend to differentiate ethics and morality. Ethics is more theoretical, it is viewed as a branch of philosophy. It is often understood as moral philosophy. Ethics relates to the study of the right and the good. *The Webster's World Dictionary* defines ethics as "the study of standards of conduct and moral judgment; code of moral of a particular person, group, religion or profession, etc."[1] Clark et al say, "Ethics is the study of morality. Ethics is the philosophical and theological analysis of morality"[2] The word ethics comes from the Greek *ethos*, which means character. Ethics seems to refer to the "individual character of a person or persons." If ethics is theoretical, morality is more "specific and practical," it describes the actual "living out what is right and good." The word morality comes from the Latin *moralis*, which means custom, manners, or habits. Morality points to "the relationships among human beings."[3] It relates to behavior or conduct where a person is able to distinguish between right and wrong in conduct. A moral person is one who conforms to the general accepted standards of goodness or rightness in conduct. It is often associated with sexual conduct.

In normal life, we often use the words ethical and moral or unethical and immoral interchangeably. We speak of a person who is moral and ethical as one whose actions or behavior is good and unethical and immoral if one's behavior is bad. Traditionally, we use the word immoral mostly in relations to sexual behavior. "Morality is the dimension of life related to right conduct or behavior." Our ethical and moral language includes words like good, bad, right, and wrong. What are the relations of these words to each other?

---

[1] Victoria Neufeldt, ed. *Webster's World Dictionary*, Third College Edition. New York, Webster's New World, 1991, 466.
[2] David K. Clark and Robert V. Rakestraw. *Readings in Christian Ethics: Volume 1: Theory and Method.* Grand Rapids, MI: Baker Books, 1994, 18.
[3] Jacques P. Thiroux, *Ethics: Theory and Practice*, 2nd edition. Encino, CA: Glencoe Publishers Co., Inc., 1997, 2.

Based on the meaning of the two words and popular use of the terms in everyday language, we will use the terms ethics and morality interchangeably in this book. This will help to connect faith and practice, theology and ethics. I will use morality, ethics to mean a person whose behavior is aligned with his/her character, and they are not in opposition to each other.

Principles and values

Principles are broad general guidelines that all people everywhere are to follow. They are fundamental truth, law, doctrine, or motivation, force upon which orders are based."[4] These principles become the guide for people to make moral choices that the community or society consider important for their social life and coherence. They are a body of rules that people must follow.

Value on the other hand, relates to something that has worth for a person. I will define value as the worth of a thing, the quality of a thing. What a person value will be something that s/he cherishes, and it has a special significance in the life of that person. It is related to the "good." Value is inherent, or intrinsic or relational, extrinsic to a thing or person.[5] In its ethical sense, it is the social values or principles, goals, or standards held or accepted by an individual, class, society to govern their practices and conduct. I will use the words values and principles as the fundamental religious beliefs, philosophy, traditions, cultural, social, moral, standards, principles, and body of rules that guide the behavior of a community. Such values reflect one's passions and perceptions, solicit total loyalty, guide the way we reason and inform our basic convictions on moral matters.[6]

Social ethics

Social ethics lays the foundations for us to live harmoniously in community or society. Immoral behavior threatens the wellbeing of society. Due to

---
4 Neufeldt, ed. *Webster's World Dictionary*, 1070.
5 Nicholas Dent, "Value" in *The Oxford Companion to Philosophy*, ed. Ted Hendrick. Oxford: Oxford University Press, 1995, 895.
6 Glen Stassen & David Gushee, *Kingdom Ethics: Following Jesus in Contemporary Context*. Downers Grove: InterVasity Press, 2003, 59.

its social implications, ethics is always social in nature. Our communities shape our moral life. In addition, we all have a social responsibility to our communities. Social ethics are defined by societal and cultural norms or values. Most of our social ethics today are driven by our cultural and moral values. However, it is the Christian story and God's character that give grounds for our social ethics. God's moral laws have implications for our social live. Our Christian values based on God's character and nature form the basis for our Christian social moral vision. The goal of our moral vision as Christians is to transform the moral values and lives of people in our societies to reflect the divine will. I will use social ethics in this book to mean the social implications of God's blessing to us as humanity and our moral obligation to society to promote its wellbeing and shalom.

Character and virtues

Character comes from the Greek *Charakter*, which was a mark impressed on a coin. It later came to mean a distinctive mark, trait, quality, attribute, and a pattern of behavior or a person's personality by which a thing or a person is distinguished from others. Character entails a comprehensive set of ethical and intellectual dispositions of a person. It is the distinctive qualities or set of qualities that make somebody or something distinctive from the other.[7] It is an essential part of a person's nature. It is pivotal to the moral life. "Virtues are the qualities of a person that make that person a good person in community, and that contributes to the good of the community, or to the good that humans are designed for. They are qualities of character."[8] Virtue describes one's character while virtues are specific qualities linked to a person's actions.[9] Character and virtues are related. Virtues give concrete form to character. Virtue involves "attitudes, intentions, desires, the inner will, an inner disposition to act in beneficent ways."[10] I will use character

---

[7] Michael J. Meyer, "Character" in Robert Audi, ed., *The Cambridge Dictionary of Philosophy*, 2nd ed. Cambridge: Cambridge University Press, 1999, 129–130.
[8] Stassen, *Kingdom Ethics*, 32.
[9] Stanley Hauerwas, "Virtue" in *Readings in Christian Ethics*, 249
[10] A, F. Holmes, "Goodness," in *New Dictionary of Christian Ethics and Pastoral Theology*, David J. Atkinson & David H. Field, eds. Downers Grove, InterVarsity Press, 1995, 413.

and virtue as the inner qualities and traits patterned after God's character that are essential for the moral life. The Bible encourages us to develop character and virtues that are necessary for the moral life.

I will now look at African ethics by exploring its nature, character and the religious, cultural, social, and moral values that gave its shape and meaning.

Part 1

Foundations for African Theological Ethics

CHAPTER 1

The Anthropological, Social, and Religious Foundations of African Ethics and Morality

Introduction

When one looks at ethics books written by Africans on African morality or ethics, it is often difficult to see how much of African moral, cultural, and religious values these authors use as basis for developing African ethics. Often times the authors would mention the role African traditions, cultures, and religion play in African morality. However, one is disappointed to find any of these values consciously used or applied to the subject of African ethics and morality. We hope we can correct this shortcoming by attempting to address the problem by asking the questions: What shapes and forms the basis of African morality and ethics? What are some of the religious, cultural, and moral values that shape African morality? In this chapter, we will develop the thesis that African cultural, religious, and moral values are central to African morality. In our attempt to answer the above questions and support our thesis, we will explore the nature of African ethics; examine some of the African cultural and moral values that shape African morality, and what we can learn from the African moral and ethical traditions as we reflect on African Christian ethics and morality. We will begin by looking at the nature of African ethics and morality.

The nature of African morality and ethics

As we look at African morality and ethics, it is important to ask the question, what is African morality like? What cultural, moral, and religious values give shape to African morality and ethics? To answer these questions we will like to look at three schools of thought that scholars hold about the nature of African ethics. These can be classified as:
- The anthropological nature of African ethical values (cultural values)
- Social and humanistic nature of African ethical values (moral values)
- Religious nature of African ethical values (religious values)

The diagram below will illustrate these schools of thought. We will look at each value in turn.

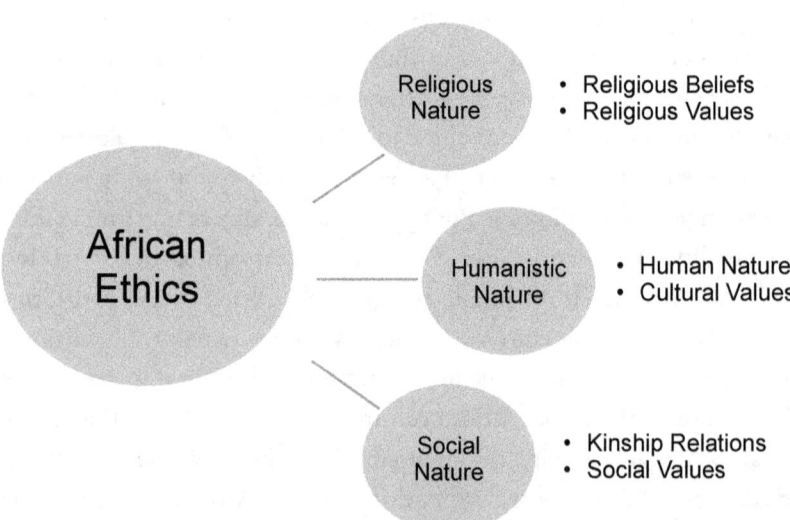

Anthropological nature of African ethical values

African moral values are largely based on cultural values expressed through traditions and customs. One of the central African cultural values is the human being. Human beings occupy a central place in the African universe after God, the divinities and the spiritual forces. The value placed on the human being explains why he is put at the center of life. Africans value people! This centrality of humanity's position in creation becomes a critical determinant factor in African morality. The African moral life consists in seeking the wellbeing of one's fellow human being. Any activity that disrupts this fundamental goal is considered reprehensible in the community. Some of the central cultural values that are deemed valuable and cherished are community, hospitality, solidarity, harmony, cooperation with other human beings, and respect for elders just to mention a few. These values shaped all the relationships and moral responsibilities that the community expected her members to embrace and live out within the society.

Central to these cultural values are the traditions, taboos, mores, proverbs, and customs that have developed over the years as the people interacted with each other and lived together. To ensure the community's survival and wellbeing, the leaders of these communities developed rules and regulations that ensured their safety and wellbeing of the people.

African scholars such as Kudadjie and others, who have written on African ethics and morality, have rightly observed that African morality has been shaped by African cultural values, traditions and customs.[1] These traditions are enshrined in their customs and taboos and they form the bases for the moral laws of the people of the particular community. These traditions, customs, and taboos are expressed by cultural values such as hospitality, purity, integrity, solidarity, honor and shame, respect for the elderly, and many others. These cultural values are foundational for the behavior of individuals and the community as a whole.

The traditions or cultural values are binding on every member of the community. Members of the community have moral duty or obligation to ensure they follow the traditions. The community punished any member of the community who violated the moral laws set out in the traditions. Traditions served as strong moral sanctions for the community's

---

[1] Kudadjie does not rule out religion as not having any place in African morality. He admits that religion does play a role in people's behavior, but it is not the primary motivation for morality in Africa. The primary motivation for morality for him is traditions and customs.

behavior. The laws and traditions determine one's behavior in a particular situation. Thus, the whole idea of right and wrong actions is based on what Kudadjie describes as "communal spirit"[2] or what we call solidarity or the "*ubuntu*" philosophy.

The essence of this methodological framework for ethics is anthropological; that is, it focuses on human customs and traditions. The human person is at the center of this kind of ethics. Human beings become the measure and focus of all ethical action. Moral decisions are made for the good of the human person and for the good of the whole community. African writers point out the anthropological nature of African ethics. Mbiti says African morality is on "man-on-man level rather than on the God-to-man plane of reality."[3] Although they believed God is behind the moral laws, it is nevertheless, the human ancestors and the deities who see to it that the moral laws are kept. On this Mbiti writes:

> Even if…God is thought to be the ultimate up-holder of the moral order, people do not consider Him to be immediately involved in the keeping of it. Instead, it is the patriarchs, living or dead, elders, priests or even divinities and spirits who are the guardians or police of human morality.[4]

Commenting on Akan morality, S.G. Williamson makes a similar statement. He says, "The customs and traditional ways of life sanctioned by the spirit-ancestors and the gods provided the framework of the Akan ethical code."[5] Again, we note from Williamson's statement the anthropological nature of African ethics. Its focus is on humanity's wellbeing. Its sanction has its force on the authority of the ancestors, elders, and leaders of the

---

[2] See J.N. Kudadjie, "Does Religion determine Morality in African Society? A View Point" in *Religion in a Pluralistic Society* ed. J.S. Pobee, Leiden: E.J. Brill, 1976, 60–77, especially page 76; Joshua W. Sempebwa, *African Traditional Moral Norms and Their Implication for Christianity* St. Augustine: Stelyter Verlag, 1983.

[3] J.S. Mbiti, *African Religions and Philosophy* London: Heinemann, 1969, 214.

[4] Mbiti, *African Religions*, 213.

[5] The Akans are the largest ethnic group in Ghana. See B.G. Williamson, *Akan Religion and the Christian faith* Accra: Ghana Universities Press, 1955, 108–109.

society. It is important to note at this point the religious dimension of African ethics and morality. We will say more about this later.

In assessing the essence of African morality, Mbiti suggests that it is more "societary" than "spiritual." The values of the community play a central role in shaping the morality of people. The behavior of a person in community is critical. This understanding of morality tends to ground morality in one's "conduct." Good behavior is mandatory in the community. Any person who goes against the moral ethos of the community is described as deviant or immoral.

Some scholars see "society," not the ancestors as the real enforcer of the moral laws. Society puts pressure on its members to conform to its norms and rules without which they will face some sanctions. People conform to moral norms out of societal pressure not because of their own character. Thus, the kind of behavior found in African communities is a "forced" behavior. While this may be true, it is the view of the author that character plays a critical role in African ethics and morality. We will demonstrate this later on in the chapter.

This particular understanding of morality by African ethicists and advocates of traditional religions is based on the African's view of the nature of humankind. These scholars believe "human [kind] by nature is neither good nor bad except in terms of what he does or does not do." This understanding of human nature according to Mbiti is a "necessary distinction to draw in discussing the African concepts of morality and ethics."[6]

The implications of this thinking are that human beings are potentially good in their nature and therefore are able to make good moral choices. What corrupt their behavior might be the environment and the things they learn from society. People shift blame often to society for the moral failures of its members rather than putting the blame on the moral agent who is responsible for his or her actions.

The central issues Mbiti and Kudadjie have raised, namely, African morality is a morality of conduct rather than a morality of being, that

---

6 Mbiti, *African Religion*, 214. The point Mbiti is making here is very crucial in developing a Christian ethic. We will take up a full discussion of this in chapter 3.

humanity is neither good nor bad, and that morality is enshrined in traditions and customs, would be contested by other African scholars. These scholars would agree with their basic argument that tradition and customs play a critical role in determining African moral behavior but will reject their assertions that character has nothing to do with African morality and that what makes a person good or bad depends on what they do or do not do.

While this may be true to some extent, it is not entirely the case. While these sentiments may be true, it is important to note that character formation is very central to the moral upbringing of children in African societies. We think character development determines people's behavior and that people are by nature sinful and as sinful human beings, it is human nature to do evil and do what is not right. It is precisely because human beings have the tendency to do what is not right that society created laws.

African families spend time teaching their children moral values and virtues at home, as they grow. The children develop some character traits and virtues when they are young. We think these taught cultural and moral values lay the foundation for their behavior in society as adults. These character traits play a major part in shaping their behavior. The societal influence and the anthropological focus as we have shown in this section have led other scholars to describe the nature of African ethics as social and humanistic.

Social and humanistic nature of African ethical values

The Ghanaian philosopher Kwame Gyekye argues that African morality is not founded on traditions and customs but is based on "social rules and norms." These rules and norms form the basis of conduct for the people of that society. The particular rules and norms are derived from what constitute right and wrong conduct or good and bad character in a particular society.[7] It this sense, "morality is intrinsically social," it is meant to foster "harmony and cooperative living" within a given community. It seeks the "interest

---

7 Kwame Gyekye, *African Cultural Values: An Introduction.* Accra, Ghana: Sankofa Publishing Company, 1996, 55.

of others," and commands a "sense of duty to others." Moral values are forms or patterns of conduct considered worthwhile and cherished by the society. These moral values become the goal of social and individual actions.[8] Gyekye points out African scholars fall into the temptation to believe that African moral values are founded on religion. These scholars assume that African

> Moral values of good and bad, or right and wrong derive from the commands of some supernatural being or beings, and their moral beliefs and principles can be justified only by reference to religious beliefs and doctrines. This view of the religious basis of African moral values is greatly mistaken.[9]

Gyekye's basic argument is that since African traditional religions are not revealed religions, Africans could not have access to God's commandments as basis for their moral system. Rather, their form of morality derives from "natural religion arising out of people's own experience and view of the world."[10] African morality is therefore, "naturalistic," it is "embedded in or arising out of, human existence in the natural world."[11] He concludes,

> African moral values derive from the experiences of the people in living together, or in trying to evolve a common and harmonious social life... The moral values of African people have social and humanistic bases, rather than a religious basis and are fashioned according to the people's own understanding of the nature of human society, human relations, human goals, and the meaning of human life.[12]

---

8 Gyekye, *African Cultural Values*, 55.
9 Gyekye, *African Cultural Values*, 56.
10 Gyekye, *African Cultural Values*, 56. By natural religion, Gyekye is referring to natural revelation as opposed to "revealed" revelation.
11 Gyekye, *African Cultural Values*, 56.
12 Gyekye, *African Cultural Values*, 57.

Some of these moral values include social solidarity, cooperation, community, generosity, compassion, and hospitality. We can see the overlap of these moral values with the cultural values I mentioned earlier. They serve a social goal to maintain the wellbeing of society.

The importance of the value of community and solidarity in African morality rule out any form of individualistic and egoist ethical tendencies found in many of the western cultural and ethical values. These communal values—"sharing, mutual aid, caring for others, interdependence, solidarity, reciprocal obligation, and social harmony"—"underpin and guide the type of social relations, attitudes, and behavior that ought to exist between individuals who live together in a community, sharing a social life and having a sense of common good."[13]

The members of the community have the moral responsibility to promote and advance the common shared values, interests, and goals of the community. Their loyalty to these common values is mandatory; they must seek the wellbeing of the community and not just their individual goals. Selfishness is not a value that is acceptable in African cultures. In fact, there are so many stories exposing the folly of selfishness. Any person who is insensitive to the needs and feelings of others and only thinks of himself or herself is not admired in the society. The values of cooperation, solidarity, reciprocity are very important values for the community. There are social mechanisms to ensure that people do not become perpetually dependant on the generosity of the community.

We will now turn to one of the critical issues in our discussion, that is, the place and role of religion in African morality. Is religion central to African morality? To what extent is religion the foundation for African morality? What are some of the religious values that give shape to African morality? It is very important we address this issue if we will attempt to develop African Christian ethics that is biblical and theologically grounded.

---

13 Gyekye, *African Cultural Values*, 35.

Religious nature of African ethical values

The scholars we have mentioned earlier on, Kudadjie, Mbiti and Gyekye, although they do not think the primary foundation for African morality is religion, nevertheless, they admit that religion can not be detached from African morality. In fact, Mbiti is on record by his well-quoted statement; "Africans are notoriously religious." Religion, he thinks, permeates every aspect of their life, which includes their moral life! Both Kudadjie, who thinks traditions and customs rather than religion, forms the basis of African morality and Gyekye, who strongly argues that African ethics is intrinsically social and humanistic, admit that religion play a critical role in African morality. Gyekye, for example, claims the "African heritage is intensely religious." His assertion that, "the African lives in a religious universe: all actions and thoughts have a religious meaning and are inspired or influenced by a religious point of view"[14] is significant. If what he says is true, then one cannot dismiss the claim that religion is at the core of African morality. If truly all the actions, thoughts of Africans are inspired and influenced by religion, then the African's moral actions are inspired and influenced by religion as well.

Gyekye in fact admits that religion plays some important role in the moral lives of individuals and even society as a whole. Africans, he points out, hold God as the overlord and moral lawgiver of human society, and therefore, "religion constitutes part of the sanctions that regulates moral practice" although "the moral values of the African society did not derive directly from religion."[15]

Religion plays a critical role in the moral life of the African people as we find in the moral lives of people in other cultures. Gyekye asserts, "Religion provides sanctions for the moral obligations and responsibilities of the members of the community." Africans sometimes link

> Misfortunes suffered by individuals or groups as punishments
> for their unethical behavior; but they could also be warning

---

14 Gyekye, *African Cultural Values*, 3.
15 Gyekye, *African Cultural Values*, 57

that people ought closely to examine their moral behavior. The warnings embody moral rules and accepted norms of conduct. Religion controls conduct through the application of sanctions by the supernatural powers, which are accepted to see that proper conduct is maintained and rewarded and offenses punished.[16]

Religion therefore played a critical function in African moral practices. This is very important as we develop African Christian ethics. It shifts the emphasis of the foundation of ethics from anthropology to theology. God is the foundation and center of biblical and theological ethics not human being. Our overall thesis for part 1 of this book is to underline the theological nature of biblical ethics; God is the basis for the moral life. For Christian ethics, the cross is central to the moral life. We will discuss this in chapter 4.

What are the religious values that shape African moral life? What African morality strives for is goodness, wholeness, and purity, which are some of Africans' core religious values. These religious values have their source and foundation in God. An African maxim expresses this idea: "goodness is the prime characteristic of God." Goodness, the Bible affirms is the central nature and character of God. Here, goodness has dual essence. The meaning is a moral one. First, it reflects God's moral character as good as opposed to evil or bad. The second meaning of "good" depicts God's benevolence, generosity, and providence. He graciously and generously provides for all the material needs of his people including giving rain and fertility in people and for the land, averting misfortune and disasters as well as healing the diseases of people.

Other religious values include compassion, mercy, generosity, and kindness and being just. These virtues are seen as some of the character and nature of God, which humans must emulate in their relationships with other fellow humans. These religious values are foundational in the moral lives of African people. The extent to which they are applied in their

---

16 Gyekye, *African Cultural Values*, 17–18.

day-to lives depends on how much they have internalized these values in their personal lives. Vices are not encouraged. These include stealing, lying, suicide, immorality, killing, cheating, and laziness.

The concept of immortality of the human person was the religious motivation for the good life. The African want to live and do good so that at his or her death he can join the ancestors and enjoy a blissful life.

Africans believe God is a great moral lawgiver and that God gave all their moral laws to them. These beliefs are shared by other cultures outside of Africa as well. In this case, God is the source of all moral laws. These are reflected in the African traditional names given to God. For example, the Kikuyu of Kenya's name for God, *Ngai* means "He who divides." It has something to do with God's character of being just and fair in his distribution of resources. Elders who are given the moral responsibility to judge cases were to demonstrate the same character of God to be fair and just. In fact, these leaders are selected because of their impeccable character. God, therefore, is seen as the model of the moral life.

I think African theologians are more helpful to us when it comes to African morality more than African philosophers and secular scholars. Against the view that sees morality as originating from society, common sense, or experience, Idowu argues religion is at the core of African morality.

> Our own (referring to the Yoruba tribe) view is that morality is the fruit of religion and that to begin with, it is dependent on it. [Hu]man's concept of deity has everything to do with what is taken to be the worth of morality. God made humans; and He implants in him the sense of right and wrong. This is a fact, the validity of which does not depend upon whether man realizes and acknowledges it or not.[17]

The notion that religion underlines African ethics is a widely held view. This tends to give authoritative sanctions for these moral laws to be obeyed. They are not negotiable, as far as people are concerned. To violate them

---

[17] B. Idowu, *Oludumare, God in Yoruba Belief* London: Longmans, 1963, 145.

incur serious consequences from society, from the ancestors and from the gods or God depending on the seriously of the moral violations committed.

Secondly, the religious nature of African morality is expressed by the religious role ancestors play in African cosmology. In fact, there is a strong believe among African's that these ancestors are the custodians of the moral laws given to them by God. Their duty is to ensure the living adhere to these moral laws so it will turn out well for them. They are strict in demanding compliance to the moral laws. They punish any person who breaks the laws.

The ancestors themselves are examples in keeping the moral laws and the traditions and customs of the people. They are therefore human models or examples of the moral life. The living must emulate their upright, unselfish lives, their generosity, and uncompromised determination to see to the wellbeing of the community. The ancestors lived exemplary moral lives while they were on earth. They have left for the future generations a legacy to follow. Thus, the African religious beliefs in God and the ancestors provide religious sanctions for the moral obligations and responsibilities of the members of the community.

African moral values as bases for character development

In our previous sections, we asserted that African ethics is anthropological; it focuses on humanity's wellbeing. It is also social; it builds and nurtures social relationships that foster harmonious human relationships for the wellbeing of society in general. It is also religious. It has its basis on the moral laws given to the community by God, which are expressed by their traditions and customs. It has religious sanctions and builds on religious values such as love, goodness, mercy, purity, and so forth. In essence, the African ethical system pursues the wellbeing of the human person.

In addition, Africans cultures place a high premium on good character. Gyekye puts it succinctly: "Good character is the essence of the African moral system, the linchpin of the moral wheel."[18] A person's character plays a pivotal role in the quality of moral life one leads. What a person does emanates from his/her character. We can say that the motivation to do what is right and obey moral rules all depends on the quality of one's character. The same could be said of the person who break moral rules and do not have any urge to do what is right. Character is acquired and there is need to develop and nurture it. We will later show how this is done through some cultural activities and moral values taught by families to their children.

In the African ethical systems, what is morally good is what brings about human wellbeing. African morality is preoccupied with human welfare. In societies that thrive on "harmonious human relations, what is morally good is what promotes social welfare, solidarity, and harmony in human relationships."[19]

Some of the moral values that will enhance the wellbeing of society include "truth, truthfulness, faithfulness, dependability, loyalty, honesty, probity," "kindness, compassion, generosity, hospitality, kindness, benevolence to strangers and friends alike. The idea of truthfulness is capture in many African languages as "a single-tongue person."[20] Nobody would want to be a person who has a "double mouth."

In addition to the above, wisdom is one of African's priced values. It is required for guidance in good behavior. A counterpart to wisdom is courage. Young people learn wisdom from the elderly by watching and listening to them. Courage carries a moral force. A person may need moral courage to resist evil or to repudiate evil. Self-control is vital to keep the society in peace. All these values were critical for the moral life to ensure the community's wellbeing.

Love is another value that is central to the African moral life. Love is expressed through concern for others, and actions that bring peace, justice, dignity, respect, and happiness."[21] Children are taught to love others and

---

18 Gyekye, *African Cultural Values*, 65.

19 Gyekye, *African Cultural Values*, 57.

20 C. A. Ackah, *Akan Ethics: A Study of the Moral Ideas and the Moral Behavior of the Akan Tribes of Ghana*. Accra: Ghana University Press, 1988, 25.

21 Gyekye, *African Cultural Values*, 58.

share what they have with them when they have the opportunity to do so. Love is a central African cultural, social, and moral value. All people admire a loving person!

Other values include obedience and submission to authority, moral upbringing, obedience and respect, co-operation and mutual help, patience, contentment, justice, gratefulness, well doing, love of fellow humans, and self-control.

These values and virtues form the basis for character development in many African families. One of the central features of teachings that go into the training and upbringing of African children is to develop good character of the family members. These values are modeled for children through the family that serves as the primary source for moral training. The goal for teaching all these values and virtues are to develop the character of people so that when they grow up, these values would guide the way they behave and live meaningful and fruitful life in community and contribute the welfare of society.

Africa is a society of honor and shame culture. Every family would like to protect its family honor and good name. Whatever will bring shame to a family is avoided. Because of this honor and shame culture, the family will endeavor to uphold to high moral standards that bring a good name for the family within the communities in which they are part. Every member of the family is expected to behave in his/her relations with all persons, in such a manner that what s/he does will not bring discredit to the family.

How character is developed

African communities use various means to teach these moral values to develop character. One of the commonest ways is through stories. These stories carry some moral lessons that the family would like their children to have. Different communities use different stories. Among the Akan people of Ghana, the Ananse stories are the most popular. The Ananse is the proverbial Spider, whose ingenuity and craftiness is admired, but it often landed him in trouble. The stories were meant to help to instill certain attitudes, and moral responsibility that are essential for living and those attitudes and behaviors that need to be avoided because they will not help a person if they chose to follow that path. The stories encourage virtues to follow and vices to avoid. The merits and the consequences are clearly discerned from the stories.

Other means Africans use for moral training and development of character are naming ceremonies. For example, when a child is born to an Akans family in Ghana, the child is named on the eighth day after birth. The central feature of this ceremony or ritual is to teach the child about truth and honesty. Early in the morning on the eighth day, some few members of father and mother's families and some friends will gather in the parents' home. An elder will preside over the ceremony. We use drinks for this ceremony. However, before they are shared or drunk, the elder will carry the baby in his arms. Two glasses are placed before him, one half-filled with water and the other half-filled with alcoholic drink. He will say something like this:

> 'Baby, you are welcome to this world. Have a longer stay, just do not come, and exhibit yourself and return. Your mothers and fathers have assembled here today to give you a name. The name we are giving to you is Nana Kwame Amoako. We call you Kwame; because that is the day of the week, you were born. We are naming you after your grandfather Amoako. Your grandfather has gone to be with his ancestors, so we call you Nana. You must follow his good example. In view of this, come and put up a good moral behavior that reflects the good behavior of your ancestors. Again, we are attaching your father's name Nkansah-Obrempong to your name. Follow the footsteps of your father, come, study hard, and grow up to become a noble person.

> Then the elder will call the child's name given to him/her by the parents—Nana Kwame Amoako Nkansah-Obrempong and he will dip his finger in the water and puts it on the tongue of the child, saying, "When we say water, let it be

water." Then he will do the same calling the child's name and dipping his finger in the glass with alcoholic drink and put it on the tongue of the child and say "when we say drink let it be drink.'

He will repeat this three times after which the drinks are served. The meaning of this part of the ceremony is that the child is expected to learn above all else to speak the truth and be honest always. S/he should not mean water when s/he means alcoholic drink or vice versa. When s/he says water, let it be water, when s/he says drink let it be drink.' S/he should mean whatever s/he says and avoid falsehood, deceit, and dishonesty. As the child grows, this truth is emphasized and implanted in him or her that honest dealings with his or her fellow humans are imperative. The friends and other relatives present at the ceremony as witnesses also have moral responsibility to discipline the child when s/he is misbehaving at anytime.

Other occasions and events where these values and virtues such as patience, courage, respect, obedience to authority, social responsibility, and many others are emphasized are during rites of passage. African children are brought up to develop good character that will result in a virtuous living. Children trained to develop virtues such as honesty, self-control, generosity, patience, selflessness, respect for older persons are all considered very important character traits. Character formation is central to African moral training because "Character is seen as the engine of the moral life."[22]

While African ethics seeks to build up virtues that enhances human life, and promotes harmonious relationships with communities, bad acts that undermine human wellbeing, and promote strife, dissention and conflicts are discouraged and sanctions are placed on those who engage in such behavior. In African communities, these vices or acts include "backbiting, selfishness, lying, stealing, adultery, rape, incest, murder, and suicide." Some of these acts such as incest, suicide, rape, are considered taboos in African societies.

---

22 Gyekye, *African Cultural Values*, 176.

Other anti-social values or vices discouraged include falsehood, unfairness, insincerity, double-dealings, hypocrisy, ingratitude, ungratefulness, selfishness, self-interest, laziness, or tardiness, immorality that is often associated with dirt, or filthy life. Worthlessness, futility, useless things; adultery—taking somebody's wife, illicit sexual intercourse with a married person, witchcraft, greed, mischief against fellow humans, pride, strong character.

The communal values shared by African communities require "sharing, mutual aid, caring for others, interdependence, solidarity, reciprocal obligation, and social harmony."[23] Any individual living in the community and only thinks about him/herself is considered antisocial. Selfishness in not welcomed in African communities. African morality is communal and social. It is not individualistic. African ethics as Gyekye points out is "social and non-individualistic morality." It is preoccupied of the human wellbeing. As human communities, we are dependent on each other as expressed by an African proverb: "The left arm washes the right arm and the right arm washes the left arm."

Our exposition so far challenges the assertions made by some African ethicists that African morality is related to conduct and not to character is not valid. That a person is what he does and not what he is, is not true. At best on cannot give what one does not have. An African proverb says, "A crab cannot give birth to a bird." If a person is morally bankrupt, his actions will reflect that bankruptcy. Character or "being" therefore precedes doing. Character development is essential if we would develop any authentic ethics that will have lasting effects on society. We will see this as we examine the scriptures later on in chapter 4.

So far, we have outlined the nature of African ethics and laid out the values that have shaped African ethics and morality. The question we will like to address now is what significance does this have for our quest to develop African Christian ethics? Is there anything, principles, values, we can learn from the African moral traditions today. Our answer is affirmative. Let us

---

23 Gyekye, *African Cultural Values*, 35.

now sketch some of the significance and implications of our discussion for African Christian ethics.

The significance and implications of African ethical and moral values for Christian ethical reflection

As we conclude this chapter, we will like to underscore the significance of the African moral systems for Christian ethical reflection. Indeed, some important values have emerged from the discussions on African morality that are critical for Christian ethical reflection. First, the important role humanity occupies in the African ethical system is note worthy. The goal of African ethics is to enhance humanity's wellbeing. The social nature of African ethics and the focus on building strong social relationships should be taken very seriously in any Christian social ethics. The goal of our moral life should be to encourage and enhance strong social relationships. This is vital for a harmonious community.

This means any authentic ethics must promote and enhance our social lives and our obligations to each other as humanity. It means we need to give a lot of attention to community or social ethics rather than on personal ethics. This in not to say that personal ethics is not important, it is important. If ethics will have impact on communities and societies then we need to refocus our ethical ideal and values. We must ensure that communal moral values, goals, aspirations, and social well-being of society are not sacrificed in the name of individualism and personal ethics. We need to balance community well being and social welfare with individual wellbeing. We need to develop community values rather that personal values that we share together as humanity. These values then will be what govern and shape our moral life. This would help us build strong social ties where we have moral responsibility to each other within the human family.

The second element that comes out is the relationship between faith and practice, theology and ethics, religion and ethics. It is interesting to note even scholars who do not share the view that religion plays a critical role in African ethics could not dismiss the idea that religion is critical and central to African ethics. It will be important to emphasize the place of religion in ethics in a world where secularism and other ideological philosophies are challenging the place of religion in public life. There is only one moral lawgiver, God! All that we aspire to become morally will be an impossible task on our part without God. Our faith then must have huge implications for our behavior. This is the essence of biblical ethics. I will discuss this in chapters 4 and 5. Meanwhile the tension between ethics and religion will continue, but as Christians, we must be bold to assert the critical role religion has to play in our moral life.

Thirdly, if character is the engine of morality, then it is important that any ethical system we develop must think and reflect seriously on how character development must be encouraged. We should create space for its development in our homes, communities, and churches. It is interesting to note the similarities of the moral values that Africans hold on to with biblical values that are giving to us in Scripture. If these values are taught in African moral discourses, then, it underscores the importance of Christian discipleship where we seek to intentionally develop and build the character of Christians to develop Christian virtues that scripture teaches us to cultivate. What we are, have a lot to do with how successful we will be in living lives that are pleasing and honoring to God. As members of the family of God, we are to bring no shame to our family. We must uphold the honor of the family. Every act and behavior of all members must uplift the family dignity and integrity. Christian communities have a heavy obligation to discipleship.

Lastly, it is important to address the place of authority in Christian ethical and moral reflection. The moral responsibility to uphold traditions, customs, taboos, so there would be harmony and peace in communities are very important. Rules and values are important. We must affirm them and encourage society to uphold them for our own good. We live in a world where people are not so much comfortable with authority and they tend to undermine it. In a relativist society where there are no absolute, laws that must be binding on people, may become more difficult to enforce because most people may refuse to submit to authority. However, we all need to have some form of laws or rule to guide behavior so we can live in peace and in harmony with one another. Therefore, the issue of obedience and submission to authority is critical in any ethical system we would maintain and foster social cohesion. We must encourage and affirm all these important African cultural, moral, and religious values, and incorporated them in our ethical and moral formation and life of our Christian communities and society.

Conclusion

African ethics is anthropological; it focuses on humanity's wellbeing. It is also social; it builds and nurtures social relationships that foster harmonious human relationships for the wellbeing of society in general. It is also religious. It has its basis on the moral laws given to the community by God, which are expressed by their traditions and customs. It has religious sanctions and builds on religious values such as love, goodness, mercy, purity, and so forth. In essence, African ethical systems pursue the wellbeing of the human person.

We have also attempted to show the cultural, social, and religious values that has given shape to African morality and the importance of good character as foundational for African morality. Some these values include community, hospitality, integrity, truth, honor and shame, solidarity, respect for the elders, compassion, faithfulness, hospitality, generosity, dependability, honesty, justice and many others are values the Bible critically affirms. These must shape our ethical behavior.

The values we indicated have strong biblical foundations and we should endeavor to assimilate them in our African moral discourse. We must seek to encourage and promote these values. They must form the bases and foundations for moral training of our children. The truth is, they are intrinsic to the African life, and when affirmed, we can have a society that cares for one another and seeks the wellbeing of all.

However, these African cultural, social, and religious values are under attack from other external cultural and social values that are eroding these traditional moral values. Western cultural and moral values are exerting a lot of pressure on African morality. We will turn to this in the next chapter.

CHAPTER 2

Foundations of Western Morality/Ethics

Introduction

The nature and character of African morality and ethics are based on its religious, cultural, and social values. In this chapter, we will seek to explicate the nature and character of Western morality and ethics and the values that underpin its ethics. In doing so, we will examine some philosophical traditions and cultural values that have shaped western morality in the hope of understanding how people make ethical judgments and decisions and what inform those decisions and choices they make. First, we will explore some of the philosophical traditions that shaped western modern thought and moral perception; western cultural values; examine some theories of moral judgments and show the value and relationships between the foundations of Africa and western ethics.

Religious and philosophical traditions and western morality

Every ethical and moral system has some basic presuppositions and principles that underpin behavior of people. In this section, we will like to address the question "what are the fundamental philosophical and religious traditions that have given shape to western moral reflection? What is the nature and character of western ethics? What are the resultant values that gave shape to western moral practices? First, let us examine the religious and philosophical traditions that lay the foundation for western ethics. The diagram below will illustrate our point.

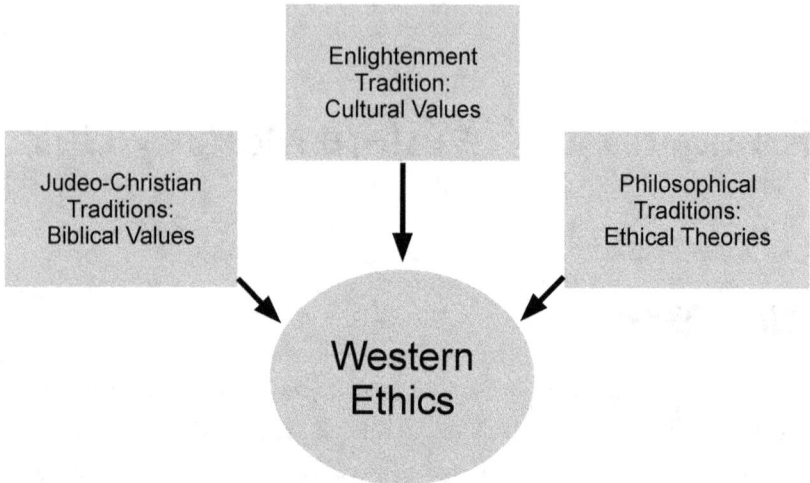

The legacy of Protestantism and enlightenment

Protestantism: its influence on Western morality/ ethics

Protestantism has played a major role in shaping western ethics. Medieval philosophies[1] gave birth to two theological systems, natural and revealed theologies. These philosophies sought to hold together reason and faith. Natural theology has its roots in classical Greek philosophy of Plato and Aristotle and revealed theology has its source in biblical revelation. Men like Anselm developed theologies that saw faith and reason as bedfellows. The Roman Catholic Church, which was the dominant church in the medieval era built, its moral theology from the works of Thomas Aquinas using both natural and revealed theology. Natural law's basic "premise is that human

---

1 See John Haldane, "Medieval and Renaissance Ethics," in *A Companion to Ethics* by Peter Singer, ed. Oxford, Blackwell Publishers, 1993, 134–142.

moral beliefs have a rational foundation, in the form of general principles of right conduct that reflect a determinate and rational human nature."[2]

The Reformation of Luther and the other reformers gave birth to the Protestant movement. This movement continued to emphasize the Bible as the sole foundation for Christian theology and for the moral life. The place given to the Bible as the authority in matters of faith and conduct is seen in most Protestant statements of faith today. The ethical life of the church, its moral responsibilities to the state, in dealing with economic, political, social matters were shaped by the biblical message given to us in Scripture. The Bible was central to the development of theology as well as morality and ethics. The reformers maintained a close link between theology and ethics. In fact, ethics was the natural outflow of theology. Faith and theology they maintained are intrinsically bound together.

The moral code for the Christian living was the Bible. For almost 300 years between the Reformation and the enlightenment, the ethical system in the west was based on the Christian Scriptures, which were largely based on biblical moral values and principles. How did the enlightenment change all that? We will now turn our attention to the enlightenment and the role it had on shaping the moral thinking and discourse in the west.

The enlightenment: its influence on Western ethics

If there is a single philosophical tradition that has shaped western thought in general and in particular morality, then is it the enlightenment philosophies of the 16th and 17th centuries. The modern secular outlook has its foundation in the rational enlightened philosophies of those centuries. These philosophies shaped western ethics. Two ideas characterized this period, namely, reason and scientific investigation of our world. During this period, there was a common belief that science could explain everything in our physical world in terms of causes. There was an underlying assumption of the rationality of the universe and the power of reason to understand it.[3] Reason, rather than faith was moved to the center of how people

---

2 Stephen Buckle "Natural Law" in *A Companion to Ethics* by Peter Singer, ed. Oxford, Blackwell Publishers, 1993, 173.
3 Colin Brown, *Philosophy and the Christian Faith: A Historical Sketch from the Middle*

come to know truth. The medieval beliefs in a Supreme Being, spirits, and supernatural forces were considered outdated beliefs. Humanity has become more rational and therefore has become of age.

The enlightenment gave birth to the idea of the "rational autonomous self." There was a revolt of "reason against religion, political and social authority." There was a strong sense to break away from traditionalism and all forms of authoritarian rule. What resulted in the end is a self-sufficient individual, who believes in her or himself and his or her selfish interest. Humanity became the measure of all moral good. Unlike the medieval and the Reformation eras where the scripture and tradition were the authority that governed the lives of the people, this was not so.

In what ways did the enlightenment influence western moral discourse? The enlightenment made a radical shift and put emphasis on humanity as the moral agency and not God. Humans became the measure and law to themselves. God was removed from the center of ethics. What they considered "law is not the expression of the mind of God, but of the will of the people."[4] What constituted right was a person's freedom, the individual's right to property, security, protection from violence, life, liberty, and happiness. The Bible's impact on morality diminished. Brown's observation is right: philosophy made the Bible irrelevant, and reason took over revelation.[5] Right and wrong became the judgment of the individual. There are no moral absolutes. All moral values are relative and have no moral binding on anybody. The authority of the Bible as the foundation for ethics was questioned and in some of the humanistic ethics that were developed later on, the proponents rejected the scriptures as the source for morality.

Enlightenment philosophies rejected the medieval and reformation theologies where they held faith and reason together. Reason became the primary source for "legitimacy" and "authority." However, in fairness to the philosophies of that time, we must say, "reason has its legitimate place

---

Ages to the Present Day. Dowers Grove, IL: InterVarsity Press, 1968, 48.
4 Brown, *Philosophy and the Christian Faith*, 39.
5 Brown, *Philosophy and the Christian Faith*, 44.

in science and everyday affairs. It has its true function in grasping and evaluating what was set before it." However, we must reject its notion that it is the sole criterion for truth.[6]

Through reason, philosophies at this time reached some moral values that were compatible with Christian moral teaching. By means of right reasoning these philosophies have discover the right way of acting and living. The scholars at the time believed human beings possessed "innate power of moral knowledge." Human beings are rational beings who think and can arrive at right conduct outside of revelation. The idea that human beings possess "moral faculty sense" by which humanity intuitively can discern what is right or wrong set the stage for rationalist and intuitionist theories of moral reasoning which became a dominant feature in western ethical systems. In this period, ethicists saw the human conscience as an innate faculty that revealed God's moral laws as these were imprinted on the human souls as one created in the image of God. Ethicists synthesized idea of virtues from Greek philosophies and their counterparts in Christian thought into a set of rational foundations to ethics.[7]

The moral thinking that developed because of the enlightenment is clearly articulated by Kant. This ethics was based on the assumption that the human being is a

> Free agent who bind himself through his reason to unconditional laws, it stands in need neither of the idea of another Being over him, for him to comprehend his duty, nor of an incentive other than the law itself, for him to do his duty.[8]

This assumption underpins many humanitarian ethics who claim to do their duty for its own sake. This ethics is motivated by the obligation one

---

6 Brown, *Philosophy and the Christian Faith*, 44.
7 Peter Singer, Ed. *A Companion to Ethics*. Oxford: Blackwell Publishers, 1993, 173 ff.
8 Quoted in Brown, *Philosophy and the Christian Faith*, 100.

feels, that it is right to love and serve others as themselves. This obligation is not dependent on circumstance and personal likes and dislikes.

Kant's ethical works influenced many ethical theories developed in the west by ethicist. Notably is his emphasis on "human freedom, the dignity of man, and to "the view that moral obligation derives neither from God, nor from human authorities and communities, nor from the preferences of desires of human agents, but from reason."[9] These are seen in modern universal principles for justice, the respect for persons and human rights. The enlightenment created some new cultural and moral, social, economical and political values, which became what defined the attitudes, behaviors, and aspirations of the people of the west. The import of that culture has influence the west ever since. The current postmodern and secular societies we find in the west with its rejection of objective truth, relativism, and no moral absolutes all have their roots in the enlightenment tradition. Let us now look at some of the cultural and moral values that emerged from the enlightenment.

The nature of western ethical and moral values

The enlightenment also provided a set of cultural values for the west as they rejected the aristocratic monarchies and traditions found during the medieval period. Some of the values have been mention earlier on. These values have at its core the individual person. As Lukes rightly asserts, "individualism is the common characteristic of Roman law and Christian morality."[10] The focus on the individual's autonomy underscores the humanistic nature of western ethics.

Individualism in the history of America has its source in Protestantism. The highest form of individualism in Protestantism is expressed theologically in the Reformation teaching of the "priesthood of all believers." The emphasis here lies not so much on the individual's ability to know truth

---

9 Onora O'Neill. "Kantian Ethics," in *A Companion to Ethics* by Peter Singer, ed. Oxford, Blackwell Publishers, 1993, 175.
10 Steven Lukes. *Key Concepts in the Social Sciences: Individualism*. Basil: Blackwell, 1073, ix.

but on his responsibility before God. Luther's emphasis of the individual standing before God because of personal faith is a classical illustration of the reformation's contribution to the development of individualism. Thus, individualism is seen as a product of the Reformation and the Renaissance. For both the Protestant and the Renaissance emphasized the autonomous individual.

Arieli has argued that, "Protestantism is the fountain of all modern religious and political liberty. It had broken the chains of authority and had engaged the human mind to a bold vindication of its own rights in opposition to all blind obedience of whatever kind."[11] He states further, "yet individualism was not the sovereignty of the individual over himself and the aborgation [sic] of all authority. True freedom required the individual to subject his will to the universal law of truth. Moral freedom recognized order as the true law of reason to which to subject itself."[12]

Bellah and his colleagues identified three other important core values that are central to the American culture, namely, success, justice, and freedom.[13] The authors purpose was to deepen Americans understanding of the various traditions that have shaped the American character which Tocqueville called "habits of the heart," and how these traditions provide or fail to provide Americans with solutions to the kind of moral problems facing Americans today.[14] They demonstrate how these three traditional values have contributed to shaping the concept of individualism in western society.

What underlies all the three basic values of the American people is individualism. Success is viewed in terms of the individual's ability to

---

[11] Yehoshua Arieli, "Individualism: A European Concept Crosses the Atlantic" in Donald Capps and Richard Fenn, eds. *Individualism Reconsidered: Readings Bearing on the Endangered Self in Modern Society* (New Jersey, Princeton Theological Seminary: Center for Religion, Self and Society), 22.

[12] Arieli, "Individualism" in Donald Capps and Richard Fenn, *Individualism Reconsidered*, 22.

[13] Robert Bellah et al, *Habits of the Heart*, 22–26. See William A. Dyrness, *How Does America Hear the Gospel* (Grand Rapids, Michigan: Wm. B. Eerdmans Publishing Company, 1989), 30. Here the author argues that American middle class is distinctively "philosophically pragmatic, temperamentally optimistic, and psychologically humanist."

[14] Bellah et al, *Habits*, 21.

amass wealth while justice is to provide equal economic opportunity to an individual to develop his or her potential. Similarly, freedom means to be your own person in the sense that you have to define who you are, decide for yourself what you want out of your life, and free from all possible form of coercion or conformity to family, friends, or community. Freedom then means, one must separate one's self from the values imposed by one's past or by conformity to one's social milieu, in order for one to discover what one really wants. Freedom is seen as one exercising control over his or her own life. The authors traced individualism to both Protestantism and republicanism. I think what these writers say about America is true for many western nations. The issue of freedom, success, competition, and justice are fundamental values in many western cultures.

How did reason, the enlightenment cultural values, and humanistic philosophies derived from the enlightenment influence and shaped modern ethical discourses in the west? We will examine some of the philosophical thinking that has influenced western ethical theories that are having influence on other cultures around the world today.

The influence of philosophical thought on western ethical theories

The ethical theories we will discuss below are attempts to answer some fundamental questions in ethics; what ought I to do? How do I live? These theories are applied to answer these fundamental questions. These theories form the part of ethics we call normative ethics. Normative ethics is concerned with guiding people's actions by way of norms or principles. In the history of ethics, two main approaches have emerged in terms of moral reasoning in the west: the nonconsequential or deontological and teleological or consequential. These theories are derived from and grounded on western cultural values. We will look at each approach below.

Deontological or non-consequential approaches to morality

The deontological approach to ethical reasoning derives it name from the Greek word "deon," which means "duty." It is often called "duty ethics." For example, Kant believed only acts done from duty are morally right. The basic question deontologists' address is what is right in itself? Deontologists believe morality is governed by moral rule that must not be broken even if doing so would bring better consequences. To find the right and to act on it from the motive of a purely good will is to walk the path of moral duty. For example, I must not lie. When I am confronted with temptation to do so, I sense the categorical imperative as a claim upon my will. I ought to tell the truth for truth's sake. With that pure motive, without self-interest, if I decide to tell the truth morality has prevailed.

Thus, for the deontologist, decision-making focuses on regulative principles, rules that establish the basic ground rules for action. Right or good action is determined by one's obedience to a set of rules or norms that regulates one's behavior. Actions are to be judged by their intrinsic good or bad not on the consequences they produce. One's action is good by obeying the rule irrespective of the consequences, which may not be in the interest and wellbeing of the individual involved. The law stipulates what is good and what is right. The law must be followed.

Action involves norms and rules, expectations of behavior that can be expressed as moral imperatives. The divine command theory is an example of deontological theories where God's commands are to be obeyed by human beings regardless of the consequences. What is good and right is what God has stated is good and right. The "law" is the proper form of formalizing this. What is fundamental is justice and fairness to others and these must takes priority over notions of human happiness and wellbeing. The theory asserts the minimum duties, the part one has to play in ensuring the wellbeing of the human community, the requisites of human life, the unbreakable limits set to action. Examples of institutions that use this reasoning are the courts of law. Christians use this kind of reasoning more often.

There are two categories of non-consequential or deontological theories: Act deontological and rule deontological. Act nonconsequentialist asserts there are no universal moral rules or laws. What exist are particular actions, situations, and people about which we cannot generalize.[15] What underlines act deontologist's decisions is "intuition." Since there are not general rules or laws to guide a person's actions, one depends on what one thinks or feels to be good or right. This intuitionistic approach to moral reasoning is individualistic at heart. It also reflects other ethical theories such as emotivism and noncognitive morality. Emotive moral theories state that ethical words and sentences do two things it expresses people's feelings and attitudes, and it evokes or generates certain feelings and attitudes in others.[16]

The second category of theories is the rule non-consequential or rule deontological. The rule deontological theory works on the assumption that there are basic rules that under girds morality. However, who determines the rules? Here rules are believed to have their source in a Supreme Being outside of the human person. In the Christian circle, all moral laws are attributed to God. The Bible provides the moral values Christian must follow. He sets the moral standards. These groups of ethicists are called rule-deontologists.

The deontological theories give proper place to rules and standards as the bases for morality. This makes it easier for people to know what they can do and what they cannot. People are not left to guess and figure out what they must do in a situation.

There are however some weaknesses that must be addressed: (1) Sometimes these laws are so abstract and remote from our everyday life that they do not make sense to the modern mind. The formal principle can never embrace concrete reality and there is the tendency is to introduce constantly more and more specific laws to deal with new moral issues. One becomes preoccupied with a mass of rules and deductions (and ceases to attend to the nature of what is actually going on). (2) There is the temptation

---

15 Jacques P. Thiroux. *Ethics: Theories and Practice*. Encino, CA: Glencoe Publishing Co. Inc. 1977, 57.
16 Stanley Grenz, *The Moral Quest: Foundations of Christian Ethics*. Downers Grove: InterVarsity Press, 1997, 51–53.

to assume the more concrete, specific sense of the principle (application) the more the principle is universal. (3) This might lead to legalism if it is not sensitive to the context that has given rise to the situation at hand.

Teleological or consequential approaches to morality

This term teleological comes from the Greek word *telos*, which means "purpose," "goal." The basic thrust of this approach is concerned about "result" or "consequences." A good moral decision is judged by the result or the consequences of the action. Consequentialists determine the rightness and wrongness of an act by its outcome. Consequentialists are concerned with actions that will bring about the greatest amount of good and the least amount of evil. This approach justifies principles or rules extrinsically. In every situation we find ourselves, one has to determine which course of action will result in the greatest balance of good over evil.

There are two key consequentialist approaches, namely ethical egoism and utilitarianism. They both agree that human being must act to bring about good consequences. The difference between the two theories has to do with the question about who is to benefit from the said moral action. The ethical egoist essentially says that human beings ought to act in their own interest while the utilitarian says that human beings ought to act in the interest of all concerned. For example, if Fifi has a chance to embezzle some public funds, if he is a consequentialist, he will try to predict the consequences of his action, which might be losing his job and going to prison and so, he will decide not to embezzle the money. If he is egoist consequentialist, he will try to predict what will be in his own interest and perhaps steal the money or not steal the money. He might reason that it will not be in his best self-interest to break the law, subject himself to punishment, or infuriate the government by his action. If he is a utilitarian consequentialist, he will try to predict what will be the interest of all the people concerned and not steal the money.

But, who's good should we seek to advance? The answer is my own. This approach to ethical decision is called ethical egoism. What is ethical egoism? It is not selfishness. For example, if this person is stabbing people in the back to advance his personal interests, everybody will hate him and this can become harmful to the egoist's self-interest. Ethical egoism is "a philosophical-normative, prescriptive theory."[17] Ethical egoism says each person's sole moral obligation is to advance the agent's own welfare. One always has to act in such a way to bring about the greatest amount of good over evil for one's self. Ethical egoists think first of their own long-tern rather than short-term interests. It is expressed in three basic forms. The first is universal egoism—The universal asserts everyone should always act in his or her own self-interest, while individual egoist thinks that everyone else should act in my self-interest; and the personal egoist avers that I ought to act in my own self-interest.[18]

Institutions that use this kind of consequentialists' reasoning are in the public, economic, and political arenas—especially in policymaking, business planning, and legislative actions of the governments.

While there are merits for people to think about the consequences of their actions and the effects it bring on themselves and others these theories have some problems or weaknesses that must be pointed out.

- The problem with this theory is that it uses people as means to achieve one's own ends. It also makes altruism often degenerates into self-promotion.
- It exaggerates our capacity to predict and control the results of our actions.
- It reduces the value realm to what is quantifiable.
- Some things are bad and others are wrong regardless of their consequences.

Utilitarian theories of moral reasoning

Jeremy Bentham (1748–1832) an English law student and John Stuart Mill (1806–1873) are the key proponents of this theory. The theory derives its name from "utility," which means "usefulness." The utilitarian believes an

---

17 Jacques P. Thiroux. *Ethics: Theories and Practice*. Encino, CA: Glencoe Publishing Co. Inc. 1977, 48.
18 Thiroux. *Ethics*, 48.

act is right or good if it is useful "in bringing about a *desirable* or *good* end."[19] This theory uses the principle of utility to determine the rightness and wrongness of an act. An act is right and wrong depending on the degree to which it is useful or harmful to the greatest good of individuals or a community. One has to ask the question with every action, does this particular action bring about the greatest good for the greatest number of people? If it will not, then it is not something one must do. If it is, then one must do it.

There are two main forms of utilitarianism: act utilitarianism and rule utilitarianism. "Act utilitarianism states that everyone should perform that act which will bring about the greatest good over bad for everyone affected by the act."[20] It is concerned not with rules as the basis for human action because they think each human situation is unique and different and each person is different. Each individual must assess the situation he or she is in and try to figure out what action would be the best to do to bring about the greatest amount of good consequences with the least amount of bad consequences, not just for him/herself, but also for everyone involved in the situation. This leaves the moral decision entirely on the discretion of the person involved. This position relativizes moral values.

> In assessing the situation, the agent…must decide whether, for example, telling the truth is the right thing to do in *this* situation at *this* time. It does not matter that most people believe that telling the truth is generally a good thing to do; the act utilitarian must decide for the particular situation he or she is in now whether or not it is right to tell the truth. In act utilitarianism, there can be no absolute rules against killing, stealing, lying and so on, because every situation is different and all people are different.[21]

---

19 Paul Taylor, Ed. *Problems of Moral Philosophy*, 2nd ed. Belmont, CA: Dickenson, 1972, 137.
20 Thiroux. *Ethics*, 49.
21 Thiroux. *Ethics*, 42.

On the other, rule utilitarianism postulates that everyone should always follow the rule or rules which will bring about the greatest number of good consequences for all concerned." It is based on the assertion that there are "enough similar human motives, actions, and situations to justify setting up rules which apply to all human beings and situations."[22] They think it is dangerous to leave moral action to individual discretion without giving them some form of guidance and set rules that will help bring order and stability to society. This could result in utter chaos.

This approach is also called situation ethics. The situation determines the rightness and wrongness of an action. For example lying may be right when lying will accomplish the greatest good for the greatest number of people than not lying.

Most western ethical systems see utilitarianism as alternative system for political and social action. Most public policies of many western nations are based on the principle of utility.

The problem with such an approach is the potential danger for the individual's rights and concerns to be discarded for the good of the community. It overrides the concern for justice for the individual. The other problem for this approach is the assumption of our ability to anticipate the results of our actions. We need to admit that we cannot anticipate all that will result from every act we make we will really know what balance of good over evil will ensue from those moral actions. We cannot determine all the consequences of our actions. That is impossible.

Others have found consequentialists, utilitarians, and the autonomous theories as inadequate to address the moral issues confronting our world today. There has been a shift toward community and virtue and character development as essential components for moral discernment in our day. We will now turn to this approach of ethical reasoning.

---

22 Thiroux. *Ethics*, 50.

Character and virtue ethical theories/approaches

The ethical theories discussed so far all focus on "doing" or "acting." So far, all of the theories fall under what we call ethics of doing. One of the shortcomings of normative ethics of doing is that it does not deal with attitudes and motivations from which actions spring. This is a very important aspect of the Christian's decision-making process. These theories construct a theory of moral obligations by focusing on human action. Morality of "moral duty," "obligation," and "what ought to be" are not tenable anymore in our present context. These theories ignore the important role character plays in morality. Many western ethicists are moving in this direction emphasizing the place of character as grounds for the ethical life.[23]

In our opinion, ethical decisions are best made because of who we are. Our being is the fountain from which our actions and behavior spring. This understanding of ethics is consistent with biblical ethics. We will deal with this later on in chapter 4. The locus of ethics then lies somewhere else; in who we are (ought to be) rather than in what we do. Of cause, we need to emphasize that what we are will determine what we do and what we do is always a reflection of what we are.

The ethical life is not primarily a function of the actions that people engage in but a function of the kind of people that engage in the actions. This understanding of ethics turns our focus from actions to character and virtue and speaks about actions that emerge from the virtuous person. Today many ethicists are abandoning the ethic of doing and searching for an ethic of character, virtue or being.

Ethics of being is concerned with what we should be or what we should prefer. The concept places conduct secondary to character. Conduct is important both as an expression of character and as a means in developing character. Ethic of being gives primacy to value judgments. Moral obligations are derive from judgments about motives, which are based

---

23 Stanley Hauerwas, *Character and the Christian Life: A Study in theological Ethics*. San Antonio: Trinity University Press, 1985, Stanley Hauerwas, *A Community of Character: Towards a Constructive Christian Social Ethics*. Notre Dame: University of Notre Dame Press, 1981, Alasdair MacIntyre, *After Virtue*, Notre Dame: University of Notre Dame Press, 1981, Glen H. Stassen and David P. Gushee, *Kingdom Ethics: Following Jesus in Contemporary Context*. Downers Grove: InterVasity Press, 2003.

on character traits or virtues, and integrity of the moral agent. The moral person is to develop certain character traits from which moral decisions are made. It is from this well of values, virtues that gives the basis for the actions of a person.

In summary, our discussion on normative ethics has led us to see how people today use the deontological, teleological or the utilitarian approaches to make ethical decisions. We see the emphases on these different approaches are different. While the deontological theories emphasize right actions, right traits, the teleological theories on the other hand emphasize on what is good, what we value as the basis for making ethical decisions. While the deontologists stress traits—that are virtuous, (from which one's actions spring) as well as rules, standards and principle that govern one's actions the Consequentialists stress values or desires. All however are concerned about the good of the person. They are concern about what is referred to as "the good life."

In normative ethics, the good life becomes the converging point for both the deontologist and the consequentialist. The good life then becomes the foundational principle of the moral life. Our conception of the ethical life is connected to our perception of the good life. The good life is the life of obedience to one's duty.

So far, we have explored the foundations of western ethical and moral systems and the values that shaped them. We have also looked at the many theories that were developed to address moral problems because of these values and philosophies. Now we would like to explore what elements in the western ethical systems are similar to the African moral systems. This dialogue will help our integration as well give us the opportunity to learn from each culture. We will look at the relationships that exist between the two cultures.

The relationship between the foundations of African and western ethics

A quick look at the two ethical systems show the place of cultural values, traditions and religion have in shaping the moral life of people. These traditions and cultural values have provided in a great way the foundation for the different ethics found in these cultures. There are other fundamental similarities. In both ethical systems, the human person is central to the ethical system. Both African moral values and the western moral values are anthropocentric. They focus on the person. In Africa, the human community is emphasized while in the west the individual is the focus. Both cultures underscore the social importance of ethics.

At the core of these ethical systems are relationships. We live in a community where we are constantly engaging each other in different ways, so our relationships with each other and how we behave and respond to one another is very important for the well-being of the community. We must say here that there is need to balance individual moral values with that of the community values. The community values, which are embedded in the customs and traditions, must be spelt out clearly, so everybody knows what these values are. The balance between community's interests and the individual's interests is critical for both cultures.

While African ethics is grounded on the authority of the traditions, customs, taboos and sanctioned by the ancestors, who are considered the custodians of the moral law, western ethics seem to reject largely all forms of traditions and laws as unnecessary for morality. The place given to the individual as the measure of morality reduces western morality to personal opinion about right and wrong. This makes morality too subjective without any objective criteria for making decisions. The sole role given to reason as the only authentic means for moral choice can be problematic. It is based on the assumption that "reason" is infallible. It presupposes that human mind are perfect and they can reason and come up with right decisions. This thinking undermines the biblical teaching of the sinfulness of humanity. It is critical for the issue of authority to be addressed when it come to African ethics. I think the west can learn from Africa. We cannot reject authority. We all have some authority over us in real life; at home, school, work place, at church and so forth. We must have some forms of authority under which one may submit oneself; otherwise, we will be living in a country where impunity and lawlessness reign.

Significance and implications of the findings for Christian ethical reflection in Africa

There are certain western cultural values that are very beneficial for ethical reflection in the African context. Some of the cultural values that may be helpful for our ethical discourse include the ideas or concepts of equality and freedom, the eternal value of the individual, human dignity, self-development and empowerment, respecting the rights of individuals, and justice. These values are affirmed by biblical teaching. When these ideas are understood from the perspective of God and biblical morality, they can contribute immensely to our ethical reflection on the issues facing the church in Africa today. Of course, when these concepts are not understood from Christian biblical and theological perspectives, its secular tendencies could lead to moral conflicts for the church.

On the side of western philosophical traditions, some of the ethical theories outlined in the chapter may be helpful but we must use them critically and we must evaluate them in light of the teachings of God's word. In particular, in the areas of public policy by government institutions and agencies, the theory of utility would be beneficial where decisions are made not to benefit an individual but the whole society. More importantly, character and virtue ethic will be very important to incorporate in the moral community to build and develop character of people to help them live to fulfill their moral responsibility in society as they serve God and their fellow human beings. We will apply some of these principles in the second section of the book.

Conclusion

In this chapter, we examined the nature of western morality as well as the cultural values and philosophical traditions that have shaped this morality. We noted that the Protestant tradition played a critical role in western morality during the medieval period. However, it was the enlightenment tradition that had the most important impact and influence on western morality. The enlightenment provided both the philosophical and the cultural and social values that have shaped western morality to date. While religion is, still acknowledge in many western ethical systems, it is not the predominant determinant of moral values.

The moral philosophical traditions reject religion as the basis for morality. What determines people's behavior is the personal values they believe will make them happy and fulfilled in life. This individualistic focus on ethics found in the west is foreign to African morality. Since these traditions reject any form of authority or rules as a guide for human behavior, morality is left to the individual to decide.

Secularism that seeks to remove religion from public life has become a dominant cultural influence on western ethics and most of the ethics formulated today in the west are ground on secular values. This is in contrast to both biblical ethics and African ethics. Both are grounded on social laws and values that are binding on the community.

However, there are some critical cultural values such as the dignity and worth of the individual person, freedom, fundamental rights, empowerment, and justice have important place in ethics. Again, these values reflect some of the biblical values and idea even though we reject the secular ideologies and assumptions behind some of these concepts. For example, while freedom is a biblical concept, it has its limits and boundaries when it comes to moral behavior and conduct. Biblical freedom is not a license for self-indulgence and immoral behavior. In addition, ethical theories such as deontological and utilitarian approaches can be helpful in dealing with matters of public policies and welfare issues.

So far, the two cultures we have examined have developed their moral systems with humanity at the center. We have emphasized the anthropological and social nature of these moral systems. The ethical systems are based on the assumptions; that human beings are good and through good reasoning, they can reach good moral decisions. This raises many questions for us today. The moral degradation we find in our societies today tends to prove these assumptions wrong. What may account for this moral degradation in our society? We believe it is important that we discuss the nature of human beings as we think of Christian ethics. The next chapter will address the human being and the moral life.

CHAPTER 3

Human Nature and the Moral Life

Introduction

In this chapter, we will examine the place and role human nature plays in moral discourse. I will argue that one's anthropology will affect one's ethics. It is important that we explore the relationship between human nature and morality. For us to develop an African Christian ethics, it is critical to have the right, understand of human nature, and show how that nature impinges on morality. By way of illustration, I will examine the particular views of human nature from the three contexts and show how such understandings have influence African, western, and biblical ethics. I will show that biblical ethics is closely linked with theological anthropology; that is, the biblical view of the human condition necessitated the redemptive work of Jesus Christ, which forms the basis, or foundation of biblical ethics.

To illustrate my assertion above, I will examine the African view of human nature and two western philosophical views of human nature in some details and show how these views shaped their views of ethics and morality. My choice of the idealistic and the humanistic views of humanity, which are rooted in western cultural values and ideals, were because of their growing impact and influence on our African people today. Then I will later examine the biblical view of humanity by contrasting the biblical view with the other two views. I will then show how the biblical view of humanity; his sinful nature and helplessness, shifts the basis of ethics to theology and not anthropology.

African views of human nature and its impact on morality

Africans believe the human being is created neutral; he is neither good nor evil. Danquah believes human beings are born with pure and uncontaminated soul. He rejects any idea that Adam and Eve's sin affected human beings in any profound and negative way in relation to human nature. He thinks the notion that humans are born sinners is a figment of human imagination. He writes:

> The Akan do not imagine that man ever could have had a fall. His (the Akan) conception of the *Nkrabea*[1] and *Hyebea*[2] for each particular individual precludes any such possibility of one man's soft heart or one woman's indiscretion making all the rest, even their countless generations to suffer a fall.[3]

The implication of Danquah's statement is that Adam's fall or sin did not affect the rest of humanity or his own *destiny* and *fate*. This particular understanding of human nature is based on the belief that each person has direct access to the source of all life—God Almighty. All that humanity needs, therefore, is to have "an exemplar or an inter-medium who will take him/her near to the source or make the source better understood."[4] The only person who can change one's destiny and fate is the person himself or herself. In short, Adam's sin did not change human destiny and fate.

Secondly, since Africans reject "original fall" of human beings, they also reject any such thing as "original sin." Humans, according to the African

---

[1] *Nkrabea* is the Akan word for destiny, fate, appointed lot, manner of death Christaller, *Dictionary*, 28ff. It is a message one gives to his maker about how his life would be on earth before he comes to his existence. This message is only known to the person who gave it to God.

[2] *Hyebea* means predestination, fate—Christaller, 262. It also means destiny, decree of life, manner of life as ordained by nature or God (*hye* means to order, make, and law). This finally culminates in one's *Nkrabea*.

[3] J.B. Danquah, *Akan Doctrine of God*. London: Frank Cass, 1968, 82.

[4] J.B. Danquah, *Akan Doctrine of God*, 82.

belief, are born with the purest soul[5] and with a destiny ordained and endowed for him directly from God. There is no evil in the soul for the soul is considered to be "part of the source (that is God) and maintains its pristine goodness of sacredness unimpaired."[6] The implication of this is that the essence of a person's being is derived directly from God. For example, Idowu's comment below reflects this understanding of humanity sharing in the deity.

> This is to say that man is made a rational being, intelligent, equipped with a sense of purpose; there is something of the divine in him which makes him addressable and responsible (capable of response) and therefore, there exists in him the possibility of his spirit being in communion with the Divine Spirit.[7]

In speaking about the soul, Danquah claims, "So far as the *okra* (soul) is concerned, no evil stains or singes its goodness, but evil can arrest its growth to its full destiny if the spirit[8] is not prepared for its entry.[9] Sin is understood as one failing to fulfill or realize his destiny and not as an act against the nature and character of a Holy God. Human beings are imperfect not because of sin; rather, they are "imperfect because their fullness in goodness is not complete."[10] Danquah also says about the soul:

> It is a part of true being, or it is in the path to share in true being, it is in its nature divine, and no contamination with sin or evil is possible for it. The evil soul is a chimera of our own imagination.[11]

---

5 *Okra* is the soul, the inner ego of the self.
6 J.B. Danquah, *Akan Doctrine of God*, 85.
7 See B.E. Idowu, *African Traditional Religion: A Definition*. London: SCM Press, 1973, 55.
8 The Akan word is *sumsum*. It refers to the personality, ego, looks, and individuality of a person. It is the opposite of the *okra*, soul, the latter being inner, and the former worldly.
9 Danquah, *Doctrine of God*, 86.
10 Danquah, *Doctrine of God*, 82.
11 Danquah, *Doctrine of God*, 86–87. Danquah's statement about the soul echoes some of

The above statement reflects the basic position of the African belief on human nature. It sees the soul as perfect and uncontaminated with sin. Human beings have inherent in their beings, moral "goodness." With the possession of destiny and fate, humanity could live in harmony with each other so they can fulfill their moral obligations.

By focusing on the horizontal levels of human relationships, African ethics loses its vertical dimensions. Humans are the center of everything, not God. Human existence is viewed as other oriented, her existence is complete only when it is understood in the larger context of other existence. Ethics becomes communal. Morality is therefore to conform to the social norms, customs, and traditions. African ethics therefore, can be described as humanistic. The foundation of African morality is non-supernatural for it is pre-occupied with human welfare.[12]

The African view of humans undermines the seriousness of sin and its effects on both human nature and creation as a whole. We reject this high view of humanity. Instead, we will show later on in this chapter that sin affected human nature and creation as a whole and this makes it impossible for us to make good choices and we always follow the desires of our hearts, which are always prone to selfishness; what we think is good and best for us.

We will now turn our attention to examine the western view of human nature and show the impact such views have on ethics in the west.

Western views of human nature: the idealist and humanistic views of human nature and their impact on morality

Reinhold Niebuhr said, "It is not unfair to affirm that modern culture, that is our culture since the Renaissance, is to be credited with the greatest advances in the understanding of man."[13] Niebuhr's observation is very

---

the themes outline in idealistic, humanistic, and Thomistic philosophies.
12 Kwesi Wiredu, *Philosophy and an African Culture*. Cambridge: Cambridge University Press, 1980, 6.
13 Reinhold Niebuhr, *The Nature and Destiny of Man: A Christian Interpretation*, Vol. I.

important for our discussion of ethics. He underscores how modern culture has shaped the west's understanding of humanity. The way modern philosophical schools of thought understand the world and reality and how human beings relate to all these realities has contributed to the west's understanding human nature.

The idealists view of human nature and its impact on morality

The idealists argue that ethical behavior is a general human accomplishment. They believe every human being possesses a moral code and at least some bits of moral conscience. What is central to the idealists thinking is the place they give to the "mind" and "ideas." They understand the human being primarily as a rational being. What is unique, therefore, in human being is the mind. The mind is distinguished from the body, and it is defined as "the unifying and ordering principle, the organ of the *logos*, which brings harmony into the life of the soul as *logos,* is the creative and forming principle of the world."[14] This understanding of the mind and the separation of the body from the mind have certain implications for the idealist's view of human nature. First, rational being is associated with the divine as a "creative principle." Humanity is put on the level with God. The human person as a rational being is perfect and there is no defect in his/her personality. Secondly, it reinforces and projects dualistic view of the human person. Everything associated with the human body is evil, while the mind or the spirit is good. However, what is of concern to us is the central place it gives to the mind. The mind in idealism is the ultimate ideal.

The idealists' thinking of Kant developed into what is known as "autonomous ethics."[15] Kant postulated that ethics must be an autonomous

---

London: Nisbet and Co. Ltd, 1941, 7.
14 Niebuhr, *Nature and Destiny of Man*, 7.
15 Etymologically "autonomy" comes from two Greek words *autos* (self) and *nomos* (law or rule). It means the power of self-determination and freedom from alien domination and constraint. Thus, autonomy stands in opposition to heteronomy or the subjection to the determination of another. However, perhaps we need to draw a distinction between "autonomy in ethics" and "autonomy of ethics." With regard to the former, the individual has freedom and power to bind the self by a law, which the self promulgates. By the autonomy of ethics, we mean "the doctrine that morality is independent of religion, of custom and convention, and indeed of any other sphere of life or form of authority."

discipline, a statement that resulted in creating a gulf between theology and ethics. We can know and do the right independently without having any knowledge of God. Kant puts this in categorical terms.

> ...hence, for its own sake morality does not need religion at all (whether objectively, as regards willing, or subjectively as regards ability [to act]); by virtue of pure practical reason, it is self-sufficient.[16]

Brunner describes the spirit of the enlightenment's view of humanity by the words of Brunner:

> The spirit of typical 'modern' man is relativistic and skeptical. He is weary of all systems, averse to all doctrines, and contemptuous of all creeds, that is he has a habit of mind which meets every ethic—and not the Christian ethic alone—with the 'superior' attitude of one who is too 'advanced' to care about this kind of thing.[17]

Thus, morality is a question of one's will to do good. The whole concept of human "free-will" was very important in Kant's thinking. His ethics is based on this. The question that confronts us now is, to what extent is human "free will" capably of making ethical decisions?

Augustine one of the prominent African Church Fathers says this on "free-will," "To will or not to will is in the power of man who will or will not only in such a way that it does not impede God's will or vanquish his power."[18] The whole question of free will becomes important in Thomas Aquinas' understanding of morality. Aquinas was one of the prominent

---

See John E. Smith, "Autonomy of Ethics" in *A New Dictionary of Christian Ethics*, eds. J. Macquarrie and James Childress. London: S C M Press, 1967, 53.

16 Emmanuel Kant, *Religion within the Limits of Reason Alone*, trans. By T. M. Greene and H. T. Hudson Harper Touch Books, 1960, 3.

17 See Emil Brunner, *The Divine Imperative*, Trans. by Olive Wyon. Philadelphia: The Westminster Press 1937, 17.

18 Robin Gill, *A Textbook of Christian Ethics*. Edinburgh: T. & T. Clark, 1985, 57.

Roman Catholic Theologians whose theology influenced Roman Catholic Church's moral and social ethics Aquinas' ethics consists in a Christianization of Aristotelian ethics in which all ethics resides in the movement of the rational creature towards God. In this system, the intellect plays a central role in morality.

Aquinas observed that intelligence is ordered and sustained by the will and especially by freedom. On free will, he says, "Free-will is rooted in reason, which proposes to the will the objects of its efforts and the motives of its actions."[19] Reason is the foundation and motivation for moral action. Roger Mehl has made a good observation about Thomastic ethics as to its source:

> On one hand, moral action flows forth from within man. It expresses the spirituality and the freedom of man. On the other hand, it is determined by objective and external norms, and receives its orientation from a supreme end that acts upon freedom without contradicting it. For this freedom is that of a rational being who, insofar as he has been created such, is normally ordained to this supreme end.[20]

He concludes, by saying, "…Thomastic ethic does not take its departure in the new life into which man enters by justification. It is rooted in an anthropology in which man is by nature ordained to being."[21] For Aquinas moral decision is the result of rational being exercising his free will in matters of morality.

The reformers struggled with the idea of free will. Luther, for example, with his emphasis on the corruption of human nature, saw free will differently. Luther argues that human being as a descendant of Adam, lives in constant state of sin, so that even his best aspirations are corrupted by sin. In this case, it is difficult to say truly that human will free.

---

19 Roger Mehl, *Catholic Ethics and Protestants Ethics*, Trans. by James H. Fartey. Philadelphia: The Westminster Press, 1971, 28.

20 Mehl, *Catholic Ethics*, 30.

21 Mehl, Catholic Ethics, 31.

The influence of idealism upon Christian theology in general and in Christian ethics in particular has come chiefly through the version of post-Kantian idealism. The proponents argue,

> The Christian gospel is not the proclamation of redemption from sin by the self-offering of the God-man but a way of life consisting in observing the ethical teachings of Jesus of Nazareth in efforts to bring about the Kingdom of God on earth.[22]

Idealists fail to take the effects of indwelling sin in human beings with sufficient seriousness. This attitude is reflected in their interpretation of Christ's redemptive work. Christ's death on the cross was not, they say, "redemption from sin" but only served as a moral example for us to follow in order to bring in the kingdom of God. Sin is undermined in idealistic thought. To undermine the effect of sin on human nature and the human race as a whole is to show a low view of the atoning work of Christ to deliver his creation from the power and dominion of sin. The idealists claim every human being possesses a natural knowledge of the good or what they called a "moral common sense" or "conscience." Citing Romans 1:18–20 and Romans 2:14–16, the idealists have argued that human beings possess a knowledge of the "the good" and "the bad" among even non-Christians. Their knowledge of "good" and "bad" make them responsible for their behavior. Some theologians have used these passages to argue that the *imago dei* in man has not been affected by sin or by the fall, thus building ethics on the foundation of reason and natural law.[23]

The basic outlook of idealism is anthropocentric, with the mind and reason as the most important element in the human person. However, the nature of sin and the corruption in human nature make this high view

---

22 See P. Helm. "Idealism" in *New Dictionary of Theology*, eds. S.B. Ferguson and D. F. Wright. Leicester: Intervarsity Press, 1988, 327.

23 The Roman Catholic view is that the Imago Dei in man was not fundamentally affected by original sin. Man only lost some supernatural powers but the *Imago Dei*, which includes reason and freewill, was not affected. The reformers' view was that "original sin" affected the core of human nature.

of the idealist's "human being" impossible as Luther rightly points out; "human nature is far too corrupted by sin for it to be a reliable source of ethical judgments."[24] Brunner describes this ideal view of human being as the "error of the natural man."[25]

The humanistic view of human beings and its impact on morality

Twentieth century humanism believes that human beings are the apex of the evolutionary process and that human beings have sole responsibility for their own fulfillment and betterment. This philosophy can best be described by the ancient axiom that humans are "the measure of all things." Humanists see human nature as a "set of inherent distinguishing characteristics, including ways of thinking, feeling, and acting."[26] Humanists hold an optimistic view of human nature. The human being is a "single organic being, and must be seen as a whole. Human acts are expressions of human nature and this nature is common to all human beings. Human nature manifests in acts, which may be judged as good or bad.[27] Human beings are morally not evil, but good and therefore they are capable of doing what is good. This idea can best be described with the maxim: "I can, therefore I ought." Humanists place emphasis on "human power" and "freedom," and humanity's ability to actualize her potential. By having the ability to think consciously and rationally, human beings are able to control their biological urges and achieve their full potential. Human beings are responsible for their actions and destiny. They have the freedom and the power to change their attitudes and behavior.

The humanists object to any authoritarian or divine command in legitimizing the moral life. David Little observes that what makes an act moral is not obedience to some external imperative, but rather one's freedom to decide and choose to make and keep human life human.[28] The

---

24 See Robin Gill, *Textbook*, 64.
25 Emil Brunner, *Divine Imperative*, 64.
26 http:// en.wikipedia.org/wiki/human_nature. Accessed January 20, 2011.
27 Weiss, *Human Freedom*, 11–12.
28 See Roger Hazelton, "Humanistic Ethics" in *A New Dictionary of Christian Ethics*, eds.

central idea in humanism is the freedom of the individual and his ability to choose and act freely. This ability to choose freely makes human beings unique in this world. Hazelton's question reflects this central theme of humanistic ethics when he asks,

> Here freedom as self-motivation can only mean non-accountability to any higher or lower determining power, that human beings can and do know, seek and realize their own real good without relying upon any standard or support beyond themselves—Is this not still the hall mark of any humanistic ethics?[29]

Humanistic ethics is anthropocentric at its core because of its view about human nature. The idea of seeing the human being as essentially good and not evil or corrupt in his "human nature" underlies the whole humanistic ethics. However, this "good" in human beings is not to be understood as an intrinsic goodness, but as a bestowed "goodness."

The fact of sin and the corruption of human nature are again not taken seriously by the humanists. In fact, they ignore the evil side of human nature. Human beings are credited with such high moral powers and with freedom to choose, act, and live right. We know that this is not the case in real life. While Christians will agree and not deny human freedom and free will, for without which ethical decisions would be possible, they, however, see human freedom as a gift rather than as a right. To speak of free-will and humanity's ability to choose is something that is contrary to normal life experience. Human beings are very often slaves of their own lower natures, or raw instinct and passion, unable to do the good they wish to do, thus making their situation one of helplessness and hopelessness. One cannot resist the force of one's own natural impulse.

In a passage remarkably reminiscent of Paul's description of the internal conflict between good and evil in Romans 7, Weiss admits, "We constantly

---

J. Macquarrie and J. Childress. London: SCM Press, 1986, 282.
29 Hazelton, *New Dictionary*, 282.

commit absolute wrongs in the endeavor to do what is relatively right and we constantly do what is relatively wrong in doing what is absolutely right. The conflict is inevitable: it is part of the tragedy of man."[30] It is true in real experience that there are inhibitions in people that make it difficult for them to move naturally towards perfection. Kingsley Martin points out that "Men are more naturalistic, violent, and stupid than we thought they are. We control the earth and air, but not the tiger, the ape and the donkey inside ourselves."[31] This phrase, "inside ourselves" reflects the corrupt nature of the human being, which can only be rescued through the redemptive work of Christ.

In our examination of all the three views of human nature discussed in this section, we observed that the outlook is anthropocentric. The human being is placed at the center of life. Humans are depicted as perfect, sinless, and possessed minds and will, which are capable of making moral decisions. The question of sin and its effects on the human nature and the whole creation have not been taken seriously in all the three views. This, I see as one of the fundamental weakness of "anthropological" or humanistic ethics. The influence and power the power of sin over humanity is ignored. This however is critical to morality. Biblical ethics takes seriously the condition of the human being when it comes to morality. I must also point out that while Africans will recognize the place of God in its ethics, in practice they derive their ethics from traditions and customs that are embedded in society. The idealists and the humanists push God out of ethics all together.

Having laid down the foundations for both African and modern views of human nature, we will now examine the biblical view of human nature. In doing, this we will focus on Paul's teaching on human nature. This will give us a comprehensive view about how the Bible views human beings. Paul also helps us to see clearly the relationship of human nature to morality.

---

30 Paul Weiss, *Man's Freedom*, 221.
31 Kingsley Martin, *Objections to Humanism*, ed. H.J. Blackham. London: Constable, 1963, 102.

The Biblical views of human nature

Old Testament view of human nature

The Bible sees humanity in relation to God. Human beings are created by God to occupy a unique place in the world. They are created in the image of God to have dominion over the rest of creation (Gen. 1:26). Human beings were created as free beings with the ability to love, which is the very essence of God's nature. However, this God-nature in humans changed because of sin. Sin altered human beings relationship with God and changed their attitude towards each other. Sin changed the inner disposition of human beings—their attitude towards God and their attitude towards each other. From this time in human life, things were not the same. Evil and violence dominated human life. Wickedness and moral degradation increased on earth, human thoughts became consistently very evil. The earth became corrupt in God's eyes and it was filled with violence and depravity everywhere. (Gen. 6:1–14). Human beings ceased to reflect God's love and holiness. Prophet Jeremiah states the condition of the human being succinctly: "'the human heart is most deceitful and desperately wicked. Who really knows how bad it is? But I know! I, the Lord, search all hearts and examine secret motives. I give all people their due rewards, according to what their actions deserve'" (Jer. 17:9, NLT). Humanity in their rebellion constantly disobeyed God's laws and lived contrary to God's moral standards. The Old Testament did not have that high confidence in human nature and human ability as advocated by idealists, humanists, and African scholars' views about human nature.

New Testament views on human nature

What does the New Testament say about human nature? The fullest account on human nature in the New Testament is found in the Pauline epistles. For the purpose of this section, we will only concern ourselves with Paul's view of human beings as it relates to ethics. It is primarily Paul's understanding of human beings; their nature and status, which provides the reason for Christ's redemptive work for humanity and this forms the basis for biblical and theological ethics.

In dealing with Paul's view of human nature, we need to note that Paul's anthropology has its basis in the Old Testament, particularly

Genesis chapters 2–3. While Paul had a high view of humanity (Rom. 2), he nevertheless, considered human beings as fallen creatures who needed God's redemption. Paul held the view that Adam's sin resulted in moral corruption. He lost his fellowship with God. Human nature became corrupt because of Adam's disobedience to the commands of God. The corruption affected the whole person, mind, will, and heart, resulting in a change in human social behavior. The author of Genesis describes the state of humanity vividly. "Now the Lord observed the extent of people's wickedness and he saw that all their thoughts were consistently and totally evil" (Gen. 6:5, NLT). Adam's sin resulted in the corruption of humanity's social behavior, which is linked to violence. Again, the scripture says, "Now the earth has become corrupt in God's sight, and it was filled with violence. God observed all this corruption in the world, and he saw violence and depravity everywhere" (Gen. 6:11–12, NLT).

With this understanding and background, let us now look at Paul's anthropology with particular attention to the effects of Adam's sin on human nature and the moral life.

The impact of Adam's sin on human nature

Paul did not speculate about the origin of sin and he assumed the reality of sin's power in human experience. Adam's sin affected the whole human race as well as the created order. Although Paul never taught about "original" sin per se, he taught about the universality of sin and its impact on humanity (Rom. 5:17–19). Paul states that both Gentiles and Jews are under the power of sin (Rom. 3:9–18). Both Jews and Gentiles are slaves of sin. Quoting from the Psalms and Ecclesiastes, Paul argues that there is no good person and there is no one who is good. He concludes with an astonishing remark, all have sinned, both Jews and Gentiles, and have come short of God's glory (Rom. 3:23) and holiness.

Paul argues humanity and the created order are sold under the power of sin. In Paul's view, we should not understand sin primarily as an individual act but as a cosmic power or a sphere of existence into which humankind has been placed. Humanity is under the dominion of sin. Sin has enslaved and subjected humanity to its rule and control. Paul shows how sin has affected creation and subjected it to corruption and futility (Rom. 8:20–22).

Adam's sin affected not only himself and posterity, but it also affected the physical creation. All were subjected to decay and corruption. The environment that was perfect and beautiful changed to become a hostile and imperfect one because of sin. The whole cosmos was subjected to the rule and power of sin—it was "enslaved to corruption." Paul points out that the only way this corruption and decay can be removed is at the final redemption of the children of God. Paul's view of the effects of sin on both human nature and man's environment is radically different from that of the idealists and Africans' views on the created order. The Bible affirms humanity's sinful nature, contrary to the views we have discussed earlier.

Sin affected the whole person. Human beings have become slaves to sin. Contrary to what we saw with the African and western views of human nature, the biblical view holds that human will is affected by sin therefore human will is subjected to the power of sin.

Human beings possess corrupt and sinful nature

The biblical view is that human beings possess corrupt and sinful nature. Humans do not just commit sinful acts; human beings are sinners. Our sinful nature is expressed in our sinful deeds. For in Adam, all humans are constituted sinners (Rom. 5:19). The ascription of Adam's sin to his posterity has been discussed in almost all works on biblical anthropology and soteriology.[32] How did Adam's sin affect us? In what way are we guilty with Adam in his sin? Paul answers this question in Romans 5:12–21.

In Romans 5:12–21, Paul shows a parallelism between Adam and Christ where he presents the two men as the "representative heads" of the human race. Paul's presentation gives us some insights on the nature of our solidarity in sin with Adam. Paul draws a parallel between Adam's disobedience, sin and their effects on himself as well as his posterity[33] and Christ's obedience

---

32 John Murray, *The Imputation of Adam's Sin*. Phillipsburg: Presbyterian and Reformed Publishing Co. 1959; H.C. Theissen, *Lectures in Systematic Theology* rev. ed. by V. D. Doerksen. Grand Rapids: Wm. B. Eerdmans, 1979. 186–190; Herman Ridderbos, *Paul: An Outline of His Theology* trans. J.R. DeWitt. Grand Rapids: Wm. B. Eerdmans, 1975, *Paul*, 91–135.

33 Paul's view is in direct opposition to the Akan's view of Adam's sin and its effect on human nature.

and righteousness and their effects on the human race. Paul says all people are condemned and so death reigns over all people because of Adam's sin. Consequently, death reigned from Adam until Moses; even over those who had not sinned in the likeness of the offense of Adam, who is a type of him who was to come" (Rom. 5:14).

Paul's teaching is clear. He stresses the fact that all people share in the sin of Adam and as a result, they have been placed under the power of sin and death. Paul implies in this passage that Adam's sin was imputed to his posterity just as Christ's obedience and righteousness is imputed to those who show faith in Him. The idea of solidarity is a cultural value that Africans understand very well. The principle of solidarity is embedded in scripture. God's dealings with people were not exclusively individualistic (see Gen. 6:12; Joshua 7). He dealt with human beings in terms of corporate relationships.

For Paul our solidarity in Adam's sin is a result of our biological descent from him. The whole human race originated from Adam and that Adam was our natural father. Adam is the natural parent of all humanity. As our representative, his sin was our sin. In him, all men sinned and we were constituted sinners. Does this view of humanity have any implications for biblical and theological ethics? How does this view of humanity affect biblical ethics and morality? In the section below, I will discuss how this view of humanity does affect biblical ethics.

The implications of biblical view of humanity for morality

I think this view of human nature has a definitive impact on morality. It challenges the assumptions and the claims made by idealists and humanists about human nature; that is not affected by sin. It also may explain why we still have so many moral problems in our world today. It all has to do with human nature. For us to have an ethics that is going to transform attitudes and behavior, we need to take seriously the problem of sin and its effect on human nature and behavior.

Paul assumes in his biblical view of humanity that human beings are essentially moral beings with ability to distinguish between right and wrong. Paul emphasizes the reality of a natural moral law written on the hearts of every person (Rom. 3:14–18). The human being as a moral person has certain moral obligations and responsibilities. Thus for Paul, a person was not created neutral. Paul's view of a person as a moral being is related to his teaching about human conscience. The possession of conscience by every person is evidence of the validity and universality of humanity's moral nature. The conscience provided or enabled the Gentiles to live a life similar to the Jews according to the law. It awakens in them the awareness of the moral laws of God, which were written on their hearts. Paul associates the conscience with humanity's moral awareness (Rom. 2:15; 9:1; 13:5 c.f. 1 Cor. 8:12; 8:12; 1 Tim. 3:9; 4:2).

However, Paul points out that the conscience can be fallible and corrupt. For example, a weak conscience can lead to sin (1 Cor. 8:9), it can be deadened to the extent that it is not responsive to sin and wrong (1 Tim. 4:2).

For Paul, there is a close relationship between our corrupt human nature and our fallible and corrupt conscience. Human beings are depraved because of Adam's sin.[34] This does not mean that the unregenerate person is totally insensitive in matters of conscience, of right and wrong. Such a view will contradict Paul's statement that the Gentiles have the law written on their hearts, so that "their conscience also bears witness and their conflicting thoughts accuse or perhaps excuse them" (Rom. 2:15).

Paul will argue that humans cannot choose freely because their wills are controlled by sin (Rom. 6:17 cf. 2 Tim. 2:25–26). The human mind is corrupt (Rom. 1:21, 1 Cor. 3:14; 4:4). The human body subjected to sin's

---

34 Schleiermacher, although he accepted the consequence of original sin, he, however, denied there was any creative relationship between the primal sin of Adam and ours. He argued that universal sinfulness is not due to any altered change in the nature of our first parents that was brought about by their transgression. Sin arose in Adam from the very condition of human nature, but it did not affect any change in human nature. In fact, the sin of our first parents was in itself but a simple and trivial event. See F. Schleiermacher, *The Christian Faith*. Translated by H. Mackintosh and J. S. Stewart, (Edinburgh: T&T Clark, 1928), 291, 302.

power (Rom. 6:6, 12; 7:24; 8:19, 13) and human desires are sinful (Rom. 1:26–27 cf. Gal. 5:24; 2 Tim. 3:2–4).

Humans cannot choose freely because their wills are controlled by sin (Rom. 6:17 cf. 2 Tim. 2:25–26). The human mind is corrupt (Rom. 1:21, 1 Cor. 3:14; 4:4); their bodies subjected to sin's power (Rom. 6:6; 12; 7:24; 8:19; 13) and their emotions or desires are sinful (Rom. 1:26–27 cf. Gal. 5:24; 2 Tim. 3:2–4).

Adam's sin resulted in two things with respect to human beings. First, the whole person became corrupted. Sin corrupted the mind, the heart, and the will so that sin manifests itself in our sinful deeds in the body and in our members. Secondly, Adam's sin subjected humanity to slavery and bondage to sin. The human body was subjected to the power of sin to the extent that it has paralyzed the inner being—the mind, heart, and will—so that it is unable to offer any resistance to coercive power of sin in the body. We will discuss these two aspects of our nature in turn.

The corruption of sin in the "inward being" makes the moral life impossible

The moral life is made impossible of the effects of sin in our inward being, nature. Paul describes the effects of sin on our moral life by citing the moral degeneration of the life of the Gentiles. Paul attributes the moral perversion of the Gentiles to their ignorance and lack of true knowledge about the true God. The apostle makes a clear and close link between the actions of the Gentiles and their minds by claiming that their degenerate conduct was the result by the worthlessness of their minds and the hardening of their hearts (Rom. 1:18–32).

By depending on their depraved minds that led to depraved thinking, the Gentiles ended up in unacceptable worship and perverse sexual activities. Their corrupt nature affected their morality and worship. They gave themselves up to all forms of idolatry they reached the height of all impiety. Their depraved minds and hearts led them to engage in unnatural sexual behavior. The "desires of their hearts" were given to impurity and they dishonored their bodies among themselves. The "women exchanged natural function for that which is unnatural," and the "men abandoned the natural function of the woman and burned in their desire toward one another, men with men committing indecent acts and receiving in their own persons the due penalty of their error" (Rom. 1:, 23, 27). God's wrath was poured out upon them, which resulted in more sins. For God gave them up to depraved mind.

In his comment on Romans 1, Cranfield suggests that this passage is "not a description of especially bad men only, but the innermost truth of all of us, as we are in ourselves."[35] The universal validity of the Gentiles' moral depravity is the experience of all men. This passage, therefore, refers to the whole human race. The fallenness and sinfulness of fallen man as a whole is what Paul has in mind here. Cranefield says that Paul here "declares the truth about all men."

The emphasis of Paul on the mind and the knowledge of God in relation to our moral life are very important for ethics. While Paul admits the role of the mind in ethical decision making, as the other philosophical thoughts believe, Paul however, characterized the mind as deprived and given over to worthless thinking. Cranfield points out that "a depraved mind" depicts a mind that is so "deliberated and corrupted as to be quite untrustworthy guide in moral decisions."[36]

Paul also underscores one basic fact or ground for morality, namely, one's relationship with God. Paul attributes the heathen's indecent behavior to lack of true knowledge of the one true God. Their wrong conception of God led to a "corruption of morals."[37] The thoughts of the Gentiles about God were perverted and corrupted. This resulted in the "darkening of their hearts." They lost the light of divine knowledge and became destitute in understanding. The consequence of this lack of divine knowledge is darkness—their whole moral state became darkened. Their

---

35 C. E. B. Cranfield, *The Epistle to the Romans* (I.C.C) Vol. I. Edinburgh: T&T Clark, 1975, 104.
36 Cranfield, 128.
37 Charles Hodge, *Commentary on the Epistle to the Romans*. Grand Rapids: Wm. B. Eerdmans, 1947, 34.

distorted knowledge of God led to a perverted and distorted moral life. Ridderbos' comment on the corruption of human nature is insightful: "For not only is the inward man given up to a darkness and ignorance in his relationship to God, but he is also perverted and inclined to all unrestraint and reprehensible activity in his moral self-determination."[38]

The indwelling sin in the human body makes the moral life impossible

Paul shows that the indwelling sin in the human body makes the moral life impossible. Sin affects the human mind, heart, and will so that the mind is incapable to lead a person into right moral judgments. In Romans 7, Paul adds another dimension of the effects of Adam's sin on humanity. He claims the whole of humanity is sold out to sin so that people cannot do the good they will to do. In this passage, Paul views sin as a power, which holds our bodies and its members and subjects them to slavery.[39] Paul claims in this pericopy that sin takes captive of our bodies, members, our 'flesh' and renders the "inner man" powerless to do the good one wishes to do. Even the good person who desires and wills to do what is good and right is subjected to this bondage of sin. Ridderbos describes this condition adequately when he says,

> Although man is disposed and inclined to do the good even then because he is flesh, because of his inclusion in the whole of the human solidarity in sin he is nevertheless frustrated in a decisive manner in doing what is good.[40]

Romans 7 is a classical passage illustrating humanity's bondage to sin and his ethical inability to do what is good. The passage shows the moral

---

38 Ridderbos, *Paul*, 122.
39 Ridderbos, *Paul*, 124.
40 Ridderbos, *Paul*, 125.

conflict that goes on in humans and they need of a total supernatural power to break the power of sin over their lives. The picture Paul paints in Romans 7 of humanity is that of a sense of moral failure. All humanity falls short of the moral standards of God. Paul recognizes the constant conflict between self-will and the demands of God's law upon us. Paul had already shown that we cannot fulfill the moral laws of God for all have sinned and come short of God's glory (Rom. 1:18–3:20). The impossibility of keeping the whole law is Paul's argument for salvation by faith in Christ for both Jews and Gentiles. Human beings have the desire to do what is good and right but the power of sin was present to frustrate this desire. This was not only Paul's experience but also the experience of the whole human race.

He affirms the abiding realization of the futility of human effort in fulfilling God's moral law. What is true of everyman is also true of Paul. His experience and struggle with sin and his moral inability are not unique but typical of everyman. Paul understood the indwelling nature of sin in his members resulted in his moral failure to keep the law of God. The description of this hopelessness is graphically described by Paul in Romans 7:14–20:

> …But I am of flesh sold into bondage of sin. For that which I am doing, I do not understand for I am not practicing what I would like to do, but I am doing the very thing I hate. But if I do the very thing I do not wish to do, I agree with the law, confessing it as good.… For I know that nothing good dwells in me that is in my flesh, for the wishing is present in me, but the doing of the good is not. For the good that I wish to do, I do not; but I practice the very evil that I do not wish. However, if I am doing the very thing I do not wish I am no longer the one doing it, but sin, which dwells in me. (NLT)

Paul blames the moral failure of humanity on human depravity—nothing good dwells in me—and on sin that dwells in humans. These two are responsible for human moral failure. I should point out Paul is not shifting responsibility for humanity's sinful behavior from humanity, for he had pointed out elsewhere that all human beings are guilty before God.

Paul recognizes the enslaving power of sin at work in us to paralyze our efforts to do what is good and right. This moral predicament leads to his cry: "Oh what a miserable person I am! Who will free me from this life that is dominated by sin?" (Rom. 7:24, NLT). His answer is emphatic Christ!

Conclusion

In concluding this chapter, it would be appropriate to tie together the four views of human nature we have discussed so far. We should observe that the Biblical view of human nature agrees at certain points with the African, the idealistic and humanistic views of humans. The agreement is found to certain degree in the dignity of the human being who must be loved and treated with respect and that human being have the capacity to rationally distinguish between good and bad, right and wrong. However, there are serious disagreements between the other three views about human nature and the biblical view. This difference is fundamental to the Christian faith and it is very important for morality. While the other three views believe in the "perfection" of humans, both the OT and NT especially, Paul argues that human beings by nature are wicked and sinful. Human beings are corrupt, they have a depraved nature, and this makes it impossible for them to live the moral life without God's enabling power and help!

Again, while the two philosophies stress man's ability to choose and human will as the essence of personality and that what is basic for action is information, Paul teaches that sin has affected the whole person, mind, will, and heart. Sin has affected creation and our environment so that we cannot create a good environment for our moral action as is believed by African, the idealistic and the humanistic philosophies views of the human being. These views on human nature do not take seriously the problem of sin and its effects on human nature and on our moral ability. In fact, all these views reject such thinking. Human beings are sinners and they live in a world where powerful forces seek to induce them to sin. The cure for our sinful nature comes only through a change in our human condition that can only happen by God's power and deliverance.

So, what is the solution to human humanity's moral inability? According to our examination of biblical teaching and for Paul, the solution to human depravity and human moral inability is the cross of Jesus. Paul's victory over his moral inability was found in Christ (Rom. 7:25). The cure for humanity's moral inability is not in oneself but in God. It is because of God's grace made available through the atoning work of Christ that humanity can live morally and overcome sin's power. Christ became our sin bearer. He broke the power of sin and released us from sin's domination. His death gave us the power to live the new life and this can only be appropriated by faith in Jesus Christ—this is the indicative aspect of Paul's theological ethics.

Salvation enables us to live the moral life. Marshall observes salvation has ethical significance for our lives. Salvation negatively delivers us "from moral failure, moral guilt, and sense of moral impotence." However, on the positive side, it is the "ability to make headway in the moral life, the sense of waxing moral power and achievement."[41] The Christian life is a life redeemed from the infectious power of sin. As Beker puts it: "Sin has become an impossible-possibility—impossible, because of the victory of Christ over sin, which is mediated to us through the Spirit and possible because Christian life remains threatened and liable to *Anfechtung* (attack or temptation)."[42]

The ethical and moral teachings of the Bible are related to a sinful human nature. It is precisely the nature of human beings as sinful and the redemption that Christ offered them to live a new moral life that form the basis of all the ethical commands in the Scriptures. From our investigation we have observed that the human condition, that is, human enslavement to sin, the moral corruption of human nature, human depravity and human wickedness necessitated God's redemptive work through Jesus Christ and effected by the power of the Holy Spirit that the moral injunctions in the Bible are built. We will endeavor to demonstrate this concept in the next two chapters.

---

[41] L.H. Marshall, *The Challenge of New Testament Ethics*. London: Macmillan, 1950, 250.
[42] J.C. Beker, *Triumph*, 217.

CHAPTER 4

Foundations for Biblical and Theological Ethics: Old Testament

Introduction

In this chapter, I will explore the character and nature of biblical ethics. The key questions I will endeavor to answer are what is the nature and character of biblical and theological? What is the foundation for biblical ethics? Is biblical and theological ethics primarily anthropological in nature, or ethics is primarily theological? I hope in answering the questions I will be able to argue for the close connection between theology and ethics, faith and our moral life. I also hope to address the question of authority in moral discourse.

The foundations of biblical and theological ethics

We saw in the three previous chapters that both African and western ethics are largely anthropological, humanistic and socialistic in nature. They are both largely shaped by their cultural and humanistic values. Humanity is at the center of their moral systems. Human reason in the case of the west and human traditions, in the case of Africa ethics are the foundations of these ethics. This is different with biblical ethics. The primary foundation of biblical ethics is theological in nature. Biblical ethics has its nature and foundation on the triune nature and character of God as revealed to humanity in the Scriptures. God clearly makes his character and nature known in his dealings with Israel in particular and humanity in general through his dealing with the nations surrounding the nation of Israel. In these biblical accounts, we see God, not humans as the center of the moral life. This makes religion a core component of biblical ethics. Since our concern is to develop a Christian ethic, it is important for us to lay the foundation upon which such ethics rests. We will begin our discussion by looking at the nature and character of biblical ethics.

The nature and character of Old Testament ethics and morality

Two main elements characterize Old Testament ethics and morality. These are theological and sociological. The diagram below illustrates the two important foundations for Old Testament ethics. We will discuss each in turn in this section.

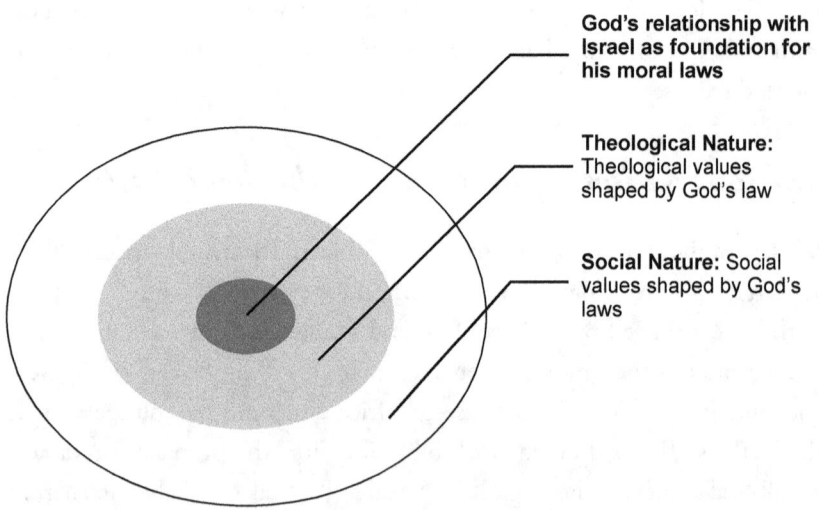

The theological nature and character of Old Testament ethics

The nature of biblical ethics is theological not anthropological. God is the focus and foundation of biblical ethics. Scholars who have written on Biblical ethics make a clear distinction about the nature of biblical ethics and philosophical, humanistic, and secular ethics. Kaiser makes some distinction between the nature of biblical ethics, especially Old Testament ethics and philosophical ethics. He argues that while philosophical ethics is abstract and anthropocentric, biblical ethics is concrete, it is rooted in religion or theology; it is personal and communal—both individuals and communities are to respond to God's laws in obedience. It is internal, it is universal, and it is eschatological. Philosophical ethics lacks these characteristics of biblical ethics.[1] The primary subject of the moral laws is God, first, then human beings, not the other way round. This does not mean that biblical ethics has no place for the human person. This theological foundation has social implications for the moral lives of the people.

The theological nature of biblical ethics is clearly elucidated by scholars such as Chris Wright in his remarkable book, *Old Testament Ethics for the People of God*.[2] Wright argues that Old Testament ethics is essentially theological. Ethics and moral values in the Bible are related to God— to "his character, his will, his actions, and his purpose."[3] Old Testament ethics is based on God's character as creator and covenant keeping, faithful God. These words "covenant keeping and faithful" carry some moral connotations about the character of God, but also it says something about his place in morality as the moral lawgiver. The moral values given in the Bible reflect God's moral values, values that are dear to his heart and are part of his being. Israel was warned by God not to follow the moral values of the surrounding nations, which God disapproved.

---

1 Walter C. Kaiser, Jr. *Toward Old Testament Ethics*. Grand Rapids, MI: Academie Books, 1983, 4–12.

2 In this section of the book, I am heavily indebted to Christopher J. H. Wright's work on *Old Testament Ethics for the People of God*. Downers Grove, IL: InterVarsity Press, 2004. I find his work very important and critical for laying a biblical and theological foundation for ethics in the African context.

3 Wright, *Old Testament Ethics*, 23.

Old Testament ethical teaching is theological in nature. Chris Wright points out that what lies at the heart of Old Testament laws and exhortations is Israel's worldview. He sees three basic motifs underlying Israel's worldview, which forms the matrix for both Old Testament theology and ethics: "the Lord as God of Israel, Israel as an elect people in unique relations with the Lord and the land Israel believed the Lord has promised and given to them."[4] These three motifs delineate the theological, the social, and the economic nature of biblical ethics. God, Israel and Land are the three pillars of Israel's worldview that informs her theology and ethics. Wright looks at Old Testament ethical teachings from a theological (God), social (Israel), and economic (land) perspectives.[5]

At the center of Old Testament, ethics is the covenant that provides the theological ground for Old Testament ethics. The covenant underlines God's unique relationship with Israel. God in his love, mercy, and compassion chose Abraham, their ancestor and promised him that he will make him a great nation and through him bless the rest of the world. In addition, we can see at the heart of the Abrahamic covenant is the intrinsic moral obligation for Abraham and how he trains his children. God expected Abraham to train his children to "walk and keep the way of the Lord and do what is right and just" (Gen. 18:19). The covenant sets the terms upon which Israel's relationship with God will be maintained and nurtured. For the covenant to work, Israel must show the same commitment and loyalty, or faithfulness to the covenant as God is. We must point out here that Israel's call to action to be faithful to the terms of the covenant is predicated on God's own character of faithfulness and loyalty in fulfilling his promises to their ancestor Abraham.

Israel's understanding of her unique relationship with God provided the foundations for its ethical life. Israel's relationship with God demands that they walk and live in a way that is consistent with God's character and nature. The law that was given to Israel at Sinai was predicated on this relationship and set out the grounds for the moral demands God made on

---

4 Wright, *Old Testament Ethics*, 17.
5 Wright, *Old Testament Ethics*, 17–19.

Israel. Through the law, God placed certain moral obligations on Israel that reflects his moral values—ones that were different from the cultural values of the surrounding nations. Israel must live and conduct herself in a certain way that is consistent with the terms of the covenant that was based on God's own character. They were to be a holy assembly to God (Ex. 12:16). Israel must now walk in obedience to the divine will that was revealed at Sinai and expressed in the Torah. Israel was to be a holy community and their covenant status must translate into proper conduct toward others. God ratified the covenant with the whole nation of Israel at Mt. Sinai culminated in the given of the law (Ex. 20).

Israel must live in obedience to God's moral values by separating herself from all that is profane or defiled, including the worship of idols, values of the surrounding nations God abhorred. They were to consecrate themselves for God's use. As a covenant, community there was no dichotomy between temple life and daily life. Their faith in God must translate into holy and just living within the community. The Torah provided guidance and instructions so that the community might apprehend and live out the implications of being in this covenant relationship with God. The covenant provided the theological foundation for the ethical life.

Wright argues that through the mighty acts of God in his dealings with Israel and the surrounding nations, the Israelites came to know who God is. God is unique and different! He is not like the gods of Egypt or like those of the other nations (Deut. 4:35–40). God is unique in his character and nature and the values he accepts; he is holy, just, and righteous. Old Testament ethics is founded precisely on the "identity" and "character" of God.[6]

In the Old Testament God's character and nature become the moral foundations for Israel's behavior. Israel was to be holy in everything just as God is Holy (Lev. 11:44–45; 19:2; 20:7–8). Leviticus 20:8: "Keep all my laws and obey them, for I am the Lord, who makes you holy," is very instructive in terms of humanity's moral capacity or capability to live a good moral life without God. In this verse the writer shows that the power

---

[6] Wright, *Old Testament Ethics*, 25.

to live holy life or morally does not reside in human beings but in God. This faults all humanistic notions that human beings have the power in themselves to live morally.

Another characteristic of Old Testament ethics is that it is founded on God's actions. Wright underscores this. God's acts of grace to redeem Israel from slavery in Egypt becomes the bases upon which the later ethical injunctions rested. He acted first to redeem Israel from slavery. Then he puts his ethical demands on the Israelites in light of his act of redemption. God acted first by redeeming Israel from their bondage and then cut a covenant with them in which their response was to obey his laws in response to his grace and mercy shown to them. In Exodus 19:4–5, God said to the Israelites:

> You yourselves have seen what I did to Egypt, and how I carried you on eagles' wings and brought you to myself. Now if you obey me fully and keep my Covenant, then out of all the nations you will be my treasured possession....[7]

The command to Israel to obey the Torah was based on God's prior action. He delivered them, made them his people, and then called them to keep his laws. The declaration or the preamble to the Decalogue affirms this: I am the Lord thy God who brought you out of Egypt, out of the Land of slavery," repeatedly served to introduce the divine injunctions about the moral life of the covenant community (Ex. 20:2). Israel's keeping of the law was based on God's prior action and it was in response to what God has already done for them. This is the foundation of OT ethics. "Grace is the foundation of our salvation" as well as for our ethics. God's grace comes first, then our human response. Israel's relationship with God was dependent on God's "redeeming grace" and it was "sustained by his "forgiving grace."[8]

Some biblical ethicists have described these acts of God as the foundation for God's moral demands or laws for his people as the indicative and

---

7 Wright, *Old Testament Ethics*, 28.
8 Wright, *Old Testament Ethics*, 29.

imperative notions of biblical ethics. What this simply means is that God's gracious acts of redemption (indicative) becomes the bases for his moral demands (imperative) to those he has redeemed. This structure is found throughout the Bible. In both the Old and New Testaments, the indicative is always the grounds for the imperative.

Wright observes Israel knew from "the beginning that the survival of their relationship with the Lord depended on God's faithfulness and loyalty to his own character and promises, and not on their own ability to keep the law."[9] Wright continues, "Ethics becomes a matter of response and gratitude within a personal relationship, not of blind obedience to rules or adherence to timeless principles."[10] The laws served a purpose of creating and maintaining vital and vibrant relationships among the Israelites and with God. The goal of OT laws was to foster good social relationships.

The laws were given by God to nurture and grow this relationship with Israel. Israel was to "keep God's law as their response of grateful obedience to their saving God." Ethical obedience is a response to God's grace, not a means to achieving it."[11] This is the foundation of biblical ethics throughout the entire bible. We will see this later on in chapter 5 as we discuss New Testament ethics.

The Old Testament ethical teachings are embedded in Israel's history and story. It is in this story that the Israelites came to understand themselves as God's people with a mission to the rest of the nations. In this narrative, Israel sees herself as "a community of memory and hope. It was in remembering and retelling of their past, and the hope that this generated for the future, that Israel most learned the shape of its own identity and mission and the ethical quality of life appropriate to both. Israel's community and morality was shaped by Israel's story."[12]

---

9 Wright, *Old Testament Ethics*, 29.
10 Wright, *Old Testament Ethics*, 25.
11 Wright, *Old Testament Ethics*, 27 and 28 respectively.
12 Wright, *Old Testament Ethics*, 26.

Biblical ethics was grounded on the authority of God's laws/word not in human reason

The ethical response of Israel was not only based on what God has done for them. It was also based on his spoken and written word to them. The Decalogue was in fact God's word to the Israelites. The torah was considered the revealed word of God. It was to be written down, "kept, stored, read, and observed carefully." Israel is constantly reminded in Deuteronomy to obey the words or the commandments of God that Moses was giving them.

> They were not to add or subtract from it (4:2). They must use it as a map or a path, and not turn away from it (5:32–33). They must allow its message to influence their daily life from breakfast to bedtime, in person, in the home and in the public arena (6:6–9). Israel stands in a unique relation to God and has the privilege of having received God's revelation, his very word to guide them in the way they should live (Ps. 147:19–20).[13]

This is very important when it comes to Christian ethics in particular. We must emphasize the place of the written word, the Scriptures must be central to our ethics. The written scripture must be the foundation for our ethical motivation as well as well as our ethical living. The written word that reveals the will and purposes of God is the bases for our moral response and action. God's written and spoken word should guide us on how we must live and behave. If we reject this written word as the bases for our moral behavior, we run the risk of living a life that would be displeasing to God.

This has implications for Israel and for our lives as well. The word of God was "within the reach of the ordinary person." It was not the preserve of few elites (Deut. 30:11–14). God's word "was not a mystic secret for the initiated, but a light to guide every member" of the community. OT ethics is grounded on the dual premise that God has both acted and spoken and

---

13 Wright, *Old Testament Ethics*, 31.

therefore, Israel must respond in obedience to Him. We must teach God's word and explain its moral implication for our lives.[14]

How was Israel to respond to such a righteous, holy, and just God? "What ought to be the substance, quality and bases for Israel's ethical behavior? Israel's response must be theological not anthropological. Israel ought to reflect the character of God himself.[15] "What God is like is to be seen in what he does or has done. What God has done is a revelation of the character and nature of God. Wright observes this is

> Why *knowing God* is a very important theme in the OT, it means more than just knowing what God has done (the stories), or knowing what God has said (the teachings). It means knowing the Lord in person, as a living character; knowing what his values, concerns, and priorities are; knowing what brings him joy and what makes him angry.[16]

Jeremiah 9:23–24 is an instructive passage on what it means to know God. How then should a person who knows the Lord and knows that he delights in kindness, justice, and righteousness do? The person who truly knows the Lord will display these characteristics and show the same qualities in his life and actions. To know the Lord means to do and love righteousness and justice and to maintain that God delights in these things. These ethical standards and values derive from the very character of God's nature. The person who knows God must imitate and reflect his character.

God had freed the Israelites from slavery in Egypt as a proof of his compassion, love, and faithfulness. Israel is to do the same in her treatment of slaves and other vulnerable people in their society. (Ex. 23:9; cf. 21:2–11, 20–21; Deut. 15:15). This same principle is mentioned in Leviticus 19:2. God tells the Israelites to be holy for he is holy. It is a call to be like him in character and deeds. Here again we see the indicative as the grounds for the

---

[14] Wright, *Old Testament Ethics*, 30–32.

[15] Wright, *Old Testament Ethics*, 36.

[16] Wright, *Old Testament Ethics*, 36.

imperative. What God does, His people must do the same. We must reflect the character and nature of God as his children. As the general adage goes: Like father like son." Humanity should reflect the character of their Maker. God makes this possible through his decisive work in Christ.

What does it mean for Israel to be holy? We are often "incline to think that holiness is a matter of personal piety or in the OT setting one of ritual cleanliness, proper sacrifices, clean and unclean foods," as so forth. The kind of holiness that reflects God's own character is none of these. It is rather a practical one. "It includes generosity to the poor at harvest time, justice for workers, integrity in judicial processes, considerate behavior to other people (especially disabled people), equality before the law for immigrants, honest trading and other very earthly social matters." Our quality of life must reflect the character and Being of God who is holy (Lev. 19). Israel must "walk in the ways of the Lord" (Deut. 4:5–8).[17] She must do what God does in relating to humanity with justice, righteousness, mercy, compassion, and love.

One major motivation for Israel's ethical life was the personal experience of people who have experienced the goodness and the blessings of God in their lives. Because of what God has done for the individual, the person acts in gratitude to God and therefore do the same to others. Personal experience of God's goodness is turned into motivation for ethical behavior that responds out of gratitude and love (See Lev. 25:35–55, Deut. 6:5, 20). Our experience of receiving mercy, compassion, love, care, favor, honor, are all motivation and ground for our behavior and response to others. Reciprocity is a biblical moral value. God expects his people to show his love to other as He has shown and extended his love to us.

In summary, what God's acts, words, plans, and his character and nature all provided the bases for OT ethical and moral foundation. The law that regulated Israel's behavior and relationship towards God, their neighbors as well as their environment, sums this up. The word of God not reason was the foundation for the moral behavior of the people. Human we affirmed is not sufficient and capable to empower us for the moral life. We must

---

17 Wright, *Old Testament Ethics*, 39.

submit our wills and actions to God's moral values and laws. Our obedience to God's will and laws are for humanity's good and survival.

As human beings, we are created free. However, our freedom is subject to authority. We cannot reject authority and hope to live in a harmonious environment. Submitting to authority and to God's will does not mean one has lost his or her freedom. In fact, true freedom comes by one submitting to God's Spirit and will. Where the Spirit of God is there is liberty. Biblical ethics is not only based on external commands. It is also grounded on the internal outworking of one's relationship with God. In fact, this is the basis of the external laws. Submitting ourselves to obey God's moral laws is essential to the wellbeing and survival of the human race. So far, we have shown that Old Testament ethics is theological rather than anthropological. We are now ready to explore the social implications of the theological foundation for biblical ethics.

The social nature of Old Testament ethics/morality

In addition to its theological character, Old Testament ethics and morality has a social orientation. Israel's moral life was both toward God and towards the community and the nations around her. In other words, Israel's theological understanding has universal moral social import for the community and the nations at large. This was seen in the way God judges the nations around Israel that violated his moral laws and values.

God chose Abraham for a purpose. He promised to bless him and his descendants. However, he also intended to bless the whole world through Abraham. Israel's moral laws were to shape the social lives of the community. The whole purpose of the laws was to explicate both the theological and social dimensions of God's acts. The social values of the law are clearly shown by its emphasis to enhance and ensure a just social order. The laws show concern for the vulnerable and oppressed in society, its commitment to justice and righteousness, not in the sense of right standing with God but in a social ethical sense, sexuality, and economic justice.

In choosing Israel, God expects Israel to share the blessings He give her with society and the surrounding nations. They were not to learn "the ways" or the behavior of the surrounding nations. Rather, they were to influence the moral and social lives of the nations with the righteousness, justice and mercy God has shown them. Living around societies characterized by rottenness and moral decay, God expected Israel to demonstrate through her love for righteousness and justice to influence the moral lives of the communities around them. The Church must chart the course of our moral lives not the society with its moral values that opposes God and his laws.

God's choice of Israel as His "treasured possession," had an "ethical agenda" or what Wright calls, "social affairs."[18] The law was to gauge the "moral and spiritual health of the whole community."[19] The law was not meant for only an individual's piety. It had a broader social purpose. As Wright rightly observes:

> God's purpose [for the law] was not to invent a production line for righteous individuals, but to create a new community of people who in their social life would embody those qualities of righteousness, peace, and justice and love that reflects God's own character and were God's original purpose for humanity.[20]

The law shaped Israel's social relationships within the community of God's people. It was the basis for their social life and interaction. The ethical values that formed the bases on Israel's moral life derived from the Law, which was a reflection of God's character and will. God's laws have social implications for human society. We will look more at this in part 2 of the book as we address specific issues related to ethics. As the moral laws placed moral obligations on Israel's social life, so, it is today. Our understanding of who God is, his character and nature of righteousness, justice and peace places on us moral obligation to live, practice and make sure that these values are encourages and practiced in our human relationships in society. We must reflect the Character of God and his nature in our societies today.

---

18 Wright, *Old Testament Ethics*, 50.
19 Wright, *Old Testament Ethics*, 51.
20 Wright, *Old Testament Ethics*, 51.

Israel's social and moral life was shaped by her religious ethos, the knowledge of the will, purpose, and character of God. The law shaped the social values and moral lives of the people of Israel. This fact underlines the social and the relational nature of OT ethics. We will briefly look at this characteristic of OT as a relational ethics.

The relational nature of Old Testament moral laws and ethics

I have mentioned earlier that "relationship" is at the core of all biblical laws and morality. I will illustrate this assertion with one of the basic laws of the Old Testament, the "Decalogue," or what is commonly called the "Ten Commandments." A close examination of the Ten Commandments shows that at the center of the laws is relationship; the laws address humanity's relationship with God and with their fellow human being. For example, the first four commandments concerns humanity's relationship with God. It addresses how we can nurture and maintain a vital covenantal relationship with God.

By acknowledging that God is the one who delivers us from the oppression of the evil one and from sin, we are to worship no other gods but Him. To go against this law will disrupt our relationship with God. This will incur God's wrath and punishment since God really punish sins of disobedience. This punishment will be extended to generations who live after they are gone. The ones who endeavor and strive to maintain this relationship, God promises his love to them and their generations after them.

The other commandments relates to our attitude toward God. We are to respect Him in the way we use His name. Lastly, we must keep the Sabbath rest, which he has set aside for us to keep it holy. Again, we must note that the command to rest is predicated on God's own action of resting on the seventh day after he created the heavens and the earth in six days. This underscores the importance of taking rest from our work so that we can be refreshed and not burn out. Each of these laws represents boundaries and values that God has set to define his relationship with his people Israel.

Jesus said this is one of the greatest commandments. Jesus summed up these commandments as "Love the God your God with all your heart, all your souls, and all your mind." (Matt. 22:36–38).

The next six commandments form the bulk of the Ten Commandments. They relate to our social relationships, relationships with parents, which is the basic unit of society. The law commands respect and honor for parents if we want to live long as children, relationship to our fellow human beings by respecting the sanctity of life, the need for moral integrity and responsibility. We must respect the marriage bed and not defile it by sleeping with somebody other than one's spouse, responsibility to respect the property of others by not stealing, to speak the truth by not giving false testimonies against our neighbors which will stain relationships and lastly not taken by force from our neighbors what is not ours. In other word, the scripture demands we have respect for both "private" and "public" properties. These six commandments deal with values that define the boundaries for dynamic healthy human relationships. This forms the second part of the greatest commandment. Jesus summed up these principles as "Love your neighbor as yourself" (Matt. 22:39).

All the other laws found in the Old Testament are in fact expansions of these basic dual moral responsibility of humanity—our relationship with God and our social and moral responsibility for the wellbeing of our fellow human beings. For example, Exodus 21 deals with how we should treat our slaves (workers) justly and how we should deal with personal injuries caused by a person to another. Chapter 22 deals with protection of personal property and rights, social responsibility to widows, orphans and the disadvantaged; Chapter 23 deals with issues of justice and fair judgment and speaking the truth and giving true testimony about our fellow human beings. All these have the goal of building strong social bonds that make for a harmonious community.

More recently, scholars like Michael Schluter and John Ashcroft have emphasized the relational and social nature of biblical ethics.[21] Their basic

---

[21] Michael Schluter and John Ashcroft, eds. *Jubilee Manifesto: A Framework, Agenda and Strategy for Christian Social Reform*. Leicester: InterVarsity Press, 2005.

argument is that Christianity is a relational religion; it is about relationships. In setting up a biblical and Christian framework for social reform, they argue that our "understanding of key biblical values and concerns such as love, justice and righteousness is fundamentally about relationships."[22] This relational outlook of biblical social vision they argue provides a paradigm to help guide us in "our social, political, and economic life which ensures that relationships are sustained rather than undermined."[23] These values are essential and critical for our social engagement in society. Using the Bible as the measuring yard for ethics would help us correct some of the wrong notions we have about these concepts and biblical values that our cultures may have distorted.

Others who have written on the relational aspect of Christianity include Graham Cole. Cole claims that Christianity is a relational religion and so is its book, the Bible. The Bible is a relational book. Christianity provides the frame of reference for us through its stories for our social engagement and vision for society. The purpose of the Bible is to help us "establish and maintain a relationship with God" through faith in Jesus Christ and with one another.[24] The Bible has much to say about relationships. These relationships help to foster social bonds that are necessary for a healthy society.

Not only are Christianity and the Bible relational religion and book respectively, God himself, who is the source of Christianity and the Bible is a relational Being. Relationship is core to his essential nature as the triune God. The relationship that exists between the triune God, expresses this essential nature of God as social being. Humanity created in his image share this relational nature with God. Human beings are essentially social creatures. The capacity for need and desire for relationship is built into us. Relationship is fundamental to our being human.[25] We are social beings. We need each other for life to be meaningful. This social orientation of our

---

22 Michael Schluter and John Ashcroft, eds. *Jubilee Manifesto*, 27.
23 Michael Schluter and John Ashcroft, eds. *Jubilee Manifesto*, 27.
24 Graham Cole, "Christianity as a Relational Religion," in Michael Schluter and John Ashcroft, eds. *Jubilee Manifesto*, 38–39.
25 Guy Brandon. *Free to Live: Expressing the Love of Christ in an Age of Debt*. London: SPCK, 2010, 14.

humanity has ethical implications for our lives as we have seen in the Old Testament. Relationships bring with it responsibility.[26] Our relationship with God brings some moral responsibility. We are to fulfill his purpose by creating a just society where we will reflect his righteousness and justice by taking care of the weak and vulnerable in society. This is our social moral obligation.

Old Testament ethics is social. It shaped Israel's social, political, and economic vision. These activities have relational elements to them. Our social, political and economic endeavors all deal with relationships. We have moral obligation to ensure that as we engage in these activities we do them for the betterment of humanity, in other words, we do them with the goal of building healthy relationship that will enhance the wellbeing of our fellow human beings. There is one more aspect of Old Testament ethics I need to mention. Old Testament ethics has an eschatological perspective.

The eschatological nature of Old Testament ethics

The Old Testament did not assume that Israel would meet God's moral ideals and bring justice and righteousness to the nation and the surrounding nations as well. This is clearly demonstrated by the moral decay that led Israel to captivity. Old Testament ethics has both present and future dimensions to it. The future element is Israel's anticipation of the Messiah, who will come to bring renewal and restoration to Israel's moral decay and restore true, justice, righteousness, and peace, underscores the eschatological dimension of Old Testament ethics.[27] Grenz points out the repeated call by the Old Testament prophets to Israel to live right was based on God's future work to restore the moral integrity of his people through the work of His Son, Jesus Christ.[28] He argues the prophets

---

26 Graham Cole, "Christianity as a relational Religion," 47. See also Brandon, *Free to Live*, 14–16.
27 Walter Kaiser, Jr. *Toward and Old Testament Ethics*. Grand Rapids, MI: Academie Books, 1983, 10–11.
28 Stanley J. Grenz. *The Moral Quest. Foundations of Christian Ethics*. Downers Grove, IL: Inter Varsity Press, 1997, 105.

> Vision was to announce God's intentions for the future to call Israel and the surrounding nations to an ethical response in the present. The hope of participating in God's kingdom entails grave ethical implications. It meant that moral decisions carried consequences for the future.[29]

Only those who live righteous and holy lives, whose hearts are pure and their hands clean will participate in God's kingdom and stand on his holy mountain (Dan. 12:2, Ps. 24:3–4). This eschatological dimension of biblical ethics is a reminder to us that the moral decisions we make today have eternal consequences. The decisions may meet some temporary needs we may have now, but they may cause us big problems in the future.

Conclusion

What are some of the biblical moral values that emerged from our study on the nature and character of Old Testament ethics that are critical for our contemporary ethical reflections? The central notion of Israel's unique relationship with God as the basis for their moral behavior was critical for her moral life. Ethics is relational it must seek to build strong relationship with God and with society. Biblical values such as love, righteousness, justice, obedience, faithfulness, loyalty, holiness, peace, mercy and impartiality (to name a few) are some of the values that are essential for our ethical reflections today. These values reflect the character and essence of God. Faith and morality must be bedfellows. Our faith and relationship to a holy, just, righteous, loving, and merciful God must shape our social ethics.

God and his values were central values that shaped Israel's social and moral life. Since humanity bears the image of God, we are to reflect his character and nature in our moral lives. The power and ability to do so come from God's deliverance and the freedom He gives us in his Son, Jesus Christ. I will attempt to apply these values to some of the moral question and issues I will address in the second part of this book. I will now look at the nature, characteristics, and values that shaped New Testament ethics.

---
29 Grenz. *The Moral Quest*, 105.

CHAPTER 5

The Nature and Character of New Testament Ethics and Morality

Introduction

In the previous chapter, we established that Old Testament ethics is essentially theological. It is grounded on the character and nature of God as revealed to us by his dealings with Israel and the surrounding nations and recorded for us in the Scriptures. In the OT, God was at the center of Israel's ethical life. How then can we characterize New Testament Ethics? If we can say this in a brief statement, I will say New Testament ethics is Christological: it is grounded on the redemptive work of Jesus Christ. In this chapter, we will explore this Christological theme of New Testament ethics by looking at its foundations, its relational nature, its model for the ethical life and the power that makes this ethical life possible and the values that shaped it. To do this we will examine the ethical teachings of Jesus by trying to discern its character, Paul's ethics, and the place of the Holy Spirit in the Moral life.

The nature and character of New Testament ethics

The nature and character of Jesus' ethics

The Old Testament provided the basis for the ethical teachings of Jesus and the subsequent moral reflections of the early Christian community.

Consequently, Jesus' ethics has a lot of resemblance with Old Testament ethics. At the core of Jesus' ethics is its theological foundation. Jesus builds his ethics on the unique relationship he had and shared with his father, God. Jesus' ethics was grounded in the acts of God's love and grace in redeeming humanity and restoring them to obedience and right fellowship with God. Jesus begins his ministry and teaching by calling people to repentance, saying, and "Turn from your sins and turn to God, because the kingdom of heaven is near." (Matt. 4:17). He understood the effects of sin on human morality and He called people to renewal and transformation that will lay the foundation for their moral living.

For Jesus ethics is not based on just external—laws, but it emanates from the internal being of a person. Was Jesus here making a case for "intuitionism?" I don't think so. Jesus recognizes the need for an inner transformation of the human heart, which is reflected, in his call to repentance. I think what Jesus had in mind is character. Character is the wellspring from which all human actions ensue. Jesus' ethics primarily concerns character; it has to do with the heart. Jesus emphasized the role and place of the heart in both character formation; our "being" what we are and in our behavior, conduct; our "doing," what we do. For Jesus, what we are affects what we do. Being for Jesus precedes doing.

For example, Jesus describes the deceitful behavior of the false prophets using the analogy of the tree and the kind of fruit it bears. This is true for our moral lives as well. Jesus points out:

> You can detect them by the way they act, just as you can identify a tree by its fruit. You don't pick grapes from thorn bushes, or figs from thistles. A healthy tree produces good fruit, and an unhealthy tree produces bad fruit. A good tree can't produce bad fruit, and a bad tree can't produce good fruit. Therefore, every tree that does not produce good fruit is chopped down and thrown into the fire. Yes, the way you identify a tree or a person is by the kind of fruit that is produced. (Matt. 7:16–20, NLT).

The same thought is reiterated in this passage:

> A tree is identified by its fruit. Make a tree good, and its fruit will be good. Make a tree bad, and its fruit will be bad; for a tree is known by its fruit. You brook of snakes! How could evil men like you speak what is good and right? For whatever is in your heart determines what you say. A good person produces good words from a good heart, and an evil person produces evil words from an evil heart (Matt. 12:33–35, NLT).

Jesus' words are very instructive. For Jesus, the moral life is not grounded in the law as an external authority imposed on a person, to which one must submit. The ethical life emerges from a transformed life, from a heart that is clean and pure. This comes about because of the cleansing power in his blood. It is because of an intimate relationship with the Father of all goodness and truth. The condition of the human heart is very critical for the moral live. Having the capacity to reason is not enough for one to do the right or behave in a right way. It takes a transformed heart to do that!

Several theological themes underlie the ethics of Jesus. We will examine some of these themes now.

Theological themes that form the foundation for Jesus' ethics

Jesus' ethics as kingdom ethics

The covenant was central to Old Testament ethics. Similarly, the kingdom of God was central to Jesus' ethics.[1] His moral teachings focused on how people who have come into the kingdom ought to behave and live in society. The kingdom expresses the reign and the rule of God. God's moral values determine the moral lives of the people who live under his rule. How are

---

[1] Stanley Grenz. *The Moral Quest. Foundations of Christian Ethics.* Downers Grove, IL: Inter Varsity Press, 1997, Glen Stassen et al. *Kingdom Ethics.*

we to live when we have actually come under the rule of God? Those who are in the kingdom must live lives that reflect the values of the kingdom of God. For Jesus this kingdom value is not happiness, which is a central value in humanistic and secular ethics but the pursuit of God's kingdom. Humanity is to first seek God's kingdom and righteousness (Matt. 6:33). Righteousness is a moral value that must shape our moral live. Another kingdom value is goodness. "Goodness begins with the heart which is the well spring of actions" (Mark 7:21; Luke 6:45).[2]

How is the community of faith supposed to behave? The believers are to join a community of disciplined followers of Jesus who put his teachings into practice. The community's life is to be shaped by the teachings of Jesus Christ in particular the Sermon on the Mount. The Sermon on the Mount called for a life of uncompromising fervor in discipleship. The community of Jesus' disciples was to be a model community living in obedience to God: they were to be the salt of the earth, the light to the world, a city on the hill (Matt.5:13–16). These moral metaphors underscore the social dimension of the moral teachings of Jesus and the moral responsibilities Christians have towards the Christian community as well as their moral responsibility to society. Believers whose lives have been transformed have to influence the moral life of the societies in which they live. Failure to influence these societies will result in their own unproductivity, and eventually lose their moral authority over that society. Those societies would ignore them. Rather, Jesus exhorts Christians to "let their lives shine for all" and "let you good deeds shine out for all to see, so that everyone will praise your heavenly Father." (Matt. 5:16).

An examination of Jesus' teachings in the Beatitudes shows that Jesus' is not just concerned about a legalist observance of the law. He moves beyond that and addresses the motive, attitudes and motivations for people's actions. For example, one needs not to kill someone physically to commit murder. If a person is fixed with rage against someone, he is guilty, the same way a person who has committed an actual murder is guilty. In the same way, one needs not to commit physical adultery. If one looks lustfully at a woman or

---

2 Grenz, *The Moral Quest*, 110–111.

a man, one is guilty the same way as the one who has committed an actual adultery (Matt. 5:21–29). These issues of morality relate to the heart. Jesus' kingdom ethics impinges on all aspects of human relationships—marriage, divorce, money, possessions, riches, giving, fasting, vows, revenge, prayers, and so forth (Matt. 6, 7, and 19:16–22). Some of the kingdom values we find in the Sermon on the Mount includes truth, humility, justice, goodness, mercy, purity of heart, compassion, love, peace, caring for the needy, selflessness, suffering for the good. The New Testament writers later on emphasized these values in the moral exhortations to Christians.

Jesus' ethics as family ethics

Jesus' ethics was an ethic that emphasized family moral values. Christians are members of God's family. Through repentance and faith, the believer receives God's grace and forgiveness. Through this new birth we become God's children (John 1:12–13). As God's children, we are to reflect the nature and character of God, our heavenly father in all we do and say (Matt. 5:44–45, 48; cf. Luke 6:32–36). What is foundational to this family ethics is family resemblance. As the adage goes, "like father, like son." An Akan maxim expresses the same thought this way: "The crab does not give birth to a bird." Family membership involves certain privileges and responsibilities. The responsibility involves family loyalty and solidarity to stand with, care for, and forgive each other.[3] It also means upholding the family moral values so that one does not bring dishonor to the family name. The idea of belonging to God's family has far reaching ethical implications for our social life as well. We are to love and treat one another with respect as brothers and sisters (Matt. 22:37–40); we are to forgive one another (Matt. 18:21–35). Secondly, Jesus' ethics of family emphasizes spiritual ancestry over physical ancestry (Luke 3:7–8; John 8:31–59). The blood of Christ links us together as brothers and sisters. Christ's blood runs through us. This breaks down any tribal, ethnic, or racial inclinations we may have against each other. In Christ, we have become one big body. Our family is no longer based on earthly kinship ties, but that of God's (Matt. 12:50). By

---

3 Grenz, *The Moral Quest*, 113.

seeing ourselves as family; Christians in particular and humanity in general (God being the creator of all) places certain moral obligations on us for our present live as we live in a divided world where there are ethnic, racial and tribal tensions all around us. We must do all we can to live in peace with each other as family. The last theme that underlined Jesus' ethic is the concept of imitation.

Jesus' ethics as the ethics of imitation

Jesus embodied the kind of life that we should live as God's redeemed people. As Christ's disciples, we are expected to reflect his character, to be Christlike. This does not mean that we should imitate every detail of Jesus' earthly life. Jesus wanted his followers to imitate his life. He pointed to his own example as the pattern for our moral behavior (John 13:13–15, 34; 15:12). What we should imitate is his "character, attitudes, priorities, values, reaction, and goals. Then we seek to be Christlike by reflecting on what we know to be true of Jesus in the choices, actions, and responses we have to make in our own lives"[4] In Philippians 2:5, Paul clearly points this out that we should have the same attitude as Christ by being humble and having preferential care for the needs of others.

The ultimate motivation for the moral life "lies beyond mere patterning of one's conduct after the example of a great leader. The motivation arises from the kind of devotion that connects disciples to the Lord at the deepest level of their person."[5] Conduct flows from character but true character arises from devotion. Devotion to Christ then becomes the wellspring for the development of Christ-like character in his disciples.

Jesus' ethics is an "ethics of being" rather than an "ethic of "doing." Character is central to Jesus' ethic. It relates to one's inner disposition, who a person is, or who we are in Christ. Transformation of our being is essential for the moral life. Jesus illustrates this with the analogy of the good tree and the good fruits it bears. It was not a legalistic ethics. It is innate to the person. It comes from within and derives from an inner source of

---

4 Wright, *Old Testament Ethics*, 38.
5 Grenz, *The Moral Quest*. 115.

goodness, which is a result of a transformed heart. It is rooted in good character. Goodness is the central moral value in Jesus' ethics.

Now we will look at some of the New Testament writers and their moral teachings. We saw that Christ's moral teaching laid the foundation for the moral exhortations of the NT writers. I will examine the theological foundations of Paul' ethics in the next section.

Theological themes that shaped Paul's Ethics

The Christological ground for Paul's moral indicative

One fundamental premise for Paul's ethics is Christ has been a radical change in the believer's nature because of his relationship with Christ. Through faith in Christ through his death on the cross, Christian has received a new life in Christ and therefore he must walk in newness of life. Paul demonstrates this in his epistle to the Romans. In Romans 6, Paul deals with a fundamental misunderstanding of the Christian doctrine of grace, which his critics maintained, would lead to antinomianism (lawlessness). They accused Paul of saying that sin provides more incentives for God to show his grace towards sin.

For us to understand Paul's question in Romans 6:1, we need to go back to chapter 5:20–21. There, Paul says the law was given in order to increase sin. Paul asserts that the law came to increase sin because its function is to expose sin and even to provoke it (c.f. Rom. 7:7–12). Paul then makes the claim that "But as people sinned more and more, God's wonderful kindness became more abundant" (Rom. 5:20, NLT). It is clear that Paul's question, "…Should we keep on sinning so that God can show us more and more kindness and forgiveness?" Romans 6:1 is attempting to address his assertion in 5:20–21. If sin therefore promotes God's grace, kindness, and forgiveness, the critics reasoned, why couldn't we go on sinning so that God will get even greater opportunity to show us more kindness? Thus, the critics of Paul were distorting his teaching, by twisting his teaching as an excused for permissiveness and as an incentive to sin more.

Paul exposes the fallacy of his critics by pointing out explicitly why every Christian must be holy and live a good moral life, pleasing to God. Paul renounced such perverted teachings of his critics by stating strongly that there is something incongruent about the Christian who had died to sin to continue to live in sin (Rom. 6:3). Paul proves that his teachings about God's grace or kindness produces righteousness, holy living, not sin. In doing that, he relates his doctrine to morality. Righteousness for Paul was not just a static, abstract notion, but personal and relational, not juridical but ethical.[6] Paul's critics were trying to separate Christ's work for us and Christ's work in us. Righteousness and ethics for Paul are inseparable.

The Christian's union with Christ and the moral Life

One of the theological themes that shaped Paul's ethics is his concept of the believers' union with Christ. Romans 6 makes this clear. The structure of Romans 6 provides a natural division of the text marked by two rhetorical questions in 6:1 and 6:15 respectively.[7] These two sections, however, deal with the same kind of problem, namely, whether the Christian should continue in sin in order for God to show more grace to the sinner. Alternatively, to put it another way, should we continue to sin because we are not under law but under grace (Rom. 6:15)? There are two basic ideas that connect 6:1–14 and 6:15–23. These are, "Christians must give themselves completely to God" (NLT) and Christians are "not under law but under grace."

What then is the central argument of Romans 6? In Romans 6:1–14, Paul begins his argument with a basic proposition found in 6:2—"How shall we who died to sin keep on living in it?" (My own translation). Using the Christian tradition of baptism, Paul asserted we are united with Christ in his death and resurrection and showed how this union with Christ affected

---

6 .See J.A. Ziesler, *The meaning of Righteousness in Paul: A Linguistic and Theological Enquiry*. Cambridge: Cambridge University Press, 1972, 201; Paul Schubert. "Paul and the NT Ethic in the Thought of John Knox," *Christian History and Interpretation*, eds. W.R. Farmer et al. Cambridge: CUP, 1967, 378 n. 4.
7 R.C. Tannehill, *Dying and Rising with Christ*, 8–9.

the behavior of Christians. He develops his argument by working out the implication of the believers' union with Christ to his day-to-day living:

> Do not let any part of your body become a tool of wickedness, to be used for sinning. Instead, give yourself completely to God since you have been given new life. And use your whole body as a tool to do what is right for the glory of God... Before, you let yourselves to be slaves of impurity and lawlessness. Now you must choose to be slaves of righteousness so that you will become holy.... But now you are free from the power of sin and have become slaves of God. Now you do those things that lead to holiness and result in eternal life (Rom. 6:13, 19, and 22, NLT).

The second argument developed in the next section of 6:15–23 begins with another question: "Don't you realize that whatever you choose to obey becomes your master? You can choose sin which leads to death, or you and choose to obey God and receives his approval" (Rom. 6:15, NLT). By using the slavery imagery Paul points out the truth that Christians had been freed from the power of sin and they are now free to serve a new master, namely, God, and righteousness.

Paul's argument here is a theological one with the intention of drawing out some moral implications from his teaching that God in Christ has changed and broken sin's power over the Christian through the death and resurrection of Jesus Christ. Paul's main argument here concerns the death and resurrection of Christ and how this has both changed the believers' relationship to sin and his moral life.[8] In doing this, Paul uses three sets of imageries: baptism, participation, or union with Christ, and slavery to illustrate the truth that the Christian's relationship to sin has changed. He is now a slave of God to do righteousness as opposed to a life of sin.

Our union with Christ has certain implications for our moral life as well as our relationship to sin. Our union with Christ calls all believers to a new righteousness, to be servants of Christ instead of servants of sin, a

---

8 Dunn, *Romans*, 308.

call to walk in this new moral life. Christ's death therefore is not just simple deliverance from evil; i.e. moral and physical, but also it is a participation in his very life and righteousness. We are to reflect his character and nature.

Paul is saying the believer is freed from the power of sin. He is acquitted from sin because the "old man" or the "old self" has died. Thus, Paul is teaching that those who in baptism have died and identified themselves with Christ's death have put sin behind them and begun a new life. Paul is rather simply continuing the thought of Romans 6:6a where he asserts that our old self is crucified with Christ so that we are no longer servants of sin.

By participating in Christ's death through baptism, the believer appropriates for himself the atoning work of Christ. Christ's death is effective as atonement for sin. However, not only did it have the efficacy of atoning for sin; it also had the power to break sin's rule over the life of the believer and gives him the power to live and serve the righteous God. It is the fact that God has justified us that is the basis of this new freedom to resist sin's power in our daily lives.

In baptism we have become new creatures (2 Cor. 5:17) and have been adopted into the family of God, new humanity formed and fashioned according to the nature of the new age. The things, which belong to the old age, namely, sin and death, have been rendered powerless by the death and resurrection of Jesus Christ. The Christian is called upon to live a new life (v. 4) which characterizes the new age; we are exhorted to live in newness of life.

Here Paul forges a link between justification and conduct. Paul shows a close association between his doctrine of justification by faith and our ethical life. For Paul, justification is not just a morally barren doctrine. Paul argues the justification by faith in Christ and our being in Christ have important moral implications. This implication is brought to bear by the close link Paul makes between justification and sanctification in 6:19, arguing that righteousness should lead to holiness not immorality.

Paul further uses the death and life analogy to elaborate his argument by pointing out this in v. 10. Here he talks about Christ's death. "The death he died" was a "once and for all" death to sin; "the life he lives" is a life lived "for" or "with respect to" God. Christ has died to sin (v. 10) we died to sin (v.

11) and Christ is living to God (v. 10) and we are living to God (v. 11). The thought then is that Paul is conveying the idea that the Christian had died to the power of sin. Thus, Christ's death was a death to the power of sin.[9]

Paul's argument can be summed up this way: if Christ's death was a death to sin and his resurrection was a resurrection to God, and if we have been united with Christ in his death and resurrection, then we have died to sin's power and risen to live for God. We must consider ourselves so. We must see ourselves as people who have been delivered from sin's power to live in righteousness. To return therefore, to the old life is unthinkable. We have been ushered into a new life, a life yielded to God and not to sin!

Thus through God's action we have been made partakers of Christ's life. God had made Christ the head of a new humanity and like Adam; we have entered into a new organic relationship with Him, which calls for a new life-style.[10] We cannot say that we have participated in Christ's death and resurrection and yet live in sin. Our death and resurrection with Christ means we participate or share in the very nature and life of Christ.

The theological and Christological grounds for Paul's moral imperatives

Paul's imperatives were grounded upon his understanding of Christ's death on the cross and the impact it had on human sin. Through faith in Christ and baptism, believers have been united with Christ in his death and resurrection and we have died to sin. By dying to sin, they have been released from the power of sin. Therefore, Paul urges believers to stop allowing sin to rule or have control over them (Rom. 6:12).

Since the old man has been crucified (6:6) and the body of sin destroyed and that sin's power is broken, Paul exhorts Christians to reckon their bodies as dead to sin so they can live for God (v. 11). Failure to prevent sin from controlling them in the way they live would result in obeying its lustful desires. The lusts in this case will include not only "bodily lusts" but also all the desires of the self in its state of rebellion against God. Paul states

---
9 Murray, 225; Moo, "Exegetical Notes," 219.
10 Anders Nygren, *Romans*. Philadelphia: Fortress Press, 1975, 237.

the ethical conclusion more explicitly, contrasting a life of submission to God. They are commanded:

> Do not let sin control the way you live (or sin to reign in your body, which is subject to death); do not give in to its lustful desires. Do not let any part of your body become a tool of wickedness, to be used for sinning. Instead, give yourselves completely to God since you have been given a new life. And use your whole body as a tool to do what is right for the glory of God (Rom. 6:12–13, NLT).

The grace of God has freed humanity from sin and its power and the Christian stands under the Lordship of God's grace.[11] Through the death and the life of the risen Lord, God has created a new moral possibility in Christians, a new righteousness.[12]

In Paul's view, the ongoing ethical life of Christians is simply the extension of the Christian's intimate association with Christ. It involves allowing the obedient Christ to live out his righteousness within us. The gospel demands a proper ethical response. For salvation in Christ is not complete without a Christ-like attitude and behavior.[13] Thus, Paul combines assertions about our new relationship with Christ (indicative) with imperatives to encourage us to live a life that is compatible with this new status.

---

11 B.S.J. Brendan, "Living Out the Righteousness of God: The Contribution of Rom 6:1–8, 13 to an Understanding of Paul's Ethical Presupposition," *The Catholic Biblical Quarterly* 43:4 (1981), 565–567. See also Klyne Snodgrass, "Spheres of Influence: A Possible Solution to the Problem of Paul and the Law" *JSNT* 39 (1988), 93–113, D.P. Fuller, *Gospel and Law: Contrast or Continuum?* Grand Rapids: Eerdmans, 1980, 1–64; J.D.G. Dunn, "Works of the Law and the Curse of the Law, Gal 3:10–14" *NTS* 31 (1985), 531 ff; D.J. Moo, "Law, Works of the Law, and Legalism in Paul," *Wesley Theological Journal* (WTJ) 45 (1983), 85; C.E.B. Cranfield, "St. Paul and the Law" *SJT* 17 (1964), 43–68.

12 D. Winter, "Motivation in Christian Behavior" in *Law, Morality and the Bible: A Symposium* eds. Bruce Kaye and Gordon Wenham. Leicester: Inter-Varsity Press, 1978. Wenham says, "The death to sin is not only a theological fact, but a moral step as well. The rising to life is not only a phase denoting the new dynamic of the Spirit, but also living a new sort of moral existence" 212.

13 G. Fee, "Toward a Theology of 1 Corinthians." Atlanta: SBL, 1990, 275.

God's mercies as foundation for Paul's ethical imperative in Romans 12:1–2

The mercies of God are another theological theme that underlines Paul's ethics. In Romans 12:1–2 Paul appeals to God's mercies to the Roman Christians as basis for his moral imperatives. The believers are to respond to these mercies by living in a particular way that will please the Lord. Ethics for Paul is not forced upon us. It rather comes as our loving response to God's grace. That ethics derives from God's gracious work through Christ for us is the theme of this section. The idea that ethics has its grounds in God's gracious act in Christ is expressed by Cranfield:

> …The theocentric nature of all truly Christian moral effort; for it indicates that the source from which such effort springs is neither a humanistic desire for the enhancement of the self by the attainment of moral superiority, nor legalist's illusory hope of putting God under an obligation, but the saving deed of God itself.[14]

The phrase "mercies of God" is concisely the gospel. It sums up what God has done for us. that is, our union with Christ, the decisive break we have made with sin, and the new life we have received, our liberation from both the law and the "flesh" and the indwelling power of the Spirit in us, the fact of God's faithfulness to the Jews—all theses become the ground for the exhortation in Rom. 12:1–2. Here again we find a close connection between Paul's theology and ethics. His theology (the indicative) forms the basis for his ethics (the imperatives).

However, what is the content of the imperative here? The Christians are exhorted "to give their bodies to God. Let them be a living and holy sacrifice—the kind he will accept. When you think of what he has done for you, is this too much to ask?" (Rom. 12:1, NLT). The Christian is to offer his concrete daily living to God. The word body should not be limited only to the physical body. The following verse implies attitude and behavior

---

14 Cranfield, *Romans II*, 595.

that shows that body must be understood as the whole person. The idea of presenting ourselves to God involves a free surrender to God. This sacrifice is described as living and holy. Kasemann points out that the word "holy" has ethical content.[15] It is living as opposed to dead—for we have been called into a new life, in Christ. (Rom. 6:4).

Such a sacrifice is their reasonable worship. Paul's argument can be summed up in this statement: It's right and proper—logical and reasonable—that those who have been highly favored should offer themselves to God wholeheartedly, as sacrifices, living, holy, and well pleasing to Him. To be able to achieve this end, Paul exhorts them: "Don't copy the behavior and customs of this world, but let God transform you into a new person by changing the way you think. Then you will know what God wants you to do, and you will know how good and pleasing and perfect his will really is" (Rom. 12:2). What is needed here is inner change, the renewing of the mind; a change of attitude, it is an inner disposition. This desire must be a continuous affair as indicated by the present imperative.

The transformation here is the kind that takes Christ as its pattern rather than this world. Paul recognizes" a power or force, which molds character and conduct which this age 'exercises' over people."[16] Paul does not acknowledge only the transforming power of God in changing our character but also the power of social groups, cultural norms, institutions, and traditions, which mold patterns of individual behavior. The imperative implies human responsibility is involved—the individual can accept or reject such power structures, can accept or reject such behavior patterns. They are called upon to allow the Spirit to do his work within their hearts and lives. The result of doing this is to be able to "prove what the will of God…is." This discussion can be summarized in the following diagrams.

Figure 1 below shows Paul's argument in Romans 6:1–14, and Figure 2 demonstrates Paul's argument in Romans 6:15–23.

---

15 Kasemann, *Romans*, 312.
16 Dunn, *Romans*, vol. 2, 712.

The Nature and Character of New Testament Ethics and Morality

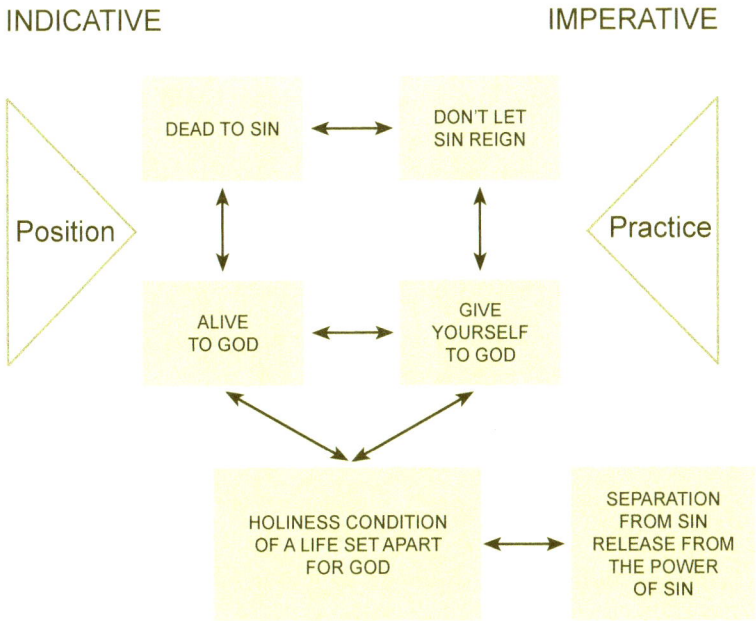

Figure 1. The indicative and imperative framework in Romans 6:1–11 illustrated

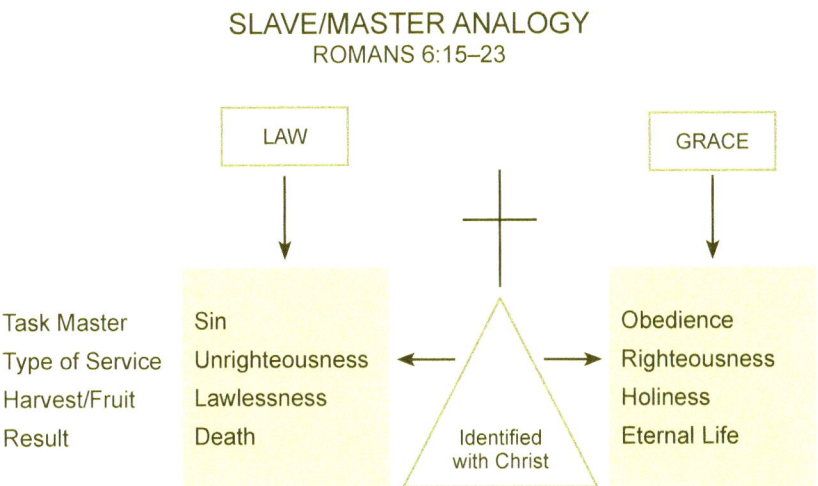

Figure 2. The indicative and imperative framework illustrated in Romans 6:15–23

The ethical implication of Romans 6:15–23 is that now that we are slaves of God we are under moral obligation to live a life of righteousness resulting in holiness which is characteristic of our new life and the nature of our new Master Jesus Christ.

The Spirit as foundation of Paul's ethics

The Holy Spirit plays an important role as the Agent of the moral life in biblical ethics. Paul's ethics is Trinitarian. In Romans 8:1–13, Paul shows the "consequences of the Spirit's activity for humanity's relationship to God's moral claim."[17] Paul contrasts life controlled by the flesh and the life controlled by the Spirit. Paul has shown that humanity in his flesh cannot fulfill the laws of God. In his disobedience to the laws of God, humanity sees its moral failure. However, through the power of the Spirit humanity is given the ability to obey the law.

Paul asserts that what the Law could not do; set people free from their sins, God in Christ has done for humanity (v. 3). Christ has set us free. The liberation has actually been accomplished. According to Cranefield, here Paul is saying that "God's gift of His Spirit to believers, by which His…. Authority and constraint have been brought to bear on their lives, has freed them from the authority and control of sin."[18]

This liberating power of the Spirit and the freedom from condemnation are described by Paul as "God's decisive deed in Christ."[19] The believer is set free so that by walking according to the Spirit he might fulfill the demands of the Law (Rom. 8:4).

A life yielded to the Spirit has the fruit that leads to life. The Spirit frees us from the power of the law and enables us to serve God in a new way by empowering us to obey God in love (Rom. 7:6). However, a life in the flesh leads to death and opposes God's will (Rom. 7:8). He urges them to live according the Spirit and not to the flesh. Living according to the flesh will lead to death, but living according to the Spirit will lead to life and peace.

As a result of the Spirit's work in liberating the believers from the law and sins' power, Paul tells them they are under obligation to the Spirit to live a life characterized by the Spirit; a life of obedience to the will of God (v. 12). The Spirit characterized life creates certain virtues in us such as love, self-control, kindness, goodness, faithfulness. These virtues are important values for the moral life (Gal. 5:19). The biblical writers talk about other

---

17 T. J. Deidun, *New Covenant Morality in Paul*. Rome: Biblical Institute Press, 1981, 70.
18 Cranfield, *Romans*, 377.
19 Cranfield, *Romans*, 378.

virtues such as humility, endurance, gentleness, righteousness, compassion, purity, goodness, peace, tolerance, unity, and patience. All these virtues are necessary ingredients for the moral life (1 Tim. 4:12, 6:11, 2 Tim. 2:22, 3:10, 1 Pet. 3:8, 2 Pet. 1:5–7, Col. 3:12–17, Phil. 2:2–3, Eph. 4:2–3, 32, Gal. 5:22–23, Rom. 14:17, 15:4–5, 2 Cor. 6:4–10).

The Spirit brings transformation in the Christian's life and empowers him to live and fulfill God's moral laws. Christians are called to a life that is led by God's Spirit. The Christian's moral life demands an arduous and continuing modification of the self, still present in this world and still exposed to the powers of this age. It demands "living by the Spirit" and constantly putting to death the deeds of the body (v. 13). For Paul, therefore the Christian life is a life yielded to what God has done in Christ (indicative) and what he now does in us through the Spirit of Christ (imperative). It is also important to note how difficult it is for human beings to live and do what is right by themselves or through the "power of the will." For such a life is impossible! We cannot have that high confidence in humanity ability to live righteously without the enabling power of the Holy Spirit!

The ethical life entails life in the Spirit (Rom. 8:4). The Spirit provides the divine power necessary for Christian living (Rom. 8:2–4, Gal. 4:6). Living by the Spirit prevents the believer from gratifying the desires of our sinful nature (Gal. 5:16). It is the Spirit who guides us into right conduct, as well as enable us to discern God's will and perceive what constitute proper behavior (Rom. 8:4–9, 13–14; Gal. 5:16, Col. 1:10). The Spirit produces in us character that reflects the triune God's character. The Christian life then is a call to a life of holiness, justice, and righteousness.

The indicative and imperative relations to eschatology and the Spirit

It is generally accepted by New Testament scholars that Paul viewed the Christian life as "a life between the times."[20] Therefore, the interrelatedness of the indicative and imperative should be understood in the context of

---

20 J.C. Beker, Paul the Apostle, Triumph, 275.

Paul's eschatology.[21] Even though the Christian has experienced freedom from sin's power, yet there is a sense in which the total aspect of this is in the future when sin will be totally removed from our midst. Thus, the full realization of what Christ's death and resurrection has done for us will not be fully realized in this life.

For Paul, Christ's entrance into human history, his death and resurrection ushered in the new age. By ushering in the new age, the end time hopes have begun to be experienced by Christians, though this is not fully realized. The giving of the Holy Spirit on the day of Pentecost ushered in the new age. Peter interpreted Pentecost as a fulfillment of prophecy of the end time expectation.[22] The interpretation of the giving of the Spirit as an eschatological fulfillment opened the door for the believer to enter into the eschatological life or the end times. This eschatological hope motivates Christians to live holy and godly lives (2 Pet. 3:11).

Geerhardus Vos and others[23] have pointed out the relationship of the Spirit to the indicative and imperative in Paul. Vos attributes the believer's union with Christ to the Holy Spirit (the indicative). The Spirit affirms and attests to justification as an accomplished fact. However, the same Spirit effects or produces the fruit of righteousness in the believer (the imperative). Therefore, the Spirit of God unites and shows the relationship between the indicative and the imperative. On this Ridderbos writes of the Spirit:

> Being in the Spirit is not a mystical but an eschatological, redemptive-historical category. It means, you are no longer in the power of the old *aeon*; you have passed into the new

---

21 T.J. Deidun, *New Covenant Morality in Paul*, 239. Here Deidun points out to the contrary that "far from resolving the paradox of indicative-imperative relationship the dialectic of Pauline eschatology only sharpens it, for rightly understood, it reinforces the indicative, yet it does not remove the imperative—on the contrary, it sanctions it with the threat of death (ct. Rom. 8.13)" While Deidun is right in saying that eschatology sharpens the paradox of indicative-imperative, nevertheless, it is eschatology which makes a close association of the Pauline indicative and imperative possible in Paul's writings.

22 Acts 2:14–21.

23 See Geerhardus Vos, "The Eschatological Aspects of the Pauline Conception of the Spirit," 225–237, Neil Q. Hamilton, "The Holy Spirit and Eschatology in Paul." Edinburgh: Oliver and Boyd Ltd, 1957, 26–27.

one, you are under different authority. This is the indicative of redemption, the proclamation of the new state of life, and it can be followed by the imperative: If we live by the Spirit, let us walk by the Spirit.[24]

In concluding our discussion on the relationship of the Spirit to the indicative and imperative relationship, Dennison's conclusion is appropriate:

> Therefore, the union of the indicative and imperative cannot be dialectical and distinctively existential as Bultmann understood, because the Holy Spirit brings to bear upon believers a new covenant consciousness, which is eschatologically conceived in the actual redemptive-historical work of God the Father through his Son, Jesus Christ. Eschatologically speaking, the Holy Spirit brings the covenant community consciously into union with Christ (indicative); the same Spirit performed and secures in us conscious works of righteousness (imperative) so that we are holy and blameless before the throne of a holy and just God.[25]

Thus the close association of the indicative and imperative are made apparent for, "the eschatological and theocentric conception of the Spirit unify the indicative and imperative by bringing the fullness of life upon the believer through the actual historical-redemptive work of God."[26]

The indicative gives a full force for the imperative in biblical ethics. The Spirit unifies both the indicative and the imperative in the believer. The indicative serves as a motive force for all biblical moral injunctions. Since the imperative serves as a corrective factor to misbehavior and a sanction to right living before the Lord, both the indicative and imperative are to be viewed as essential parts of the gospel and ethics. However, it is

---

24 H. Ridderbos, "When the Time Had Fully Come" *Studies in New Testament Theology*. Grand Rapids: Wm. B. Eerdmans, 1957, 52.

25 W.D. Dennison, "Basic Structure," 75–76.

26 Dennison, "Basic Structure," 76.

undoubtedly the indicative aspect of salvation as much as anything else that gives the theological basis for NT ethical exhortations. As Deidun has rightly said, "It is on the ground of who Christians are—dead to sin, justified and liberated from the law and sin that the Christian imperative finds ground and *raison d'etre.*"[27]

The community of God as a moral community

How can we develop virtue and character within the Christian community? Narrativists agree that stories and traditions can powerfully shape a person's character and influence his/her patterns of behavior. This is true for all cultures and communities.

To answer the question above, Christian character may best be developed within the community of God's people where the behavior of the Christian is determined and shaped by the stories and the experiences of the larger community—the church. As the Christian submits him/herself to the teachings of Scripture (Story) and daily determines to obey the will of God by yielding his/her life to the promptings and wooing of the Holy Spirit, Christian character will develop which will reflect in his/her conduct.

The Holy Spirit will shape the person's character and develop in them certain moral values or virtues such as self-control, patience, endurance, godliness, and love that are necessary for their moral life (Gal. 5:22, 2 Pet. 1:5–9) in contrast to the works of the flesh that produces certain vices in the person's moral life (Gal. 5:19). These virtues are necessary for us to produce or live a life of moral excellence (2 Pet. 1:5–9).

Those who commit themselves to live faithfully to the Christian story will develop Christian virtues and character as expressions appropriate to their Christian convictions. Character/virtue therefore becomes a central concept for moral reflection. The self is trained through the narrative of the community's story to be morally upright. Character formation is not a result of any one narrative; the self is constituted by many different roles of stories. Character development involves a constant conversation between

---

27 Deidun, *Covenant Morality*, 242.

our stories that allows us to live appropriately to the character of our existence. We must conform our lives to God's ways.

Character should develop from the Christians' convictions and the community's stories/narratives provide the means to express the moral significance of integrity without assuming any one moral principle. Hauerwas points this out; "the necessity of character for the morally coherent life is recognition that morally our existence is constituted by a plentitude of values and virtues, not all of which can be perfectly embodied in any one life." Character is forged by giving coherence to our behavior. Character then, involves an analysis of the nature of the self.[28]

An ethics of character centers on the claim that an agent's being is prior to doing. This is not to say that what we do is unimportant or even secondary, but rather that what one does or does not do is dependent on one possessing a self, sufficient to take personal responsibility for one's actions. What is significant about us morally is not what we do or do not do, but how we do what we do.

As persons of character, the kinds of situations we encounter and how we understand them, are a function of the kind of people we are. However, there is a sense in which we are also shaped by our communities or societies. It takes community or society to shape a person with integrity of character. We all derive our integrity or character from our communities—villages, towns, cities, family, friends, and workplace. These communities shape most of the values we form in life. So, when an individual cuts herself or himself from his/her roots and community and become an autonomous individual one is made to lose his or her moral compass.

Integrity of character is shaped when we see our lives, our loyalties, and ourselves as part of a larger story that shapes our community. However, from these stories come certain principles that shape a behavior. While virtue ethics is important, we cannot neglect principles because many virtues do correlate with principles and ideals. Any society without principles would not allow virtues to flourish.

---

28 Stanley Hauerwas, *Community of Character*, 134.

Nurturing and cultivating virtues as the critical component of New Testament ethics

Virtues are character traits that enable us to contribute to community—to the particular society in which we live. In nurturing and developing character and virtues, we need to focus on discipleship. Christian discipleship must be intentional and focused on nurturing Christians in building Christian Character and values. We must emphasize community and model these values for people to see. Communities help to promote and ensure the sense of belonging and one's responsibility to the community to help it reach its goals and ideals.

There are certain virtues that should shape our character and behavior. Jesus expresses these virtues in the Sermon on the Mount. The virtues Jesus taught in the Sermon on the Mount include humility or meekness, righteousness, mercy, purity of heart, peacemaking, suffering persecution for justice and Jesus' sake (Matt. 5).

Apostle Paul taught similar virtues: humility and gentleness, righteousness, kindness, compassion, love, forgiveness; purity or goodness, peace, tolerance, unity, patience, endurance, joy (Col. 3:12–17; Phil. 2:2–3; Eph. 4:2–3,32; Gal. 5:22–23; Rom. 14:17, 15:4–5; 2 Cor. 6:4–10). Having these virtues speaks of what it means to be a follower of Jesus. These virtues are what characterized the reign of God.

In addition to these biblical virtues, the NT encouraged certain moral values that shaped its ethics. These values include sharing of resources with the needy and the less fortunate in society, solidarity, hard work, truth telling, love, compassion, and mercy.

Most traditional western virtues emphasize the four Greek virtues, courage, justice, temperance or modesty and prudence. Some add to these four, faith, hope, and love. God's forgiveness, peace, and justice become normative for all human societies. Biblical virtues are good for the wellbeing of human societies—peacemaking, hungering for justice, doing mercy, integrity, humility, and caring for the poor and those mourning. These qualities in us become the foundation for our moral practices.

It is not enough to teach rules and principles about right and wrong; we need to nurture the kind of virtue and character that lead people actually to do the right and avoid the wrong. We must model what it means to be a person of integrity, justice, or faith within the community's moral life.[29]

Character transformation as goal for biblical ethics

The goal of biblical ethics or the moral life is to become like Christ. That is, looking at the world and things from Christ's perspective. It is conforming to the nature and character of Christ, by reflecting his nature in all we do, say, and think. We must have the mind of Christ. This calls for the renewal of our minds.

"Like begets like" (James 3:11–12). We share in the divine nature and we have escaped the evil and rottenness around us. Therefore, we must reflect God's character. (1 Pet. 1:3, 2 Pet. 3:11). In reflecting God's character, we must do what God does, doing good and right always. In doing good and right always we become his children (1 John 2:29).

Conclusion

In this chapter, I started with the thesis that the character and nature of New Testament ethics is Christological. Jesus' example, love, compassion, mercy, and justice were some of the foundational values that shaped his ethics. The New Testament writers' goal was to show the implications of the Gospel and their relationship to Jesus for their moral lives. We saw that New Testament ethics was relational. Both Jesus' ethics was grounded upon his intimate relationship with His father. His life was patterned after God's character and nature. He called his followers to be perfect as their heavenly father is perfect. The followers of Jesus must reflect his life and character as he reflected the character and nature of his father.

Paul and others worked out the implications of our relationship with Jesus and the moral responsibility that relationship places on the believers

---

29 Stassen and Gushee, *Kingdom Ethics*, 32.

and the community of God's people. We saw Paul's moral imperative were based on his indicative of what God has done for us in Christ. Not only is Christ the model for the ethical life he is also the source for the moral life. New Testament ethic's goal is to developed godly character that results in Christlike life. Christians must develop godly values and virtues that are foundation for their moral life. Some of these virtues include mercy, compassions, faith, truthfulness, faithfulness, patience, longsuffering, joy, etc… These virtues are essential for our moral lives.

Now we are ready to integrate our discussions of the three contexts we have examined. We suggest the indicative and imperative structure as the theoretical framework or paradigm as the foundation for African theological and biblical ethics. We will discuss this in the next chapter.

CHAPTER 6

Integrating African, Western, and Biblical Ethical Norms/Values for African Theological and Social Ethics

Introduction

African and western ethics are humanistic ethics. This humanistic tendency in both African traditional and western ethics is based on the assumption that human beings are created perfect, sinless and possess a mind, which has the ability to make moral decisions. With these basic presuppositions, African and western ethics focus on human beings' ability for the moral life and not on God's power. Most of their moral values are shaped by their cultural, social and moral values. Some of these values are founded on biblical moral values, while others conflict with biblical moral values. We affirm those that reflect biblical values and I intend to use these values as we address some of the ethical issues we will deal with in part 2 of this book.

The central place given to human beings and human reason as basis for moral decisions need correction. While the moral values of humanistic ethics has some value for human well being and mat be good, it nonetheless misses the core foundation of morality, which has it basis in the triune God as we have seen from our examination of biblical ethics. Biblical ethics has the triune God, his nature, character and his divine will as the model and source and power for the moral life. Biblical ethics is theological it is based on God's character and nature.

In African and western philosophical ethics, both the source of ethics and the power for the moral life have their answers in human beings. Humanity is the measure of all moral standards. The foundation of African and western ethics is non-supernatural; its focus is primarily on human welfare. It was inadequate and had failed to help people to live consistent moral life.

In these traditions, moral norms, rights, or wrongs are determined by customs and traditions, which are expressed in their cultural, social, and moral values. What determines wrong or right by a particular society is sometimes questionable. For example, under certain conditions and situations immorality may be acceptable when it has to deal with sexual relationships with the fertility gods or for a wife to raise children for her infertile husband. Killing a stranger or an enemy in some traditional African societies was a good thing as far as that person is not from one's tribe or clan. However, the Bible clearly teaches that God abhors both immorality and murder.

What is right becomes relative depending on the values of the particular community. One cannot speak of universal moral values to which humanity must submit. This is what has caused the present moral malaise we find ourselves regarding some of the moral values and issues confronting the world today.

The reason for this moral problem is the secular outlook our modern ethics embrace. McVeigh rightly points out that the problem that faces African and western ethics both past and present is religion.[1] By setting aside religion as basis for the moral life, ethicists have contribution to this problem. Our moral failures towards each other is not primarily a human problem, it is a theological or religious one. For all moral pollution is primarily against a Holy God who is the lawgiver and he is very concerned about the quality of our human relationships. All moral laws have their origin in God and they obtain their validity and authority from God.

To develop an ethical system that is Christian and biblical in its outlook and values, we must take seriously the role of religion in ethics. Religion

---

1 McVeigh, *God in Africa*, 101.

cannot play a peripheral role in shaping our behavioral patterns. It must be central to our moral discourse. While it is true that some communities think and believe there, is a relationship between the Supreme God and the ethical conduct of people and recognize God as the source of many of their customs and moral laws, yet the belief in and fear of God play a very limited role in governing the people's moral actions. Smith rightly observed that:

> Among numbers of Africans there is, as we have seen—in great things if not in small things—a fear of God and what God will do if certain laws are broken. As a control of behavior, this fear is generally feeble.[2]

What gives African ethics its drive and motive are the ancestral and community sanctions. People fear the consequences of their action against the ancestors or the divinities and they are forced by society to conform to its moral laws, which are expressed in the customs and traditions of the particular community. What is needed is not fear of the ancestral spirits but a new inner compulsion or motivation for morality. What we need is a new motivation based on a deeper understanding of God. This is essential in developing theological ethics in the evangelical church in Africa.

Some ethicists have suggested that what we need to guide our actions is a "new understanding of restraint of conscience."[3] While the conscience can play some role in our moral life, I point out in chapter 3 that the conscience is weak and can mislead one in making good and right choices. The conscience is not standard for morality. God is the standard for our ethical action.

Thus, the key to real moral behavior is one's conception of God. Our reverence for God's moral laws and our love for the right and good should motivate our ethical actions. This inner compulsion or motivation comes because of the Spirit regenerating our sinful and corrupt nature and creating

---

[2] Edwin W. Smith, *African Beliefs and Christian Faith*. London: Lutherworth Press, 1936, 117.

[3] McVeigh, *Conceptions of God*, 100.

in us a new nature. The Spirit of God creates in us the desire and the ability to love and to do God's will, which is set forth in his moral laws found in the Scriptures.

Our study of the indicative and imperative structure as the basis for biblical ethics revealed several important truths, which are very crucial for developing ethics in Africa. I will point out some of the methodological as well as the hermeneutical implications of the indicative and the imperative framework for ethics in the African context.

Methodological implications of the indicative and imperative for African theological social ethics/morality

African Christian theological and social ethics must have solid theological and biblical foundations. The biblical indicative and imperative structure should provide this foundation. In this paradigm, the Triune God's decisive act in Christ to redeem humanity from sin and its power forms the foundation for the moral life. God's character and nature is at the core of such ethics. He is the model and standard for the moral life. Biblical and theological values are therefore very important and central to this ethics. These biblical and theological values give shape to our moral values and ethics.

In addition to these central biblical and theological values, there are some cultural, religious, moral, and social values from both the African and western context that are helpful for the kind of ethics we are seeking to develop. Values such as justice, solidarity, truthfulness, hospitality, human dignity, and interdependence, to mention a few, are important values that are critical for this kind of ethics. These African and western values we argued have their source in the Bible.

The following diagram illustrates the critical elements I think are crucial for the foundations for African theological and biblical social ethics. Here I will attempt to integrate the Africa, western and biblical ethical values as foundation for African Christian social ethics, which I will then discuss.

Integrating African, Western, and Biblical Ethical Norms/Values

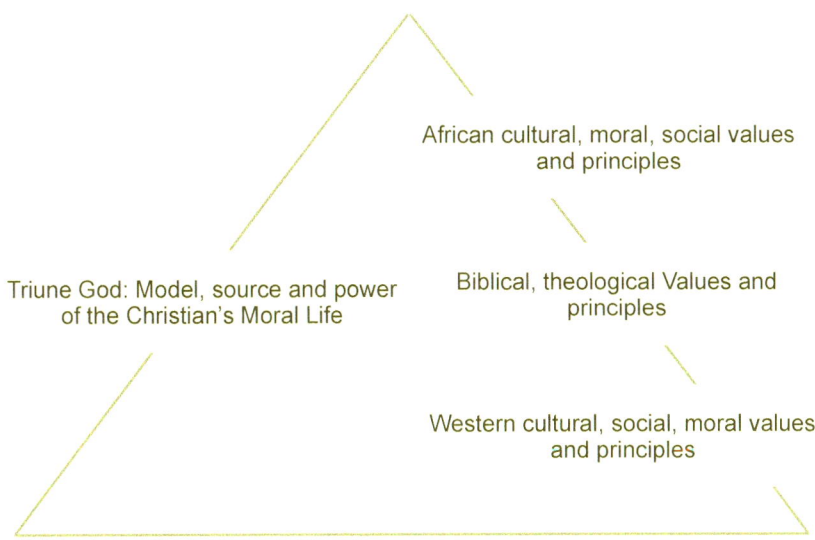

Diagram illustrating the theological, biblical, social, cultural, and moral foundations of African social ethics

Triune God: Model source and power for the Christian's moral life

This study has shown that Biblical ethics we find in both the Old and New Testaments are theologically grounded. Both foundations relate to God's relationship with humanity based on his decisive redemptive work. This we characterized as the indicative and imperative framework in both Testaments. The theoretical frame of biblical ethics is theological. However, its practical goal is social. This twin truth of biblical ethics is critical for African theological ethics.

It is therefore important that the moral life becomes viable when it begins with one having a special relationship with the Triune God, Father, Son and Holy Spirit. This relationship puts one in the position to be empowered by the Triune God to live a life that is please to God.

Since the Triune God is the model, source, and power for the moral life, he becomes the standard and measure of all ethical perfections. We must reflect his character, nature, not just human traditions, and customs become the standard for morality. This means, we have to submit all our cultural, customs, and moral values to that of God's moral values, which are found in the Scriptures. All our moral values must be subjected to the authority of God's word, the Bible.

In the Bible, we see a close connection between ethics and theology, faith and practice. This is the primary reason why we cannot set aside religion in ethics. It must be of necessity a central feature of ethics.

The Christian's relationship with the Triune God has certain moral implications his/her daily moral life. God has changed the Christian's disposition to sin and its power over him/her and has give him/her His divine nature or being so he can live to please God in all areas of life.

Mott rightly observes,

> Our ethical behavior is to correspond to what God has enabled us to be by adoption and grace based on God's historical, once-for-all act in Christ's death and resurrection.[4]

The only evidence we have to prove that we are recipients of God's grace is to live a life that is consistent with grace, that is, holiness. God's grace for us and in us must not be taken for granted. Neither should we use it as pretence for immoral behavior. Grace, rather, should motivate us to strive for moral integrity. We need to present ourselves to God as a living sacrifice, holy and acceptable to God (Rom. 12:1–2).

The Spirit as Power for the Ethical Life

The Holy Spirit makes our new birth possible. He is also the one who gives us the ability and the power to live the ethical life. The grace of God and the Spirit of God become for the believer the source of the moral power or enablement.

---

[4] S.C. Mott, *Biblical Ethics and Social Change*. Oxford: Oxford University Press, 1982, 24.

The Christian is under moral obligation to yield his or her life to the Holy Spirit. Paul emphasizes the constant tension that exists between the flesh and the Spirit for supremacy in the Christian's life. We must decide which to obey, the flesh, or the Spirit?[5] Obeying the flesh or the Spirit has some moral consequences. Yielding to the Spirit leads to holiness and life while yielding to the flesh leads to unrighteousness and death.

The Spirit enables us to put away anything that hinders the Spirit's activity in our lives to grow in holiness. Through God's action in Christ, Christians have been liberated by the Spirit and are set free from condemnation. Christians are therefore, exhorted to walk in the Spirit (Rom. 8:4). The Spirit indwelling the believer marks the beginning of the Christian's moral life. What the law could not do in that it was weak because of the flesh, Christ through his Spirit accomplished (Rom. 8:2). Thus by depending upon the Spirit, we can fulfill the demands of the law. The flesh should not govern the Christian's behavior because "the life giving principle of the Spirit has freed you in Christ Jesus from the control of the principles of sin and death."[6] Paul, therefore, encourages us to crucify the flesh which suggests that it is still alive in us but we can control its domination over our lives by crucifying it daily by the power of the Spirit (Rom. 8:13).

The Spirit both regenerates and gives guidance as to how these principles of the Gospel should work in a given situation by empowering the Christian to put these principles into effect. It is God's Spirit working in us that we receive the power to obey his moral laws and commands. Ezekiel's words are instructive:

> Then I will sprinkle clean water on you, and you will be clean. Your filth will be washed away, and you will no longer worship idols. And I will give you a new heart and new right desires, and I will put a new spirit in you. I will take out your stony hear of sin and give you a new, obedient heart. And I will put

---

[5] Helmut Thielicke, *Theological Ethic: Foundations* Vol. 1. Grand Rapids: Wm. B. Eerdmans, 1979, 83.

[6] Romans 8:2 (Berkeley Version).

my Spirit in you so you will obey my laws and do whatever I command (Ezek. 36:25–27, NLT).

Thus, the source of our ethical power is not in the strength and reason of human being but the Spirit of God. The role of the Spirit as the giver of a new life and as a source of power for the Christian moral life is very crucial in developing evangelical ethics in Africa.

Secondly, the absence of the Spirit's role and place in ethics will leave us with an ethical system that is based on human effort. This ethic will end up in moral defeat because there is no source of moral power in human beings to do the right and overcome our evil thoughts and desires as we have pointed out (Col. 2:21–23). We must therefore, emphasize the role of the Spirit in our ethical task as the source of our ethical power and daily appropriate this power by submitting to his guidance and leading.

Thirdly, Paul reminds us of the continuing threat that the flesh poses to the Christian, and this we need to avoid. The exhortation to crucify or mortify the deeds of the flesh through the Spirit speaks of only one possibility of life for the Christian by which he can achieve moral victory. This understanding of the tension between the flesh and the Spirit and the exhortation to crucify the flesh will reject any attempt of espousing any form of "perfectionist ethics."

Barclay shows this tension vividly. He says that the flesh and Spirit dualism reveal

> "The situation of believers transformed by the power of the new age and enlisted in the service of the Lord and yet required to live out that service in the midst of the lures and temptations of the old age by a constant renewal of their obedience to the truth in faith."[7]

---

7 Barclay, *Obey the Truth*, 215.

The moral life is not an act of human will or power but by the Spirit. By saying this, we are not denying the place of moral effort on the part of the Christian or human beings in general.

Indicative and imperative: Having a Proper Balance

This study points out the indicative and imperative are closely associated in biblical ethics. In applying this methodology, we need to ensure that we put proper emphasis on both the indicative and imperative without attempting to reduce the force of the other. It is very important that evangelical ethics focus upon a balanced and biblical formulation of the indicative and the imperative. There are certain dangers associated with emphasizing one aspect of the biblical framework in Africa and elsewhere.

Dangers in emphasizing only the indicative

In our ethical task if we emphasize the indicative only at the expense of the imperative, we are in danger of having an ethical system that would lead to pietistic moralism or perfectionism. This problem of over-realized eschatology was the problem of the Corinthian church, which Paul had to correct. The Corinthians by emphasizing their position in Christ lived as if they were already living in the kingdom (1 Cor. 4:8). Yet, there were all kinds of moral problems within the assembly and Paul had to deal with these moral problems, as we must in Africa.

Another group of Christians who tend to emphasize the indicative more is the holiness movements. Their failure of recognizing the tension between the "not yet" and the "already" leads some of them to espouse an ethic of perfectionism. We should constantly remind ourselves of the threat of the flesh, which the imperative summons us to crucify. African converts need to be told this frankly. The Bible warns us about over confidence in ourselves. The one who thinks he stands must take heed lest he falls! (Gal. 6:1).

Dangers in emphasizing only the imperative

If by emphasizing the indicative, we end up in pietistic or perfectionist ethic, emphasizing the imperative will lead to a legalistic ethic or legalism. To emphasize the imperative only, will rob ethics of its theological basis and will lead us to the autonomy of the ego. Human beings will be completely thrown back on their own resources for the attainment of salvation or moral righteousness and the Gospel as a source of the moral life will lose its exclusiveness.

For instance, when the Galatians Christians emphasized the imperative more it led to legalism in the church. Emphasizing the imperative will place us in a situation where the "self" is given autonomy leading to the self-creation of the self, thus freeing ethics from its theological control and dangerously placing reliance upon ecclesiastical conformity as it happens so often in many African churches.

In order to prevent the autonomy of the self, we must put proper emphasis on both the indicative and the imperative as basis for biblical ethics. To avoid any form of pietistic moralism, again we need to emphasize equally on both the indicative and the imperative. Nevertheless, there is an important sense in which the indicative precedes the imperative in Paul. In Paul, being precedes deeds. For Paul, good works always are the fruit of one's new life and not vice versa.

I will need to make certain observations about the indicative and imperative framework before we end the discussion. Firstly, the indicative and imperative formulation in both the OT and the NT emphasized the priority of grace for ethics. Both the source and the power for the moral life is God Himself. God alone is the initiator and the fulfiller of the moral life. Grace, therefore, must be seen as having a two-fold efficacy, God's power working for us on the one hand and God's power working in us on the other hand. African Christian ethics, therefore, must begin with the cross. Any ethical system that does not begin at the cross will turn out to be legalistic and humanistic in its outlook. It will be a product of mere human effort to earn righteousness from God, a task the Bible says it is impossible.

Secondly, our ethical task must be theological rather than anthropological. Biblical ethics has God as its center. It focuses upon a Holy God who by the death and the resurrection of his son Jesus Christ has entered into a relationship with humankind. Ethics is based on God's redemptive indicative. Thus, African Christian ethics must free itself from all humanistic tendencies. Biblical ethics is theologically motivated.

The Trinitarian nature of biblical ethics clearly show that the source from which such moral efforts spring is not humanistic. Rather, biblical morality finds its basis on the saving deed of God Himself. Biblical ethics is not based on the promotion of the self in attaining moral superiority. Human wisdom as a means to achieve moral approval from God is alien to biblical ethics.

The indicative and the imperative framework do not only outline the ground for ethics but it also sets out the parameter within which our ethical action must be measured. In this ethical system, God, not humans, becomes the standard of our moral life. Human actions or behaviors are patterned after God's conduct (Rom. 15:1–3, 7). For instance, we are called to accept one another, particularly the weak in faith, because God has accepted us (Rom. 14:3). Thus, any ethical system that will have human beings as the standard for behavior is unbiblical and not Christian.

Thirdly, the theological nature of biblical ethics presupposes and emphasizes the centrality of God's revelation of Himself and the unfolding redemption of the human race. The appeal for true knowledge of God's word and his nature and our current position in him is very important in our ethical task. For example, in Romans 6, Paul three times appeals to the Roman Christians' knowledge about what God through his Son has said about their new relationship with Christ and the implications of that for their old life of sin. Our knowledge of what God has done for us and in us, his word and actions, and our relationship to him as scripture teaches us becomes crucial for ethics.

Therefore, any authentic African Christian ethics should give a central place to God's special revelation of himself to humans through his Son, which is recorded in the Bible.

Not only is the Bible crucial for ethics but also faith in God's word and submitting ourselves to the authority of God's word to inform our practices and our moral life is equally important. We must not only derive our ethics using God's word. We must also believe what God's word says about our new situation or condition. Both our knowledge and faith in what God has said and done for us should govern our actions.

The indicative and imperative framework: Hermeneutical implications for morality and ethics

The primacy of a Christian counter-community and discipleship

The indicative and imperative structure in biblical ethics has both methodological and hermeneutical implication for African Christian ethics. It is very clear from our discussions that the biblical imperatives were not primarily addressed to unbelievers but to the community of faith. The inactive and imperative framework work has implications for creating a counter-Christian community and for Christian discipleship.

Hays describes the community of faith as a "counter-community of discipleship."[8] The Christian community as a counter-community of discipleship speaks of the moral responsibility the Church has towards society. Christians must provide the standard for society and its moral norms. We must not conform to the cultural and moral values of our communities that are contrary to God's moral laws. Rather we must rescind those values.

The concept of the "community of discipleship" is very important in our ethical task. It underscores two important aspects in our ethical task. These have to do with community and discipleship.

First, in our ethical discourse our primary attention must focus on community; our corporate obedience as the body of Christ or community of faith to God's moral laws.[9] This radical understanding of ethics cautions

---

8 Richard B. Hays, "Scripture-Shaped Community: The Problem of Method in New Testament Ethics," *Interpretation* 44/1 (January 1990), 47.
9 Hays, "Scripture-Shaped Community," 47.

against placing more emphasis on individual character formation at the expense of the community's corporate moral life of obedience to God's will. This does not mean we are not concerned about the individual's moral character. It is important. The focus must be communal. As the community practices its values, individual characters will be affected.

This agrees with the communal nature of African ethics, which is best characterized as social ethics. The social nature of African ethics ensures corporate observance of the moral laws and taboos by the entire community for the social wellbeing of the community. In Africa, ethics was not an individual matter but a corporate responsibility, which was realized and accomplished in the society. Sempebwa comments on the problem of an ethics that is individualistic in this statement:

> The belief in individual ethics makes it difficult for a person to relate one's individual moral convictions to the other inhabitants of the earth…. Individualistic ethics is powerless before the demands that go beyond the brother at home, next door, and thus Christian love in the wider scale tends to evaporate into a mild feeling of universal benevolence.[10]

African cultural values, which place emphasis on community life, rule out any form of personal individualistic ethic. This leads to egoistic ethics that has no place in African social ethics. Rather, African ethics points to and affirms a "corporate moral engagement and responsibility"[11] for the benefit of the community and not for the individual's benefit.

Similarly, biblical ethics is corporate ethics. It has a social goal. The corporate or the social nature of biblical ethics is also emphasized by Wright. In discussing, the ethics of the Old Testament Wright says this:

> It is not simply a compendium of moral teaching to enable individual to lead a privately upright life for God…it addressed

---

10 Hays, "Scripture-Shaped Community," 237.
11 Hays, "Scripture-Shaped Community," 237.

the individual as part of the community and their purpose is not just individual purity but the moral and spiritual health of that whole community. For God's purpose as we have seen, were not just righteous individuals, but a new community who in their social life would embody those qualities of righteousness, peace, justice and love which reflect God's own character and were his original purpose for mankind.[12]

What we have said about Old Testament ethics, that is, its social character can be said about the Church, the new community of God through which God wants his righteousness demonstrated through its corporate life in society. God has created a new community through which his moral laws will be achieved corporately. The goal of the Christian life is for all believers to grow to maturity and become like Christ in our moral life and character (Eph. 4:13).

The problem of emphasizing the Church's corporate moral responsibility is more pronounced in evangelical Christianity. The evangelical tradition has generally tended to teach an almost purely personal ethics to the exclusions of community ethics. Such an understanding of ethics tends to make the Christian ethical teachings to be regarded as a body of abstract principles necessary for maintaining the fabric of society but with no impact on the lives of the members of that society. Thus, we are to create biblical communities where ethical ideals can be realized and where the individual finds his/her moral identity and strength in the communities' moral values as we find in African communities.

Second, the indicative and imperative combination in biblical ethics has hermeneutical implications for discipleship. Christian discipleship is central in our ethical task, that is, to bring all believers to a place where they will be seeking to live under God's word.[13] The essence of discipleship

---

12 Christopher J. Wright, *An Eye for an Eye: the Place of Old Testament Ethics Today*, 34–35.

13 See Wayne Meeks, "A Hermeneutics of Social Embodiment" in *Harvard Theological Review* 79 (1986), Gerherd Lohfink, *Jesus and Community: The Social Dimension of Christian Faith*. Philadelphia: Fortress Press, 1984.

is following Jesus. We are to live and conduct our lives as Jesus did (Rom. 6:4; 15:3). In discipling new Christians, we need to explain to them what their relationship with Christ means for their individual as well as corporate moral living. Our knowledge about who we are; the fact that we are justified and have died to sin—to its lusts and passions—are basic truths that we must teach, explain, and emphasize during the period preceding and after baptism. The Old Testament placed the responsibility of parents and the community to train up their children to "walk in the ways of the Lord by doing what is right and just" (Gen. 18:18–19, Deut. 6:1–9). This is what the Christian discipleship must entail. We must train believers to live right within the community of faith as well as in society so we will reflect our family values as children of God.

The Christian faith must apply to the ethical issues and challenges we face in our walk as Christians. Part of our maturity is to apply the faith to moral issues that confront us. If I may borrow from Beker, Paul was a "pragmatic hermeneutician."[14] He applied the Gospel to particular problems in different ethical situations he encountered. For example, in Romans, Paul's doctrine of justification by faith for both Jews and Gentiles has some ethical and social import: namely, the unity of both Jews and Gentiles into one family as God's children. This basic unity is established as a result of faith in Jesus. This understanding that God has made them one should then guide their behavior towards each other. As people having the same Lord (Rom. 14:7–9), they are not to be judgmental of one another, instead of pleasing themselves, they are to please their neighbor for this is what their Lord did (Rom. 15:1–3). Based upon this unity, they are to accept one another in order to promote peace and growth of the body Christ (Rom. 14:15:19).

Given the complex ethical problems of our period in redemptive history, we need to apply Paul's hermeneutical methodology. We should apply the "gospel" to every ethical situation in which we find ourselves. We should work out the ethical implications of the gospel for the daily

---

14 J.C. Beker, "Paul's Theology: Consistent or Inconsistent?" *New Testament Studies* 34/3 (1988), 370.

ethical problems we face. V.P. Furnish clearly points out that in Paul "one finds not a 'Pauline ethic' but Paul the pastor/counselor," reflecting on how the truth of the gospel forms and reforms the lives of those who are in Christ, and urging his congregations to be conformed to the truth within the particulars of their own situation.[15] Thus Paul's hermeneutics was not just "an abstract individual activity of the apostle, not the activity of learned rabbis instructing their disciples in a rabbinic school but a pragmatic ecclesial conscious building which takes place in and for the body of Christ where under the guidance of the Holy Spirit the members "find out," "test," and "approve"...what is the will of God, what is good and acceptable and perfect (Rom. 12:2).[16]

By applying this Pauline hermeneutical principle, the church in Africa can deal effectively, biblically and theologically with the enormous ethical issues that confront her today.

Character as the moral engine for both African, western and biblical ethics

Theologians and humanistic philosophers generally agree that what is important about human beings is what they do. This implies that conduct is always a safe and sure clue to character. Many people today have very good and commendable conduct. For instance, a person who behaves honestly is acting rightly. However, if he does so simply and solely because he thinks that honesty pays him in the end, he is nothing more than an opportunist at heart. There is no high sense of dignity within him, his conduct is right but his character is base. At best, he reflects an egoistic ethical tendency, only thinking about self.

Paul, in fact, acknowledges that there can be false obedience which can lead to right conduct (Colossians 2:20–23). The Romans, however, were

---

15 V.P. Furnish, "Belonging to Christ: A Paradigm for Ethics in First Corinthians" *Interpretation* 44/2 (April 1990), 146.
16 Beker, "Paul's Theology," 370–371.

not like that. They have genuinely "obeyed with all your heart the new teaching God has given you" (Rom. 6:17, NLT).

The Roman Christians have experienced an inner transformation in their sinful nature (Rom. 6:2, 11, 18, 22). They have been freed from sin, they have their minds renewed and transformed (Rom. 12:1–2). The Roman Christians were given a new disposition. They have become slaves to righteousness and not to sin (Rom. 6:18). Christians are "right-wised" and have been enabled to live a new life. It is as a result of this new life received in Jesus Christ and the constant yielding of Christians to this righteousness received that they will achieve holiness (Rom. 6:19).

The idea of conduct deriving from one's character is central to the indicative and imperative structure of biblical morality. The Biblical writers affirmed that one's conduct stemmed from the disposition of one's heart. For humankind to have a right disposition for a godly life, their hearts have to be changed. This meant that the life that is dominated by sin must be destroyed. Christ, by his death and resurrection did that for us. He died to sin that through our baptism and union with Him, we might receive a new life—a new inner disposition. For good works are always a fruit of one's new life, new life can never be the fruit of moral living.[17] Martin Luther, the great reformer, expressed the same idea when he says, "Good pious acts never make a good pious man, but a good pious man produces good pious acts."[18]

The fact that the imperative always follows the indicative is of particular significance for ethics. It implies that character precedes conduct. This is clearly shown in the indicative/imperative combination in Paul. Paul's moral exhortations were based on the reality of the believer's present situation, that is, "what you are." For example, in Romans 6, Paul emphasizes the present reality of what the Roman Christians are. They are dead to sin and alive to God. This present reality should affect, therefore, their moral life. They are not to allow sin to rule their lives (Rom. 6:3, 11–14). Again, by the fact of their new status or position with God (as justified) and their

---

17 See Ridderbos, *Paul*, 254–255.
18 Quoted in L.H. Marshall, *The Challenge of New Testament Ethics*. London: Macmillan, 1950, 65.

union with Christ through baptism (indicative), they are called upon to manifest this righteousness in holy living (imperative).

Christians have received the Spirit and have been made the sons of God (Rom. 8:12–25 cf. 1 Cor. 15:30–34; Phil. 3:12–21). Because of the grace they have received, they are exhorted to receive one another in the Lord (Rom. 16:2); not to think more highly of themselves than they ought to do; they must be humble (12:3). Because they are children of light and not of the dark, they are exhorted to proper behavior (Rom. 13:11–14).

In our ethical task, therefore, we must make sure that we help people to transform and develop their character. We must emphasize the need of conversion and the regeneration of the hearts of men. We should begin at the cross. Any ethical system that does not take seriously the transforming power of the Spirit in making the moral life possible will lead to legalism. Of course, such an ethic will fail because it will lack the moral power to enable humankind to do what is right. Paul has made it clear in Romans that the grace of God expressed in the Law and in creation did not produce the corresponding conduct in humanity. An ethical system that undermines the transforming power of God within man's heart is not only bound to be legalistic but also dangerous. This ethical system will end up deifying humans and their moral achievements rather than glorifying God for providing the power to live the moral life. Such ethics will rob God of his exclusiveness in biblical ethics.

Theological Ethics: African, Western and Biblical Principles and Values

I spent a lot of time on the theological component of our model because of its importance in biblical ethics. Now I will turn my focus on both the African and western contribution to our ethical task.

As I pointed out in chapters 1 and 2, there are many cultural, social, and moral values found in the moral teachings in both African and western contexts that may be helpful in dealing with some of the contemporary issues we will be dealing with in the second part of the book. These include the values that are affirmed by biblical values and teachings. For example, in the African context I am thinking of communal values—"sharing, mutual aid, caring for others, interdependence, solidarity, reciprocal obligation, and social harmony." These values or principles "underpin and guide the type of social relations, attitudes, and behavior that ought to exist between individuals who live together in a community, sharing a social life and having a sense of common good.

We must discourage anti-social values or vices such as falsehood, unfairness, insincerity, double-dealings, hypocrisy, ingratitude, ungratefulness, selfishness, self-interest, laziness, or tardiness, immorality, which is often associated with dirt, or filthy life. Worthlessness, futility, useless things; adultery—taking somebody's wife, illicit sexual intercourse with a married person, witchcraft, greed, mischief against fellow humans, pride, and stubbornness. The Bible teaches against these vices.

Some of the western cultural values that may be helpful for our ethical discourse include the ideas or concepts of equality and freedom, the eternal value of the individual, human dignity, self-development, and empowerment, respecting the rights of individuals, and justice. These values are affirmed by biblical teaching.

In particular, in the areas of public policy by government institutions and agencies, the theory of utility would be beneficial where decisions are made not to benefit an individual but the whole society. More importantly, character and virtue ethic will be very important to incorporate in the moral community to build and develop character of people to help them live to fulfill their moral responsibility in society as they serve God and their fellow human beings.

In fact, all of the African and western cultural, moral and social values must be subjected to the scrutiny of the Scriptures, since we hold the view that Scripture is the primary authority for the Christian's moral practice. This engagement of values will enable us to ensure the meanings of these values are consistent with the teachings of the Scriptures.

Conclusion

In concluding our discussion on the methodological and the hermeneutical implication of the biblical indicative and imperative as foundation for African Christian ethics, I have to say that these two grammatical moods provide for us a paradigm for theological ethics. The indicative and imperative provide the framework for ethics, namely, the ground, the motivation, and the empowering agent for ethics. The ethical ground for Christian action according to Paul and other biblical writers is the eschatological act of God in Christ's redemptive work. Ethics, therefore, is theological; it has its source in God not in human beings or in human abilities. Our ethical efforts should always be a response to God's grace and not as a meritorious act. The indicative and imperative emphasize the priority of grace in ethics and place more emphasis on character as source from which ethical actions flow.

What is the implication of the indicative of our union and relationship with the triune God for our moral behavior? How can the truth about "who we are" our "being" form as basis for how we respond to the moral challenges we face in our times? What does it mean to reflect morally God's character and nature in relation to these issues? In the next part of this book, I will endeavor to apply these truths to some of the social moral problems we face today. I will use some of these principles, biblical and cultural values that reflect God's nature and character to address some of the broad ethical issues facing the church in Africa today. I will seek under the guardian of the Holy Spirit, find out, test, and approve what is the will of God, what is good and acceptable and perfect will of God in these issues.

Part 2

Contemporary Social and Ethical Issues

CHAPTER 7

Politics and Governance

"One head does not go into council" (An Akan proverb)

Introduction

Politics and governance, namely bad politics and governments, are two most critical issues that are considered the major causes of all the evils facing our African societies and the continent of Africa today. These include wars, ethnic conflicts, abusive use of power and authority, nepotism, bad use of natural, human, and economic resources, poverty, lack of basic infrastructure and many others. It is therefore very important for us to address these issues by applying some of the moral values and principles we affirmed in part 1 of this book. We will draw from some of the valuable and essential cultural, moral, and biblical values and principles to address these issues.

At the core of our discussion on politics and governance are human relationships. Politics and governance address how governments relate with its citizens by using the authority and power primarily given to them by God and secondly by its citizens to seek, promote, and advance their wellbeing. We are therefore addressing the social dimension of our ethical life as Christians in particular and humanity as a whole. In general, both identities fall under the authority and power of the Creator of the world, whose citizens we are.

What must motivate and shape our moral behavior, actions, and engagement in the areas of politics and governance is our unique relationship with God. The Triune God being the model and source of our moral life and we being his subjects or children of God, by creation and redemption respectively, are to reflect and imitate the behavior and character of God. How God rules and uses power becomes the standard for our moral actions. God's politics and governance reflect his being and character as a loving, compassionate, righteous, and just God. Our views on politics and governance must therefore be shaped by our Christian convictions on the moral character of God as the loving, righteous, and just King. Our concern in this chapter is not to examine political ideologies or to argue about which of these political ideologies is morally right and which is not. It is rather to examine the moral dimension of politics and governance as it relates to the wellbeing of citizens so they can experience God's shalom. Of particular interest to me, is how leaders use political power, authority, and governance on the one hand. On the other hand, the moral issues relating to how the government uses each nation's natural resources to enhance the lives and wellbeing of their respective African communities.

We have argued in the first section of this book that the Triune God is the model for our ethical behavior and that we are to emulate the character and nature of God in all that we do and say. If that is the case then, in the area of politics and governance, the Triune God is the foundation for how we exercise political power and govern a people. Any other way of exercising political power and governance other than God's way will be morally bankrupt and destructive. This chapter will explore the notion of God as the just, loving, compassionate, and righteous ruler or king and show how his righteous rule and governance become the foundations for our modern political and governance systems.

We will also draw some insights from African and Western cultural and moral values in relation to politics and governance that we think enhance the wellbeing of the citizens. Based on our understanding from these contexts, how should government use the power and authority given to them in managing and utilizing the resources available to her—human, natural, political, educational, and economic—for the wellbeing and development of her citizens?

In the sections that follow, we will define the terms, politics, and governance. We will then examine African traditional political systems, especially the roles played by rulers, kings and chiefs, and their functions and moral responsibilities to the community and society. We will finally look at the biblical model of the ideal King, the Triune God, and show how his rule of righteousness, peace, and justice must be the foundation upon which our political engagement and governance is established.

Defining politics and governance

The Oxford English Dictionary defines politics in many different ways. I am only interested in the definition that is relevant for this discussion. It defines politics as "the science or study of government and the state or the activities or policies associated with government, esp. those concerning the organization and administration of the state, and with the regulation of relationships between states;" and as "public life and affairs involving matters of authority and government."[1]

The word politics comes from the Greek word *politikos*, which means "citizen," "civilian." It later came to mean a "process by which groups of people make collective decisions." More technically, it means the "art of science of running governmental or state affairs" including governance.[2] In this study, we will use the word politics to mean the behavior and regulation of social relations involving authority or power, the management of public affairs and resources—human, intellectual, natural, technological, economical, etc—and the methods and tactics used to formulate and apply policies that affect the wellbeing of the citizens.[3] Since the way of running government and the affairs of the state concerns the lives of its citizens, how decisions are made, how leaders behave, how power and authority is exercised, how policies are formulated may all have ethical implications for the wider society.

The second term we would like to define is governance. The *Oxford English Dictionary* defines governance as "the action or manner of

---

1 http://www.oed.com/view/Entry/237575?redirectedFrom=politics#. Accessed February 2011.

2 http://en.wikipedia.org/wiki/Politics. Accessed January 2011.

3 http://en.wikipedia.org/wiki/Politics. Accessed January 2011.

governing." This includes "controlling, directing, regulating or influencing conduct of life or business as mode of living, behavior, demeanor," and lastly, as discreet or virtuous behavior."[4] These definitions of governance will be relevant for our discussion.

In this work, we understand governance as the "process of decision making and the process by which decisions are implemented (or not implemented)."[5] The word governance is used in many contexts, which include corporate governance, international governance, as well as, national and local governance. To show the difference between governance and government, one can say governance is basically, what a government does and government is the instrument or institution that does it. Governance is the right use of resources—human, natural, technological to build and create a peaceful environment for human wellbeing.

Both politics and governance are two important concepts that are very critical for our social stability and well-being. Therefore, God is very interested in how we do politics—rule and how we govern—and how we use resources to build society so humanity may experience God's blessings and shalom.

A close look at the African continent shows negative expressions of these two institutions, politics and governance, are the causes of the many evils we find on the continent today. The continent of Africa has been known for its political instability and bad governance for a long time. This trend still exists today. We continue to see political instability in Africa and corrupt governments that have plundered and raped African nations of their wealth which they have stacked in foreign banks in the West. We will now turn our attention to some of the causes of these problems.

---

4 http://www.oed.com/view/Entry/80307?redirectedFrom=governance#. Accessed February 2011.

5 http://www.unescap.org/pdd/prs/ProjectActivities/ongiong/gg/Goverance.asp. Accessed January 2011.

Understanding politics and governance in contemporary African societies

Human nature and its influence on politics and governance

In this chapter, we begin with the assumption that human nature is sinful, evil, and that there is need to check human behavior and actions. This is because of the reality of sin in the world. Human governments or civil governments are necessary because of human sinfulness. Paul teaches in Romans 13:1–7 that governments are put in place by God to administer justice, to punish those who do wrong and reward those who do right. This sets out the moral obligations governments and citizens have towards each other.

Since governments are part of humanity, they are fallen as well. They also have sinful tendencies and many times pervert justice and so governments, too, need to be checked because they fall under the domain of the powers and authorities that control the affairs of this world, which is Satan. The Bible teaches Satan is the god of this world. He tries to use the world's political, cultural, economic, and moral systems to advance his purposes and goals. Therefore, we must be watchful and careful so we do not fall into his craftiness.

Human nature also has bearing on one's political theory. For example, most modern political theories are grounded on humanistic philosophies that see the goodness of the human person. These philosophies argue that all humanity needs is to create a conducive environment for human progress. Therefore, great efforts are put in by political ideologies to create systems that would advance human progress and wellbeing. In doing this, most of them have not paid attention to the moral concerns these systems raise. Our humanistic tendencies and the quest for freedom and the dignity of the human person have all influenced the way politics and governance morally functions in our societies.

For example, we are fighting for peace in our communities and the world at large and yet not all our movies and actions are geared toward enhancing and promoting peace. What we find in our society is more violence on our movie screens. The values we are teaching our children are not those that build and enhance peace but those that promote violence. This is why we find so much violence in our societies and in our world today.

One's view on human nature will "ultimately filter into one's "political system of thought."[6] In fact, the Bible is of the opinion that political power has the tendency to be corrupted and abused because of the evil and greedy hearts of leaders. This is why God warned the Israelites about how the king they have asked for will treat them and their children. The king was going to be exploitative and harsh (1 Sam. 8:11–17).

Politicians in Africa are known for telling lies, leaders who lack integrity and are egoistic. They do not keep their promises and they use people as a means to their political ends. They are greedy and selfish and only think about themselves and how they can amass wealth and property and hold on to power so they can enrich themselves. The bottom line is that most of our present day politicians lack character, which is the engine that drives morality. They have acquired the vices that they were taught to avoid in life. They are known to be the most corrupt people in society. Their behaviors and lifestyles have affected many in society and corruption has become a virus in many African countries. If character is essential to a moral life, then we must ensure and demand that the people we entrust the affairs of our lives and our nations to must be people of noble and godly character and not just lawbreakers.

This behavior and attitude will have a huge moral impact on our children and the future generation if we do not act to stop it. We are not teaching our children to value hard work and industry. The actions of our governments are teaching our children to be corrupt by looking for easy ways of making money through cheating and stealing. Honesty and integrity are no longer moral values we cherish. Today most people believe one of the easiest ways to make millions of money in a short time is to be in politics. This is because politicians have access to all the nations' resources and they can exploit them as much as they can and want.

---

6 C. A. J. Coady. "Politics and the Problem of Dirty Hands," in *A Companion to Ethics*, ed. Peter Singer. Cambridge, MA: Basil Blackwell, 1991, 373

Many people in Africa think politics is a dirty game. Therefore, in politics, people play rough; in politics, one finds the "necessity of lies, cruelties, and murders."[7] Modern philosophers and political scientists aver for the "necessity for dirty hands in politics." Such thinking requires political practitioners to "violate important moral standards which prevail outside politics."[8] The idea to exempt political leaders from the moral order is widely held by politicians.[9] They argue that the political environment is morally corrupt. This environment deserves "moral scrutiny and criticism and the changes that may result from such criticism can eliminate the necessity for those type(s) of corruption in the future."[10] Therefore, politicians sacrifice at the altar all the moral values found in their cultural setting, upholding the dignity of the human person, and promoting life and the wellbeing of the community.

I personally do not share this view. Every sphere of our human existence is corrupted because of the presence of sin and evil in our world, but this does not justify our evil behavior. We are still accountable for our moral choices and decisions. As I have pointed out Christians are to be a counter-community of disciples of Jesus. We must change and set moral standards in our political environment that reflects God's character and promotes the wellbeing of humanity, not to destroy them.

We must begin to affirm and honor leaders who have integrity and are honest in their dealings. Those who are corrupt, we must expose and shame. Since honor and shame are important African cultural values, we must begin to use these values and principles to deal with bad leadership and governance in African societies.

There is a sense in which our colonial legacy has affected and shaped African politics and governance. Most of the moral attitudes of government and its governance structure have their roots in our colonial legacy. In the section below, we will deal with the question, in what specific ways did

---

7 C. A. J. Coady. "Politics and the Problem of Dirty Hands," in *A Companion to Ethics*, ed. Peter Singer. Cambridge, MA: Basil Blackwell, 1991, 373.

8 Coady, "Politics" in *Companion*, 373.

9 Coady, "Politics" in *Companion*, 374.

10 Coady, "Politics" in *Companion*, 379.

the colonial past with its western values influence African politics and governance? We will discuss the moral influence of the colonial legacy on political and governance in Africa. We will focus more on how the colonial government exercised and used power.

The African colonial legacy: its cultural, social, and moral values that shaped African political morality and governance

African political morality was shaped by two important western values: power and materialism. How the west understood power and used it affected the political morality of African governments. Their conception of power as control, domination, and suppression became a dominant feature in African politics leaving a legacy of authoritarian and autocratic leaders in many African countries. Power was a means to an end. Using power, they were able to control and exploit the wealth and resources of those they conquered and ruled. With the concentration of power in the central government, they were able to control resources, reward those who were favorable to them and punish those who disagreed with them.

In addition, there is also the legacy of materialism expressed by the many properties and wealth the colonial leaders acquired during the time they ruled African nations. This colonial legacy became a model for the leaders who took over leadership from the colonial powers when these African countries received independence. This second aspect relates to the issue of governance. We will look at these broad values in turn.

First, what is power? The word carries an aura around it[11] but simply put, power is "the ability to do or act;" it expresses "vigor, force, strength, authority or influence."[12] When it is used for a person, it denotes a person having force, influence, or authority. When it is used in politics, it denotes

---

11 Göran Collste, "Moral Justification for Power," in Stewardship: *Management, Ethics and Ecclesiology*, ed. Sven-Erik Brodd. Uppsala, Sweden: Church of Sweden Research Department, 1993, 53

12 "Power" in *Webster's New World Dictionary* (London: Pocket Books, 2003), 505.

a person with political power, force, authority, or influence over its people. The word governance is closely related to political power. It is the manner in which people with political power or authority use resources and implement decisions that affect the lives of the citizens of a nation. Power is both a relational and a possessive concept. Whoever possesses it can either use it for good or for evil. Its exercise always affects relationships.

My concern about power relates to institutionalized power as it is expressed through local or centralized political structures. Politics in Africa, therefore, has to do with the accumulation of wealth and exercise of power in society.

African leaders understand political power as domination, control and as a means of acquiring wealth and property. The political structures of many African countries were modeled after the political and administrative/governance structures of the colonial powers that ruled over them. Most of these created central governments where all decisions concerning the people are made by a select group of people who were the loyalists of the person in power. These people served the interests of those who put them in the position and took care of their own interests as well.

The administration established law enforcement agencies that were put in place to curtail the power of nationals who resisted the oppressors' rule, looted their resources for their personal gain, and compelled them to submit to the brutal rule of their masters. What we see today in African socio-political life is a replica of what went on during colonial rule in Africa.

The colonial governments' model of ruling became a pattern for African leaders who took over leadership from the colonial administrations immediately after independence. This model included coercive tendencies, intolerance towards those who opposed their rule and activities, and finally, the use of excessive force through state power and machinery to subdue dissenters and opponents. The colonial administrators used their power to dominate and exploit, and amassed great wealth for themselves. They took the best lands for themselves and built economic empires for themselves. The ruling class mostly benefited from policies they made. They were selfish and greedy. The lasting effects of this trend are most evident in many countries today.

In Africa, it is common to see the government in power using the state apparatus and law enforcement agencies to harass and subject its citizens to torture, forced imprisonment, and abuse of their fundamental human rights and dignity. This pattern of the state abusing its power coupled by bad governance; the selfish and greedy exploitation of the country's resources for the individual's wellbeing is a common practice in many African countries.

In post-independence Africa, the State continued to use its machinery to declare dissenters and opponents as traitors, people who must be punished or even killed. Those in power developed propaganda machinery and policies that control national media, and freedom of expression and association, in this way cramping all dissident voices within the society.

Leaders in their quest to hold on to power have changed constitutions and laws of their nations so they can stay in power for life. This attitude is rooted in African traditional cultures, where kings sit on thrones for life and after their demise; power is passed on to their sons, making government and governance a family affair.

African political and civic leaders exercise power in absolute terms. They love power and often power gets into their head, and they find it difficult to give it up. Lord Acton's old adage that "power corrupts and absolute power corrupts absolutely" is very true of many African leaders.

The unfortunate thing is that in most cases, the Christian Church stood behind these despotic governments and praised the leaders for their dynamic leadership and the stable and peaceful conditions their leadership has created. Yet, in many places where this has happened there were torture camps, police brutality against citizens, grand corruptions of all shapes, depleted resources and public policies that did not benefit the masses of the nation. Yet, the Church sang the praises of these leaders, and, in return, received favors from these leaders which included material provisions such as land, money, and so forth.[13]

---

13 Paul Gifford, *African Christianity: Its Public Role* (Bloomington and Indianapolis: Indiana University Press, 1998) gives examples of this pattern of religious complicity in chapters on Ghana, Uganda, Zambia and Cameroon. See also Gifford, *Christianity and Politics in Doe's Liberia* (Cambridge, U.K.: Cambridge University Press, 1993).

Western materialism is the second value that influenced African governance systems. The colonial administration was very interested in the natural resources of Africa and exploited them for themselves and their countries. While they put some governance structures in place to regulate public life and affairs, most of their private dealings were not scrutinized by anybody. Therefore, they were able to make deals and indulged in all kinds of activities that were morally questionable, yet, nobody raised a voice against them. Those who were in public life and could not get themselves into certain activities used their loyalists to front for them to conceal their business dealings. All these factors contributed to the problem of governance in terms of proper and accountable use of resources in Africa.

These materialistic tendencies of the colonial leaders and their use of political power to exploit and acquire resources for themselves and their friends laid the foundation for political leaders in Africa to loot the resources of their countries with their cronies and benefactors. These attitudes of leaders raise grave moral concerns that need to be addressed.

The colonial political elite enjoyed the unaccountable exercise of power. So long as they pleased their patrons, they got away with their evil deeds. They put in place patronage systems that handsomely rewarded people who were loyal to the leader or power broker.

But the problem is not all the fault of the colonial administration. The African religious and cultural legacy themselves have also shaped the Africans' perception of power and governance.

African legacy: the religious and cultural values that shaped the African's perception of power

The African's understanding of power relates to some aspects of African religio-cultural traditions and worldviews that show an inherent tendency towards authoritarian rule as well as sacralized authority of the political office. Busia observed that traditional understandings of solidarity had an inherent tendency towards authoritarianism.[14] Two particular African values account for this, namely solidarity and loyalty. African leaders insist on solidarity and loyalty to the point that any dissenting voice is considered unacceptable. People who disagree with leaders find themselves on the wrong side and they are labeled as opponents and enemies of the government. Such people receive the full fury of the government's power machinery.

The late Ghanaian theologian Kwame Bediako makes a similar observation that the issue of authoritarian governments in Africa's post-independence era should be understood in religious terms. The problem of authoritarianism, he argues, has to "do with the legacy of certain important religious aspects of the African traditional world-view as they relate to authority, power, and political governance, particularly the tendency of traditional society to sacralize authority and political office."[15] Bediako argues that an African ruler can enforce his will on his subjects because he is "the axis of their political relations," in his very person as a symbol of their unity and the embodiment of their values.[16] So, the leader is given great respect and honor, values that are cherished by Africans.

Bediako's assertion that authoritarian governments in Africa reflect the legacy of religious values of African traditional worldview has another dimension as well. In many African societies, he argues, "the ruler fulfills an important function as the intermediary between the living and the ancestors and the gods." Africans believe "royal ancestors are not dead; they have simply joined their grandsires in the realm of the spirit-fathers, from where they continue to manifest interest in the affairs of the society through the channels of mystical intervention by the appropriate rituals."[17] The West does not often appreciate this spiritual dimension of power, but there is a spiritual dimension to power. Westerners might agree on the

---

14 That is one of the main arguments in K. A. Busia, *Africa in Search of Democracy*. (London: Routledge & Kengan Paul, 1967).

15 Kwame Bediako, "De-Sacralization and Democratization:" Some Theological Reflections on the Role of Christianity in Nation-Building in Modern Africa," in *Transformation*, 12 (1995): 8.

16 See also M. Fortes & Evans-Pritchard (eds.), *African Political Systems* (London: KPI, 1987), 16.

17 Bediako, "De-Sacralization and Democratization," 7.

abstract notion that God is power, but they have little concrete sense of how the whole spiritual realm affects the exercise of power here on earth. Its influence may be good or evil. African rulers believe this, and some of the most notorious autocrats like King Saul in the Old Testament have practiced magic arts in the attempt to maintain their hold on power and defeat their political enemies.[18]

This background on African views of authority explains why some leaders exercise power as if they are demigods. Their particular understandings are rooted in the conception of the ancestors and the sacral role they play in the lives of the living. If African leaders will exercise power in a more, appropriate way, then, power has to be desacralized and God must be seen as the source and model for the right use of power.

The moral roles, character, and responsibility of leaders/kings in African societies

In the traditional African political system, the authority of the chief or king derives from the people, so there is a close relation between the ruler and the ruled in the matter of exercising political power.[19] Without the people, the chief is powerless. This is affirmed by African sayings like, "A chief is a chief by the people," by the Basotho," or "chieftainship is people" by the Lovedu of Transvaal, or by the Ndebele of Zimbabwe who say "The king is the people."[20]

The king sits on the stool of the ancestors to protect, provide, and ensure the progress and prosperity of his people. He and his council must

---

18 Accusations and rumors circle a number of leaders, but in the case of Mobutu of Zaire, these practices were well documented. See, e.g., Michela Wrong, "The Emperor Mobutu," *Transition*, No. 81/82 (2000), 92–112; and Wyatt MacGaffey, "Aesthetics and Politics of Violence in Central Africa," *Journal of African Cultural Studies* 13:1, In Honour of Professor Terence Ranger (June 2000): 63–75.

19 Kwame Gyekye, *African Cultural Values. An Introduction*. Accra: Ghana: Sankofa Publishing Company, 1996, 110.

20 Gyekye, *African Cultural Values*, 110.

embody the cultural and moral values of the community and ensure that the traditions and values are followed.

The chief depends on his subjects for political power and for the stability of his rule. Consequently, he must respect the wishes of his subjects, he could not rule without the consent of his people and there are limits or checks on how he exercises power. This practice may speak to some of the leaders who impose themselves on their people through political fraud and manipulations. No wonder we have such chaos on the continent because of leaders who have imposed their will and rule on the majority who do not support them.

Political power is always given. The people give it and it must be exercised for the wellbeing of those who gave it and not for the benefit of those who are given the privilege of exercising it. In Traditional African political systems, "the common people ... were the basis of all properly constituted authority."[21] When despotic and authoritarian leaders arise in traditional African societies, they were mechanisms put in place to remove such people from power if they were not meeting the needs of the community. It was not always possible for the king or chief to abuse his power.[22]

Gyekye argues that "in the traditional African political practice the will of the people plays a significant and crucial role, for the chief has to rule with the consent of the people." The will of the people in African political systems were exercised in the councils of the chief/king and public meetings where people had a chance to express their opinions on matters affecting their lives and wellbeing. Decisions were made by consensus and they concerned the wellbeing of the people. In African societies, no king was imposed on the people.

Most African societies generally believed that the king is both the political and spiritual leader of the people. He was to seek the wellbeing of the community, by protecting, providing and defending the people in the kingdom from all that threatened their wellbeing—such as hunger, diseases, attacks from other communities, curses, and so forth. Since community

---

21 Gyekye, *African Cultural Values*, 111.
22 Gyekye, *African Cultural Values*, 110.

and relationships are valued, consultation and consensus were valued in decision-making. There was a direct representation of political authority. The king was accountable to the people and misrule or abuse of his power against the will of the people was not tolerated.

The role of the king in African society was to provide for and ensure the wellbeing and the prosperity of the community. When he failed to discharge his duties, the elders removed him from power. This traditional provision to check the arbitrary use of the king's power is losing its efficacy today. We do have kings who are abusing their power and they are still in power because of corruption of the elders. The traditional chief has the responsibility to ensure provision, protection, prosperity, and progress of his people. The role of society, through the elders, is to hold him accountable and ensure that he fulfills his moral obligation to the community.

How do the values and responsibilities of the chief or king in the African society relate to the moral role and responsibility of kings in the bible? I will turn to the biblical values and principles that shaped the moral and political values we find in the Bible.

The moral role and responsibility of kings/ governments in the Bible

The moral character of the model king and his responsibilities

We begin this section by making the claim that God determines and sets the political boundaries of every nation and that all political values must reflect his values and will (Deut. 32:8, Acts 17:26). In this regard it is important to note that the "social nature of humanity" and the "sociopolitical organization that flows from it is part of God's creative purpose for his human creation."[23] God puts a moral demand on all political institutions to socially order their nations and communities in a manner that its people could enjoy the peace or shalom, of God whether these political leaders know God or not. We see how God judges the leaders of nations other

---

23 Wright, *Old Testament Ethics*, 214.

than Israel for their evil rule and how they governed their people. God cares about how we structure our politics and social relationships so they will promote righteousness, justice, and peace.

God himself is the ideal and model King who rules the world in justice, righteousness, peace, and love. These values are part of his essential being. He requires that those who rule follow his example and character and model these values in their rule. These values are essential criteria for kings and rulers. To be effective in politics, leaders and kings must humble themselves before God and heed to God's instructions so they can fulfill their mandate as rulers.

In Deuteronomy 17:14–20, God gives a blue print for the behavior of a king. God is concerned about the wellbeing of the people and he expects the political leaders to do the same:

> You will soon arrive in the land the LORD your God is giving you, and you will conquer it and settle there. Then you may begin to think, 'we ought to have a king like the other nations around us.' If this happens, be sure that you select as king the man the LORD your God chooses. You must appoint a fellow Israelite, not a foreigner. The king must not build up a large stable of horses for himself, and he must never send his people to Egypt to buy horses there, for the LORD has told you, 'you must never return to Egypt. The king must not take many wives for himself, because they will lead him away from the LORD. In addition, he must not accumulate vast amounts of wealth in silver and gold for himself. Moreover, when he sits on the throne as king, he must copy these laws on a scroll for himself in the presence of the Levitical priests. He must always keep this copy of the law with him and read it daily as long as he lives. That way he will learn to fear the LORD his God by obeying all the terms of this law. This regular reading will prevent him from becoming proud and acting as if he is above his fellow citizens. It will also prevent him from turning away from these commands in the smallest way. This will ensure

that he and his descendants will reign for many generations in Israel (NLT).

This text is a paradigm for politics today. It expresses the divine will for politics. God is seen here as the one who chooses a king. They are appointed and placed in authority by God (Rom. 13). The king is a fellow human being from his own people or nation. There are certain things a king should not do. He is not allowed to build up large stable of horses for himself. He should not lead his people to rebel against God's commands and word. He must not marry many wives because his wives will turn his heart away from God. Lastly he should not accumulate vast amounts of wealth for himself, that is in silver, gold or property (Deut. 17:14–17).

The Bible prescribes what he should do whilst in office. First, he must make a copy of the law of God for himself and he must read it all the days of his life as a king. He must fear the Lord, keep his words, and live by them. In modern political terms, he must live by the constitution of the land and uphold its laws and statutes. He must humble himself and not think that he is better than his fellow citizens are. When he fulfills all the Lord requires of the king, then he will secure his rule for many generations to come (Deut. 17:18–20). These instructions from the LORD are very important for politics. They must be the values that underline our political ethics. Here we begin to see and understand the relationship between religion and politics.

Wright is accurate in pointing out that "The Bible, therefore, makes no unnatural separation between 'politics' and 'religion,' though neither does it identify them. Politics and religion are "essential dimensions of what it is to be human." "The political task of maintaining a just social order is a human duty under God."[24] Every political leader and those in leadership must know this truth and must live and act on this truth.

Righteousness and justice are biblical moral values that characterize the life and being of God. God's people must express the same character in their political activities and relationships. The passion to imitate God's character

---

24 Wright, *Old Testament Ethics*, 215

has implications for our political life. We must dismantle the politics of oppression and exploitation and replace it with that of freedom, justice, and equity. This is what God did to the oppressive regime of Pharaoh, king of Egypt. Wright observes, God through Moses 'dismantles the politics of oppression and exploitation" by the King of Egypt, Pharaoh and introduced "a politics of justice and compassion."[25] Our political ethics, therefore, must reflect these biblical values: justice and compassion.

God gave the king certain moral responsibilities. The king it was to ensure that justice was done among his people especially for the poor and the down trodden in society (Ps. 72:1–4). He had to have compassion and pity for the weak and needy and while seeking to rescue or deliver them from their oppression. He had to save his people from oppression and from violence, because God valued their lives (Ps. 72:12–14). Food, prosperity, refreshment, and honor had to be the characteristics of his rule. He was not only to be a blessing to his nation, but he had to be a blessing to the other nations as well. This aspect deals with international and foreign relations. The king's foreign policy must be both a blessing to his people and the nations they relate with (72:7–11, 16–17).

The king was to be an example in loving justice and ruling with equity. In addition, the king was to show high standard of integrity and honesty. For example, Psalm 101 sets the moral values that must characterize the lives of those who rule, as a "kind of agenda for good government."[26] These values include love, justice, blameless life, life of integrity, hate crooked dealings, dishonesty, reject perverse ideas, and avoid anything evil and many others listed there by the Psalmist.

There is a strong stress on interior attitudes and dispositions of the king. Character is critical here. The Psalm is concerned with the moral character of the king, the ruler. He must walk blameless before God and before his citizens. The Psalm highlights the virtues of integrity and honesty as critical for kings and rulers. These qualities and virtues are not only required for

---

25 Wright, *Old Testament Ethics*, 227. Wrights quoted Walter Brueggemann, *The Prophetic Imagination*. Philadelphia: Fortress, 1978, 16–17.
26 Andrew Mein, "Psalm 101 and the Ethics of Kingship," in *Ethical and Unethical in the Old Testament*, ed. Katharine Dell. New York, T & T Clark, 2010, 59.

the king but they are also necessary for those who work in his court, his government. The king must have good character. Good government and governance come out of good character.

The king is to be an example in integrity and honesty for his courtyard. He is committed to living a blameless life—a life of integrity. He must refuse to look at anything vile and vulgar, hate crooked dealings, reject perverse ideas, and stay away from every evil. He will not tolerate deceitful liars, and proud people in his courtyard. Psalms 101:6b-7 is significant. "Only those who are above reproach will be allowed to serve me. I will not allow deceivers to serve me, and liars will not be allowed to enter my presence" (NLT). We mentioned in the first part of the book that the Triune God is the model for our ethical life. Here, the king is seen as the 'moral exemplar who models the divine virtues [of integrity, honesty, faithfulness] to his courtiers, and they in turn reflect the royal reflection of the divine character."[27]

The moral implications of the ideal king for political practice and governance

The leader must live and lead to reflect the nature and character of God. Our politics and political activities must have social goal, service. Our politics must be a politics of service, so must our leadership be servant leadership. Servant leadership is modeled for us by our Lord Jesus Christ and by all the servants of God. The model of political authority and leadership God requires is servanthood (Heb. 3:5, Num. 12:3). In Deuteronomy 17:14–20, the king is strictly forbidden to exalt himself above his brothers but serve them in humility. Kingship is servanthood (1 Ki. 12:7). Jesus himself was the model servant leader with authority and power yet he taught his disciples not to lord it over those they lead but to serve them as he had served them.

Humanity, in general, has both social and civil responsibilities to serve the state and each other. But our acts of service must be done lovingly,

---

27 Mein, "Psalm 101," 64–5.

righteously and justly. This is what God has taught us to do. When we fail to live this way, we are violating the will of God for our lives as human beings.

Human power is delegated power for the benefit of society

All authority is the Lord's and it belongs to Christ. Authority has its source in the Trinitarian God. Every human being and power is under the authority of God. All human authority is derived authority. Human authority is not absolute. Political authority must be exercised within the limits set by God. "All human authority is relative to, accountable to, and addressable by, God."[28] Therefore, all political power must be exercised according to God's dictate and for the benefit and service to humanity and not for the benefit of the leader.

True political authority comes from God and not just from the people (2 Ki. 11:17; 14:19–21). Since the authority comes from God, the king's power is limited by the one who obviously appointed him. True power and authority is God's alone. No human person should attempt to assume that power and authority for him/herself.

Leaders must be humble in their service to humanity. They should use their power to enact laws and policies that address the social, political, religious, and economic concerns that affect the moral wellbeing of their citizens.

Rulers are put in their positions to defend and protect the vulnerable in society and to provide for their needs. Government policies must address the needs and wellbeing of its citizens. Leaders are not to make policies that advance their own agendas and prosperity. Rather, they must serve the people with integrity. Power is abused when leaders fail to act on issues that affect the moral wellbeing of people within the society. Governments' inaction in making good policies to address societal problems is abuse and misuse of power. Many African leaders abuse power in this way. They fail to address the pressing issues facing their respective countries and citizens.

Leaders do not have absolute power. They have delegated power. For that reason, they must exercise their power for the purpose it was given.

---

28 Wright, *OT Ethics*, 248–249.

God placed them in positions of power so they will provide for the needs of his people. They are to serve the people, not themselves. God will hold leaders liable if they abuse their power and mandate.

Leaders have this command from God to seek justice and defend the cause of the poor and widow, the marginalized and destitute, the alien and strangers. When leaders neglected their duties to these people and sought after their own gain, God punished them. God requires kings and leaders to rule with justice, righteousness, and mercy. These qualities must be reflected in the way leaders rule and administer the resources of the country.

The king or leader must ensure that right policies are formulated for the well being of people under his/her rule. Governments must ensure that such policies are just, and they serve the best interests of society and not their own desires and selfish interests. Governments must enact laws, make policies, and allocate resources justly. This must happen at all level of society. Such policies must include, just laws, ensure the rule of law, and protect the basic human rights of citizens. It is important therefore, for us to keep an eye on government policies as they largely affect the lives of our citizens so that these policies may promote their wellbeing.

Human leaders are not sacred
We must seek to de-sacralize the African conception of power that often makes rulers behave as demigods. Both OT and NT writers de-sacralized power. The monarchy in ancient Israel provides instructive examples of the impact of the Hebrew prophetic religion on the notion of authority and the exercise of power in human society. Bediako points out that the Old Testament de-sacralized all human authority and power. Kings were mere humans among fellow humans and they can be summoned to appear before God. The implication of this was to say that there is a higher kingdom, the Kingdom of God to which all other kingdoms must bow and submit.[29]

Kings and emperors who highly thought of themselves are gods were all destroyed by their pride and arrogance. Examples of such kings are plenteous in the bible such as Pharaoh, Nebuchadnezzar, and Herod.

---

29 Kwame Bediako, "De-sacralization and Democratization," 8.

We must continue the de-sacralizing of authority and power in our own contexts as Jesus and other prophets did. In doing this, we recommend "Jesus' way. Jesus engaged and involved himself through a new way of overcoming the conception of power at his time, that of domination. He introduced a new and unique concept of power—the power of forgiveness over retaliation, of suffering over violence, of love over hostility, of humble service over domination…. Jesus' conception of power is non-dominating power."[30]

By his death on the cross, as Bediako observes, Jesus de-sacralized all human and worldly power "relativizing its inherent tendency, in a fallen universe, to absolutize itself. …the Cross desacralizes all the powers, institutions, and structures which rule human existence and history—family, nation, social class, race, law, politics, economy, religion, culture, tradition, custom, ancestors—stripping them all of any pretensions to ultimacy."[31]

Bediako thinks the recognition that power belongs to God can liberate politicians and ennoble politics. Leaders who exercise power and authority must follow the "way of Jesus." The way of Jesus is "the way of non-dominating power." The mind of Jesus concerning power is "not a dominating mind, not a self-pleasing or self-asserting mind, but rather a serving mind, a redemptive mind, a servant mind."[32]

Christian theology sees God as the source of all power. Biblical teaching affirms that true use of power is non-dominating. It is only when leaders acknowledge this and see the people they lead as fellow humans that they can serve them and make laws and policies that address their wellbeing. It is only when this is achieved that we can have leaders whose public policies would benefit the wellbeing of citizens.

---

[30] Kwame Bediako, "De-sacralization and Democratization, 8."
[31] Kwame Bediako, "De-sacralization and Democratization, 8."
[32] Kwame Bediako, "De-sacralization and Democratization, 8."

Humans tend to abuse power and authority

Human sinfulness makes it easy for humanity to abuse power. The tendency for control and the greed for more are all recipe for one to misuse power. In particular, leaders have the propensity to become exploitative by using their power to amass wealth and oppress the poor and their citizens. As a result, God in his wisdom places a limitation on the king's power, in terms of what he can and cannot do (Deut. 17:14–20).

Kings and rulers must be reminded constantly about the obligations they have to their citizens and not to themselves. The immoral use of power to intimidate, brutalize people, and exploit the resources of the nation for personal benefit is unacceptable to God.

Christians must play a prophetic role like that of the OT prophets by warning and reminding kings and presidents, civil leaders, religious leaders, and all public officers about the responsibility to serve the interest of the people they are serving. It is important to remind leaders of their divine responsibility. The prophets of Israel constantly reminded the kings when they erred and departed from God's laws and ways. This is costly work, as we see in the fate of many of the prophets.

Political leaders must use power the way God himself uses it. God exercises power with compassion and love, seeking to advance the prosperity and wellbeing of his people and creation. Political leaders must develop a concept of power that demonstrates "compassionate love that resists tragic suffering." Leaders must use their power to reduce the sufferings of humanity. God has raised them up as leaders for this purpose. They must not use their God-given power and authority for their own personal interests. If they exercise compassion towards the marginalized and destitute, they find this to be "empowering power," thus providing the ability to transform people and institutions.[33]

Leaders who have such godly attitudes would enact policies that will improve the living conditions of people and give them and their children hope for the future. As McFague rightly points out the right use of power

---

[33] Wendy Farley, *Tragic Vision and Divine Compassion* (Louisville, KY: Westminster Press, 1990), 86.

is not "the power of control through either domination or benevolence but the power of response and responsibility."[34] Johnson aptly describes the right use of power as expressing vitality: "empowering...stirs up and fosters life and one that builds up and transforms people, and makes them into better people."[35]

The right use of power is when one responds to human needs and seeks to address the wellbeing of citizens. In short, all who exercise power must do so in love. Love is the most profound and constructive motivation and foundation of power (1 Cor. 13). Love is what motivates God to exercise his power to bless and to deliver. Love must underline our exercise of power and governance.

We must promote a new political and governance culture that values people rather than one that uses them as a means to an end. Politicians must love their people and seek their wellbeing. They must show integrity, honesty, truth speaking, shunning evil ideas, and show unrelenting commitment and concern for the wellbeing of their people and nations. We all have a part to play in nation building.

Governance as stewardship, empowerment and partnership with God

Block points out that governance underlies the political nature of our lives as humans.[36] Good governance is grounded on the theological truth that "The earth is the Lord's, and everything in it. The world and all its people belong to him" (Ps. 24:1, Ps. 89:11; NLT). So, nations, its people, and all the natural resources they have are entrusted to politicians and leaders as stewards. God will hold them accountable for how they exercise these stewardship responsibilities.

---

34 McFague, *Models of God*, 85.
35 Johnson, *She Who Is*, 269–70.
36 Peter Block, *Stewardship: Choosing Service over Self-Interest*. San Francisco, CA: Berrett-Koehler Publishers, 1993, 5.

Bad management, corruption, and administration of resources have plundered many African nations into a moral dungeon, which they are struggling to get out of. The earth's resources belong to God as Creator and how politicians and leaders use these resources are of a major concern to God. As creator, he has absolute control over his creation and he is concerned about how humanity uses the resources he has given them. The principle of stewardship requires that "the gifts of human life and its natural resources and environment be used with profound respect for their intrinsic ends."[37]

God is concerned about how we use the resources he has given us because of his goodness to us. Those who are charged with the responsibility of managing these resources are expected to manage them according to God's purposes.

Therefore, leaders, governments, civil servants and politicians are appointed by God and are given the responsibility to manage the resources for the common good of society. They do not own them. God is the owner. The Bible calls these people stewards. Who are stewards? The word originally concerned the "management, direction, or administration of a household with its variety of concerns." It later came to mean the "administration of an entire state, particularly in the military and economic areas." Its common meaning today has to do with the "careful and responsible management of something entrusted to one's care" or a "responsibility given to a person to take care of something owned by someone else"[38] or "management and administration of the property of others"[39] So, stewards are not owners of the things over which they are appointed stewards. They hold those things in trust. Stewards cannot use God's resources as they wish. They must manage the resources according to the wishes of the owner.

The Bible sets forth the character of stewards. Stewards are to be faithful, honest, and diligent, have integrity and skillfully competent in how they

---

[37] http://www.ascensionhealth.org/index.php?option=com_content&view=article&id=90:principle-of-stewardship&Itemid-171. Accessed February 2011.

[38] http://en.wikipedia.org/wiki/Stewardship, Accessed February 2011.

[39] Vine, W. E., *Vine's Expository Dictionary of Biblical Words*. Nashville: Thomas Nelson, 1984.

use the resources entrusted to their care. This will help to avoid waste so that the resources give their optimum value. Five key values are important: "faithfulness, wisdom, shrewdness and diligence (Luke 16:1–9), and recognition of one's role"[40] as a steward (1 Cor. 4:2–3, 7). Faithfulness, not accumulation of wealth, or greed is required of good stewards. Humanity is given the privilege and responsibility to manage God's world and resources. God himself cares for and upholds creation (Gen. 2:15, Col. 1:11–15). He requires that those who have been entrusted with responsibility to manage resources remain faithful as he is. We will talk more about this in chapter 12.

Stewardship carries responsibility. In responsibility, we see another principle. This principle of responsibility comes with accountability; too much responsibility comes with much accountability. Jesus taught his followers to use the resources and blessings they have received from God to serve and meet the needs of others (Matt. 25:31–46). Jesus told his followers "Much will be required from those to whom much is given and much more is required from those to whom much more is given" (Lk. 12:48b, Lk. 12:41–48, NLT). Leaders must account for the way they use resources entrusted into their hands for the benefit of others. God will hold them accountable for their stewardship. Part of proper governance is to ensure that there are proper systems put in place for accountability.

Seitz asserts, "Stewardship is an activity of God." It is grounded on God's activity as creator and Lord over creation. It is also rooted stewardship in relationship and stewardship is a partnership with God."[41] God calls humanity to collaborate with Him when he appoints us as stewards. Thus, stewardship, empowerment, and partnership are embodied in God's own acts in his dealings with humanity. He calls and empowers us through the Holy Spirit, by giving us abilities and gifts to accomplish the work he calls us to do. In addition, he collaborates with us by continuing to give us the resources we need to accomplish his plans and purposes for his creation.

---

40 Lane R. Seitz, "Stewardship: Managing God's resources for the Growth of the Kingdom." Unpublished Doctor of Ministry Dissertation. Pasadena: Fuller Theological Seminary, 1991, 22; See Ritva H. Williams, *Stewards, Prophets, Keepers of the Word in the Early Church.* Peabody: MA, Hendrickson Publishers, 2006, 75

41 Seitz, "Stewardship," 25.

For Paul, "faithful stewardship is characterized by an imitation of Christ's self-emptying solidarity with humanity."[42] Christ used all the resources and power he had for the good of humanity by redeeming them form evil, sin, and death. He is our example. He calls us to identify also with the weak, poor, and alienated. He calls leaders to care and seek the welfare and good of the people by using the resources he has provide for their good.

Jesus set an example, of self—sacrifice, serving others instead of one's self. Egoism is not good for community building. Greed, selfishness and irresponsibility are vices that must be avoided in good stewardship or governance (Lk. 12:13–21). God demands that those who govern concern themselves with the wellbeing of the common good of others and be faithful stewards of his resources.

Leaders must be transparent in their dealings. Integrity and character is essential for good governance. This value is expressed as transparency and accountability. We must wisely use our human resources—knowledge, experiences, talents and gifts—to build and develop nations and their people towards their common good and wellbeing. This must be done in an open and fair manner.

God who is the ultimate owner of the world and its resources will hold each person accountable for how they have used the resources put under their charge in this world. This is an eschatological dimension to the issue of accountability. If we fail and manipulate the system to run away from it, one cannot avoid being held accountable before God in the future when He will judge all human action and intentions.

For good governance to occur, we must reject "patronage and the ideology of benevolent patriarchalism."[43] Good governance must seek to empower the grass root people to take responsibility for their own lives and not depend on the government or leader for their daily needs. Governments must move resources closer and closer to the people in order to empower them. They must call the people to accountability and not control or dominate them. Governments must be examples in modeling good

---

42 Ritva H. Williams, *Stewards, Prophets, Keepers of the Word in the Early Church.* Peabody: MA, Hendrickson Publishers, 2006, 76.

43 Williams, *Stewards,* 92.

governance. Accountability is central to good governance and stewardship. Stewardship focuses on "service rather than control."[44] Government leadership in good governance will motivate citizens to take their social and moral responsibility to society and the nation seriously and in this way take on their political role in nation building. For good governance to take place leaders must replace "self-interests with service" as the basis for holding and using power." The ideas of stewardship, empowerment, partnership, and accountability deal with power distribution. It can help reduce abuse of power in politics and governance.[45]

Conclusion

I set out in this chapter to explore two critical moral issues—politics and governance—that have affected African morality in profound ways. In particular, we looked at the values that have shaped our politics in terms of political power and governance from African and the western perspectives. Later we examined the biblical values for politics and governance and made certain observations that I believe will serve as a criteria and model for our political ethics and for good governance in African societies. These principles and values are based on God's own character and nature. They are God's values set up for kings to help guide their rule and behavior. If we follow these biblical values and principles which are love, justice, righteousness, integrity, honesty and compassion and shun certain socials vices like greed, dishonesty, evil, perverse ideas, and pride which destroy leaders, we will have political systems that will seek and promote the wellbeing of its citizens. We will have political systems that help its citizens to experience God's shalom.

---

44 Block, *Stewardship*, 19.
45 Block, *Stewardship*, 27.

CHAPTER 8

Economics and Poverty

"Inequality is not just bad for social justice; it is also bad for economic efficiency." (Growth with equity is good for the poor, Oxfam, June 2000)

Introduction

Economics is so central to human activities and it has become a dominant force in human life. It affects every domain of our human existence—individual, family life, and national life. Economics and poverty affect the way we think about ourselves and the world in which we live. There is always the tendency of rich nations to look down on poor nations. The economically powerful nations often use their economic power to intimidate, control, and manipulate the less fortunate nations. This is seen at the level of international politics. There is a sense in which the poor see themselves as unworthy and lose self-respect and dignity because of the way the rich often treat them. Again, economics and poverty are relational issues which we must deal with.

At the global level, poor nations lose the rights of sovereignty, often times, and the west dictates to them using economic sanctions and other means of power to subject them to their ways of doing things. In this process, poor nations lose their dignity as humans who can make independent, rational choices that can shape the destinies of their own nations. Therefore, at both the local and international levels, economics and poverty raise certain moral concerns that we can discuss.

There is so much inequality in terms of resource acquisition and distribution in many African communities. How we use and distribute resources is flawed by injustice, exploitation, and greed. This has left many communities in Africa impoverished for a long time.

This state of affairs of economic injustice and poverty has forced many people to engage various forms of economic activity that are morally questionable. This chapter will deal with some of these moral concerns of injustice, greed, exploitation, and the economic values that have shaped our present day economies. The first section will deal with economics. We will attempt to draw on some biblical values that must shape the moral vision for our economic life. The second section will address the issue of poverty. We will discuss its sources, its effects and provide some biblical and cultural values that will help in dealing with the problem. Finally, we will discuss some concrete steps the government can use to deal with the problem.

Modern economic systems and its values

Economics undergirds our value systems which are shaped by our cultural values. These values are expressed in the accumulation of property, power, prosperity, wealth, consumerism, production and so forth. Modern economic systems and theories are based on western humanistic and utilitarian philosophies that see wealth as the source and means to all human happiness.

Wealth is one of the central economic values in every community. Africans place much importance on wealth because of the important value it has for families, community, and the state. Some of the following African proverbs exemplify the value Africans attached to wealth. One proverb states "money is sharper than a sword," emphasizing that money opens doors and helps one to overcome problems and hurdles. Another one expresses wealth as the ultimate possession and human pursuit "when wealth comes and passes by, nothing comes after."[1] Wealth brings fame and respect that enhances a person's social status and gives one the opportunity to move up the social ladder. Africans tend to celebrate wealth that comes as a result of an individual's hard work which is in itself one of the vital

---

1 Kwame Gyekye, *African Cultural Values*, 98.

economic values in African culture. This view of wealth by Africans is not unique to just Africa for wealth is valued in every culture. The danger comes when it is seen as the most important thing in life as is suggested by the African proverb.

Wealth is valued and individuals and communities are encouraged to pursue it. However, so it does not become self destructive, generosity is also highly encouraged within African communities. The wealthy in society are to use their wealth to contribute to the welfare of their family's community and society because African moral values see selfishness as a vice, as an egoistic ethical value that must be avoided and rejected in any form.

In fact, the Bible affirms wealth as part of God's blessing for humanity. However, the Bible rejects the idea of making wealth the ultimate value or the source for human happiness. Jesus also rejected and challenged this thinking. Jesus' statement that life does not consist in the abundance of things one possesses is a reminder to us that wealth is not what life is all about. Wealth does not bring happiness neither is it the ultimate achievement in life. True wealth is spiritual, being rich toward God and toward our neighbor.

To achieve this goal of creating and accumulating wealth as a central economic value, modern economics concerns itself with "efficiency and clever calculations."[2] Modern economic theories focus on the principle of utility, profit making, and efficient production of goods and services. The kind of questions modern economics ask are not questions to do with morality, but rather they are questions that deal with how they can make more profits. This tends to lead to greed, exploitation, and extravagant life styles. These values raise certain moral concerns for our lives. The Bible warns against such a life style.

This economic view, called the neoclassical economic view is the product of the enlightenment and the industrial revolution views of humanity as rational autonomous individuals who are "motivated by preferences, each

---

[2] Roelf Haan, *The Economics of Honour: Biblical reflections on money and property*. Translated by Nancy Forest-Flier, Geneva: WCC Publications, 1988, 2.

making choices independently"³ about what is good for them and would make them happy.

People make choices in terms of "their aims [and goals], not in terms of their genes, their upbringing, their emotions, or the norms of society to which they belong [character]. In the standard model of economics, all depends on calculation and on preferences between alternative outcomes."⁴ What drives economic activities is the utilitarian nature it serves. The economic outcome is important.

Humanity is made in the image of God. They are free to make choices, as God is free. However, they are responsible for the choices they make. Human beings find their "fulfillment in serving God, not in going their own way. Human choices require "a change of our values, our objectives, our preferences."⁵ They must conform to the purposes and will of God. Human economic activities are grounded upon God's own gracious act in giving to humanity a good earth with all the rich resources it has to support human economic endeavors. Biblical economic values clash with neoclassical economic theories.

Our economic decisions are driven by our cultural values; it is individualistic, utilitarian, and egoistic. They are motivated by the individual's economic needs, right price for the commodity and if the individual has the power to afford it. It is egoistic. It is based on individual costing, self-satisfaction and pleasure. The person involved does not often think about the cost others have to pay and the moral conditions surrounding the production of the commodity for him or her to enjoy. Our present economic thinking is shaped by secular ideologies that have their roots in the enlightenment tradition that focuses on the choices of the individual as an autonomous rational being. It has nothing to do with biblical faith.

Thus, it often neglects the human and the moral dimensions of the economic processes, the sacrifices people make that morally affect their

---

3 Britton and Sedgwick, *Economic Theory*, 25.

4 Britton and Sedgwick, *Economic Theory*, 72.

5 Britton and Sedgwick, *Economic Theory*, 73

lives through these economic activities. We propose that the ultimate goal for any good economic policy should focus on "enriching the quality of life and human relationships in any given society"[6] Economic activities must become servant to human needs rather than human beings becoming servants to their economic systems.

Human beings and human dignity is more precious than money and riches as demonstrated by an African proverb: the human being is more beautiful than gold." The fleeting nature of money is expressed by another African proverb: "Money has wings" or "money does not stay in one place." What is truly of value is people. Money by itself cannot help any person unless people make that happen. Human beings give money its value as expressed by another proverb: "It is human being that counts; I call upon gold, it answers not; I call upon cloth, it answers not; it is human being that counts."

In our modern economics, politics play a critical role. Most of the economic policies are crafted by the powerful economic nations, the technocrats, and the influential people in society who often times have no relationship with the great number of people in society who are poor and living in abject poverty. Some of these economic policies favor the rich and powerful nations while leaving the poorer nations poorer.

The richer nations exploit the resources of the poorer nations paying them very little for their raw materials, which they use for their industries and later on sell the finished products, back to them 100 times more than they bought the raw materials. This form of economic exploitation and injustice by powerful nations has rendered many developing nations economically poor.

These unjust economic systems are based on exploitation on the one hand, and the mismanagement of natural resources on the other hand. Their aim is to benefit a certain class of people—the powerful, affluent, rich, and privileged few—rather than the good and wellbeing of majority

---

[6] Paul Mills, "The Economy," in *Jubilee Manifesto: A framework, agenda, & strategy for Christian social reform.* Ed. Michael Schluter & John Ashcroft. Leicester: InterVarsity Press, 2005, 217.

of the citizens. Economic justice and the right use of natural and human resources have moral implications for the lives of the citizens of any nation.

The current economic issues and the moral concern they raise can best be understood in relationship to God rather than today's very secular view. This 'world' perspective looks at economic issues as consumers interested in certain products that they can buy because the price is right. It does not count the real cost of the product, all the sacrifices people have to make, and the working conditions they were in to produce the product. This is what Haan's refers to as "cost-consciousness" based on his analysis of 2 Samuel 23:13–17 where David's responds to what his officers did by sacrificing their lives to get him water to drink from the well of Bethlehem. Their enemies, the Philistines were in Bethlehem at the time. Three of his mighty men, when they heard of his need and request, voluntarily went, broke through the enemies' lines, and got him the water. When they brought the water to him, he poured it before the Lord as an offering rather than drinking it.[7] Morally, David could not "drink the blood" of his soldiers because of the sacrificed involved in what they did. Do consumers consider this "cost-consciousness? Probably not!

Our concern in this chapter is not to look at economic systems to decide how right or wrong they are. Our concern is to look at the moral dimension of economics, in particular, the processes by which resources are used by those in power who are entrusted with God's resources to enhance the wellbeing of a nation's citizens. As I have said before, the Christian and humanity's moral action is predicated upon God's own acts. We will now explore how God looks at economics and poverty. I will offer some biblical economic values and principles that can help us first develop a Christian moral vision for just economic practices and secondly, one that teaches us how to deal with poverty. I suggest the following biblical economic values that are rooted in God's character and African economic values—justice, mercy or compassion, and generosity in using wealth.

---

[7] Haan, *The Economics of Honour*, 1. See his analysis of 2 Samuel 23:13–17, on pages 1–5.

God the Economist

Meeks asserts that God's character and works makes Him an Economist although what he means by the term differs from what it means to those who practice and study economics.[8] If his assertion is right that God is an economist, which I think it is, then the Christian faith must relate to all aspects of our economic lives.

God as the creator of the earth and all the wealth in it is concerned about human well being. He provides in creation all that humanity needs to enhance and sustain its life. As people created in his image, He has given humanity creative abilities to invent, to develop and actualized their potentials. He has given resources in all spheres of human affairs, especially in economics, which is central to all human activities.

Humans were given dominion over creation, to increase, multiply, and fill it. God expected humanity to grow not just numerically but also economically. As humanity increased, more resources were needed to sustain the growth and increase. So, our economic mandate is enshrined in the creation mandate.[9]

God is interested in how resources are accessed and shared, that we provide a favorable environment for workers, access to and availability of work for all, as well as fair sharing and distribution of the goods and services available for the wellbeing of all members of a community or nation. God is very much concerned about how we engage in these economic activities so they fulfill his purposes and intentions for humanity, which is their wellbeing. In our economic life, God is concerned about our moral behavior, that is, how we make our wealth. This means in God's economy, there is a close link or relationship between economics and ethics. Our economic life must reflect the character of God's righteousness, justice, and holiness.

Since these are God's concern, the Bible addresses economic issues in both the Old and New Testaments. In the Old Testament, God and the prophets spoke so much about Israel's economic activities, pointed out

---

8 M. Douglas Meeks, *God the Economist: The Doctrine of God and Political Economy*. Minneapolis: Fortress, 2.
9 Wright, *Old Testament Ethics*, 156–168.

how God was displeased with them by setting aside His commands, and exploited the poor and the weak in society by those who were in positions of power.

There are many references to the economic dimension of human activities in the entire Bible. By economic activity, we mean what human beings do to produce and sustain life. Our concern in this chapter is not to vouch for any particular economic ideology or system. We are concerned about the moral integrity of these economic activities that seek to promote the wellbeing of people.

Our economic policies are tinted by our fallen human nature. "Sin is always present in human economy no matter what the economy's structure"[10] may be. Our economic systems are exploitative, motivated by greed and covetousness and injustice. This results in ill-gotten wealth and possessions. The Bible speaks so much on economic injustice and exploitation by the powerful who leave a majority of the people impoverished. The powerful in Israel committed such evil against the people of Israel. This violation of God's laws and instructions by the leaders threatened the "household's economic viability." God saw this behavior as evil. Thus, economic exploitation of the poor is a moral evil that must be rooted out and dealt with so ardently. These structures must conform to the principles set forth by God.

Corruption, which has been attributed to the course of poverty in Africa, is contrary to the nature and character of God. Human corruption is related to human fallenness. It has its source in sin. Humanity's sin brought both spiritual and physical corruption to God's creation, so that the earth, which is the major source for our economic activities, became corrupted as well. However, God has delivered humanity from sin and its corruption. He calls people to a kind of life that reflects his character of justice, righteousness, and peace.

These qualities and values must shape all our economic activities. God is concerned about how we make our money. The wisdom tradition saw economic growth and prosperity as the gifts of God (Prov. 3:9; 10:22).

---

10 Meeks, *God the Economist*, 10.

However, they were also aware of the dangers of excessive wealth and the temptations brought about by acute poverty.[11]

God is the source of all economic resources

We begin this section with the thesis that God, the creator of humans, the heavens, and the earth, is the sole owner of the world and all the resources and the people in it. The land—which houses natural resources, minerals, rivers, seas, mountains, and the heavens that all produce most of the material for human technological development—is the economic engine of the world's economies and is a gift from God to human beings. God has the moral authority over how his land and the economic resources it produces must be used. The land is meant to be a blessing for humanity, that they may enjoy, is fruitfulness and its wealth. God challenges the legitimacy of those who shamefully deprive others of their property (Mic. 2:1; Isa. 5:8) and give them access to the means and source of production and wealth. To address economic injustice, we must take a serious look at who has access to the land and empower the weak and the marginalized to have access but also the means or capital to engage in productive economic activities.

Land is one of Africa's major economic assets/resource and the liberal allocation of land resources for the benefit of the individual and communities for the sake of economic development carries major economic value.[12] We find this to be true as one of biblical economic values. The land is God's gift to humanity. He also gave Israel land as an economic resource. Through the jubilee economic principle, God ensures first that land continues to be the economic backbone for the family and secondly it buffers the poor from losing their lands to the rich and powerful.

Land is very central to all economic endeavors. It is the source of most of the raw materials—agricultural products, minerals resources—gold, diamonds, crude oil, etc; natural resources—rivers, forests, animals, mountains, etc, we use in most of our economic activities. Its proper use,

---

11 Wright, *An Eye for An Eye*, 82.
12 Kwame Gyekye, *African Cultural Values*, 97.

access, and distribution are very critical for economic development and prosperity of any nations. God is the ultimate owner of the earth (Ps. 24:1, Ps. 115:16, Ps. 8:6). He has entrusted it to humanity and he will hold him accountable for his stewardship (Gen. 1:26).

Jesus and economics

Most of Christ's teachings in the New Testament focused on human economic activities. His illustrations employ the idea of a household servant's role as steward in charge of his master's house. In many of these parables, the servant or steward is given some money to invest. How he invests the money as well as how he makes his profit and handles the other servants or workers under his care are all very important to the master. He is expected to invest the resources entrusted to him to make more profit for his master but also to treat the other servants with respect and compassion (Lk. 12:42–47, 19:11–27).

Although, traditionally, the Luke 19 passage has been interpreted by biblical scholars as teaching about stewardship; our accountability before God in the way in which we use the gifts, talents, and possessions he has given us, I would also like to think of the text as dealing with economic practices.

The idea that the noble gave those servants money to invest while he was away and the fact that he expected some profits from them at his return underscores the economic grounds for my interpretation. Profits are important. God expects that we increase the resources we invest. He does not, however, set out how much profit we should make. He accepted whatever profit the servants made. What he did not accept was the servant who did not engage in any economic activity or work. Moderate profits are acceptable in our economic ethics. We have to recoup our investment but the profits have to be fair and just. They must be earned justly and not through exploitation and greed.

Jesus also spoke strongly against the economic values that pervaded his society which led to the exploitation of the poor to the extent that they became even poorer. The central values that shaped the economic activities in Jesus' day include obsession for wealth, lovers of money, greed, stinginess, hoarding, and lack of generosity. We see this in the way he castigated the religious leaders. He described them as greedy and self-indulgent (Matt. 23:25) and warned them against the folly of greed and wickedness (Lk. 11:39).[13]

A clearer account of Jesus' teaching against an economics of greed and hoarding is the story of the rich fool. The background of the story is a man who shouts from the crowd asking Jesus to ask his brother to share his father's estate with him. Christ's answer to the man is instructive. First, Jesus did not want to be part of this problem. However, his response reveals some hidden motives of the man, which is greed. Jesus said "Beware! Do not be greedy for what you do not have. Real life is not measured by how much we own." He then gives this illustration of the rich fool in Lk. 12:16–21.

What is central and relevant for our discussion is that this rich farmer has a bumper harvest of crops that season. He was "unwilling to sell the excess produce on a saturated market" because it would prevent him from making more money or profit. Then he realized he did not have enough space to hoard the excess goods for a lean season when he could make "a killing" in profits. Therefore, he decides to tear down his existing inadequate barn to build a bigger one where he could store all the excess goods and eventually take rest. But when his efforts were complete, he was told that his life would be demanded of him and he would die that very night. Therefore, he could not enjoy the wealth that he spent his life accumulating for himself. Jesus concludes his story with these words: "Yes, a person is a fool to store up earthly wealth but not have a rich relationship with God."

> Greed is a grievous moral problem. But consumerism is the value that has shaped our modern economics. [Stassen says] Greed is a spiritual and a moral disorder. [It is] rooted in a fundamental misunderstanding of the value of possessions and of the role that possessions can play in a person's life, greed

---

13 Glen Stassen and David P. Gushee, *Kingdom Ethics*, 411–415.

misleads men and women into ascribing inordinate value to that which is not worthy of it.[14]

Simply put, greed leads to idolatry. Jesus said a man couldn't serve God and wealth at the same time. Both of these realities demand total loyalty of the person and it is morally impossible for a person to please two masters at the same time as Jesus insists (Matt. 6:24). I agree with Stassen *"greed encourages a lifestyle of luxury, pride, hoarding, self-indulgence, oppression and lack of generosity."*[15] The story of Jesus about the shrewd manager who decides to reduce the debts of his master's debtors reveals some important biblical values for our economic ethics. Here we see a radical shift from the idea of profit making that do not give priority to human relations corrected. The situation this manager faced changed his perception about economics. What really is important is not profit, but good thriving relationships. He decides to change his tactics and attitude to address economic injustice. He realized that his future would be more secured if he makes friends with his master's debtors they will take care of him later on in life when he does not have a job. The rich man admired his clever manager's behavior and attitude. Jesus commends him for his shrewdness and attitude: "I tell you, use your worldly resources to benefit others and make friends. In this way, your generosity stores up for you in heaven" (Lk. 16:1–9, NLT).

The NT writers were aware of OT economic value that resisted all forms of economic injustices and exploitations of the poor and weak by the economic barons. They reiterated that God hates exploitation of the poor by the rich for the purpose of self-enrichment (James 5:1–6).

Associated with corruption, exploitation is another vice called selfishness. This vice according to the NT writers such as James has its roots and source in the Devil. It has a twin ally called jealousy. Both jealousy and selfish ambitions are describe by Apostle James as worldly values, they are unspiritual and motivated by the devil" (James 3:15–16). These values are not of God. God is not selfish. He is jealous in defending what is good

---

[14] Glen Stassen and David P. Gushee, *Kingdom Ethics*, 415.
[15] Glen Stassen and David P. Gushee, *Kingdom Ethics*, 416. The italics are that of the author.

and in line with his character and repudiates what will bring disgrace and dishonor to his name. Both of these vices we pointed out are not acceptable within the African communitarian society. It is destructive and does not build up community. They have negative impact on our economic values; they breed greed.

The antidote to covetousness and greed which is a form of idolatry, is the "fear of the Lord" (Col. 3:5) which engenders the wisdom of contentment." In summary, both the OT and the NT speaks on our economic activities. There are certain biblical values that give the moral foundations for our economic values and practices. The theological and biblical foundation for economic practices is based on the fact that all the resources we have are God's gifts to humanity for their wellbeing. God requires that there is a fair, just, and evenhanded distribution of the economic resources he has given us for the benefit of all humanity. This means we need to ensure economic justice that seeks to care for the poor and needy in our societies. Biblical economic values decry "distributive economic injustices" and vouches for economic values that reflect God's economic value: righteousness, justice, compassion, and generosity by replacing these biblical economic values with our unjust social economic systems based on greed, hoarding, and consumerism. Biblical economics requires we repudiate an "economic ethos that ratifies the deceitfulness of wealth" and makes it our economic Mammon, or idol.[16]

How do economic activities relate to poverty and the moral and ethical issues poverty raises for African Christians? In the section following we, will deal with the problems of poverty. Our concern is not to prove with statistics that poverty is a reality in Africa. We hold the view that poverty is a global problem, and we find it all around us wherever we are. There are many researches done on global poverty all over the world and we need not fill these pages with those statistics. Our concern here is how we can morally utilize the resources made available by God to human beings to enhance their lives and wellbeing and reduce poverty in Africa. I will turn to poverty and draw on some African communal and biblical values to address

---

16 Glen Stassen and David P. Gushee, *Kingdom Ethics*, 426.

the moral concerns poverty raises for the African Christian community and society.

Defining poverty

What is poverty? It is difficult to come up with a simple definition of poverty because of its complex nature. Poverty may be described as absolute expressing some fundamental or basic material deprivation and relative depending on different living standards and cultures. I will define poverty generally as a condition where people are involuntarily deprived of certain basic human needs essential for life such as food, clothing, medical care and housing and such conditions reduces them to become beggars. I will also add the deprivation is not just material, that is critical but it is also spiritual deprivation.

The basic word for the poor in the Old Testament carries the idea of "wrongfully impoverished or disposed." The primary understanding of poor in the Bible is economic. Therefore, the poor are those who are "economically impoverished because of a calamity or exploitation" by the rich and powerful in society.[17] This understanding of poverty is very important. It underlines the basic ethical and moral concern we have in dealing with the problem.

But, poverty is more than just material deprivation, as it is understood in contemporary societies. It includes also spiritual deprivation and relational deprivation. The "lack of *relational* support—the absence of those to whom you can turn for emotional encouragement—is as critical as lack of financial resources."[18] It isolates the individual from the family and community. Schluter points out there are a close link between financial deprivation and relational deprivation. Lack of financial resources most times makes one sever relationships with friends and family because one does not have the resources to give gifts, entertain or play a role in community affairs.[19] His

---

17 Ronald J. Sider, *Rich Christians in an Age of Hunger*. Dallas, TX: Word publishing 1990, 39.
18 Schluter, "Welfare," in *Jubilee Manifesto*, 176.
19 Schluter, "Welfare," in *Jubilee Manifesto*, 176.

observation is very true in Africa. This is the worst experience an African can face. It robs one of his or her dignity and usefulness to the family and community. An African proverb illustrates this idea, "poverty splits and divides the family" or another that says poverty has no friends."

Poverty is a global problem. It is not just an African issue. An African proverb says; poverty is like honey it is not harvested in one particular place alone." Poverty is everywhere in the world and no one particular place has monopoly of it.[20] This means we look at the issue both locally and globally.

Poverty is shameful in Africa. It deprives one of his or her dignity as a human being. Poor people have no social status and most times, they do not participate in the social life of the community. Poverty results in abuse of the poor, distortions, and exploitation of the poor. This creates a moral problem. It is an ethical issue that has to do with social injustice and exploitation that destroys the quality of human relationships and the abuse of the poor.[21] Several African proverbs affirm this thinking about poverty in general and the poor person in particular. The "poor person" an African proverb says, "has no friends," or "the poor man's corpse is buried in the morning" or the poor man [is] buried by the road side." These proverbs expressed certain cultural attitudes towards the poor person who is not shown respect and is easily ignored or dismissed because he is poor. On the contrary, the rich are treated with respect and they are honored at their funerals.[22] What are some of the common causes of poverty in Africa?

Causes of poverty

Corruption is one of the main causes of poverty in Africa according to research done by many multinational agencies working in Africa. This corruption has a global perspective that contributes to it. There seems to be corroboration between African political leaders who are the most notorious for grand corruption, and western liberal economic systems that gives

---

20 Kofi Asare Opoku, *Hearing and Keeping: Akan Proverbs, African Proverbs Series*, Vol. 2. Ed. John S. Mbiti. Accra, Ghana: Asempa Publishers, 1997, 55, No. 259.
21 Wright, *Old Testament Ethics*, 168.
22 Opoku, *Hearing and Keeping: Akan Proverbs*, 56–57, Nos. 268, 269.

these leaders safe havens for them to keep their ill-gotten and stolen wealth in their banks and financial institutions. Because of greed, these western financial institutions lose the moral integrity and power to challenge this evil of corruption. In most places in Africa, these multimillion-dollar business corporations from the west, collude with national leaders to loot and rape the resources of many developing countries' economies with the masses paralyzed and unable to do anything to save their country from these powerful forces.

Then there are natural causes such as failed rains, blight on crops, or crop failure, which affect production, and consequently decrease economic prosperity. Africa, being an agriculture-oriented economy faces this challenge year after year. Because of failed crops and low crop yield, many Africans are unable to feed their families and generate enough financial resources to educate and provide the necessary basic needs of their families. The government through corruption is not able to buy enough food to feed the people. As a result, many have died of hunger. The problem of poor harvests has caused many African farmers to slip into abject poverty over the years. Some have had to sell their lands and have lost their basic economic base for survival.

Both in the Bible and in many African societies, laziness and slothfulness are seen as some of the causes of poverty (Prov. 6:6–11, 12:11, 19:15, 14:23, 20:13, 21:17, 25, 24:30–34). We must be very careful not to think that laziness is what has caused poverty in Africa. A significant African cultural value is hard work. Many African cultures believe hard work is the medicine to cure poverty and misery. Africans are very hard working people but get very little pay for their efforts because of the greed of the rich and powerful. The foremost problem I see is the unjust economic systems that operate in our world today where those who work hard are paid very little for what they produce. Inequality, unfair, and unjust trade, is the cause of poverty in many African nations who sell their raw materials to local cartels, cartels fronting for developed nations, and they are paid very little in return for their hard work and raw materials. These kinds of exploitations of the poor by the rich and powerful nations raise a moral concern for our economic activities in our world.

The other cause for poverty is oppression. In both the Bible and contemporary society, oppression by the powerful and their greed to grab all that they can grab, using state power and machinery is another major cause of poverty in the scriptures and in contemporary African societies. Poverty is caused! It is not a divinely imposed condition, or one that is simply the result of faults on the part of the individual—though it may include human fault at personal, community, and political levels in regards to its causes, impact, and continued existence. The primary cause of poverty is exploitation of the power of the weak and helpless. These powerful people are selfish and delight in keeping others poor so they can control them.

Two of the major causes of poverty in the Bible were oppression and exploitation of the poor by the rich and powerful in society. Wright points out five areas in which economic oppression took place in the Bible. These are true today in our contemporary society because human nature is the same everywhere and throughout time. In the Bible, the economically powerful exploited the socially weak and vulnerable. These vulnerable classes included those who had lost family or land or both: widows, orphans, and aliens (2 Ki. 4:1–7). In the exploitation of the economically weak, victims accumulate debt which leads to loss of land, exorbitant interest rates/charges and royal taxation and conscription (Ex. 22:25, 1 Sam. 8:10–18), exploitation of the ethnically weak (Ex. 22:21, Lev. 19:33), royal excesses in taking huge taxes from the peoples, corruption and abuse of power, a life characterized by extortion, robbery, oppression of the poor and needy, ill treatment of aliens and denying them justice. (1 Ki. 11–12, 21, and Jer. 22:13), judicial corruption and false accusation of the poor to rob them of their possession and inheritance (1 Ki. 21:7–16, Amos 5:7, 11–12, Isa. 10:1–2, Ps. 82).[23] We find that these many causes mentioned in the Bible are a reality in our societies today.

---

23 Wright, *Old Testament Ethics*, 170–171.

Dealing with poverty in contemporary western and African societies

Welfare systems in the west

The West deals with poverty and meets the needs of vulnerable individuals or groups through state welfare programs or systems. Social structures and legal mechanisms are put in place to determine who qualifies for welfare and who does not. In this way, the government is able to reduce its budget. This is often more applicable to nationals who are citizens of the land.

But often orphans (or fatherless), widows and immigrants or aliens who live among them do not qualify for welfare. These people lack the "socially supportive structures" of both nuclear and extended "family to help them cope with their economic and social stress."[24] The people of Israel, as the chosen people of God, were expected to care for these three categories of people—aliens, orphans and widows (Ex. 22:22; Lev. 19:34, Deut. 27:19). In our contemporary African cultures, we would like to add children and women to the group of vulnerable individuals within any given society. These people lack the social protection and economic advantages others have in society or natives have.[25] The Israelites were to love the alien as they love themselves, because they were aliens themselves in Egypt. It is obvious that God was referring to Israel's experience as aliens in Egypt. It was a reminder of their experience in Egypt; of how the Egyptians mistreated them and how they cried out to God for justice and deliverance from their oppression. If they did not like their bad experience in Egypt as aliens, then they had to treat other aliens well. It reflects the principle of the golden rule: "Do to others what you would like them to do to you." Our act on caring for aliens is reflected in God's behavior of delivering Israel from Egypt. Imitating the just character of God in dealing justly with the poor, alien and widows is imperative. This was a general Bible value advocated for in both the OT and NT. The NT writers urge Christians to care for widows and orphans as well as the poor (Gal. 2:10, 1 Tim. 5:3–8; James 1:27).

---

24 Schluter, "Welfare," in *Jubilee Manifesto*, 176.
25 J. P. Burnside, et al. *Religion and Rehabilitation*. Cullompton: Willan Publishing, 2004, 14.

Schluter points out some problems western welfare systems create such as a "dependency mindset," which diminishes community responsibility and puts a huge amount of pressure on government resources. This financial burden on the government might be passed down to its middle class citizens in the form of taxes. This might increase poverty. Any social welfare system either in relief or in providing services for the needy must be a temporary measure to prevent dependency that might entrench poverty. We must create opportunity for people to have work so they can support themselves. Work is critical for poverty alleviation. This will also restore human dignity for the people who live on welfare so they can also help those who are needy. Secondly, we must endeavor to balance providing welfare support to individual and families "without undermining the family structures that were meant to take responsibility for it."[26]

Caring for the poor in African societies—community and human solidarity

Unlike the west, where welfare systems are centralized government systems to deal with poverty and to meet the needs of those in the communities, African societies tend to deal with the issues through its communal systems. Gyekye has rightly argued that the African communal system is fundamentally socio-ethical and not economic. "It is a social and ethical arrangement aimed at finding ways of adequately and realistically responding to the needs and wellbeing of the individual members of the society and defining what sorts of relationships should hold between them as they function in society."[27] He describes the role of the traditional chief as being overly concerned for the welfare of the people. He had the responsibility to meet material and physical needs of his people. Therefore, the African traditional political structure was a social welfare state.[28] Most of the revenue collected by the rulers as taxes was used to care for the needs of the people. Our current political structures do not have welfare systems

---

26 Michael Schluter, "Welfare," in *Jubilee Manifesto*, 176.
27 Gyekye, *African Cultural Values*, 96.
28 Gyekye, *African Cultural Values*, 105.

for the poor and needy in society. This makes life more difficult for the poor in Africa which leaves many excavating for food in dumpsters.

The other way in which the poor are cared for is through the extended family and kinship systems. These means provide the economic support for families who are struggling financially. But it is becoming increasingly difficult because of the fast rate at which poverty is spreading widely in Africa.

Nevertheless individuals who have access to land to work to make some income and those who are in any kind of employment are under a moral obligation to use some of the proceeds or income to help some of the less fortunate people in their family and even contribute to support some of the less fortunate in their community. The wealthy person in any family or community is expected to help and show concern for the wellbeing of the family, community and even the state. Therefore, wealth is highly valued in African communities.

In summary, the Africans' value of sharing a common social life and their commitment to the social life or common good of the community along with their sense of mutual obligations to care for others, their sense of interdependence on and solidarity with the community provide mechanisms for people to deal with and take care of the poor within their communities. This is made possible through the extended family and clan systems as well as through the generosity of the affluent members in the society who are under moral obligation to help those who are poor within their community.

The Biblical mandate to care for the poor

The role and the responsibilities of the rich in society towards the poor

God, who is rich, watches over the poor. He is passionate about her or her wellbeing. Therefore, whoever takes care of the poor is doing it for the Lord. Proverb 19:17 says, "He who is kind to the poor lends to the Lord" (Prov. 19:4, 7). God's own act to redeem Israel form Egypt is an act of God freeing Israel from both economic oppression and exploitation. He also liberated religiously from the worship of false gods. At the exodus, God ended Israel's economic oppression and brought economic justice to them. God gives them a land and promises to bless them in that land. It is in light of his blessings to his people that he commands the rich to take care of the poor within their borders. Our action to take care of the poor is again predicated on God's action and care for the poor.

Therefore, in both the Old and the New Testaments, the people of God are instructed by God to care for the poor among them and provide for their welfare and needs. The rich are to honor and treat the poor with respect because they bear the image of God in them. When the rich despise the poor because of their economic status, they are indeed despising the creator, who made the poor (Prov. 14:31). Apostle James argues, God has chosen the poor in this world to be rich in faith as well as the ones who will inherit the kingdom he promised to those who love Him (James 2:5). God created both the poor and the rich. The grounds for our action to take care of the poor and respect them is based on the greatest commandment "love your neighbor as yourself" (James 2:8b). There are other New Testament passages that instruct Christians to take care of the poor. In Acts 9:36 and 10:31, we see the writer commending the generosity of two individuals who gave to the poor. Paul encouraged Christians to help the poor (Rom. 15:21, and Gal. 2:10).

The condition of the poor-aliens, widows, orphans, the weak or vulnerable—is a test for true Christian piety and one that drives the moral vision of Christians. True religion has a social responsibility to the weak and marginalized. Our economic life is a communal one not an individualistic agenda so is our use of our wealth. It must be used for the good of society. The rich and poor need each other.

The proper use of wealth and treatment of the poor in society

There are certain Biblical and religious values that lay the foundation for proper use of wealth. Wealth and prosperity is a gift and blessing of God to humanity. Both the Old and New Testaments see wealth and prosperity as an act of God's grace, which should prompt a response of generosity of God's people toward those found in need. Wealth is not evil or bad in itself. It becomes dangerous when it takes control over us and becomes the passion for which we live. "The love for money is the root of all evil." Money has an inherent power to dominate our souls and passions. But material wealth when put in proper perspective can be a blessing to humanity (Matt. 6:19–21, Heb. 13:16).

God would not condone the behavior of the rich mistreating the poor. He is the source of their blessings. He blessed them so they would in turn become a blessing to the poor. The rich are warned not to exploit the poor by charging interest on their loans (Ex. 22:25, Lev. 25:35–37, Deut. 23:19). The prophets were harsh on the rich in the nation who oppressed the poor, subjected them to humiliation, and loss of their dignity as human beings. God's judgment was brought upon them as a nation and he sent them into captivity beside their religious corruption (Amos 2:7, 5; 10–15, 6:1–7). Amos warned they would not enjoy the wealth and houses they build on the back and sweat of the poor (Amos 5:1).

The poor were on Jesus' mind. Several times Jesus asked the rich people who wanted to follow him to sell all the property, give them to the poor, come, and follow him (Matt. 19:16–24, Mk. 10:17–22, Lk. 18:18–30). Jesus taught his disciples to imitate God's mercy and compassion when they lend money to poor. They were encouraged to lend money to the poor, those who could not pay them back (Lk. 6:33–36). Christians lend and they should not expect anything back. This is the nature and character of God. He gives and he does not expect us to pay Him back. This principle stands against our cultural and economic values that seek for profits on our investments. When Christians do this, they are truly reflecting the character of their heavenly Father. It, however, goes against our cultural and economic values. Nevertheless, it is God's way! We are to show respect for the poor (James 2:1–9). This injunction is grounded on the command to love your neighbor as you love yourself. Mistreating and dishonoring the poor is essentially dishonoring God, the poor man's creator (Prov. 14:31). "So you see, it isn't enough to have faith. Faith that doesn't show itself in good deeds is not faith at all—it is dead and useless" (James 2:17b, NLT).

Wealth must be used to meet the needs of those who are needy among us so there will be no poor among us (Deut. 15:4). The rich are instructed to be generous to the poor and lend them as much as they need and not become hard-hearted or tightfisted (Deut. 15:7). This injunction is tied to God's promise of blessing his people in the land He has given them. As we have pointed out, the blessings we received are gifts from God. Often times we think we have made our fortunes by our own strength and sweat, so others must suffer the same way we did to become rich. And we close our hearts to the needy and the poor among us. Israel was warned not to think that the wealth it would make came because of their ingenuity and hard work, so they become proud and forget God. God reminded them that he is the person who gives them the power to become wealthy. Therefore, our wealth, much like that of the Israelites, is not to be used selfishly on ourselves, but we are to use it to care for the poor and those who need help in our communities (Deut. 8:9–18). There is more blessing in giving than in receiving, as taught by our Lord and King, Jesus Christ (Acts 20:35).

The early Christian community practiced this model of life where there were no needy people among the community of faith because the rich among the group learned to share their wealth with the rest of the community (Acts 4:34). They overcame the selfishness and greed that are central vices in our culture. They truly understood the concept that all they have is God's. Therefore, they did not hold their wealth back. They put it to the service of God and for the well-being of humanity.

God's imperative and the motivation for Israel's generous treatment of the poor are threefold according to Schluter. It was based on Israel's "shared experience and imaginative empathy" (Deut. 16:11–12), the expectation of divine blessings (Deut. 14:29), and direct obedience to God's commands (Deut. 26:13)."[29] All these three principles should guide our resolve to care for the poor and needy among us so we can deal with the problem of poverty in Africa.

As I have intimated, any attempt to help the poor must be a temporal measure. We must endeavor to give a more permanent solution to help

---

[29] Schluter, "Welfare," in *Jubilee Manifesto*, 184.

them meet their needs and be able to help other people who might need their help. Therefore, we must focus on empowering them to become economically independent. In the next section, we will look at some biblical models and values for poverty alleviation or reduction.

Biblical models for just economic relationships, poverty alleviation, and economic empowerment

Jubilee is God's command to the Israelites to cancel debts (Lev. 25, Ex. 20:8–11, Deut. 5:1–15) owed to them by fellow Israelites who could not pay their debts. This was to prevent them from slipping into abject poverty because of their debt. Similarly, individuals or families who have sold their land to another Israelite for reasons that were beyond them, were to receive their land back. Since Israel was an agrarian community, land served as the economic engine that brought prosperity to the people. Getting their land back meant the individual regained access to a means of production so they could become economically independent. Having access to that means of production meant they now had ability for capital creation that would enable them to meet their basic economic and financial needs without having to depend on others or the community. Jubilee, therefore, ensured justice in work relationships and prevented the wealthy from amassing large tracts of lands through which they could oppress the poor and subject them to unending poverty.

Jubilee—the principle of release for the land was extended to the poor. Jubilee was time of release for the people, in relation to remission of pledges for financial debts (Deut. 15:1–3, 13–15). Again, this was to give people a new lease of life to begin afresh without having the financial burden of large loans on their heads. Many often struggled to pay off these debts due to their meager financial resources. The Jubilee principle kept individuals from becoming perpetual debtors. Our faith in God results in a social responsibility to our fellow human being who is in need. We have an obligation to take care of the needy amongst us. This is true religion. Faith must result in concrete actions, that is, showing concern for the poor and needy people around us making their lives more pleasant to live.

The other model for poverty alleviation was through the tithes. Tithes were set aside for God, and were to be used to keep up the Levites as they served God in the temple. (Deut. 14:22–27). However, every third year the Israelites were to give a special tithe that had to be given to the poor—Levites, aliens, widows and orphans (Deut. 14:28–29; 26:12–15). The purpose of this tithe was to make sure that the poor and the underprivileged in society were cared for, had something to eat, and were satisfied. The principle is clear. We need to take care of the physical and material needs of the less advantaged in our society. This is our social and moral responsibility.

Another way in which the poor and needy within the Israelite community were catered for was through the first-fruit offering. The first-fruit offerings were to be given to God to thank him for the blessings he had bestowed on Israel through the good land he gave them, but also to remind them where they came from. In this context of blessings and thanksgiving they were to share that blessing; "all the good things the LORD your God has given to you and your household with the Levites and the foreigners living among them. Therefore, the poor were beneficiaries to and participants in the rejoicing and free agricultural produce associated with the first-fruit offerings (Deut. 26:1–11).

The sabbatical fallow was a law that allows the land to fallow every seven years without any work done on it. This was another provision to take care of the poor. The poor were allowed to eat the produce that grew on the fallowing land including the grape and olive groves (Ex. 23:11, Lev. 25:6).

Gleaning provided another means for the poor to meet their needs. This was a very common practice. Every third and seventh year, there was the annual allowance of gleaning from crops, vineyards, and olive trees. The farmer was instructed by God to leave some crops behind as he harvested for the poor and foreigners living among the Israelites, so they could have something to eat (Lev. 19:9–10, 23:22, Deut. 24:19–22). A person who was hungry could take crops from his neighbor's farm without transgressing the laws of trespassing or stealing (Deut. 23:24).

The concept of relief is a New Testament development. Paul took a collection for the poor in Jerusalem to help relieve them from the economic hardships they were facing. He based his philosophy on Christ's own experience on earth. He reminded the Corinthians that the Lord Jesus became poor so that they might become rich (2 Cor. 8:9). In the New Testament, Christ's example in giving of himself for the redemption of humanity became the motivating factor for Christian giving to the poor and the helpless. Through the "amazing self-sacrifice of Christ," Christians are encouraged to give generously to the needy, oppressed and the poor (1 Jn. 3:16). This is also expressed in the distribution of food to widows in the book of Acts (Acts 6:1–7) and the collection of gifts by the Church in Greece for the struggling Church in Jerusalem. (Rom. 15:25–28).

While relief is good, it must be used for a short period to meet urgent needs in people's lives. If extended for too long it degenerates into dependency syndrome. We must empower people by teaching people to fish rather than give them a fish every day according to a Chinese proverb. Providing resources for economic empowerment is the key to resolving poverty in Africa, not relief aid.

So far from our discussion, we see some fundamental biblical values that must shape our social moral vision to address poverty and care for the needs of the poor among us. These values are rooted in God's own nature. Our care for the poor must be motivated by love, compassion, mercy, and justice, with the recognition that everything we have is given to us by God not only for our wellbeing but also for the welfare of others. We are blessed so we can become a blessing to others. At the individual and community levels, I think all the principles and values we have explicated in this chapter must be part of our vision. We must express compassion, mercy, love, and justice to those who need them. God requires this of us as his children. He cares for the welfare of the poor, the oppressed, and the weak. Wherever we find injustice, we must stand against it.

Before I end our discussion, I would like to suggest some biblical and theological principles and some practical steps that need to be taken to help radically transform our economic relationships and the issue of poverty.

The section below will focus on policy matters at the national level to help deal with economic injustice and its resultant poverty in Africa.

Responding to economic injustice and poverty in Africa

Empowering the poor to create wealth through dignified hard work

In Africa, starting a welfare system must be done in a manner that it would be just a temporary policy to address poverty. People who live all their lives depending on the good will of others lose their dignity as human beings. They lose self-respect for themselves. What we need to do is to help them regain their dignity as human beings by helping them to development their economic potential, so they can take care of themselves and their family and make a viable contribution to the well being and life of the community in which they live.

Most of the biblical principles for taking care of the poor through the triennial tithe, gleaning, and relief, must be seen, as temporal measures to ease the immediate needs and sufferings of the poor. However, a long-term solution must look at the principles of the Sabbath year release of land, generous lending to the poor, the ban on interests (Ex. 22:25, Lev. 25:35–38, Deut. 23:19–20) and the jubilee principles as very critical to dealing with economic empowerment and poverty in Africa.

Africans have always worked hard to provide for their needs within their respective societies. They never depended on the chiefs or kings to provide for their basic needs such as food, clothing, and shelter. That we ensure those who work hard get what they deserve, in terms of the pricing of their goods and services, is the responsibility of the government. We cannot just leave these things to the market forces that are driven by greed and exploitation. When the pricing of goods is left to the "forces of the market" and the rich and powerful nations, they tend to manipulate and control these market systems, to use them ultimately for their own selfish gain. In the end, the poor, though working hard, remain poor because they do not get what their products are worth. As a result, people get frustrated and lose hope and confidence in our economic systems.

African leaders must invest in current technologies to process our raw materials at home so those who deal in raw materials can get more value for commodities. In this way, people who are working hard can enjoy the fruits of their labor and not become victims of greedy and exploitative systems.

Hard work and while empowering people to engage in meaningful work and economic activities to create favorable social, economic, infrastructural, and good working conditions are the right antidotes to poverty. We will discuss the importance of work in the following chapter.

Capital is very essential for any economic activity; Government should take initiatives to create fair and just financial institutions that will give soft loans and credit facilities to people to be able to access capital for businesses and other economic ventures they would like to engage in. As we have seen from our discussions, the rich were asked to loan money to the poor so they could be empowered to develop themselves economically. They were not to take advantage of them and charge them exorbitant interest rates on the loans they gave. This principle needs to be encouraged within the financial markets and banks today. The current interest rates on loans make it difficult for the poor to access those financial opportunities. The rich are the only ones who can usually access these loans. So, the rich are enabled to get richer while the poor are made poorer. Interest rates must be moderate, and this will only be possible if we are not selfish and greedy in our passion to maximize profit.

The Government must ensure and create loans and credit facilities that will give some power for the poor to develop their economic base so they can meet their basic needs such as shelter, healthcare, food, clothing, and education. We must develop social economic systems that are just:

- Leaders should develop public policies that ensure proper use of resources for the good of society and not for a class of certain individuals, the rich and the privileged. In doing this, we must recognize the impact of sin on our human culture and economic activities that is characterized by exploitation, injustice, selfishness, greed, and oppression. We must address our cultural and economic values that have brought us to where we are and seek to change and replace those values with some of the principles we have learned in this chapter—God's character of goodness, mercy, compassion, justice, righteousness, and peace. We must set aside individual interests and seek the interest of the majority among us where are in need and help them.

- We must address the gap between the rich and the poor at both the national and at the international level. The inequality in income that exists between the poor and the rich is immoral. We must find ways of narrowing this if we are to succeed in reducing poverty in our world today. We must acknowledge that the poor will always be with us as far as we continue to be selfish, oppressive, and unjust. The question is whether we have the political will power to empower the poor and give them a new lease of hope and confidence.
- Samuel's model of leadership must be encouraged. Leaders must be blameless, honest, people of integrity, content with what they have, and not oppressive and thieves—stealing from the people (1 Sam. 12:3–5). It is the duty of the rich to use their power to care for the poor. More specifically, rich nations must care for poor nations. The cause of poverty in many African countries is due to trade injustices and bad economic policies both locally and internationally. We need just and fair local and international trading policies that do not only favor powerful people and rich nations. We must deal with unjust international trade and we must address the use of exploitation of resources and poor labor policies which contribute to poverty. We must demand an end to economic injustice and the exploitation of the poor as did the prophets of the Old Testament. Those in authority who are entrusted with these matters must take them seriously.
- Sin is the impulse for trade expansion that has continued to go hand in hand with economic oppression, selfishness, and structural injustice even today. Unfair trade, bad trade policies, contracts, and arrangements by international trade robs many

developing nations and the poor of the world from enjoying their own wealth as most of this wealth is exported to more developed, and often wealthy nations in the world. The basic order in economics is the order of "free market economy" which is based on natural laws that can be traced and determined through human reason.[30] We must ensure that these economic principles are not manipulated to enhance the wealth of few while leaving the larger portion of society in abject poverty.

- Population explosion in Africa is making land a scarce commodity. Many people are landless, which we have pointed out previously is the basic source of economic power and development. Given this, we need to look at other ways of creating wealth other than just depending on land. We must explore, be innovative, and tap in to the technological advances in the world today. We must innovate and create other means and ways of creating wealth in a morally appropriate ways.
- Educational institutions must play a critical role in dealing with poverty in Africa. We must train people to become entrepreneurs, people who will create jobs for others and not those who will come out of our institutions of higher education only to look to the government to give them the jobs they desire. Our education must focus on our national needs and goals.
- Lastly, we must seriously consider the spiritual dimension of economics and poverty which has its root in human sinfulness. Satan can use wealth and prosperity to turn us away from God and harden our hearts towards one another. We must submit our economic activities and systems to God so he will redeem them. We must not only deal with material depravity, we must work hard to enrich people's spiritual sensibilities by encouraging close relationship with God, who is the source of all blessings.

---

30 Haan, *The Economics of Honour*, 9.

Developing just economic policies to aid poverty reduction

- In dealing with poverty, we must remember Jesus' words that the poor will always be with us (Mk. 14, 7, Jn. 12:8). We must not get disillusioned that we can eradicate poverty completely from our world. However, we can work to reduce poverty in our world. In doing this, there should be equity and efficiency in sharing and utilizing resources for the good of humanity. Wright has argued that God gave the earth to all humanity and so, we must share the resources of the world together. He insists we cannot use the Old Testament narratives to justify "privatized, individual ownership." Individuals can have "legitimate private ownership of material goods," but the legitimacy of that property right must be grounded on the belief that the land is God's gift to the people and he is concerned for its proper distribution to the families.[31] In many African countries where we have huge tracts of land unutilized because they are considered private property, we must enact laws that could give access to people who can use the land for economic purposes so those people can create some economic stability for themselves.
- Humanity has a responsibility to work. God is a worker. The image of God in humans makes them workers. To work is what it means to be human. Wright writes, "It is thus mankind's nature, as well as his responsibility and his right, to be engaged in productive economic work with the material resources of the world." This means that we do not only have the duty to work ourselves, but we also have "a responsibility to enable or allow others to work. So to prevent another person working, or to deny or deprive him of work, is to offend against his humanity and the image of God in him, as well as failing in one's responsibility to God for him"[32]

---

31 Christopher Wright, *An Eye for An Eye: The Place of Old Testament Ethics for Today.* Downers Grove, IL: InterVarsity Press, 1983, 54.

32 Wright, *An Eye for An Eye*, 69.

- There must be equity and fair sharing of the product of all our economic activities. This calls for economic justice and compassion; two values that must underlie our economic activities. There should be economic justice and fairness for workers who produce the wealth. They are to be paid fairly and promptly (Deut. 24:14–15).
- As Christians concerned with our socio-economic state in Africa, we must affirm the viability of the smallest economic units, which is the household, in our African societies. The Jubilee principle in the Bible was a check on a few powerful and rich individuals who would accumulate vast tracts of land for themselves leaving majority of people landless. "It was an attempt to impede…to reverse, the relentless economic forces that lead to a downward spiral of debt, poverty, dispossession and bondage."[33] There must be laws to protect individuals from losing the source of their economic life, whatever that may be.

Conclusion

Economic justice is God's concern for humanity. We must take an active role in dealing with economic injustices in our world today that have left more than half the world's population in abject poverty. Locally, leaders who are in power and have been given the responsibility to protect and to see that citizens have descent lives must work hard to reduce the economic inequality that exists in many African countries and the world at large. God's concern for the poor and the destitute would not make Him overlook our moral obligation to our fellow human beings who need our help while we turn the other way. To love God and to know Him is to do justice, righteousness and walk humbly with God. True religion is to take care of the poor, of widows, of orphans, and of aliens among us. This is our social and moral responsibility as humans.

---

33 Schluter, "Welfare," in *Jubilee Manifesto*, 184.

CHAPTER 9

Work and Unemployment

Labor is "the lost province of Christian Faith" (Elton Trueblood)

Introduction

In our last chapter, I said that work is one of the major medicines that will help us to cure and deal with poverty in Africa. It is a critical human activity. However, work is one of the most sought after endeavors in human history. Yet in many countries of the world, it is the most difficult to find. The unemployment rate in many countries in the world, and particularly Africa, is so high. The youth, who form the highest population in African nations, and majority of women, are unemployed. The statistics on unemployment in Africa are staggering. For example, the unemployment rate in Kenya is so high. The unemployment rate by the end of December 2011 stood at 40%. Statistics show 64 % of Kenyan youths is unemployed.[1] Many university graduates and a huge number of the youth are unemployed. This trend is widespread in many African countries. Many people have to struggle to find work and when they do find employment they often work in such deplorable conditions that rob them of their human dignity.

This chapter will look at work and draw out some cultural and biblical principles for the necessity for people to work. In line with our argument in this book, I assert that work is intrinsic to our nature as human beings created in the image of God and to deny humanity an opportunity to work is to deny them of their human dignity or humanness. The right

---

[1] http://youthbanner.org/component/content/article/104. Accessed October 26, 2012.

for humans to work is enshrined in their status as creatures of God; creatures created in the image of God. Humanity has the right to work because their creator created them for that purpose. This understanding of work has moral implications for humanity in terms of what kind of work we engage in. It places responsibility on all humans to engage in good work that ensures the dignity of the person and brings fulfillment to the individuals involved and the community, and brings honor and glory to God. It also places responsibilities on policy makers and governments to create decent employment opportunities for her citizens. We will pursue this argument using some biblical values and principles on work and the moral responsibility that is placed on us. However, before I begin this discussion, I would like to define the term work.

Defining work

The Collins Dictionary of the English Language (1979) offers at least four basic meanings of work. Work is seen as "physical or mental effort directed towards doing or making something." It can mean a "paid employment at a job or trade, occupation, or profession." It could also mean "a duty, task, or undertaking," and furthermore as "something done, made, etc., as a results of effort or exertion." As we see, it is difficult to define work in a simple way. However, the basic idea of work has to do with exerting some kind of physical or mental efforts, to do or to make something.

Work includes jobs or labor for which we are paid. It also involves all we do to meet our physical and social needs. Work serves our basic self-interests and the interests of others as well as society. We work in order that we can provide for our personal needs, but also we are able to help make life better for others and ourselves.

The words the Bible uses for work have two basic meanings. The first group of words has no moral or physical implications. These words have to do with words that describe God's work or as a general reference to human work (Gen. 2:2, Ex. 20:9, Gen. 5:29, Ex. 5:15, Prov. 16:9). The other words in the Bible imply work is "weariness, hard, pain, trouble, and sorrow (Gen. 31:42, Deut. 28:33, Ps. 90:10, Eccl. 1:3, 2:10, Matt. 11:28, 2 Thess. 3:8)."[2]

I will sum up this discussion with Volf's definition of work. Volf defines work as "an instrumental activity serving the satisfaction of creaturely needs."[3] Work, therefore, involves all human activities that bring some form of satisfaction and meet human needs. We must point out here that not all work (that is, results in satisfaction and meets human needs) affirms human dignity (e.g. prostitution, child labor, drug trafficking, etc) although engaging in such activities may provide resources to meet our human needs and even bring about human satisfaction, but they fall short of both our cultural values and biblical ethics.

The Bible says a lot about our work and God is very much concerned about what we do for a living. Therefore, we want to construe work as any human engagement that affirms humanity as created in the image of God while enhancing their dignity as humans. In this sense work may mean paid jobs, trade, occupation, profession, agricultural work, and domestic work (the majority engaged in domestic work are not paid for their services in many countries in Africa). How do we view work? Many people in the world today have certain misconceptions and apprehensions about work. What has given rise to such poor attitudes towards work? I will address this problem below.

Some contemporary misconceptions about work

Most of contemporary understanding of work is based on a secular outlook. A majority of people in today's world divorce the true meaning and character of work from religion. Their views of work are largely shaped by secular ideologies associated with Marxism and capitalism. This is radically different from the biblical concept of work, which is laden with

---

[2] W.S. Reid, "Work" in *Evangelical Dictionary of Theology*, ed. Walter E. Elwell. Grand Rapids: Baker Books, 1984, 1188.

[3] Miroslav Volf. "Materiality of Salvation: An Investigation in the Soteriologies of Liberation and Pentecostal Theologies," in *Journal of Ecumenical Studies* 26 (Summer 1989), 447–467.

theological meaning. True work must be guided by God's will and purpose. It is to bring glory to Him as well as to bring some benefit to others and ourselves in our communities. Without this theological perspective, work will ultimately be useless and meaningless.

As I pointed out, the biblical words for work that carry the connotations of weariness, trouble and sorrow, have influenced modern thinking about work. People regard work as evil and as something, one must avoid if possible. There are those who see work as tedious and demeaning and therefore choose to shun it.

The dualistic worldview and values of the middle ages divided the world into two—sacred, which included all work and activities done within the church and secular that comprised of all other activities outside the church or in the marketplace. Secular work was regarded as "profane" that consequently had a negative impact on our modern understanding of work. What we take to be true work is work that relates to church and those outside of the church are considered secular work. Often times they do not carry any important value. They considered secular work as worldly; it does not have eternal value. People who engaged in secular work were often not respected within the Christian community and some had to resign their secular work to take up church work before they became satisfied that they were finally truly working.

Theologically, some have associated work with God's judgment on our first parents Adam and Eve in the Garden of Eden when they sinned against God. People associate work with the curse and see work as something that was originally not for humans to do. Many others see work as punishment from God. This has cast a negative attitude on work and people do not give due respect for hard work. It must be pointed out that work in itself is not a result of Adam's sin although it was certainly affected by it. I will say more about this latter.

The new wave of prosperity gospel in African societies is also contributing to this dismal attitude towards work. The emphasis on faith in God—through the means of "claiming and possessing" what one wants—is drawing many unemployed people to these churches and religious meetings. Perhaps they have developed these attitudes because of the frustrations they go through in not finding or getting work. The teaching on "hard work" is lacking in most of these churches. We must say that not all prosperity churches preach laziness or encourage it. God uses our work to bless us and provides for our needs so we can help others. People are not cultivating an attitude for work in these churches. They are only told to have faith in God and all their needs will be met. This is not what God created humanity for. He created us to work, and then, He provides the ability to make us wealthy.

Despite all the gifts humanity is endowed with, work can become empty unless humanity realizes that its true purpose is to glorify God and to offer service to others. Apostle Paul makes this very plain in speaking to both Christian masters and servants urging them (Eph. 6:5–9, 1 Tim. 6:1–2) not to be "slothful in business, but fervent in spirit serving the Lord," (Rom. 12:11), and that Christians should do all things to the glory of God (1Cor. 10:31).

This view of work means that Christians especially, and humanity generally, must always regard their work as a divinely appointed task. As they strive to fulfill this calling, they are serving God. Such understanding of work requires humanity to be honest and diligent in all that they do whether as employees or employers. The parable told by Jesus in Matt. 25:15 on talents clearly expresses this central idea that servants are to be faithful and obedient, doing all things as in God's sight. On the other hand, employers are to be fair and considerate in dealing with their employees.

Humanity reflects the image of God. All human work should be patterned after the activities of God, who is their maker. Work is part of the image of God in humanity. God himself is a worker. Work is an "essential, constitutive part of our God-imaging humanity. It is our responsibility and right (not a privilege) to be engaged in productive economic work with the material resources of the world."[4] We will discuss how we can harness and utilize these resources as means of creating jobs for our people.

---

4 Wright, *Old Testament Ethics,* 148.

Work is important

At a general level, work is very important for human survival. It helps us to meet certain human needs and aspirations. I see work as one of the ways of dealing with the problem of poverty. We work to provide for our needs so we do not become a burden to the community. Paul instructs the Thessalonians to work to provide for their own needs and not depend on others for their daily food. This is what he tells them:

> And now, dear brothers and sisters, we give you this command with the authority of our Lord Jesus Christ: Stay away from any Christian who lives in idleness and doesn't follow the tradition of hard work we gave you. For you know that you have to follow our example. We were never lazy when we were with you. We never accepted food from anyone without paying for it. We worked hard day and night so that we would not be a burden to any of you…. Even while we were with you, we gave you this rule: "Whoever does not work should not eat." Yet we hear that some of you are living idle lives, refusing to work and wasting time meddling in other people's business. In the name of the Lord Jesus Christ, we appeal to such people—no, we command them: Settle down and get to work. Earn your own living (2 Thess. 3:6–8, 10–12, NLT).

Here we see the Bible affirms the goodness and beauty of good, simple, quiet hard work. Paul commends one who works quietly and earns a living (2 Thess. 3:11). He says that believers should aspire to live quietly, to mind their own affairs, and to work with their hands. Why? He gives two reasons for this: (1) so that they "may walk properly before outsiders" and (2) "be dependent on no one." This Paul says should be our ambition in life: to live a quiet life, minding your own business and working with your own hands (1 Thess. 4:11–12). Paul also encourages those who are thieves to stop stealing and begin to do honest work with their hands so they can give to others who are in need (Eph. 4:28). He himself lived that way. He appeals to his own example. He and the other apostles worked to support themselves so that they would not be a burden to the churches they served.

The scripture is very concerned about the kind of work we engage in. Hard work is affirmed. I pointed out that hard work is as African cultural and ethical value. The African says, "Work is good." This reflects the African's basic work ethics and it expressed by hard work. Africans teach their children the value of hard work. This Yoruba saying illustrates the idea of hard work as a cure for poverty:[5]

> Work is cure for poverty
> Be hard-working my friend
> For one can become great
> Only through hard work
> When we have no supporter
> We may appear lazy
> But such a situation
> It only pays to
> Keep on working hard.

Lazy people are not encouraged in African community. Another African proverb says this of a bird that lazes around and refuses to fly to go find food. That bird, they say sleeps hungry. Alternatively, another one says, "There is no other thing you get out of laziness than poverty or a similar one that says, "There is nothing in laziness except tattered clothes." Most African thinking associates poverty with laziness. Laziness is discouraged in the Bible and it results in poverty as I have pointed out earlier (Prov. 10:4, 15, 12:24, 19:15). Humanity, therefore, has a moral duty to work. To not work and walk idly around is sin. Paul reminded the Thessalonians this truth: "for even when we were with you, we gave you this rule: 'If a man will not work, he shall not eat'. We hear that some among you are idle. They are not busy; they are busy bodies. Such people we command

---

[5] Quoted in Gyekye, *African Cultural Values*, 102. See Segun Gbadegesin, *African Philosophy: Traditional Yoruba Metaphysics and Contemporary African Realities*. New York: Peter Lang, 1991, 226.

and urge in the Lord Jesus to settle down and earn the bread they eat' (2 Thessalonians 3:10–12, 6–13).

Secondly, it is important for one to work in order to be able to provide for one's family and relatives. Children are lovingly to care for their aging parents who are unable to work (1 Tim. 5:4). The care for parents is a core moral and cultural value of Africans. They have the moral obligation to take care of the parents in their old age. Paul writes in the Pastoral Epistles, "But if anyone does not provide for his relatives, and especially for members of his household, he has denied the faith and is worse than an unbeliever." Furthermore, the person who doesn't work and provide for his/her family does not only "deny the faith" but is "*worse* than an unbeliever" (1 Tim. 5:8).

However, work also provides certain benefits. Ryken asserts, "Work provides for life's needs and wants and is a means of economic production. It carries with it constant possibility of being a curse or drudgery, but it has the potential to supply a sense of human achievement, psychological satisfaction, and service to humanity."[6] As service to humanity, we work to help those who are in need so their needs can be met. Jesus teaches about showing generosity to the needy and poor that cannot pay us back. However, such kindness has eternal rewards (Lk. 14:12–14).

Lastly, there is a missional dimension to why we work. This is very important and it is central to God's heart. We work so we can support God's mission and purposes in his world through the ministries of the church. Through our work in society, we have opportunities to build up meaningful relationships and to demonstrate love, care, and concern for the people we relate with. This relationship gives us the opportunity to live out our Christian lives in the public sphere so others would experience God's glory and love through our work.

Work results in a lot of benefits and blessings for society. In the same way when there is lack of work, it can bring a lot of hardships and difficulties for society. We see this expressed when we have high rates of unemployment. Human suffering increases, poverty levels increase, and people struggle to meet their basic human needs. It often leads to social

---

6 Leland Ryken, *Redeeming the Time*, 21

unrest and many criminal activities people turn to for survival. Lack of work and unemployment has been given as cause for crimes we find in society today because the people who are supposed to work are idle and doing nothing. They find themselves involved in criminal activities. When people have work to do, the levels of crime in society goes down. This has been proven to be the case. This is why it is so important for governments to create jobs for our youth who are prone to engage in all forms of crimes if they are idle, because they want and are looking for something to do.

God: the moral and theological foundation for human engagement in work

The idea of human work, in fact, is grounded upon the fact that God, the Creator is a worker himself. God created the heavens and the earth, giving humanity an example to follow. He continues to work and he expects human beings to work. Banks clearly shows in his book, *God the Worker*, that "The Bible is a treasure-trove of images of God at work."[7] The Creator is depicted as a potter and a builder crafting the human race. One of the prime tasks God gives Adam and Eve after they were created is work. The couple was charged with the responsibility to cultivate the earth (Gen. 2:5, 15, 20).

God is actively involved in work and he invites us to be co-workers and co-creators with Him. Pope John Paul II in his *Laborem Exercens* (*LE*) makes this affirmation: "God's word is marked by the fundamental truth that, by his work, man shares in the activity of the Creator, and continues to develop and perfect that activity as he further discovers the resources and values of creation" (*LE* 25).

Therefore, all human work is based on the analogy of God's work in creating the natural world as classically described in Genesis 1–2. In Genesis, we see God's own work. In six days, God created the world and all that is in it. At the apex of his creation was humanity. Humanity was

---

7 Robert Banks, *God the Worker*. Australia: Albatross Book, 1992, 29.

created in God's image. As one created in the image of God, the creator, work is inherent in God's purpose for humanity and it is an essential human experience.[8] As people created in God's image, they are to reflect God's activity and God's own example as a worker. This becomes the ground for their activity; they are workers!

It is important to note that one of the cultural mandates God gave Adam when he was created was to name the animals and birds and all other non-humans that God has created. God gives Adam the opportunity to participate in God's creating activities. God also gave instructions for Adam to till the land and take care of the rest of creation. This underscores the critical place work occupies in God's agenda for humanity. Work was not because of sin. It preceded sin.

In the creation story, human beings are given a mandate to work, which is intimately related to their identity as created in the image of God. Human beings, who bear God's image, are to work by ruling and serving God's creation. As God has shown his transcendence to the created order through his work, human beings must reproduce the divine likeness by having dominion over creation. They are to explore and develop the material resources inherent in creation for their sustenance and wellbeing. Human beings are called to imitate God through work, by being co-creators with Him.

In addition to this, work is ontological to our nature as human beings. As Cosden rightly observes, humans are ontologically workers created in the image of God the Worker.[9] God created humans and gave them a mandate to "fill the earth and subdue it." Wright points out that this command "inescapably entailed human work."[10] Preece asserts that "The creation mandate in Gen. 1:26–28 concerns both production and reproduction responsibility for men and women…. Economic production should provide a stable, local base enabling reproduction and economy of

---

8 McKenna, *Love Your Work!*, 66–67.
9 D. Cosden, *A theology of Work: Work and the New Creation*. Milton Keynes, UK: Paternoster, 2004, 9, 17.
10 Wright. *Old Testament Ethics*, 148.

care."[11] Humanity's foremost responsibility besides worshipping God was to work; be fruitful, fill the earth, and subdue it. God uses work to meet our needs.

Human beings were made by God to be workers. Therefore, in doing work, humanity is being obedient to God and in this way pleasing God. You can work cheerfully and willingly or sullenly and half-heartedly, but only the former pleases God. To work is part of our human nature, and an important element of our human dignity, and a source of self-worth."[12] This is why the Bible exhorts us to do all our work cheerfully and as unto the Lord.

The tediousness and ambiguity of work

Because of the ambivalent apprehension about work, it is easy to construe God's verdict on Adam in Genesis and say, "Well, that's just the way work is. It's a burden we just must bear." What is often forgotten, Lewis reminds is that

> These Bible verses are a description of work *after* "The Fall." We miss the fact that God does *not* intend for work to be dismal and oppressive. Creation is good (Gen. 1:31), human beings have been made in the image of God (Gen. 1:26–27), and we are called to share in the creative activity of God. We are invited to be stewards of God's bounty, fashioning and shaping the world with dignity and respect. Work is only boring and anxiety producing when it is unjust and oppressive—when it is focused on greed and not the glory of God.[13]

Like material possession and money, some have made work Mammon. Work has become the god of many. It takes all our devotion and loyalty.

---

11 G. Preece, "Work, Theology of" in *Global Dictionary of Theology*, eds. William Dyrness and Matti-Veli Karkkainen. Downers Grove: IVP, 2008, 941.

12 Biggar and Hay, "Bible and Social Security," 62.

13 Jim Lewis, A Theology of Work, www.thewitness.org, 2003, 1.

We have become slaves to work. This inordinate passion can destroy us and draw us away from God.

Sin indeed transformed human work. The judgment of God affected the material world: Adam's efforts to extract a living from it are met by its resistance and his sweat (Gen. 3:7–19). The perspective of humanity to reality was also altered. The first couple's eyes were opened to the reality of evil (Gen. 3:7) and closed to the reality of God's works and God's will. Human relationships in the sphere of work became corrupted as well. Wright captures this better:

> Work becomes a commodity to be bought and sold with little care or responsibility for the working human being. Work becomes a slave of greed, a tool of oppression, a means of replacing God with one's own ambition. On the other hand, work, originally a good gift of God to those created in the image of God, can become an idol when we try to find in it our identity and significance, or some ultimate meaning and purpose for life.[14]

After the curse on the earth because of Adam's sin, work became toilsome and frustrating. After the fall, work was no longer simply a joyful, privilege of our human nature, but it became a bondage and necessity: "By the sweat of your brow you will eat your food" (Gen. 3:19). The Bible shows this ambivalence of the nature of work. On the one hand, it is wearisome, bothersome and stressful. On the other hand, it is fulfilling and rewarding. It is in the context of this larger message that we find in Ecclesiastes a two-fold perspective on our daily work.

Firstly, there is a strong witness borne to the weariness and futility of work. The following passages will illustrate my point:

> What do people get for all their hard work? (Eccl. 1:3)

---

14 Wright, *Old Testament Ethics*, 151.

> But as I looked at everything I have worked so hard to accomplish, it was all so meaningless. It was like chasing the wind. There was nothing worthwhile anywhere (Eccl. 2:11).
>
> So now I hate life because everything done here under the sun is so irrational. Everything is meaningless, like chasing the wind. I am disgusted that I must leave the fruit of my hard work to others. And who can tell whether my successors will be wise or foolish? And yet they will control everything I have gained by my skill and hard work. How meaningless! So I turned in despair from hard work. It was not the answer to my search for satisfaction in this life. For though I do my work with wisdom, knowledge, and skill, I must leave everything I gain to people who haven't worked to earn it. This is not only foolish but highly unfair. Their days of labor are filled with pain and grief; even at night they cannot rest. It is all utterly meaningless (Eccl. 2:17–23).

Secondly, Ecclesiastes strongly affirms work as providing fulfillment and satisfaction for the worker. Again, the following passages underscore this fact:

> Anything I wanted, I took. I did not restrain myself from any joy. I even found great pleasure in hard work, an additional reward for all my labors (Eccl. 2:10).
>
> So I decided there is nothing better than to enjoy food and drink and to find satisfaction in work. Then I realized that this pleasure is from the hand of God. For who can eat or enjoy anything apart from him? God gives wisdom, knowledge, and joy to those who please him. But if a sinner becomes wealthy, God takes the wealth away and gives it to those who please him. Even this, however, is meaningless, like chasing the wind (Eccl. 2:24–26).

So I saw that there is nothing better for people than to be happy in their work. That is why they are here! (Eccl. 3:22).

Even so, I have noticed one thing, at least, that is good. It is good for people to eat well, drink a good glass of wine, and enjoy their work—whatever they do under the sun—for however long God lets them live. And it is a good thing to receive wealth from God and the good health to enjoy it. To enjoy your work and accept your lot in life—that is indeed a gift from God. People who do this rarely look with sorrow on the past, for God has given them reasons for joy (5:18–20).

So I recommend having fun, because there is nothing better for people to do in this world than to eat, drink, and enjoy life. That way they will experience some happiness along with all the hard work God gives them (8:15).

Live happily with the woman you love through all the meaningless days of life that God has given you in this world. The wife God gives you is your reward for all your earthly toil. Whatever you do, do well. For when you go to the grave, there will be no work or planning or knowledge or wisdom (9:9–10).

We see from these passages that hard work is satisfying, fulfilling—both for itself and for what it brings us—and it is an important part of the human happiness. A person who works feels she/he is doing something useful; accomplishing something and feeling a sense of accomplishment; s/he is using his gifts and talents; s/he sees and enjoys the fruit of his/her labors. It adds goodness to one's life in many ways. It gives a sense of purpose and meaning to your life.

These two perspectives provide for us a theology of work drawn from both the creation and the fall and a view of work that is both realistic and affirming at the same time. It invites humanity in general and Christians in particular to accept and face the more painful realities of our working life—not to imagine that we can avoid these—but at the same time to accept that we are right to find fulfillment, satisfaction, and pleasure in our work. God made us for that and gave work to us and not even the fall can take this from us.

However, this double perspective also means that while work should be for us an opportunity for fulfillment and satisfaction, it can never be, we must never let it be, the secret of our lives, the center of their meaning, or our salvation. Work will not unlock the mystery of life and it will not entitle us to the world to come.

As it happens, that is an extraordinarily important conclusion and conviction to be trumpeted in our day. Today work is worshipped and is trusted and is believed in a way that is quite remarkable. Whether it is the feminist woman who looks to work to validate her existence or the man who finds work the place, the sphere of, his real success in life, people are looking to work for things it is incapable of providing.

The value and dignity of work

The creation texts bestow sanctity on work. In Genesis 1, God is introduced to us as *God at work*. God is involved in work, being its *raison d'être*. If God works, then we can say that work is intrinsically good and has value. "Work is so natural to God's character." McKenna believes that "part of Christ's total plan in dying on the cross was to redeem our work."[15] Human beings have the responsibility and privilege of virtually replicating the works of God. Work is a significant part of what it means to be created in God's image. The human race co-creates and co-rules with God as it replenishes the earth and exercises dominion over the universe (Eph. 2:10).

God created work before the entrance of sin and evil in the world. Work was part of what it means to be human. Adam was given the responsibility by God to care for the land and the garden God Himself has planted before he fell into sin (Gen. 2:15). Therefore, work is not a punishment for human

---

15 David McKenna, *Love your Work!* USA: Victor Books, 1990, 63.

sin. It is not then surprising that the curse pronounced upon man after he had sinned bears directly on his existence as a worker: "Cursed is the ground because of you; through painful toil you will eat of it... By the sweat of your brow you will eat your food" (Gen. 3:17–19). Man does not cease to be a worker because of his sin, but his work becomes more difficult, more frustrating. In any case, it is obvious that the curse is not that man must work—he was a worker before sin entered the world—but that his labor has become laborious, grueling, and so often unsatisfying.

Therefore, the value of work is grounded upon the fact that God, the Creator is involved in work. Work is not therefore evil and something to shun. Work and labor are not in themselves evil. Rather we should see it as humanity's natural occupation in the world. Even in the state of innocence, human beings who were at the zenith of God's creation, the representatives of all creation before God, were given work to do as part of their normal existence. God designed work for us to do to realize our mandate to "subdue" the earth. That mandate involves work. Humanity has to harness all the resources God has put at her disposal to create and increase. This requires that humanity maintains and sustains itself.

Although human sin corrupted and degraded work in the sense that through work humanity will be affected physically, will become weary, and will eventually die, there is something good about work. Work is only boring and anxiety producing when it is unjust and oppressive—when it is focused on greed and not the glory of God. The religious community, if it is to be faithful to God's Covenant, must ask serious questions about the nature of work in our cities and villages.

On the other hand, work can become fulfilling if we ask some critical questions and reflect on some of the biblical principles given in the Bible to govern the behaviors of both worker and employer. Such questions may include, are we producing good and worthwhile products? Are workers paid a livable wage, with good health care and pension benefits? Are workplaces safe? Are jobs supportive of family life? Do workers have the ability to organize for necessary changes in the workplace without fear of being fired? Do workers have adequate housing? Is the globalization of work causing problems for workers and consumers? In addition, what is our responsibility as people of faith to those who have no work, or cannot work—the unemployed and disabled?

Moreover, lest we think, God is only resting and not working now. Jesus tells us, "My Father is working until now, and I am working" (John 5:17). God is the ultimate worker, who fills the act of work itself with inherent meaning, significance, and dignity. Work is part of God's original plan for humanity hence it has great value to God.

Work will be part of the world after Jesus Christ returns to reign in his Kingdom. At his return "weapons of warfare [will] be transformed into implements of productive work—plowshares and pruning hooks. That is, productive work will be part of the program when Christ returns to bring his kingdom in its fullness" (Isa. 2:4). Work has value. It transcends our lives on earth. Even in the new kingdom, we will still be working. To work is what it means to be human and what it means to be created in God's image. Since God works, we will also work in this life and in the life to come!

The rights and responsibilities of employers[16]

Since God is concerned about the way workers are treated by their employers, he sets up the moral obligations and responsibilities for employers. Because of human sin, there is a tendency for employers to mistreat their workers and deprive them of their right wages and dues. The Scriptures therefore prescribe principles and values that should govern the employer/employee relationships. These include the following:

Provide right and just conditions for work

Both the Old and New Testaments give instructions concerning how employers must relate with and treat their workers. For example, the OT instructs slave owners to give their Hebrew slaves (workers) an opportunity to freedom. They must work for six years and they must be set free in the seventh year and must not pay his master anything for his freedom.

---

16 C. Wright, *Old Testament Ethics*, 159.

The terms of service and release are clearly laid down (Ex. 21:1–6). The employer was placed under clear legal restraint and moral obligation in the way he physically treated his slaves (Ex. 21:20–21, 26–27), while those who had voluntarily entered the service of a creditor because of inability to support themselves were not to be made to work in oppressively harsh conditions." (Lev. 25:39–40, 43).

Just and timely payment for services rendered

God was concerned about the pay packet of employees. He instructs employers to pay "the wages and services of hired persons fully and promptly (Lev. 17:13; Deut. 24:14–19). The prophets condemned the oppression and exploitation of workers, especially on the issue of pay (Isa. 58:3; Jer. 22:13)." The NT speaks about right and fair treatment of slaves and workers (Lk. 10:7). Paul gives similar instructions to masters (employers) to do right and pay fair wages to their slaves (employees). They must recognized that they have a Master in Heaven (Col. 4:1, 1 Tim. 5:18)

Give adequate rest to workers

God is concerned with the health and wellbeing of the worker. He commands that workers be given time to rest, as he himself rested on the seventh day after the six days of work of creation. The "Sabbath rest, a principle and privilege since creation, was made mandatory on employers, employee and even working animals, not only on the basis of God's example in creation, (Ex. 20:11) but also on the grounds of his redemptive act (Deut. 5:15). In addition to this regular weekly total rest, slaves, and other residential and hired workers were to be allowed to enjoy all the benefits of the great festivals and cultic occasions, which added several days' break from work throughout the agricultural year (Deut. 16:11, 14). In an agricultural life of long, difficult, burdensome physical labor, such regular relief would have been invaluable."

Working conditions in most places in Africa are deplorable, harsh, and oppressive. The analyses set forth above underscore God's prescription for work and employment. Satisfactory and dignified working conditions, fair pay, adequate rest are critical for the employer to uphold. In such countries where there is worker abuse by employers, the church must stand up for the oppressed and the disadvantaged by cooperating with labor organizations to advocating for better job conditions for people.

The rights and duties of employees

The rights to work, fair conditions of employment and right to join and form trade unions are provided for in articles 6 to 8 of the International Covenant on Economic, Social, and Cultural Rights. These rights are also recognized in certain instruments of the International Labor Organization (ILO). While employees have rights to be treated well by their employers, the scriptures hold employees to account for their behavior and attitude to work. God endows humanity with certain gifts and abilities to do their work (Judg. 3:10, 1 Sam. 10:6–7), Isa. 45, 1 Cor. 12, Eph. 4:11 ff). God calls all humans to work in positions in life in which he has called them to serve him ((Esth. 4:13–14, Eph. 6:5 ff, 1 Tim. 6:1–2; Philem. 1).

Workers are instructed not to be slothful but be diligent in the work (Rom. 12:11), they should do their work as a service to the Lord (1 Cor. 10:31).

We have seen in our discussions so far the importance of work in the human existence. The Bible encourages hard work and warns against laziness. However, we find many people in our world not working. How can we make work accessible for all so that humanity might fulfill what he has been created for, a worshipper and a worker? I think we have the moral responsibility to be work creators in our world today. The responsibility to create work rests on the shoulders of all humanity but in particular, to governments who have been given the opportunity and mandate to manage the resources of our country and economy. They must work hard to create conducive environments and opportunities for people to work. In the next section, I will attempt to make some practical suggestion to ensure we create enough work for our people.

Work creation is our human responsibility as co-creators with God

The role of governments to provide work for citizens

In order to fulfill God's mandate for humanity to engage in work demands that governments provide institutions and system that will foster job creation for the citizens of their nations. This is not a privilege of the citizens of the nation, but a right! Every person who is at the age of maturity (18 years and above) must be able to get gainful employment. It is a citizen's right from the government they pay taxes, to create jobs for them. Given the fact of unprecedented population growth in many countries of the world, governments are finding it more difficult to meet the job demands facing their countries. The responsibility to create jobs, therefore, must be the responsibility of every person and institution within the nations.

Work involves harnessing the world's resources. Work creation must be one of the fundamental issues that African governments must address. The unemployment rate in Africa is too high. Many of our young people are unemployed and therefore can be used by evil people to do acts that are not beneficial to development or nation building. To address this issue, governments must make deliberate efforts to create jobs for its citizens.

However, governments, we know, do not have all the resources to ensure this happens. Governments must encourage the private sector to assist in creating jobs by giving them incentives that will encourage this kind of endeavor and cooperation. It is not enough to create jobs. It is important that there are good conditions for workers to do their work in a more humane and dignified manner. Where the government fails to do this, the Church must play the role of advocacy. The Church must remind the government of her primary responsibilities to its citizenry. The Scriptures exhort Christians to do this. The writer of Proverbs says, "Speak up for those who cannot speak for themselves, for the rights of all who are destitute" (Proverbs 31:7–9). In addition to this, the Church must ensure that Governments put in place clear public policies and plans for creating jobs.

In a more practical way, the Church can also be involved in creation work for its followers. The church can open its doors to set up skills training institutions and start small business enterprises, micro-financial to help their members create jobs for themselves.

The place of educational institutions to train citizens to be entrepreneurs

Educational institutions should teach and prepare citizens to become entrepreneurs. Our educational goals should focus on training people to meet the diverse human needs in our societies. Besides the theoretical foundation, it must have a practical goal, to give tools for people to address the problems in a concrete manner. We must diversify our educational disciplines and place more emphasis on applied science and applied technologies. This will help people to create jobs for themselves and be in positions to hire others to work for them. Job creation should be a joint venture between governments and the private sector. The government should ensure that our educational institutions are linked with the public sectors and the industries and economic and infrastructural needs so they can train for effective change to meet our economic needs. Good policies should be encouraged and plans put in place by both government and the private sector to create jobs. Educational institutions should think ahead to orientate our education systems to meet the needs in our societies. People must also develop attitudinal change. We must renew our minds (Rom. 12:1–2). We must embrace new technologies that will ensure efficiency and add value to our products so they can earn us more income.

The place and role of the Church: creating opportunities for its youth and its advocacy role

Church institutions should create employments opportunities for the youth in their church through vocational training to help create jobs for themselves. Such training will help many of our youths create jobs for themselves using the God-given talents they have. Many of our youth are skilled with various talents. We must help them develop these skills and abilities in all kinds of artisan work. God Himself as a Worker is involved in all kinds of activities: He is a composer and performer, a metal worker and potter, a garment maker and dresser, a gardener and orchardist, a farmer and winemaker, a shepherd and pastoralist, a tentmaker and camper, a builder and architect.[17] These different categories of work can serve as examples of vocations we can train our youth in to become entrepreneurs. As the church seeks to help its youth in giving them skills that would enable them to create jobs for themselves, we should learn from God's own work. Pope John Paul II points out that we are co-creators with God through work (*LE* 3.1).

We do have a responsibility to facilitate and allow people to work. To deny "other persons working, or to deny them work, is to offend against their humanity and the image of God in them, as well as failing in one's responsibility to God for them."[18] This kind of work must not be limited to pay employment only. We should be working nations and communities. There should be no room for idlers and laziness in our communities.

The church can also put pressure on governments and employers to "introduce statutory rest days and holidays, statutory terms and conditions of employment, statutory protection from infringement of personal rights and physical dignity, statutory provision for fair wages promptly paid"[19] (James 5:1–6; cf. Ex. 22:22–23; Lev. 19:13; Deut. 24:1–15).

The place and role of a labor organization to ensure job security for citizens

The world economic crisis is posing enormous challenges on job opportunities and job security around the world. Workers need to be protected from loss of jobs which in turn infringes on their right to work and earn a living. Legislations that will protect workers from losing their jobs will boost our production and will in turn ensure sustainable development in most of our African countries.

---

17 Robert Banks, *God the Worker*, 29–345.
18 Wright, *Old Testament Ethics*, 148.
19 Wright, *Old Testament Ethics*, 161.

There should be joy in work as all work is a vocation. (1 Cor. 10:31). Work calls for responsibility, self-control, and competence. There is need for workers to give themselves wholly to work. This presents the duty bearers and employers the responsibility of ensuring that wages are adequate, this is proportionate to the work done (Luke 10:7 and 1 Timothy 5:18), and are paid promptly. (Leviticus 19:13 and Colossians 4:1). Unemployment is a serious assault on human nature and churches need to initiate employment creation schemes that harness the creative potential of their youth and young adults. Economic justice is built on opportunity including the opportunity for every person to work.

Conclusion

Humanity is created to work. We have the responsibility to ensure that work is provided for all. To be idle demeans us and robs us of our human dignity. We must all engage in work that will bring honor to God as well as give us the opportunity to serve others. It is having this theological understanding of work that work will become more meaningful to us and bring glory to God. Richard Baxter lays the ax to the root concerning our attitude to work. He says, "Choose that employment or calling in which you may be most serviceable to God. Choose not that in which you may be most rich or honorable in the world; but that in which you may do most good, and best escape sinning."[20]

As one scholar summarizes our creation mandate this way:

> Man is to subdue the earth and to have dominion over its living creatures and its fruitful production.... He was to govern nature in order to develop to the full its potential for reflecting the glory of God and promote the well-being of man. Nature bore by creation and preservation the impress of the Divine

---

[20] *Treatise on the Vocations*, cited in Ryken, 31.

Mind. Man was to bring to play upon it the creative effort of a human mind fashioned in the Divine image.[21]

Every Christian should see his or her daily work in these terms. We should all see ourselves as answering this summons to use and rule the earth and its resources for the glory of God and the benefit of others. However, when a Christian offers his work to God, he is serving his Maker and fulfilling an assignment that God has given to him.

As God's image bearers, we are to use our God-given creativity and responsibility to use the earth's resources for godly purposes. We are to work and create the environment for others to work so they can fulfill their God given mandate. *God calls us to work unto His glory.* 1 Corinthians 10:31 say "So, whether you eat or drink, or whatever you do, do all to the glory of God." Our work must glorify God. Again, Paul says, "Whatever you do, work heartily, as for the Lord and not for men, knowing that from the Lord you will receive the inheritance as your reward. You are serving the Lord Jesus Christ" (Col. 3:23–24).

I end with John Piper's statement: "the essence of our work as humans must be that it is done in conscious reliance on *God's power*, and in conscious quest of *God's pattern of excellence*, and in deliberate aim to reflect *God's glory.*"[22]

---

21 Carl F.H. Henry, *Christian Personal Ethics*, 243
22 Justin Taylor, *Working out a Theology of God*, Boundless.org, 2008.

CHAPTER 10

Righteousness, Justice, and Morality

"The essence of Justice is mercy" (Edwin Hubbel Chapin)

Introduction

The evil and the injustice we see in our world today raise some ethical concerns for Christians, the Church and society. For example, immorality, corruption, inequality, oppression of the weak, economic exploitation, and all forms of discrimination in our societies all speak of the moral decay we are experiencing in our communities and in our the world today. God requires that righteousness and justice permeate our societies and so these values must become the foundations for our behavior towards each other. Christians must respond to and denounce the unrighteousness and injustices we see in our world. We, more importantly, are called by God to promote righteousness and justice, which is part of God's own character and nature in the world he has created and given to us to live in by his grace, love, and mercy.

In this chapter, I will explore the meaning of these central biblical values and show their implications for our social moral lives as Christians in particular and as humanity in general. We will also underscore the moral imperative these concepts present to us as we engage our world today to bring God's shalom to humanity to enhance their wellbeing.

Righteousness as we will argue in this paper is not only to be understood in a forensic sense, as one's stand before a holy and righteous God; but also as an ethical concept, that has moral and ethical implications for our social life. The social dimension of righteousness and justice have to deal with right relationships between human beings and God as well as that between humans and their fellow humans, in accordance with right behavior within a given community. This involves promoting the total well being of humanity as well as right and just actions to bring about this well-being. This seems to be the emphasis in the Bible.

To do this, I will first look at the modern understandings of these biblical values and show how such understandings have affected our morality. Then, I will explore the biblical and ethical meanings of the righteousness and justice. I will argue that these values are central to the character and nature of God and they are the foundation for biblical ethics. I will affirm that these values must guide our engagement in our world today as we respond to evil and injustice. The final section of the chapter will suggest some principles for our social moral engagement.

African understanding of righteousness and justice

Righteousness and justice in African cosmology are defined in terms of a person's positive behavior within a community. The concepts have something to do with a person's character or being. Righteousness and justice are seen as a foundation for right and just behavior. Since the terms carry the ideas of character, we can affirm that it assumes the person's being or personality plays a vital role in his behavior. Acting and doing what is right is the focus. Africans define righteousness in terms of "good" and "evil." But good and evil are not philosophical and abstract concepts. Rather, they are concrete concepts. A "good" person is good and "righteous" because his or her deeds are good and right. A bad person is bad and unrighteous because of his or her bad deeds.

For example, the Akan word for righteousness is *trenee*, which means "straight." The person who acts righteously is called *treneeni*. The righteous person is literally the "straight person." So righteousness is seen in moral terms as a person with "straight" and not with a "crooked" character or behavior. For Africans righteousness is a concrete moral and ethical term. It defines right actions and right behavior.

Righteousness therefore has to do with right character and right behavior of a person within the community he or she lives in. It involves doing good to people to promote their well-being and prosperity. However, right living comes because of right character. It is important to underscore the emphasis on character. The righteous person is indeed, a person of good character.

A righteous or good person must be honest, sincere, dependable, and faithful. In addition to these virtues, the righteous person must exhibit kindness, hospitality, fidelity, reliability, humility, and gentleness. I mentioned these moral values in chapter 1 as central to African morality. Furthermore, the righteous person must also be a peace-maker, they must just, and fair in all his or her dealings with people in the community as well as outside of his or her community. He must be merciful, generous, and loving. The righteous person must eschew acts such as lying or falsehood, killing, stealing, and any kind of evil. In short, the righteous person must be blameless before the community. In the eyes of the community, this person is blameless. It means that there is nothing blameworthy in his social behavior.

Justice in Africa is associated with the concept of truth telling, fairness, equity, doing what is right, right judgment, being impartial, and straightforwardness in many African cultures. It carries the idea of treating two persons the same or equally without showing any partiality. It is one of the central moral values in African. The idea of justice related more to the judicial systems in African societies. However, people are encouraged to deal justly with their fellow human beings in the day-to-day interaction with one another. This will ensure long life for them. For it is believed that people who do what is just enjoy long life. For example, the state drummer at a hearing of a dispute by the paramount chief will drum at certain intervals giving some moral advice like, If you are in the habit of doing what is just, you live long." Ackah points out this alludes to 'the justice and fairness that has characterized the long reign of the king and his long life, if he is very elderly and has reigned for many years; or it would mean he is just and fair to all...." The drummer's advice is "intended for all present to learn to be just, for justice will bring them peace and long life."[1]

Thus, these two terms, righteousness and justice are moral categories in an African world-view. They have to do with "right" and "just" behavior. Righteousness for Africans is not a concept that sees the individual's position before God but rather it is a moral obligation a person has do what is right and just to promote the well-being of fellow human beings. I will now discuss the western understanding of these terms.

Modern Western definitions and understandings of righteousness and justice

The Collins English Dictionary defines righteousness or righteous as a thing or a person characterized by, proceeding from, or in accordance with accepted standards of morality, justice, or uprightness, virtuous, or morally justifiable or right. Justice is generally defined as the quality of being just, and fair. It refers to the principle of moral rightness; equity, righteousness or the upholding of what is just, especially fair treatment and due reward in accordance with honor. "Justice is the concept of moral rightness based on ethics, rationality, law, natural law, religion, fairness, or equity, along with the punishment of the breach of the said ethics"[2] It is also used in Law to mean standards of law or the administration and procedure of law.[3] It emphasizes the principle of fairness, a principle that punishment must be proportionate to the offence—retributive and distributive justice.

As we can see from the definitions, justice is related to other disciplines such as law, politics, economics, sociology, and psychology. Justice is seen also as one of the personal virtues as well as an institutional concept. There is no scholarly consensus on the meaning of justice. Our understanding of justice may be shaped by our cultures.

---

1 C. A. Ackah. *Akan Ethics*. Accra: Ghana University Press, 1988, 69–70.
2 Justice-Wikipedia http://en.wikipedia.or/wiki/Justice, Accessed February 2011).
3 Justice: West Encyclopedia of America Law, American Heritage Dictionary. Accessed February 25, 2011.

Sandel offers three contemporary notions of justice. The first relates to maximizing welfare. This deals with promoting prosperity, improving standard of living for everyone and promoting economic growth. The underlying assumption to this notion of justice is that prosperity contributes to better living standards. Prosperity contributes to the total wellbeing or welfare of people. Utilitarianism is the ethical philosophy driving this notion of justice. The second understanding of justice connects it with freedom. At the core of these understandings of justice is the idea of 'respect for individual freedom and rights. These are expressed in some of the basic liberties we find in our contemporary civil society documents—rights to freedom of speech, food, shelter, education, health, religious liberty, respecting human dignity etc. The third contemporary understanding of justice sees it as "virtue and conceptions of the good life.[4] Stassen and Gushee add other cultural understandings or views of justice. They include "Rawl's two principle of fairness—"liberty and difference that benefit the least advantaged" or Walzer's 'complex equality' and human rights, the reduction of justice to retribution or punishment, the drive for freedom to pursue wealth that reduces justice to the dictatorship of the free market" or the drive for political control that reduces justice to 'the dictatorship of the proletariat.'"[5]

As one can observe, the word justice doesn't have one meaning. In this study, therefore we will use the term justice to mean fairness; that is creating the space and equal opportunities for everyone in society to prosper and do well without showing impartiality. In this sense, "justice requires policies that remedy social and economic disadvantages and give everyone fair chance at success."[6]

I want to point out one significant similarity and one difference between the African's notions of these ethical terms with the west. Both terms are seen in moral terms. There is basic agreement between the two views that see justice as fairness, equity, and both see the terms as related to law. The

---

[4] Michael J. Sandel, *Justice*. New York; Farrar, Straus and Giroux, 2009, 19–20.

[5] Stassen and Gushee, *Kingdom Ethics*, 346,

[6] Sandel, *Justice*, 20.

significant difference is on emphasis. While Africans give strong emphasis on righteousness because it relates more to character, which is a central ethical value in African morality, the west emphasizes justice, which is a fundamental ethical value of the west. This can explain why they are sharp disagreements between the two cultures when it comes to certain moral issues such as homosexuality and lesbianism. Why Africans are arguing on moral grounds, the west's arguments are based on justice and equity for all. One thing is sure, these two values have influence on both African and western morality.

Biblical understanding of righteousness and justice

Both righteousness and justice are relational concepts in the Bible. They have at the core the relationship between God and human beings, between humans and fellow humans and between human beings and creation. Due to its relational nature, both righteousness and justice have moral and ethical implications for our social life as Christians in particular and non-Christians in general.

The Greco-Roman culture generally understood righteousness as a principle for law—divine or human—in the world, which provides norms for the structure for life. It is used therefore in relation to tradition or custom. In this sense, righteousness means one who conforms, is civilized and observes customs. Secondly, it is used to describe a person who fulfills his obligations towards men.[7] This obligation could be religious, civil, or judicial. The term *diakaion* is linked with *kalon*, *agaton*, and *prepon* that are leading ethical terms in the Bible.

Among the Greeks, righteousness was seen as an "ethical" as well as a "political virtue." Plato understood the term in this sense. For Plato, righteousness as political virtue is finally anchored in the "soul of man." Philo also expressed the same idea in terms of "merit of virtue." Righteousness is considered the most prominent often the "chief of virtue[s]" besides

---

7 Schrenk, "Righteousness" vol. II *TDNT* ed. Gerhard Kittel, 182.

prudence, self-control and courage.[8] It also has the sense of what is "proper or fitting."[9] From the above general usage of the term in the Greco-Roman world, one can argue that the term has many meanings and nuances with strong pull towards the ethical. How did the biblical writers understand righteousness? I will look at both the Old Testament and the New Testament understanding of the term.

Righteousness in the Old Testament

Righteousness is a major concept in the Old Testament. Gerhard von Rad's statement will illustrate this:

> There is absolutely no concept in the Old Testament with so central a significance for all the relationships of human life as that of *sdqh*. It was the standard not only for man's relationship to God, but also for his relationships to his fellows reaching right down to… animals and to his natural environment… for it embraces the whole of Israelite life.[10]

The Old Testament word for righteousness is *sedaqa* (feminine) or *sedeq* (masculine). The *sedaqa* or *sedeq* is usually translated in the English Bible as "righteousness" or "justice." The root meaning means "'straight:' something fixed, and fully what it should be; a norm, a standard. So, it came to mean "rightness." When it is used in terms of human actions relationships it meant "conformity to what is right or expected," indicates right behavior or status in relation to some standard of behavior accepted in the community."[11] Faithfulness and righteousness reflect the qualities of God's actions. These become requirements for human actions.[12] The concept generally refers to being on the side of right or in the right, that is, what is right in accordance

---

[8] Schrenk, "Righteousness," 193.
[9] Schrenk, "Righteousness," 185.
[10] Gerhard von Rad, *Old Testament Theology* (New York: Harper & Row, 1962, 1965), Vol. 1, 370, 373
[11] Wright, *Old Testament Ethics*, 255–256.
[12] Wright, *Old Testament Ethics*, 258.

with some standards. This may be natural law or some assumed standards accepted in the given community including, more importantly, standards derived from God's character and God's laws (Deut: 6:20–25; Ps. 15:2; 18:20–24).[13] Faithfulness and righteousness reflect the qualities of God's actions. These qualities or values become requirements for human actions.

The masculine form *sedeq* generally expresses an "abstract principle of righteousness" or as an "abstract ideal" that is personified (Ps. 85:11, 13; Isa. 45:8). The feminine *Sedaqa*, on the other hand refers to a "concrete act" and it is bound up with concrete actions (See Isa. 56:1; 58:2) and later it was used to express the act of giving alms to the poor (Dan. 4:24).[14]

Since people's behavior in Ancient Israel is not conceived as something that must be judged in accordance with an abstract norm, but rather as a function of concrete human relations, the term righteousness is accordingly to be understood as a social phenomenon concerning relationships between two or more parties.[15] In this sense, the term refers to the fidelity to and fulfillment of demands of a relationship. This includes a vertical relationship between God and man as well as a horizontal relationship with fellow beings[16] Gerhard von Rad puts it this way:

> Ancient Israel did not in fact measure a line of conduct or an act by an ideal norm, but by the specific relationship in which the partner had the time to prove himself true. Every relationship brings with certain claims upon conduct, and the satisfaction of these claims, which issue from the relationship and in, which alone the relationship can persist, is described by our term *sdq*.[17]

---

[13] David J. Reimer, "Sdq" in *New International Dictionary of the Old Testament Theology and Exegesis*, ed. Willem A. VanGemeren, vol.3 (Grand Rapids, Michigan: Zondervan, 1997), 746–750.

[14] Weinfeld, *Social Justice*, 34.

[15] Leone Epzstein, *Social Justice in the Ancient Near East and the People of the Bible* (London: SMC Press, 1983), 45–49.

[16] Bruce V. Malchow, *Social Justice in the Hebrew Bible* (Collegeville, Minnesota: Liturgical Press, 1996), 16–17.

[17] Gerhard von Rad, *Old Testament Theology*, vol.1 (New York: Harper & Row, 1962), 371.

Thus, when a party in a relationship is faithful to and fulfills the conditions imposed on that party by the relationship, that party is considered *righteous*. In the Old Testament, for instance, Yahweh is proclaimed as a *Righteous God* (2 Chron. 12:6; Neh. 9:8; Ps. 7:9; 103:17; 116:5; Jer. 9:24; Dan. 9:14; Zeph. 3:5; Zech. 8:8). Yahweh is considered *sadiq* because he is faithful and fulfills the obligation that he has in his relationship to the Israelites. He is *righteous* because he acts as God should. He saves, preserves, restores, and vindicates the community he is bound to in covenant, as well as gives laws and statutes by which this community can be preserved and be sustained. However, he also judges and punishes those who violate the covenant. The linking of righteousness and salvation is most deeply grounded in the covenant concept. Righteousness is the execution of covenant faithfulness and the covenant promises. God's righteousness is demonstrated in God's righteous acts, that is, in covenant faithfulness to his people he vindicates and saves them.

The term righteousness therefore has a strong communal dimension within the background of social relationships. This is because the social world of the Near East is "a world where 'to live' is to be united with others in a social context either by bonds of family or by covenant."[18] Righteousness relates to human behavior and actions.

Zeisler has pointed out that righteousness is depicted as the activity or behavior of human beings and God.[19] The term, he argues has two applications in the Old Testament. First, in respect to God, it came to mean God's righteous activity—his redemptive activity—his acts which bestow salvation, creating and carrying out his covenant with Israel (Isa. 46:13; cf. 51:5, 6, 8; 61:10). It depicts God legal activity as a judge, as one who acts reliably, trustworthily, and faithfully (Jer. 9:2). These words are ethical in nature. Reliability, trustworthiness, and faithfulness are all ethical terms that define human relationships.

---

18 John R. Donahue, S.J., "Biblical Perspectives on Justice" in *The Faith That Does Justice: Examining the Christian Sources of Social Change*, ed. John C. Haughey, S.J. (New York: Paulist Press, 1977), 68–72.

19 J. A. Zeisler, "The Meaning of Righteousness in Paul: A Linguistic and Theological Enquiry" (*SNTSMS* 20:1972), 23–32.

Second with regard to humans, righteousness is seen in terms of the ethical demand on humans, a type of conduct in response to relationships within the covenant community (Ps. 106:3). This righteous activity of humans reflects that of God's. Human beings must judge and govern righteously so we can establish social justice in the community. Ethically, they are to be upright in their conduct (Gen. 6:9, 10; 7:1); they are to love what is good, speak the truth; to be obedient to the law and finally they are to be faithful to the covenant (Isa. 51:7; Ezek. 18:19–21).

Righteousness in the Old Testament is not an individualistic concept but strongly a communal concept. The concept of righteousness is therefore a dynamic concept, dealing with the right actions of God and humans.

For example, in Gen. 6 the unrighteous activities of humanity are described in terms of wickedness of heart and mind. This has a social or communal implication for the society that was expressed by "violence" in the society. The phrase "corrupted their ways" implies patterns of behavior that was against the standards or norms set by God for human behavior. In the mist of this unrighteousness stands the righteous Noah. "Noah was a righteous man, blameless among the people of his time and he walked with God.

The implication is that there was nothing blameworthy in the social behavior of Noah, and he walked with God. "Blameless" and "walked with God" explain the meaning of "righteous" in this passage. Thus, righteousness has both social and theological implications. It is seen in terms of one's social behavior towards the community, which the people find blameless. It is also a vertical relationship with God where God finds the individual's behavior blameless towards Him. Later on, God also described Abraham as blameless."

The concept of righteousness implies maintaining social justice in the society, so that equality and freedom prevail. In the Old Testament, the social ideal along the lines of mercy, kindness, and truth is often associated with righteousness, (cf. Ps. 33:5, 85:15; Jer. 9:23; Hos. 2:21, 12:7; Mic. 6:8).[20] The prophet Ezekiel makes the ethical and moral dimension of the

---

20 Moshe Weinfeld, *Social Justice in Ancient Israel and in the Ancient Near East*

term clear. The righteous person is the one who does good to the neighbor to release him or her from enslavement and anguish. Weinfeld points out that in Ezekiel for example, righteousness denotes proper and correct behavior, including matters pertaining to religion and cult.[21] The righteous man according to Ezekiel is the one who "refrains from oppression, from seizing pledges, from theft, from usury, and from performing injustice"[22] (Ezek. 18:7–8, 12–13, 16–17). All these describe the person's behavior and actions towards fellow human beings.

The idea of performing righteousness is not confined to abstention from evil; it consists primarily in doing "good" that is giving bread to the hungry and clothing the naked (Ezek. 18:7, 16). Meeting the needs of the needy among us is a righteous act. Righteousness in the sense of deeds of kindness to the poor, the orphans and the widows and those suffering are also found in the Wisdom literature. (See Job 29:23–25).

God is righteous Himself, that is, he is righteous in keeping his covenant agreement with Israel. Relationship is central to the concept of righteousness in the Old Testament. Schrenk points this out this clearly.

> It should be emphasized particularly that righteousness implies relationship. A man is righteous when he meets certain claims, which another has on him by virtue of that relationship. Even the righteousness of God is primarily seen in His covenantal rule in fellowship with His people.[23]

He goes on to say that the idea of righteousness as a "concept of relationship… already, includes both the forensic and ethical elements and the idea of saving action."[24]

(Jerusalem: The MagnesPress, The Hebrew University, 1994), 29.
21　Weinfeld, *Social Justice*, 17. See note 26.
22　Weinfeld, *Social Justice*, 18.
23　Schrenk, "Righteousness," 195.
24　Schrenk, "Righteousness," 195.

A summary of the meaning of righteousness in the Old Testament

Our study of the concept of righteousness in the Old Testament shows that righteousness has at least five aspects or facets. Not all of these aspects or facets are present each time the concept is used. Usually only one aspect of the concept is signaled by a word. The five aspects of the concept of righteousness are:

a. Forensic: Humans are declared righteous or guilty by God. It has a legal flavor where the judge declares a person innocent or guilty (Deut. 25:1). It has both positive (where God declares a sinner righteous) and negative (where God condemns or pronounces the sinner guilty) sides.

b. Righteousness means standard, norm, or law. Righteousness is seen as a standard, norm, or correct yard. The law shows this. We have a hint of this use of righteousness in Gen. 18:19.

c. Righteousness relates to conduct: Righteousness underlines right conduct in a relationship. Righteousness is described as right conduct or behavior in a relationship. Conduct is right when it conforms to the standard. Right conduct is the result of obedience to the standard. As we have pointed out with the case of Noah, he was a "righteous man" because he was seen as blameless among his people (a matter of observable social behavior), and he walked with God. A righteous man is defined by the phrases: "blameless among the people" and "walked with God." Both of these statements refer to conduct. It shows right conduct towards society and right conduct in relation to God. Both of the statements also describe a relationship. In short, righteousness is a matter of right conduct in a relationship as a measured standard. Retribution: It is the administration of punishment for injustice in conduct. Examples of these are is Gen. 2:7 and Gen. 7.

d. Distribution: It is restoration, lifting up, salvation of the oppressed, the victim, and the afflicted. This is the other side of retributive justice, distributive justice. Here the victim, the oppressed, the one cast down is lifted up and restored. Example of this in the Old Testament is the deliverance of the Israelites from Egyptian bondage to the Promised Land in Canaan.

e. Fairness: It is the administration of all aspects of justice without partiality. All the five aspects of righteousness must be administered with fairness—without respect of persons.

The Old Testament emphasizes this dimension of righteousness as behavior more in addition to matters relating to justice and its administration. The concept therefore has moral implications for human behavior and activities.

Righteousness in the New Testament

Righteousness in early Christianity: its Jewish and Greek influence

The New Testament writers' understanding of righteousness derives from the Old Testament. The New Testament phrase, the righteousness of God could be traced to Deut. 33:21, which deals with the commands or justice of Yahweh. The New Testament word for righteousness is the noun *dikaiosynē*. The verb *dikaioō* carries a juridical sense of "be justified (or condemned, *katadikaioō*) by your words" (Matt. 12:37). The Greek term "justice" (*dikaiosynē*) has religious, legal, and ethical overtones. In religion, justice was often personified as a goddess, *Dike* (Acts 28:4). Righteousness therefore was construed as "a principle of law—divine or human—in the world, which provides structure and norms for life."[25] The early Christians used righteousness "both to express its message about God's saving acts and to speak of the believer's response in their relationships to society."[26]

Righteousness was employed in early Christianity to speak of both God's saving righteousness and the ethical uprightness he seeks in humans. It is both a "gift" and a "demand." There is a close association between

---

25 Reumann, *Righteousness and Society*, 34
26 Reumann, *Righteousness and Society*, 35.

righteousness and ethics in the New Testament. This relationship involves the fact that "justified" people who have experienced the action of God's righteousness are called upon to a life of righteousness. In the Gospels and other New Testament books the term righteousness have the following sense, juridical—to be justified (Matt. 12:37; Lk. 10:29, 16:15; innocence (Matt. 27:19, cf. 27:24; Lk. 23:27); fitting, right (2 Pet. 1:13; Lk. 12:57; Matt. 20:4, 7); virtue or social conduct (Phil. 4:8). God is righteous from the stand-point of judgment, a language largely taken from the OT (Rev. 16:5, 16:7, 19:2, and 15:3). For example, right conduct—the practice of love constitutes righteousness. A person who fulfils the law or the Divine will is considered righteous (Matt. 10:41, 13:43, 49, 25:37, 46).

In summary, righteousness in early Christianity relates to *sdq* themes in the Old Testament, which include the idea of vindication, God's righteousness, and the justification of human beings on the one hand and the ethical demand placed on humans on the other hand.

Righteousness in Paul

In the writings of Paul the word carries both forensic and the ethical senses. In Paul it means "the saving power of God, given in Christ through faith to persons under sin who are brought "into Christ," "unto sanctification," in a community of faith, ultimately to salvation in all its fullness."[27] Zeisler argues that because man's dilemma is both forensic and ethical, it suggests the term has both forensic and ethical senses, dealing respectively with juridical processes and with behavior in life generally and in liturgy.[28]

In summary, the New Testament shows that the term has many different meanings that include innocence, fitting, right, one who practices love, virtue, one who fulfills God's laws, right conduct, and so forth. In Paul, it takes on a strong legal connotation where a sinner is declared righteous by God based on God's grace alone. The New Testament emphasizes more the legal and forensic dimension of righteousness. Righteousness and justice are related concepts. Righteousness is many times translated as justice. I

---

27 Reumann, *Righteousness in the New Testament*, 189.
28 Zeisler, *The Meaning of Righteousness*, 18–21.

believe therefore that righteousness will always *express itself in justice*. God is not interested in our worship if we fail to give justice to those who are in need or trample on justice itself. (Amos 5:21–24; Is. 1:10–17, 58:2–7, Jer. 7:1–11). I will discuss the concept of justice and its moral implication for our behavior and activities.

Biblical understanding of justice

Aquinas defines "justice as a disposition in virtue of which a man has the firm and constant will to render everyone his due."[29] In Christian tradition, justice is the second cardinal virtue. Biblical justice is founded on the character as will of God. God's justice is related to his righteousness. Biblical justice carries the notion of equality without respect to person.[30] Burch points out biblical justice relates to the covenant, which was based on the law. Biblical justice is relational. It required obedience to God, love for one's neighbor and care for creation.

The law, which is the basis for Israel's justice system, relates to God's holiness, showing the connection between righteousness and justice. This connection is very important to emphasize. In our modern understanding of justice, justice is mostly seen in term of human rights which often pay no attention to holiness even if those rights violate God's moral laws. Violations of God's laws were violation of justice.[31] This is made very clear in the Bible especially in the OT testament where the people violated their covenant with God and as a result God accused them of injustice, which they committed against the poor, weak, widows and marginalized. The laws made provisions for the wellbeing of these people so they could be taken care of by the community. Violation of that law meant being guilty of injustice.

---

29 Karl Rahner and Herber Vorgrimler. *Dictionary of Theology*, 2nd ed. New York: Crossroad, 1981, 259.
30 M. Burch. "Justice" in A. Elwell, ed. *Evangelical Dictionary of Theology*, 2nd ed. Grand Rapids: Baker Academic, 2001, 641–642.
31 Burch, "Justice" in *Evangelical Dictionary*, 641.

There are three aspects of justice, which are related to our life in society. The first is commutative justice. This deals with an individual's relationship with others. The second is distributive justice. This relates to an individual's relations with society including family, state, and church. The third is legal justice. This concerns the individual subordinating himself to the common good.[32] These three aspects of justice are important for biblical justice addresses all three dimensions of our social relationship. In this chapter, I will focus more on the first two and discuss the third in more detail in chapter 14.

In both the Old and New Testaments injustice against the community were perpetuated by the elite and the powerful in society—namely kings, rich, priest, emperors, and many others. These injustices have to do with greed, domination, violence, and exclusion from community. God, the prophets and Jesus spoke strongly against these injustices. Justice in the Old Testament is not just a concept confined to the judicial process. Rather, it is primarily concerned with "the improvement of the conditions of the poor" and the kings and their officials were to provide a conducive environment for that to happen.[33]

Biblical justice has implications for our social, political, and economic life. Burch rightly observes:

> Biblical justice has always had a social, political, and economic dimension to it. The people of God by virtue of their relationship with a God who has revealed himself as righteous and holy, have a heritage of responsibility to each other and the world around them.... Justice must transcend all our human activities, social political, and economic.[34]

---

[32] Karl Rahner, *Dictionary of Theology*, 259.
[33] Moshe Weinfeld, "Justice and Righteousness," in *Justice and Righteousness*, eds. Henning Graf Reventlow and Yair Hoffman. Sheffield: Sheffield Academic Press, 1992, 237.
[34] Burch, "Justice" in *Evangelical Dictionary*, 642.

Jesus and justice in the New Testament

Jesus' announcement of the reign of God or the kingdom of God was based on the prophetic traditions of the Old Testament whose central message was justice and righteousness. The Old Testament prophets' message had at its center justice for the people of God. For example, Isaiah's teaching on justice was central to Jesus' teachings on God's reign and kingdom. Stassen and Gushee sum up Isaiah's teaching on justice as covering four significant areas. First, justice involved deliverance of the poor and the powerless from the injustice they regularly experience (Isa. 11:1–4). Secondly justice meant lifting the foot of the domineering power off the neck of the dominated and oppressed (Isa. 26:2–10). Thirdly, justice meant stopping the violence and establishing peace (Isa. 32:16–18, 33:5, 15). Lastly, justice meant restoring the outcasts, the excluded, the Gentiles, the exiles, and the refugees to the community (Isa. 42:1–7, 51:1, 4–7, 53:7–9, 10).[35]

Following the Old Testament prophetic tradition, Jesus committed himself to issues of justice in his teaching and ministry. Like God, Jesus has strong passion for justice and he renounced all forms of injustice against the weak, the poor, the oppressed, the outcasts, the orphans, widows, and the victims of violence. He attacks the injustice going on within the temple system, where the temple was being used as a cover-up of injustice where the poor, the weak, aliens, widows and orphans were oppressed and economically exploited (Matt. 21:12–13, 23:23, Lk. 11:42, 19:45). Stassen and Gushee point out Jesus' confrontations with the powers that be and religious authorities of his day addressed issues of justice.[36]

They argued Jesus renounced injustice of greed by promoting justice for the poor and hungry (Lk. 3:1–14, 8:14, 16:14–15, 18:18–25; Matt. 3:1–10, 13:22, 19:21, 23:16–19, 25; Mk. 4:18–19,10:17–22, 12;38–44. Jesus rejects the "injustice of domination and sought to bring about deliverance through the practice of mutual servanthood" (Mk. 10:42, 11:27–33; Matt. 20:25–26, 21:23–27, 24:45–51; Lk 12:42–46, 20:1–8, 22:25–26). Thirdly, Jesus confronted injustice of violence against the weak and the innocent

---

35 Stassen and Gushee, *Kingdom Ethics*, 349, 355.
36 Stassen and Gushee, *Kingdom Ethics*, 357.

(Lk 13:31–33, 20; 9–19; Matt. 21:33–46, 23:29–36; Mk 12:1–9); and lastly, Jesus deals with injustice of exclusion from community especially those we consider as enemies or as different from us ethnically and socially. He calls us to embrace and bring them in as being part of us (Matt. 5:43–48, 9:9–13, 15:1–9, 21–28; Mk 2:13–17, 7:24–30; Lk. 4:24–29, 5:27–32, 10:29–37, 15:11–32; Acts 1:4, 8, 2:1ff).[37]

As we can see, the triune God is deeply concerned about justice. God cares deeply about justice for the poor, the powerless, the outcasts, and victims of violence. In addition, Jesus was concerned for justice as we see him rebuke the religious leaders for committing injustice against people in the name of giving their tithes to God while failing to care for their parents and the poor, "But how terrible it will be for you Pharisees! For you are careful to tithe even the tiniest part of your income, but you completely forget about justice, mercy and faith or the love of God. You should tithe, yes, but you should not leave undone the more importance things" (Lk. 11:42, NLT).

Who's justice, God's or human justice?

Our concept of justice can be culturally construed. It makes what we call justice relative. What is just in one society might not be just in another. For example, for most of us, our cultures have formed our understanding of justice as vengeance or retaliation or getting even. This is what we call fairness. So, when we talk about justice, whose justice are we talking about? And justice for whom? In the context of our discussion when I talk about justice I mean God's justice, that is, justice as God sees it. What does God's justice entail?

Biblical justice is not about revenge or getting even with someone. It is relational. It ensures restoration of a person to wholeness. It entails treating people with dignity and respect. It means seeking their welfare and good. A biblical view of justice challenges our cultural views of justice, which are inadequate. Our view of justice must be comprehensive, if we understand the biblical notion of justice. The Sabbath and jubilee principles covered

---

37 Stassen and Gushee, *Kingdom Ethics*, 357–365.

nonhuman creatures such as land and animals that were central to the economic life of the people of God. Normally when we speak of justice, we have often limited ourselves to human rights only. We are called to create a just and righteous society where right relationships are built with each other as well as with our environment. Our human relationships are very important to God, especially how we treat each other. God hears the outcry of the oppressed, the poor, families, and workers concerning human relationships, economic activities, payment of wages, and other areas of our human existence.

When Christians hear the cry of the oppressed and the poor, what do they do? God's justice is to hear the cry of the poor, oppressed and those violated. Beyond hearing their cry, God goes further by providing for them and removing them from their oppression and misery. That is justice. As Christians, we must seek and promote God's standard of justice for all people.

We must have the characteristics of God's nature of compassion, faithfulness, mercy, kindness, and love. These qualities are necessary for our moral response to the cry of the poor and to respond to all the injustices we find in our societies today. We may close up our ears to the cries of the poor and oppressed if we do not have these qualities operating in our daily lives. God calls us to live rightly and justly. Love and compassion move us to respond to needs around us. Love and justice are related. Mott is right to say that "Justice is a necessary instrument of love" and justice carries out what love motivates."[38]

God hates "political servitude, economic exploitation, and social genocide"[39] as we see in most of our nations around the world today. These evils, political servitude, economic exploitation, and social genocide, which are perpetuated by governments and powerful people in our world, must be addressed by the Church to ensure that justice is ensured for all. We must build societies that are committed to building vibrant, healthy,

---

38 Mott, *Biblical Ethics*, 53–54.
39 Wright, *Old Testament Ethics*, 261.

and enriching relationships in our societies for the common wellbeing of all humanity.

The mandate to reflect God's character in our behavior in society

Social justice was equally the task of individual Israelites and believers in Christ, as it was for those who had the responsibility to ensure justice is administered to all. Our mandate for social justice is dependent on our own experience of God's indicative action in our lives. Having been freed from oppression, and made free in Christ, God requires that we act justly and righteously in our behavior and relationship towards each other as human beings and to his nonhuman creation—the earth. I will discuss the moral problems we face with the nonhuman creation in chapter 12.

Love is the ground for justice. Love has social importance. Love provides the basis for the worth of human life. People are to be loved because they are our fellow human beings. The incarnation restored human dignity. "As a human being, Christ shared our lot, and in him the potential glory of humanity is seen (Heb. 2:5–18)."[40]

Mercy, righteousness, and justice are the essence of God's being. Righteousness must be seen in both our public and private, sexual and social, religious and secular lives (Eze. 18:5–9). Justice is central to God's essence and the foundation for his throne and government (Is. 61:8, Ps. 33:5, 97:1, 2; 89:14). Biblical justice is attending to the needs of the poor and the weak.

Righteousness and justice are divine qualities or values that define the essence of God. God loves righteousness and justice, they are the foundation of his government (Ps. 33:5, Is. 16:5, Ps. 89:15). Righteousness and justice must be the way of life for Christians and leaders, to establish social justice and equity to improve the lives of the poor and the weak in society through policies that would prevent oppression and domination of the poor and the

---

40 Mott, *Biblical Ethics*, 46.

weak. God loves kindness, justice, and righteousness. All who know him will reflect his nature and character (Jer. 9:23–24).

God demands righteousness and justice from all human beings especially leaders

All human authorities have the primary function to promote righteousness that leads to justice for all peoples in all areas of their leadership and authority. Leaders are expected to exercise justice with integrity and impartiality (Deut. 1:10–18). The judges in Israel were to judge fairly and were warned not to pervert justice or show partiality. They were forbidden to take bribes, which is the cause for twisted judgment. The judges are encouraged to follow justice and justice alone. Moses gives the reason why maintaining justice in the land was important. It depended of their own survival in the land: "so that you may live and possess the land the Lord your God is giving you" (Deut. 16:18–20).

One of the major causes for Israel's captivity apart from their idolatry, was injustice and oppression of the poor and the weak in society by their leaders. The prophets, Amos, Jeremiah, and Isaiah all warned the kings of the impending danger of captivity because of the unjust ways they were treating their own brothers and sisters.

The judges in Israel from Samuel to the kings had the duty to maintain justice and righteousness in the land. Samuel turned out to be an ideal ruler of Israel, who did not steal, cheat, oppress, or take bribes from the people he led. He judged the people with justice but not his children (1 Sam. 12:3–4). They did the opposite. Likewise, the duty of the king was to maintain justice for the people. "The expectation was that if the king was faithful in his duty of executing justice and imitating God's own protection of the afflicted and needy, then God would grant him success and prosperity in other spheres also."[41]

---

41 Wright, *Old Testament Ethics*, 270.

The king was to ensure social justice by doing what is right and just. What is right and just was to rescue the robbed from the hand of the oppressor. He could not show violence to the alien, the orphan, the widow or shed innocent blood (Jer. 22:2–5). The king's success and the durability of his reign depended on it. The king was to abstain from certain behavior such as excessive drinking, which it became a hindrance to his ability to defend the rights of the oppressed. Rather, he had to champion the cause of the weak, those who could not speak for themselves, the rights of the destitute, the poor, and the needy (Prov. 31:4–9). The leader was raised to maintain righteousness and justice in society (1 Ki. 10:9).

Like Samuel, the ideal judge, David reigned over all Israel, doing what was just and right for all his people. David models the behavior all leaders and those put in authority by God to rule his creation must have (2 Sam. 8:15). A future dimension of this model king is the messiah who will rule and bring righteousness and justice (Is. 9:7) and judge the needy righteously and bring justice to the poor of the earth (Is. 11:4–5). The fruit of righteousness is peace—shalom—and its effects will be quietness and confidence forever (Is. 32:15–17).

Biblical justice has ethical implications for our social life as humanity. Justice has implications for the rights of citizens in general but more specifically, it has implications for the rights of the poor, the weak, the destitute, and the marginalized in society. Besides humans, we must also seek justice for the nonhuman world, the rights of creation itself—rivers, mountains, lakes, animals, plants, forests, earth, etc. We will develop some of these in our chapter on ecology. Justice pertains to human and nonhuman life since both are the handiwork of God. "Justice means essentially that we share one another's fate and are obligated by creation itself to promote one another's wellbeing."[42]

Justice is a norm for Christian life just as some of the virtues we have spoken about in the other chapters of this book. It is central to God's being and nature. Since we are to reflect and imitate the Triune God, who is

---

42 Larry L. Rasmussen, *Earth Community, Earth Ethics*. Maryknoll, NY: Orbis Books, 1996, 260.

the model for our ethical life, justice must be central to who we are as Christians. Do our actions reflect God's character in terms justice? How do we respond to the injustices we see in our world today?

The theological and biblical notions of righteousness and justice: implications for Christian social moral vision

God is righteous and just. This has implications for our social moral vision at the individual and the corporate levels. At the individual level, justice and righteousness must pervade our personal, social, political, business or economic life. At the corporate levels, the church must engage herself with the concerns and needs of society by ensuring that righteousness and justice permeates all of society's activities—social, political, and economic. They must work with the government to ensure this is done. Then at the national level, the government is one of the human agencies given the responsibility for justice. The first duty of government is to ensure basic rights for all her citizens and to provide for their needs socially, politically, and economically. Some of the steps I see church and government must take to ensure that justice and righteousness are maintained include the following:

- The government must take the ethical responsibility to ensure individual's rights are respected. Where we see oppression, injustice, mistreatment of people so they lose their human dignity and freedom, we must act to address the situation. This includes all the fundamental rights humanity is to enjoy in their social, political, religious, and economic lives. God requires this from those he has put in authority to provide leadership to his people.
- A human rights and civil society body must be established and funded by the government to be the watchdog that blows the whistle whenever and wherever they find human injustice taking place in our societies. The Church must work closely with this body by encouraging their work and by advocating for and defending the cause of the poor and the disadvantaged in society.

However, this advocacy must go beyond just the rights of people. It must be concerned for righteousness as well. The two concepts, righteousness, and justice are closely related concepts. We must equally emphasize both. God is not only interested in our being treated justly; he is also interest interested in our being morally upright.

- The Church must continue to play its prophetic role of advocacy for the weak, poor, oppressed, dispossessed, and the victimized as we see the Old Testament prophets did. We must align ourselves with the poor as God is on the side of the poor because "the poor as a particular group in society… are on the wronged side of a situation of chronic injustice—a situation God abhors and wishes to have us address. For God's righteous will to be done requires the execution of justice on behalf of the poor."[43]
- The administration of justice in society is a matter of priority to God and so social justice must be central to our life if we really know God, who delights in justice, righteousness, and kindness. Justice in the judicial system is critical for God especially justice for the poor. Judicial officials have a moral obligation to ensure the poor get justice and that judges are not manipulated by the rich to rule in their favor. This is a clear indictment on our legal systems that are infested by a virus called corruption that has eroded the integrity of our judicial systems. This has implication for our legal and justice systems in Africa. I will handle this topic in more detail in chapter 14.
- Biblical ethics "regulates the social construction and treatment of migrants and displaced people—aliens, sojourners, strangers or exile migrants." These groups of people are God's concern. They are to be taken proper care of by citizens and governments alike (Deut. 10:19, Ex. 23:9, Lev. 19:33–34). Christians have a moral obligation to provide and offer hospitality and protection to immigrants, oppressed, the weak, orphans and

---

43 Wright, *Old Testament Ethics*, 268.

the underprivileged. We must speak out for the aliens and foreigners in our mist who are taken advantage of by the citizens and provide them with hospitality, which is a one of the central African moral values. The Church must appeal to government to streamline immigration laws that treat immigrants and aliens inhumanely.
- One central problem of injustice in society is economic injustice. The church must continue to seek economic justice for its citizens. They must speak out against government economic policies that discriminate, entrench, and disenfranchise certain members of the community. They must ensure there is fair distribution of economic resources for the common good of all its citizens. God demands economic justice. The Church must work with bodies which have expertise in this area.
- All humanity must strive and promote a just and humane society by making personal commitments to this goal. We must learn to live in peace and respect each other. For "a just and humane society can exist only because its people possess such qualities as self-respect and self-acceptance, tolerance, mutual respect, unselfishness, honesty, the sense of right to duty, the desire for equal treatment, and fidelity to law."[44]

Conclusion

In this chapter, we have seen that the biblical notions of righteousness and justice are two critical biblical values that shaped biblical morality. These two moral values are essential to God's own character and being; that God's character and will is the foundation for justice. We have also asserted that these values are very important for our social moral vision. God requires that all humanity live and act righteously and justly. Righteousness and justice we saw are related to each other and we must always hold them

---

44 Stephen C. Mott, *Biblical Ethics and Social Change*. New York: Oxford University Press, 1982, 197.

together. We must move away from the cultural notion of justice in terms of one's rights to one that looks to meet the critical needs in a person's life, which deprive him or her of her dignity.

Underlying these biblical values are other values we have already mentions as critical for biblical morality. These are compassion, love, and mercy. These values are necessary for justice to be achieved. We end by affirming that socially and ethically, righteousness and justice are moral obligations God places on all humans and he expects right and just actions or behavior from individuals as well as the community or society. The righteous and just person lives a blameless life in his relationships to neighbor, society, and creation. His or her behavior towards the neighbor and the community is blameless. We must always enhance right and just relationships that build up society's wellbeing. This is our moral mandate!

CHAPTER 11

Ethnicity and Reconciliation

Introduction

Ethnicity and ethnic conflicts have increased in our world today especially in Africa. The Rwanda genocide, the ethnic wars in the Democratic Republic of Congo, and some of the ethnic tensions in Kenya are just a few examples. Politicians and other powerful entities in our nations and communities have used ethnicity to advance their political power, economic prosperity, religious status, and as means of resource allocation and development of infrastructure in certain communities. These unjust behaviors and attitudes have often generated into ethnic enmity, conflicts, marginalization, discrimination, ethnic cleansing, wars, dehumanization, and polarization of certain communities. All of these raise ethical issues for the Church today. This has brought untold evil and sufferings on communities and nations in Africa.

Ethnicity is a universal phenomenon; it's not just unique to Africa. The issue of race in many western countries is a form of ethnicity at a certain level. The moral effects of racism that result in discrimination, marginalization, dehumanization and other evils associated with racism make racism and ethnicity bedfellows. Ethnicity plays out in every aspect of human life. It is seen in politics, economics, religion, and social vision. How can we amalgamate diverse peoples within a nation state? How can the Church address this menace in Africa to encourage harmony, national cohesion, and civility in our communities and nations?

This chapter will address this pertinent ethical issue. The purpose is not to treat ethnicity as an academic subject. Therefore, I will not spend too much time discussing in detail the subject matter of ethnicity. Rather, I will focus on the moral issues raised by negative ethnicity to which we must address ourselves. As we have always done in our methodology in this book, we will explore ethnicity in Africa, emphasizing some of the cultural and moral values we can draw from ethnicity and then look at it from a theological and biblical perspective to understand the biblical values that we can learn to form as the foundations for how we relate with one another ethnically. I will then suggest some biblical and theological values for dealing with negative ethnicity in our world today. We begin by asking the question, what do we mean by ethnicity?

Defining ethnicity

There is no scholarly agreement on the meaning of ethnicity. Scholars approach ethnicity from different disciplines such as anthropology and sociology and therefore, they see the concept differently. The word ethnicity comes from the Greek word *ethnos*, which was used to describe pagans who are "non-Hellenic, and later, non-Jewish (Gentile) or non-Christian, as second class peoples."[1] In simple terms, ethnicity carries the notion of "us" and "them." Consequently, ethnicity expresses the idea of "difference and otherness." At its core is the issue of identity.

Elizabeth Tonkin et al observe that ethnicity is

> A rich and complex moral vocabulary, lay out along the dimensions of inclusion and exclusion, dignity and disdain, familiarity and strangeness-gentle, Gentile; popular; tribe; nation, national; polite; barbarous; civil, civilized; and so on.[2]

---

1 Siniša Mallešević, *The Sociology of Ethnicity*. London: Sage Publications, 2004, 1. See John Hutchinson & Anthony D. Smith, eds. *Ethnicity*, Oxford: Oxford University Press, 1996, 20.

2 Elizabeth Tonkin et al, "History of Ethnicity" in Hutchison and Smith eds. *Ethnicity*, 20.

It is precisely this characteristic of ethnicity with its emphasis on otherness and difference that degenerates to negative ethnicity whereby those who are not like "us" are considered often times as less human. This ought not to be so. To be different from someone else does not make the other person less human. Ethnicity tends to force people to exclude others just because they do not look like or behave like us. It is this ethical dimension of ethnicity that this chapter will address.

Eriksen defines ethnicity as:

> ... an aspect of social relationship between agents who consider themselves as culturally distinctive from members of other groups with whom they have a minimum of regular interaction.[3]

The identity of the individual or group is uniquely distinctive from everyone else. This explains why ethnic identity is asserting itself in many communities as a powerful force, especially in places where there are multiethnic groups as well as imbalances of power, wealth, and economic deprivation. What constitutes an ethnic group? What are some of the core elements of ethnicity?

Jenkins proposed a basic anthropological model of ethnicity that explains the various facets the term carries. He says,[4]

- ethnicity is about cultural differentiation;
- ethnicity is concerned with culture-shared meaning—but it is also rooted in, and the outcome of, social interaction;
- ethnicity is no more fixed than the culture of which it is a component, or situations in which it is produced and reproduced;
- ethnicity is collective and individual, externalized in social interaction and internalized in personal self-identification.

I would like to make two observations about Jenkins statement. First I would like to point out that ethnicity is about identity which can be

---

[3] T. H. Eriksen, *Ethnicity and Nationalism: Anthropological Perspectives*, 2nd ed. London: Pluto Press, 2002, 12.

[4] Jenkins, *Rethinking Ethnicity*, 13–4 and 165.

individual of corporate. Second, ethnicity is not a fixed concept. It changes. People change their identities due to change of circumstance and situations. As human beings, we tend to have many other identities that define us besides our ethnic identities.

Ethnicity is a social *resource* that others draw on and exploit in different contexts.[5] Some have used it as a tool to unite one ethnic group against the other causing ethnic conflicts. Often powerful ethnic communities have used power and wealth to subjugate weak and small ethnic groups as their servants. This practice is common in many Africa countries. There are other related issues such as class, race, and tribes. Ethnicity is often tied to the term tribe. Tribe connotes a distinct group of people sharing a common history, language, geographical area, and socio-political institutions. As far as these terms are used to discriminate and disenfranchise people and communities, they are morally unacceptable. In other words, the negative form of these concepts—tribalism, racism, and classicism are moral evils we must deal with in our modern societies.

Volf's category of exclusion as a metaphor of negative ethnicity is helpful. Volf proposes exclusion involves two interrelated aspects: one transgresses against 'binding' and the other transgresses against 'separating.'[6] Exclusion has the tendency to cut

> The bonds that connect, taking oneself out of the pattern of interdependence and placing oneself in the position of sovereign independence. The *other* then emerges either as an enemy that must be pushed away from the self and driven out of its space as a nonentity—a superfluous being—that can be disregarded and abandoned. Second, exclusion can entail erasure of separation, not recognizing the other as someone who in his or her otherness belongs to the pattern of interdependence. The *other* then emerges as an inferior being who must either be assimilated by being made like the self

---

[5] Richard Jenkins. *Rethinking Ethnicity: Arguments and Explorations.* London: Sage Publications, 90.

[6] Miroslav Volf, *Exclusion and Embrace*, 67.

or be subjugated to the self. Exclusion takes place when the violence of expulsion, assimilation, or subjugation and the indifference of abandonment replace the dynamics of taking in and keeping out as well as the mutuality of giving and receiving.[7]

This understanding of ethnicity that results in exclusion is morally wrong and unacceptable. Such understanding of ethnicity must be rejected because the Scriptures speak against such behavior. This is a wrong way of treating humanity. Exclusion is evil.

The reality of ethnicity in Africa

Africa is made up of many diverse people groups. This is evident in the many languages spoken in different African countries. African has rich diverse cultural heritage because of our diversity. There are three main features for distinguishing Africa's ethnic groups from each other. These are (i) a community of people with physical space and emotional attachment to this space no matter where they find themselves; (ii) a common language and myth of common descent; and (iii) common culture. All three features are what give a person his or her identity.

Africa's diverse ethnic groups have often become the cause of most of the wars and ethnic unrest we have experienced in Africa in recent decades. Ethnicity has been used as a social, political, economic, and religious tool to exclude, marginalize, and degrade others. Such ethnic exclusion has resulted in gross injustice, humiliation, shame, and indignity to certain ethnic communities in Africa.

Historically, there are factors that have contributed to these heightened ethnic identities in our time. Firstly, the colonization of Africa by the west exploited ethnicity to isolate some communities while elevating others so they can rule the nations they have colonized. Through this divide and rule tactics, they, colonialists, managed to marginalize certain communities.

---

7 Miroslav Volf, *Exclusion and Embrace*, 67.

Unfortunately, this trend did not change after African nations got their independence; it rather prevailed and remains a dominant vice in our societies today.

Secondly, the evangelization of Africa during this colonial period was done along ethnic lines. The missionaries evangelized particular ethnic groups, resulting in creating ethnic churches and denominations that are predominantly composed of a particular ethnic group. This escalated the ethnic identity crisis. The Christian church that was to be a leading player in and center of ethnic integration became segregated. Although this phenomenon is changing with some of the new Pentecostal and charismatic Churches today, we are far from dealing with the problem of ethnicity in the church.

Thirdly, politicians in Africa have exploited the ethnic dimension of our cultural and social life for political and economic power as well as resource allocation, religious agenda and even marriages. Like their colonial counterparts, African politicians have used ethnicity as a means to political and economic power, and as social control of the masses. As a result, many political leaders in Africa have isolated certain communities and have deprived them of basic infrastructure and economic development in their communities. As a result, poverty and human degradation have become the lot of these ethnic communities. When leaders are caught up in corruption and other misdeeds and are questioned, they often draw ethnic solidarity and loyalty from the ethnic communities and they escape any legal redress for the evils they have committed against their nations. This has resulted in unequal distribution of resources in many African countries. The result has been conflicts and wars.

For all purposes, the church and the political leadership have used ethnicity negatively in the context of Africa socio-economic and political sphere. Such exploitation has caused Africa many troubles and woes. The situation must change. We need to address this negative ethnicity in Africa today.

These negative ways in which people have exploited ethnicity for egoistic ends should not over shadow the positive aspects of ethnicity, which I think we must continue to embrace. Some of values of ethnicity include the positive sense of identity it provides for the individual and the group. It gives a positive self-image and confidence to a person that s/he is valuable and important. It also fosters clan solidarity and loyalty that opens doors for more opportunities for people to engage and assist each other. Ethnicity promotes unity. It tends to unite the community or the group. This unity provides the strength they need for their survival as a people group. However, we must not confuse unity with uniformity. The two are not the same. We cannot all be the same. Our diversity is the essence of being human. Therefore, we must encourage unity in diversity.

Furthermore, ethnicity ensures the welfare of the community, which means care for each other. This provides a sense of belonging that brings some joy and fulfillment to the individual and the community as a whole. More importantly, it prevents incest and inbreeding, one of the taboos in many African communities. Lastly, ethnicity ensures the continuity of the group so they do not become extinct.

Ethnic diversity: A blessing or a curse?

If Africa will live in peace and foster an enduring development and prosperity for its peoples, then it is important we address the problem of identity and difference. We must celebrate both our cultural and ethnic diversities. Our diversity is a blessing and it should not become a curse to us. Our cultural and ethnic diversities are good for building vibrant and authentic human relationships for the enrichment of our lives. This is an important fact that we must embrace as we deal with ethnicity not only within Africa but also around the world.

How can we shift our focus from negative ethnicity to begin to celebrate and enjoy our diversity? Several approaches have been suggested in the west to deal with the problem of ethnicity or "identity" and "otherness." Volf outlines three ways the issue of identity or ethnicity has been handled in the west drawing on some western, moral, cultural, social values.

The first approach is what he calls the *Universalist Option*. This approach encourages controlling "the unchecked proliferation of differences, and support the spread of universal values—religious values or enlightenment values—which alone can guarantee the peaceful coexistence of people; affirmation of values without common values will lead to chaos and war rather than to rich and fruitful diversity."

The second approach he calls the *Communitarian Option*. This approach avers for celebration of our "communal distinctive and promote heterogeneity, placing ourselves on the side of the smaller armies of indigenous cultures; the spread of universal values will lead to oppression and boredom rather than peace and prosperity."

The third approach he calls *Postmodern Option*. The postmodern approach encourages fleeing "Both universal values and particular identities [to] seek refuge from oppression in the radical autonomy of individuals; we should create spaces in which persons can keep creating "larger and freer selves" by acquiring new while losing old identities—wayward and erratic vagabonds, ambivalent and fragmented, always on the move and never doing much more than making moves."[8]

Volf observes that these approaches have its focus on *social arrangements* underlying what society or humanity have to do in order to accommodate individuals and groups in a diverse society to live in harmony with each other. He argues, while these solutions show "important perspectives about persons who live in such societies, the main interest is not on the social agents, but it is on social arrangements. Instead of reflecting on the kind of society we ought to create in order to accommodate individual or community heterogeneity," Volf proposes an approach that focuses on *social agents* by exploring "*what kind of selves we need to be* in order to live in harmony with others."[9] This approach deals with ontology. It concerns who we are.

The importance of focusing on the moral character of social agents and their engagement in society is made clear by Bauman's observation on modernity and post modernity ethics. Bauman has argued that modernity is known for its "tendency to shift moral responsibilities away from the moral self either toward socially constructed or managed by supra-individual

---

8 Miroslav Volf, *Exclusion and Embrace: A Theological Exploration of Identity and Otherness, and Reconciliation*. Nashville: Abingdon Press, 20.
9 Volf, *Exclusion and Embrace*, 20–21.

agencies, or through floating responsibility inside a bureaucratic 'rule of nobody.'" Such "fragmentary" and "discontinuous" relationships results in "disengagement and commitment-avoidance."[10] Volf thinks doing this will produce *"the kind of social agents capable of envisioning and creating just, truthful, and peaceful societies, and on shaping a cultural climate in which such agents will thrive."*[11]

In Africa, I must say we have not done very well in living in harmony and celebrating our cultural and ethnic diversity. This has been so because of our socialization process. Most Africans growing up were told negative stories about their neighbors and ethnic groups that were different from them. They were people who were not to be trusted, they were thought to have strange behavior and practices that were abhorred by their neighboring groups, and so forth. Intermarriages were often forbidden and these groups continue to see each other as enemies, even today. People were encouraged to promote the wellbeing and welfare of the group. Therefore, there was not enough interaction between the various ethnic communities. Africa really needs to work hard in dealing with this problem of ethnicity.

In summary we can affirm from our discussion of ethnicity, that ethnicity by itself is not evil. It is amoral. It has a lot of positive value. However, it can be used for a negative purpose that tends to destroy the other as it excludes them thus depriving them of their intrinsic value as human beings. It is ethnocentrism that is evil, not ethnicity. We must avoid every form of ethnocentrism in our communities as individuals and as members of society. Rather than seeing our diversity as evil and as cause for exclusion, we should celebrate our diversity as a way of enriching our experiences as humanity. We can learn so much from each other if we have a learning spirit and attitude. In the next section, I will demonstrate that our diversity is a blessing from God, as we explore ethnic diversity and God's intension and purpose for diversity in His creation as something to celebrate and not one to divide us. This is in line with our methodology for this book. God

---

10 See Volf, *Exclusion and Embrace*, 21.

11 Volf, *Exclusion and Embrace*, 21. Italics are the author's.

provides the model for our human actions. If our human ethnic diversities originate from Him, then there is a purpose for it and we must enjoy it.

Theological and biblical foundation for ethnic diversity

Humanity is created in the image of God and each human person has dignity and value that must be respected by all (Gen. 1:26–27). This character of our being demands that we treat every human being as the bearers of God's image. Every person irrespective of where he or she comes from has value. Secondly, humanity belongs to one universal parent and family, namely Adam and Eve and later Noah (Gen. 5, 10). Therefore, humanity is rightly so, children of Adam and Eve and more importantly children of God. Therefore, the Akans of Ghana say "All people are God's children; none is the child of the earth." This affirms Paul's statement in Acts 17:28 that "For we are also His offspring." This means humanity belongs to one common ancestor, Adam and Eve and later on Noah after the flood. If this is true then we are truly one big family irrespective of color, race, or creed. We must celebrate our unity and oneness. This was God's intension for humanity.

However, when sin entered the world it destroyed human relationships and brought about tensions and violence against each other. Sin entered the world (Gen. 3) and distorted the goodness of God's creation. Adam and Eve's disobedience to God's command resulted in broken relations between God and humanity, between husband and wife—where Adam blames Eve his wife instead of accepting responsibility for disobeying the Lord's command—between humanity and the environment they live in and between siblings (Gen. 4). Rather than creation making it possible for our ethnic diversity to be appreciated and celebrated, it becomes distorted into ethnocentrism and it is used as a tool by the evil one to divide and cause discord among us.

Humanity shares a common ancestry, dignity and integrity as human beings. Human beings belong to one universal family with God as the Father or the Great Ancestor of all. Enmity and strife, quarrels and dissentions, while it may occur in normal families, must not be tolerated or accepted as a norm in human relationships.

Diversity is part of the creation order. We find in creation diversity. God created diverse kinds of things. This diversity makes creation beautiful and pleasant to enjoy and admire. The diversity in God's creation was good and beautiful, e.g. diversity of color, foliage, and plants. Therefore, in the same way we appreciate diversity within nature, we must celebrate our diversity as human beings.

The first record of ethnic diversity occurs in Genesis 11 where God came down to confuse human language so they could not accomplish their plans and desire to build a great city with a tower that reached the skies—a monument to our greatness! This [would] bring us together and keep us from scattering all over the world" (Gen. 11:4, NLT). The confusion of human language by God resulted for the first time in ethnic differentiation of humanity. Old Testament commentators see this as God's judgment on the rebellion of Noah's son to "fill the earth" (Gen. 9:1). Later on we saw the ethnic animosity that followed this development in the wars and conflict ensued between the people of Israel and the surrounding ethnic groups for a long time.

Although, this episode seems like a judgment of humanity, it was part of God's divine purpose for humanity that we speak diverse languages. God's salvation includes redeeming our mother tongues or languages. This is why we are redeemed as ethnic people. Salvation does not obliterate our ethnicity; it gives it a new meaning. It does not become a tool for oppression and discrimination. However, we are giving the privilege and honor to serve others.

In Acts 17:24–26, Apostle Paul makes the claim that God is the one who is behind our ethnic differentiation. Paul emphasized some biblical truth about human origin. He points out God created the world and everything that is in it. He is Lord over heaven and earth. He also created humanity and every nation of men to dwell on the face of the earth from "one blood." Paul is suggesting ethnic groups are God's will and purpose for humanity (Acts. 17:26). Again, Paul connects human ancestry to the first humans, Adam and Eve. Thirdly, Paul affirms that God is the one who has placed humanity, nations, and ethnic groups in their respective current geographical locations. Ethnicity, therefore, is not an afterthought of God. It is central to God's purposes and will for humanity. It is a permanent feature of our being human.

The book of Revelation affirms this permanent nature of our ethnic identities. In Revelation 7:9, we see in heaven a great multitude of people from every nation, tribe, people, and language standing before the throne of God and of the Lamb. Not only are people from many nations, tribes and tongues singing and worshiping God and the Lamb, but God has also redeemed people by the blood of Jesus Christ from many nations, tribes and tongues and has made them kings and priests to God and they reign with Him on earth (Rev. 5:9). This indicates that God will not obliterate our ethnic identities. Our identities are permanent. Our ethnic identities are not intended to be used to exclude others or marginalize them. God, who is not a tribal or an ethnic God will not tolerate such an attitude from humanity.

The Cross is God's remedy for ethnocentrism

Jesus' death on the cross demonstrates his radical obedience to God as well as his self-giving love (self-donation) for or an expression of loving care towards his followers and humanity.[12] The cross becomes the basis for our relationship with one another and not our ethnic identity. The cross is an open demonstration of God's opened and outstretched arms towards humanity, reconciling them to God through his death.

Through the cross, God has embraced and received us into his family and has made us one new humanity (Col. 3:11), where he has broken the ethnic dominance that holds us captive. He breaks the evil power behind ethnocentrism and frees us from it dominion. In this new humanity, there is no Greek, Jew, circumcised, uncircumcised, barbarian, Scythian, slave, and free. All are one in Christ (Gal. 3:28–29). The Christian's identity is

---

12 Volf, *Exclusion and Embrace*, 23–24.

not primarily found in his ethnicity but in Christ. In light of this change in our identity, Paul encourages us to show love, mercy, kindness, humility, compassion and patience towards each other, by forgiving one another just as Christ has forgiven us. These biblical values are very important for dealing with the issue of ethnocentrism in our context in Africa.

The call to embrace one another is grounded upon God's act towards us as his people. In Romans 15:7–9, Paul writes, "Accept one another, and then, just as Christ accepted you, in order to bring praise to God." For I tell you that Christ has become a servant of the Jews on behalf of God's truth, to confirm the promises made to the patriarchs so that the Gentiles may glorify God for his mercy…." If God has embraced us, his enemies, and has accepted us as his children, then, we ought to accept those who are not like us and embrace them and care for their well-being. This is our moral obligation. We must act and behave like our Father in heaven who opened wide his arms to embrace all who come to him.

The cross therefore is a model for reconciliation and acceptance. The cross induces certain biblical and moral values—forgiveness, humility, love, compassion, mercy, longsuffering—etc, which we must practice. We forgive because we have been forgiven, and we show mercy because we have received mercy, we love because we have first been loved. Our acts of mercy, love, compassion, are grounded upon what God has already done for us. We need to reciprocate in kind what God has done for us in Christ to others.

Christ's death on the cross has altered our "social space." Through the shedding of his blood, He has created a new humanity and a new human solidarity and family that go beyond family, kinship, and ethnic ties. Since we are related naturally to our siblings by blood or by adoption, Christ's blood has brought us into one family, the family of God in that we have his blood running in us. Secondly, we are brought into God's family by adoption; we have been incorporated into the family of God again by his blood (Eph. 1:4–6). God has accepted all who believe in Him into his family.

The terms Jews and Gentiles are the broad distinctions made between humanity.[13] This social space created through Christ's death on the cross has erased the categories of ethnic group, gender, and class (Gal. 3:28–29). Christ's blood is the medium that made reconciliation and peace within the ethnic tensions that existed between Gentile and Jews possible. Christ is our peace. He made us one and has broken down the middle wall of division between us, having abolished in his flesh (death) the enmity—the things that distinguish us from each other—religion, culture, values—so he can create one new family from the two (Eph. 2:11–18). The result of this great work of Christ is to blur the distinction between us. "We are no longer strangers and aliens (them), but fellow citizens, with the saints and members of God's household" (Eph. 2:19). Christ is the answer to our ethnocentrism!

Triune God as model for equality and respect for humanity

Diversity is the very essence of God. God is triune; being Father, Son, and Holy Spirit. Humanity is not just created in His image. Humanity and his creation also reflect this diversity, which is the essence of God. The equality between the persons of the Triune God and the harmony and acceptance within the Godhead is a model for humanity's dealings with each other. God's intension as well as the social vision of both the Old and New Testaments are for humanity to live in unity and be at peace with each other.

God is not a tribal or an ethnic God. He is the God of the nations. The nations are his and he redeems them. God is concerned about humanity as a whole. He created our diversity as humans and He expects us to treat each ethnic group in a godly manner. The harmony, acceptance, and

---

13 Tite Tienou, "The Samaritans: A biblical theological mirror for understanding racial, ethnic, and religious identity?" in *This side of heaven: race, ethnicity, and Christian faith*. Eds. Robert J. Priest and Alvaro L. Nieves. New York: Oxford University Press, 2009, 212.

respect with the Godhead must therefore serve as a model for our interethnic relationships.

Ethnicity and reconciliation are closely linked. This is why I entitled the chapter ethnicity and reconciliation. The theological ground is the reconciling work of Christ by bringing Jews and Gentiles together as one people through his death on the cross. I will turn to the place of reconciliation in fostering ethnic harmony.

Reconciliation and forgiveness: God's solution to ethnocentrism and exclusion

How then can we foster good ethnic relationships with each other especially in our world where many ethnic groups have been excluded and mistreated by others who see them as nonhumans? How can we reconcile ethnic communities that are not in good relationships? Reconciliation of humanity is central to God's purpose for humanity. As such, it must be central in what we do as Christians in a world that is estranged from itself and from each other.

Reconciliation and forgiveness as the grounds for embracing and accepting one another

Forgiveness and reconciliation are central themes in the Bible. The whole concept of redemption is a confirmation of God's willingness to forgive and reconcile with humankind. The call to reconcile and forgive one another is grounded upon God's act of forgiving and reconciling himself to humanity, and reconciling humanity to humanity and to creation.

The goal of forgiveness and reconciliation is to open up for us new ways of connecting with God, with one another and with creation. The cross of Christ has brought us together and it forbids any person to exclude his or her neighbor. The greatest command demands that we love God with all our hearts, mind, and strength and to love our neighbor as ourselves (Mk. 12:30–31, Lk. 10:27, Jas. 2:8). This truth is made clear in the teaching of the New Testament as we saw in our discussion earlier on in this chapter.

The God of the Bible, whom we have encountered in Jesus Christ, is a God of justice, love, and peace. This three-fold attribute of God forms the bases for the Biblical material on forgiveness and reconciliation. The biblical narratives in the Old Testament, especially the Pentateuch, as well as the Old Testament prophets show God's willingness to forgive and to reconcile with His people who are alienated from Him and as a result become his enemies.

The sacrificial system of the Old Testament was God's way of forgiving the sins of His covenant people and thus restoring the Covenant relationship He established with the people of Israel and the whole of the human race. The blood, which formed the basis of the covenant, bonded Him to the people. When they sinned against Him and broke their Covenant relationship, the Israelites were able to, through repentance and blood sacrifice, gain God's forgiveness for their sins and be reconciled to him through his restoring them to fellowship and to a loving and vital relationship with him again.[14]

God did not sacrifice His justice for sins to be punished at the expense of His love and desire and willingness to forgive. Neither did He offer them forgiveness and reconciliation without their asking for it through the sacrificial systems He had instituted for them. Rather, forgiveness for the Israelites was based on the condition that they repent and perform the stipulated rituals. Harold Wells's statement is right, "reconciliation does not replace justice, but rather, reconciliation is the result of justice."[15]

The New Testament provides numerous teachings on forgiveness and reconciliation. Jesus offers a radical teaching on forgiveness. For example, in Matthew 5:23–26, Jesus teaches about reconciliation. He emphasizes the importance and the urgency of reconciliation and commands us to practice instant reconciliation. This text is set in the context of prayer or worship. Jesus says while in the midst of worship you "remember that your brother has something against you, leave your gift there before the altar, and go

---

14 The book of Leviticus gives a catalog of sacrifices that God instructed Moses to command the Israelites to perform when they sin against God so that they restore their relationship with Him. See especially, Leviticus 3–9.

15 Harold Wells, "Theology for Reconciliation: Biblical Perspective on Forgiveness and Grace" in Gregory Baum and Harold Wells. Eds. *The Reconciliation of Peoples: Challenge to the Churches*. Maryknoll, New York: Orbis Books, 1997, 4.

your way. First be reconciled to your brother, and then come and offer your gift." For Jesus, worship is not acceptable if it is done with, unresolved tension or grudge against a brother or sister stressing that reconciliation is more important than religious rituals.

Even more important is Jesus' teaching on forgiveness in Matthew 18:15–35. In this passage, Jesus outlines the process involved in forgiveness. The approach of Jesus is radical in the sense that He puts the burden on the offended and not the perpetrator to initiate the process of forgiveness. Jesus says the offended must take the initiative to reconcile with his brother. This is not what our cultures teach us. We wait for people to ask for forgive before we give it to them, if they are lucky. Most often, we vow not to forgive.

The purpose for Christ's teaching is to give the perpetrator the chance to repent and admit his fault and ask for forgiveness. This might open up a new page for reconstructing a new relationship. If the brother or sister who sinned against you listens to your complaint and repents, then you win the brother or sister. Notice the offended is to make every effort to win the brother. If the person fails to listen after taking along some witnesses and involving the Church, who is the community of faith, then that person is to be ostracized from the Church community.

Jesus further teaches that there should be no limit to how many times we should forgive a brother or sister. When he is asked, "'Lord how often shall my brother sin against me, and I forgive him? Up to seven times? Jesus said to him, 'Not seven times, but I tell you, seventy times seven'" (Matt. 18:21–22). Then he illustrates this with a parable of the unforgiving Servant whose master forgave him his huge debts but failed to forgive his fellow servant who owed him a very small debt. Rather than having compassion on his fellow servant like his master did and cancelling his debt, he grabbed his associate by the throat and threw him into prison until he paid every cent (Matt. 18:23–35). This passage emphasizes two important facts about forgiveness. First, we are debtors to God, but God has graciously forgiven us our sins. Therefore, we are to do the same. Second, forgiveness is God's nature and as His children, we must forgive others who offend us. It will be impossible for us to forgive without having compassion. Compassion is what makes forgiveness possible. This wicked servant does not show compassion and mercy towards the fellow servant. That was his sin! Jesus concludes God will not forgive any person who refuses to forgive others.

As Well observes, the biblical accounts on Jesus' teaching on reconciliation and forgiveness do not present us "with a simple or unambiguous picture." Rather, "Jesus' life and teaching are characterized by certain dialectic, for he holds together, on the one hand, a radical love of the enemy, and, on the other, forthright confrontation with the perpetrators of injustice."[16] Evil must be confronted because it is not God's nature. Yet, God calls us to do so in love.

Our mandate: Humanity is given the ministry of reconciliation and forgiveness

Both reconciliation and forgiveness are costly. The atonement was not cheap. It cost God Himself to die on the cross bearing both our sins and guilt. Likewise, we may have to make some sacrifices for reconciliation and forgiveness to take place. For us we might have to sacrifice our right to be right. If we have truly experienced the grace of God's forgiveness, then it is required of us as God's children to be channels of reconciliation and forgiveness.

Apostle Paul emphasized the practical implication of the doctrine of justification for reconciliation.[17] God's act in Christ by "reconciling the world to himself" becomes the basis for our reconciliation. For through Christ's death on the cross God has embraced the whole cosmos. We are entrusted with the ministry of reconciliation, and as "ambassadors for Christ" we are called to "be reconciled to God" (2 Cor. 5:18–20). We are further charged with the ministry of reconciliation. Christians must work to bring ethnic communities together.

Thus, the goal for resolving any conflict between certain individuals is "to gain a brother" as Augsburger points out. The Gospel is a message of

---

16 Harold Wells, "*Theology for Reconciliation*, 5."
17 Harold Wells, *Theology for Reconciliation*, 12.

having a meaningful relationship with God and human beings made in the image of God and restored to right relationship with Him through the Lord Jesus Christ.

According to Jesus' teaching, forgiveness becomes the sole condition for prayer. For Jesus reminds his disciples that they are connected to each other for they are members of a family, they are brothers. The issue here is the blood bond that is between them, which makes it difficult for them to cancel what ties them to their families.

The brother who sins must be disciplined strongly and if he refuses to listen to admonition: if he persists, he will be excommunicated, treated like an outsider. However, if there is repentance, the brother must be forgiven (Lk. 17:3). There remains a fundamental blood bond that we must restore.

In the Pauline Epistles, Paul used several metaphors to describe the interconnections that exist within the body. He argues that we are members of the same body. First, the body consists of those who are "in Christ" it is their relationship to him which makes them part of the body. This relationship with Christ is because of His death on the cross. Through his blood, we have become members of his body. Second, there is only one body; each individual member is in some way identified with and connected to the one body (Rom. 12, 1 Cor. 12, and Ephesians 4). The intimate connections of the parts of the body to one another is the basis for Paul's exhortation to speak truthfully to one another in Ephesians 4:25; it is also the ground for striving for peace in Colossians 3:15. Because believers are in fact connected to one another through their common participation in Christ, they must do nothing that would tend to drive a wedge between them. The common bond between Christians is their participation in the blood of Jesus. As a family, they are to live in peace with each other.

The goal for reconciliation and healing in the African culture is to restore healthy family and community relationships. As we have demonstrated in this paper, shame and dishonor are not good virtues and the African will do anything to prevent that from happening. It is on this basis that forgiveness and reconciliation is vital to the African's relationship. Disharmony in the family as well as the community if not dealt with could cause disaster for the family or the community. Secondly, the centrality of the family as well the community requires good relationships to maintain the solidarity that exits in the both family and community because of the blood ties that bonds them. The goal of forgiveness and reconciliation is to gain a family or a community member.

A people's values might form the basis or lay the ground for forgiveness. We must caution ourselves though, to make sure that we understand that forgiveness is not based on our cultural perception. Culture does not totally determine any individual; it has a profound influence upon one's values, perceptions, views, experiences and lifestyle."[18] Forgiveness may have many faces in different cultures. Augsburger points this out:

> Forgiveness has many faces. Each culture shapes its understanding of forgiveness from its central values. Harmony calls for a forgiveness of overlooking; justice for a forgiveness of repentance; solidarity for a forgiveness of ostracism; honor for a forgiveness of repayment; dignity for a forgiveness of principled sacrifice. Each group gives forgiveness a face composed of multiple values, framed by its unique history.[19]

We are concerned here with biblical forgiveness, which is part of the message of reconciliation. There cannot be genuine reconciliation without a genuine forgiveness. The two are closely related. Biblical forgiveness says, "If anyone is angry with his brother… your brother has something against you… be reconciled to your brother." Jesus teaches his disciples how to respond to the brother who sins against them, and who needs to be forgiven repeatedly.

In normal experience of human relationships, when deep hurt has occurred, reconciliation is costly. When we forgive, we bear the guilt of the one forgiven. "The doctrine of atonement, then, so potentially dangerous to the human spirit when misunderstood, can be a profound source of

---

18 See E. Lartey, *Pastoral Counseling*, 182.

19 See Augsburger's book, *Conflict Mediation across Cultures*, 262–263. His diagram on the polarities of response to perceived wrongdoing is very helpful. It shows how different cultures respond to wrongdoing based on their cultural values.

reconciliation among the perpetrators of crime and their victims."[20] For both victims and perpetrators all stand together before the cross in need of forgiveness for…"God is in solidarity with the suffering victim. God is not, then, the bloodthirsty patriarch demanding 'payment.' Rather, God is the vulnerable One, the self-giving One, who moves us not to revenge but to forgiveness. The guilty too are offered hope, for God, in Christ, has 'descended into hell' for them too. Here are deep wells of grace and hope, and powerful grounds for repentance and reconciliation."[21] For true forgiveness and ethnic reconciliation to take place, both perpetrators and victim must meet at the cross.

God's grace should lead us to repentance. Robert Schreiter speaks of grace that leads to repentance in this manner.

> We discover and experience God's forgiveness of our trespasses and this prompts us to repentance. In the reconciliation process, then, because God has brought to the victim reconciling grace to forgive the tormentor, the tormentor is prompted to repent of evildoing and engage in rebuilding his or her humanity.[22]

In speaking about reconciliation the words of the South African Council of Churches on the Commission for Truth and Reconciliation is worth noting:

> The Commission for Truth and Reconciliation is not another Nuremberg. It turns its back on any revenge. It represents an extraordinary act of generosity by a people who only insist that the truth, the whole truth and nothing but the truth is told. The space is thereby created where the deeper processes

---

20 See Wells, *Theology for Reconciliation*, 11.
21 Harold Wells, *Theology for Reconciliation*, 11–12.
22 Robert J. Schreiter, *Reconciliation: Mission and Ministry in a Changing Social Order* (Maryknoll, N.Y.: Orbis Books, 1992, 45.

of forgiveness, confession, repentance, reparation, and reconciliation can take place.[23]

There is no room for retaliation and vengeance. God requires us to forgive those who have wronged us. However, for true forgiveness and reconciliation to occur, there must be genuine confession, repentance, and some form of reparation. The goal is to gain a brother and to restore and transform relationships.

In concluding this section, we would like to end with Apostle James' exhortation. Those who are guided by the pure wisdom from heaven which is "peace loving, gentle at all times, and willing to yield to others. This pure wisdom is full of mercy and good deeds. It shows no partiality and is always sincere. And those who are peacemakers will plant seeds of peace and reap a harvest of goodness." (James 3:17–18).

Some practical suggestions for dealing with ethnocentrism

What are some practical changes we can make in our societies, churches, families, and organizations to ensure we address the issue of ethnicity that has polarized our countries and brought untold sufferings to the people of Africa? Below are some suggestions I would like to make.

- We must be honest with ourselves by recognizing, admitting, and confessing our own shortcomings and our ethnic biases against people who are different from us. In this sense, we must repent of our sins of omission and commission. We need to change our attitudes towards other ethnic groups. This we must do as individuals.

---

23 Cited by John W. de Gruchy, "The Dialectic of Reconciliation: Church and the Transition to Democracy in South Africa" in *The Reconciliation of Peoples: Challenge to the Churches*. Eds. Gregory Baum and Harold Wells (Maryknoll, N.Y.: Orbis Books, 1997, 28.

- We must education and create awareness among our people about the destructive nature of ethnocentrism. This will help us remove the understandings and prejudices we have formed against certain ethnic groups and people due to our ignorance and our poor socialization. We should be aware of systems that tend to exclude and marginalize other ethnic communities on political, religious, economic, social, and cultural grounds.
- We consciously and consistently must work to break ethnic barriers—socially, religiously, politically and economically. We must discourage any policy that seems to exclude others socially, economically, political, and religiously on ethnic grounds. There must be an intentional effort made by the individual, community, and nation to seek and work towards national integration and cohesion. We must build institutions that model, encourage, and affirm ethnic diversity and work towards social justice by ensuring systems are more equitable.
- We must have attitudinal and behavioral change towards ethnic communities that are different from "us." We should develop sensitivity to the language of "us" verses "them." We can intentionally do this by seeking and becoming friends of people from other ethnic communities and speak out for them if we see any form of injustice or isolation being committed against them by the powerful or the majority group.
- Where we see ethnic tensions and conflict we must take the initiative as individuals, and corporately seek to promote and enhance peace, justice, forgiveness and reconciliation. We must make these values a priority.
- We must embody in our practices attitudes that celebrate diversity, encourage it, and affirm it. We as Christians must give hope, demonstrate wisdom in our word and actions so we do not endorse and support behaviors that do not support the cardinal tenets of the Gospel of Jesus Christ.
- We must encourage inter-marriages as a way of enhancing social and ethnic integration. This will require that we intentionally

create room for us to celebrate our cultural and ethnic diversities. They can become part of our quest for national integration, reconciliation, and social cohesion.

Dealing with ethnicity and ethnocentrism in Africa: some biblical values and principles

Both the Old Testament and the New Testament instruct us as to how to deal with people who are different from us. In the Old Testament, God instructs the Israelites to show justice, mercy and compassion to the aliens, foreigners, as well as become an example to the nations surrounding them in righteousness, and justice. The prophets, especially Isaiah points to the future inclusion of foreigners and other outcasts into the people of God (Isaiah 56:3–8). We must embrace all humanity irrespective of what ethnic group they come from. The Gospel does not know any ethnic boundaries.

The New Testament's dealings with Jews and Gentiles provide for the Christian Church a paradigm to address and respond to ethnic and racial division in our world today. Some basic principles we learn from the NT include:Respect for ethnic groups that are different from us in terms of values, customs, etc. This is not only something required of the individual. This is a corporate responsibility of the group to ensure that its members respect the other group (Rom. 9–11).

- Transcend ethnic divisions because of the work of Christ on the cross to redeem humanity. All human beings are precious and valuable before God. To mistreat people or isolate them due to ethnic prejudices is a "betrayal of the truth of the Gospel." Christ died to destroy the hostility that exists between ethnic groups. He has obliterated the distinction between human beings, class, gender, etc. (Gal. 2:11–21). The Church is "the sign of God's eschatological reconciliation of the world, and therefore a community in which there is no longer Jew or Greek, there is no

longer slave or free, there is no longer male or female; for all of you are one in Christ Jesus (Gal. 3:28)."[24]
- God's intension for humanity is to create one people of God. Through the cross, God creates one new community of God's people, and family by destroying the hostility that exists among ethnic groups that has been heightened by customs, laws, ordinances, and so forth. God has made peace between The Jews and Gentiles and reconciled them to become one. (Ephesians 2:11–22).
- The church is a community that breaks ethnic barriers, by carrying the gospel to the ends of the earth and bringing all of humanity under the fellowship of the Son, Jesus Christ. Christians are called to maintain the unity of humanity in the bond of peace. We are called to live in peace with all people. The New Testament expects the Church and Christians as individuals and as community to transcend racial and ethnic differences. If the Church fulfills its social and moral vision, it will have a powerful influence on society; if it fails to fulfill this social vision, it will betray the reality and the power of the gospel.
- In Christ, God was pleased to reconciles all things to Himself, whether things in heaven or things on earth by making peace through the blood of Christ (Col. 1:20). The Church cannot reject or scorn people of any race, tribe, and ethnic group, or tongue, whether they are Christians or not Christians. The Church has been the ministry of reconciliation and therefore they must embody this in their ministry and activities in the world.

Conclusion

In this chapter, we explore ethnicity with a specific aim to address negative ethnicity that has the tendency to isolate and exclude certain ethnic groups

---

[24] Richard B. Hays, *The Moral Vision of the New Testament: Community, Cross, New Creation, a Contemporary Introduction to New Testament Ethics.* San Francisco: HarperSanFrancsco, 1996, 440.

thus marginalizing them. We must reject this behavior, as it is morally wrong. To address this negative ethnicity and to ensure that all ethnic groups enjoy their God given rights and privileges, we have suggested some general as well as some specific biblical and theological grounds to deal with the issue of ethnocentrism. We think that rather than using ethnicity to isolate and disenfranchised one ethnic group against the other, we must celebrate our ethnic diversities, for in it we will find our lives enriched. We must all develop a will to give ourselves to others and welcome them—embrace them, by readjusting our identities to make space for them.[25]

---

25 Volf, *Exclusion and Embrace*, 29.

CHAPTER 12

Ecology and Care of Creation

"We need to promote development that does not destroy our environment."
(Wangari Maathai)

Introduction

The current "massive pollution, the ozone depletion, carbon emissions, global warming, habitat and species destruction, deforestation, soil erosion and all other ghastly effects of human depredation of our natural environment" around the world and in particular, Africa raises some serious ethical issues concerning human safety and wellbeing. How humanity has exploited creation over the years has begun to have a toll on creation's wellbeing. If we do not deal with this problem, humanity might destroy itself from the face of the earth. It is in light of this that I would like to look at ecology. How can we reverse this imbalance and threat to creation's wellbeing as well as that of humanity's wellbeing?

Since environmental issues are laden with questions of values, we will have to discuss some of the values that have contributed to this ecological malaise. These values raise certain ethical concerns for our subject. This chapter seeks to address these values and moral concerns they raise for the environmental crisis we find ourselves in today.

Given the deplorable environmental conditions we find ourselves in, there is need for a clear Christian moral vision for environmental or ecological stewardship. The ethical goal for this ecological stewardship is to promote justice and shalom for all of God's creation. Human beings have the mandate as bearers of God's image to protect and care for creation's wellbeing and not to become destroyers of God's creation. In this chapter, I will outline the crisis and provide some theological and biblical grounds for being good stewards of God's creation by caring and sustaining creations life and potency.

Defining ecology and environment

The word ecology comes from the Greek words *oikos*, which means "house" or "household," and *logia*, which means a "study of." Ecology is simply "the principle and practice of keeping the household of nature in order."[1] More technically, we can define ecology as "the scientific study of the relation of living organisms to their environments" or "the study of the detrimental effects of modern civilization on environment, with a view towards preservation or reversal through conservation."[2] It is important that we maintain this interdependence and interrelationship between the organism and their environments. Disrupting this balance can cause danger to either the organisms or the environment. The world's resources are finite and limited. We must ensure we do not deplete the resources without recreating or replenishing them.

The term environment refers to the surroundings of an object. In reference to our topic, the environment involves the "circumstances or conditions that surround one, or the surroundings of all living and non-living things in which they exist. We call this natural environment. Having defined our terms, I will now discuss the ecological crisis.

---

1 Henlee H. Barnette, *The Church and the Ecological Crisis*. Grand Rapids, MI: William B. Eerdmans Publishing Company, 1972, 12

2 http://en.wikipedia.org/wiki/Ecology. Accessed April 19, 2011.

The moral dilemma: the ecological crisis in Africa

Human values and the ecological crisis

The modern threat to nature or creation is referred to as an "ecological crisis."[3] The crisis has created a moral dilemma for humanity. As human civilization advances, and economic activities soar, the earth and its resources have been affected tremendously. Our humanistic values are the basic underlying factor for this ecological crisis. These values, greediness, consumerism, power, wealth, and control have shaped the way we have exploited and used creation to satisfy these human needs. This has resulted in environmental destruction and degradation that is threatening the well-being of both human and nonhuman creation in the world. The ecological crisis has become alarming over the decades and its effects and impact is being felt all over the world. In Africa, the crisis has reached life-threatening proportions. Many factors have contributed to this environmental or ecological crisis in Africa.

As I mentioned above our humanistic values are the fundamental cause for this ecological crisis. Our modern civilization, economic and industrial revolution and the need to create wealth by extracting the earth's resources have resulted in water pollution, air pollution, deforestation, desertification, soil erosion, droughts and floods which have affected the many African countries and have resulted in famine, diseases, and deaths. Some people have argued that the ecological crisis is a result of the anthropocentric philosophy of the west that sees humanity as the center of all created values "with the responsibility to exploit nature for his purposes and ends."[4] By arbitrarily using this authority and power, human beings have contributed to modern pollution and exploitation of nature to satisfy their greed and needs.

In addition to these, the west's dualistic view of reality that undermines and "discards the basic interconnectedness between human beings and

---

3 Sigurd Bergmann, *Creation Set Free: The Spirit as Liberator of Nature*. Trans. by Douglas Stott. Grand Rapids, MI: William B. Eerdmans Publishing Company, 2005, 19.
4 Henlee H. Barnette, *The Church and the Ecological Crisis*. Grand Rapids, MI: William B. Eerdmans Publishing Company, 1972, 27.

nature or between the spiritual and the material"⁵ is a contributing factor to the way creation is treated. The exclusion of the spiritual world as reality in western thought has resulted in the de-scralization of nature in many African countries. All the sacred places reserved in traditional African communities were taken and exploited by the colonial governments that ruled African nations.

Our economic activities have contributed to this ecological crisis. The cutting down of trees for charcoal, firewood, and building of houses and structures results in soil erosion which has polluted our water systems—rivers, lakes and sea. Other natural causes such as floods and bush fires have caused soil erosion and top soil destruction to our productive lands. Overgrazing our grasslands is resulting in deserts in many regions in Africa. Besides soil erosion, human and animal sewages, industrial wastes, mining wastes, pesticides, plastics, and fungicides are pollutants that affect our water systems.

Humanity's love for materialism has played a major role in the way we have exploited the resources of the earth to meet human greed. Some philosophers such as Locke and Smith have earlier said the natural world has no intrinsic value. Smith argues, "A thing has value only when and if it serves some direct human use ('value in use') or can be exchanged for something else that has value ('value in exchange')."⁶ These beliefs, attitudes, and convictions by philosophers and religious people lie at the root of the current environmental malaise.

Global warming and other climatic changes have caused long dry spells that have affected food production in many African nations. In addition to this crisis, the land has become infertile and cannot produce more food because it has lost its fertility through soil erosion, over cropping and overgrazing.

Furthermore, western advancement in technology through its industrial development has contributed to the exploitation of natural resource and the pollution of our air and environment. Manufacturing companies comes

---

5 Norman C. Habel & Peter Trudinger, eds. *Exploring Ecological Hermeneutics*. Atlanta: Society of Biblical Literature, 2008, vii.
6 See Bouma Prediger, *For the beauty of the earth*, 84.

with toxic wastes that are dumped into water systems, into rivers, and lakes that affect the source of drinking water for many people. These industrial wastes adversely affect the environment.

Air pollution is common in many African countries. With the growth of industries and mining, many pollutants such as carbon oxides, nitrogen oxides, sulfur oxides, carbon monoxides have polluted our air causing heart disease and breathing problems in many African countries. Exploitation of mineral resources has contributed to our environmental degradation. Coupled with these are the industrial wastes and garbage that fill most African cities. These gases have polluted the air, water and caused other life threatening diseases. Wars have degraded the environment, destroying land and vegetation using heavy weaponry and bombs. Vegetations have been destroyed resulting in polluted air, water, lakes, and rivers. These conditions in our world raise certain moral issues for the Church. The Church must respond to this ethical crisis, that is threatening the survival of the human race.

Population growth in Africa has contributed to the ecological crisis—land is stretched, large portions of forest areas have been cleared to accommodate the population growth. Obeng suggests three main causes of the ecological crisis in Africa as population growth that is outstripping the earth's finite resources, the depletion of the earth's resources, and the pollution, and sheer destruction and degradation of the environment.[7] Nonhuman creatures have been moved from their natural habitat, which often results in their extinction due to unfavorable conditions in which they find themselves. Over population in most African cities have resulted in slums where environmental degradation is deplorable. The unrestrained population growth in Africa has placed enormous strain on the fertility of our farmlands, coupled with the limited agricultural lands for farming, thus causing food shortages in many African nations.

Poverty, which is the result of poor governance, lack of good development and economic policies, unjust distribution of resources, unjust international

---

[7] Emmanuel Adow Obeng, "Healing the Groaning Creation in Africa," in *Theology of Reconstruction: Exploratory Essays* 2nd ed. Eds. Mary N. Getui and Emmanuel A. Obeng. Nairobi, Acton Publishers, 2003, 11.

trade and an imbalance in political power between the rich nations of the world and poor nations have contributed to the ecological crises. People have found ways of surviving by exploiting creation for their personal advancement and economic liberation. To achieve this economic progress, trees and forests are cut down and destroyed for commercial purposes as fuel and building materials. These forests hold some of the water catchment's reserves. The effects are obvious, the dry riverbeds we find in many Africa countries today.

Religious beliefs and the ecological crisis

There is a religious dimension to this ecological crisis facing our world today. This exploitative attitude is linked to Christian traditions that see humanity as a superior creature to other created things and has authority and power over creation. Some scholars argue that Christianity's teaching of dominion and subjugation of creation to humanity compound the current ecological crisis found in Genesis 1:27–28. Some consider this as a mandate for plundering the earth for all they can get from it.

Biblical scholars have been accused of the anthropocentric bias they bring to biblical texts. Most traditional interpreters see the status and role of human beings in the Genesis 1:27–28 text over the nonhuman creation. They argue, "Humanity is given priority in relation to God, to other living creatures, and the earth itself."[8] Humanity is given the mandate to have authority and dominion over the entire creation. Unlike the other nonhuman creatures, human beings are unique creatures, created in the "image of God." They have special place in creation, distinct from the others and have superior relationship with God. They are given the privilege to rule over all other living creatures, and they are instructed to "subdue the earth." Both Hebrew words "to rule" and "to subdue" carry the notion of "forceful exercise of power" over something. Habel points out that there is no suggestion of stewardship or care in these terms. Yet, he concludes,

---

8 Norman C. Habel & Peter Trudinger, eds. *Exploring Ecological Hermeneutics*. Atlanta: Society of Biblical Literature, 2008, 6.

"The presumption that humans are to subdue or conquer all of Earth is an arrogant anthropocentric attitude indeed."[9]

Many scholars will disagree with Habel on this point by seeing stewardship and care implied in the words in the way these words are used in the Old Testament. For example, Chris Wright observes that the words "to rule" and "to subdue" "entail benevolent care for the rest of creation as entrusted into human custodianship.[10] Wright sees the word "to rule" as a:

> Delegated form of God's own kingly authority over the whole of his creation. God places the human species as his image within creation, whose authority finally belongs to God as the creator and owner of the earth. How humanity exercises this rule must reflect the character and values of God's own kinship that is characterized by righteousness, "justice, mercy and true concern for the welfare of all.[11]

Human rule over creation must be an "exercise of kingship that reflects God's own kingship. Truly, humans were given some form of rule or authority over creation (Ps. 8:6–9), but this does not mean they can use that authority arbitrarily. What is the issue here is the extent of "the scope and manner of their rule." Bergant agrees with Wright when she writes:

> They [humanity] do not dominate the rest of creation because they are superior creatures, the pinnacle for which everything was made, that being items of which everything else is measured and toward which everything progresses to fulfillment. Instead, they are representatives of God, with royal jurisdiction over and royal responsibility for the territory of God's realm. 'The earth is the Lords!'[12]

---

9 Habel, *Ecological Hermeneutics*, 6.
10 Christopher Wright, *Old Testament Ethics*, 120.
11 Chris Wright, *Old Testament Ethics*, 121.
12 Dianne Bergant, *The Earth is the Lord's: The Bible, Ecology, and Worshi*Collegeville, MN: The Liturgical Press, 1998, 7–8.

Wright has rightly observed that "The image of God is not a license for abuse based on arrogant supremacy, but a pattern that commits us to humble reflection on the character of God."[13] He is the one who cares and sustains his creation.

So, Genesis must be read together with other biblical texts. We suggest that rather than seeing humanity as over creation, dominating and subduing creation, humanity must see herself as part and parcel of the earth from which all other created beings came from and are related to. Adam, the first human was himself taken from the earth with the breath of God in him. We find God's breath in all living beings within creation. Humanity's uniqueness is found in our being created in the image of God and the command to rule the earth, fish, and animals. Humans are also dependent on the earth for their growth and sustenance. This "identification" with the earth and our dependence on it for survival should change the attitude of domination and rule to that of humility and co-dependency on creation for our wellbeing.

Secondly, others have claimed Christianity's view of the future of the present world is not a positive one. Christianity sees the present creation marked for destruction. God will destroy the earth at the coming of Jesus Christ to establish his kingdom. This has killed motivation to care for a world that is going to be destroyed eventually (2 Pet. 3:10, Matt. 24; 36–44). Again, we must point out that the restoration of creation and its redemption is part of God's overall redemptive work to reconcile the whole of creation to Himself. We are not to seek the pleasures, and the values the world offers. These things will be destroyed. These scriptures do not teach we should not care for creation.

To end this section, it is important to state that the real reason for our environmental crisis in Africa and the world at large is a result of human sinfulness. Human sin in many ways affected the earth and the environment we live in. The effects of sin on human life are worked out in the broken relationships we have with God, with one another and with creation in general (Gen. 3:1–19). This, more importantly, is reflected in our selfish

---

13 Chris Wright, *Old Testament Ethics*, 121.

and greedy tendencies we share as human beings. Our consumerism values and the desire to consume more and so produce more without caring much for the devastating effects we are creating on the environment. Humanity is always dissatisfied with what we have. We always want more. Paul speaks about contentment. Godliness with contentment is great gain (1Tim. 6:6). Therefore, consumerism is a spiritual sin. It has more implication for our lives as humans. We need to overcome it and learn how to live moderately and wisely use the earth's resources, so we can deal with the healing, restoration, and health of our Earth.

How then can we describe our current ecological crisis? The current state of our world is captured by Paul's statement in Romans 8:19–23:

> For all creation is waiting eagerly for that future day when God will reveal who his children really are. Against his will, everything on earth was subjected to God's curse. All creation anticipates the day when it will join God's children in glorious freedom from death and decay. For we know that all creation has been groaning as in the pains of childbirth right up to the present time. Moreover, even us Christians, although we have the Holy Spirit within us as a foretaste of future glory groan to be released from pain and suffering. We, too, wait anxiously for that day when God will give us our full rights as his children, including the new bodies he has promised us (NLT).

Creation is groaning not only under God's judgment, but also under humanity's manipulation and exploitation. Human beings have compounded creation's ordeal by the way we are raping and destroying it. We must stop this evil before it destroys us. How can we relieve creation from its groaning? We will turn our attention to this question now.

Responding to the ecological and environmental crises

In this section, we will explore the different ways both the West and Africans are using to address this ecological malaise. First, we will explore what we can learn from African societies and how they relate with creation.

How did Africans maintain an ecological balance and relate with nature? The traditional Africans' attitude to nature might have an answer for our ecological mess and point the way forward as to how we can deal with and care for creation and our environment today. Then we will look at some of the ways the West has tried to deal with the problem from western philosophical, cultural, and ethical perspectives. In addition to these approaches we will finally examine the theological and biblical models for ecological and creation care.

African cultural, religious, and moral values shaped their ethics for creation care

The solidarity of all life with creation

Some fundamental core values gave shape to the Africans' attitude and behavior toward creation. Central to this value is relationship. This value is expressed in the African's concept of "universal oneness," or the 'bondedness of life"[14] or "interdependence" or "interconnectedness" of all living things to each other. This interconnectedness is expressed by the "vitalism" of life that pervades all living things—nature. This is popularly called "vital force."

Nature plays a vital role in the African's life and in his growth process. It provides all that humanity needs for his growth and survival. Africans see themselves as bonded to creation or nature. Sindima puts it this way: "nature and persons are one, woven by creation into one texture or fabric of life, a fabric, or web characterized by interdependence between all creatures."[15] This sense of interconnectedness solicits a kind of attitude towards creation where the African identifies with it and sees his life bond with it. Therefore, what results from this identification with nature is respect and awe for creation. All living beings share solidarity with each other, thus we must

---

14 Harvey Sindima, "Community of Life: Ecological Theology in African Perspective," in *Liberating Life: Contemporary Approaches to Ecological Theology*, eds. Charles Birch, William Eaken, and Jay B. McDaniel. Maryknoll: Orbis Books, 1990, 138.
15 Sindima, "Community of Life," 143.

seek the well-being of all to maintain the ontological balance needed for humanity to prosper and do well.

Creation and all life are sacred

Africans believe God is the source of all life, as the creator of the world. Life is given to both humans and creation and it is the duty of all human beings to preserve life; that consists of both living and non-living. Africans hold the view there is a close relationship between people and the non-human creation. This relationship is very important for human survival. This African view contrasts the view held by many Christians who see the world in a dualistic fashion. Christians often ignore the significance of the body and the material world. Some see it as evil and temporal. Instead, much attention is given to the spiritual and immaterial world; one that is more permanent called heaven. Our desire to be in heaven often affects our appreciation for the present world. God's power and glory is revealed in creation or nature and this is expressed in the beauty we find in creation, which is made of trees, rivers, mountains, rocks, forests, animals, and birds.

Some of these non-human forms of creation especially the higher animal species such as the lion, leopard, elephant, buffalo, deer, and certain tree species, rivers, forests, mountains are seen by Africans as sacred and are viewed with awe and reverence. Some of these animals were considered as clan totems. The members of these clans could not eat these animals or kill them. In this way, most of the animals in African societies were preserved and conserved. The same applied to rivers, mountains, forests, trees, and so forth. The people did not eat the produce of these sacred objects. No pollution was allowed in these designated places. They preserve their purity. The understanding of creation as sacred made the African care for and respect creation. This sense of sacredness of creation put enormous responsibility on individuals as well as communities to respect the sacred objects, species, and spaces within the community.

Generally, Africans related in a dynamic way to nature because nature is not impersonal object, it is filled with religious significance;[16] Forests,

---

16 John Mbiti, *African Religions and Philosophy*. New York: Doubleday, 1970, 73.

rivers, mountains, rocks, trees, animals, etc. all have vital life, which is sacred and must be respected by all. Africans know that their lives, survival, and wellbeing depend on their proper relation to their environment. The need to uphold the ontological balance between creation and humanity is critical for their survival.

There is an enduring interdependence between human persons and the cosmos or the non-human creation in African thought. Africans believed God is creator of all nature. Whoever treats nature with contempt treats God with contempt. Bujo expresses the African thought this way:

> God penetrates all his creatures with his presence. Therefore, we must not treat any of his creatures (any element, plant, or animal) recklessly but deal with them in a sensitive manner, with empathy and reverence. Whoever commits a fault against a creature, commits a fault against God, the Creator himself.[17]

Nature has its own character and being. This attitude of Africans helped them to conserve natural resources and declare certain places as sacred and a no go zone for members of the community. The colonial governments that colonized African nations misunderstood this method of preservation and conservation. These powerful lords destroyed these forest reservations, water catchment areas, mountains and trees with impunity. They desecrated and de-sacralized these places with their machines and bulldozers. With time, Africans lost this sensitivity to the sacredness of nature and have exploited it for their own evil and greedy purposes as the colonial lords did. Most of them enriched themselves by exploiting nature; thus following the footsteps of their colonizers. Since we live in a global village, Africans have been affected by western dualistic, technological, and industrial advancement, which has resulted in the wanton destruction of nature in Africa by both Africans and their western counterparts.

---

17 Benezet Bujo, *The Ethical Dimension of Community: The African Model and the Dialogue Between North and South.* Nairobi: Paulines Publications, 1998, 215.

We need to restore and instill the value of maintaining the ecological balance that should exist between human beings and nature. Failure to do so would be catastrophic for human life. We must teach our children and the present generation to have reverence for nature, not to worship it, but to care for it and help sustain it for our own survival. The earth was seen as sacred and human life depended on it. Therefore, nature was respected and revered. We must recapture this sensibility of human dependence on creation.

Western ethical approaches to creation care

Eco-justice approaches to environmental ethics

The proponents of the eco-justice approach to creation or environmental ethics have argued from the perspective of creation having its own integrity and value that must be respected by humanity. The phrase "integrity of creation" is defined by Birch as "The value of all creatures in and for themselves, for one another, and for God, and their interconnectedness in a diverse whole that has unique value for God."[18]

Some environmentalists see the value of creation in its usefulness to humanity. This is often referred to as the "instrumental value of creation." Other environmentalists see creation having its own value independent of its value to humanity. This is called the "intrinsic value of creation." We agree with Carmody who says, nature does not simply exist for humanity's good pleasure. Nature has its own value and integrity. It is "the mystery of nature's being, the Christology of nature's intelligibility, the occurrence of nature in God, and nature's impersonal revelations of God all argue that nature has a right to be, a right to live, a right to flourish apart from its utilities to human beings."[19]

---

18 Charles Birch, William Eakin and Jay B. McDaniel, eds., *Liberating Life*. Maryknoll: Orbis Books, 1990, 15–16.
19 John Carmody, *Ecology and Religion: Towards a New Christian Theology of Nature*. New York: Paulist Press, 1983, 133.

The significance of Carmody's statement is its ethical implication. Nature has the right to exist, live, and flourish. Creation has an "intrinsic worth and value."[20] We must respect creation's worth and value.

The term, integrity of creation, also refers to the principle of interrelatedness of all created forms to each other. The concept of interconnectedness of human beings with the nonhuman creation is a very important truth we must affirm and ensure we instill and share this with all people. Human life entirely depends on creation. If we destroy creation, we are eventually destroying human life on earth. Equally, the life and the survival of nonhuman creation depend on human beings. This interdependence must be guarded so there is mutual benefit derived by both human beings and nonhuman creatures. Humanity has the responsibility to respect the integrity, right, and dignity of creation. The importance of humanity's dependence on creation is truly captured by Gnanakan, who says "Creation can survive without humans; *we* cannot last long without drawing from some of creation's bounties!"[21] Indeed, humanity cannot survive without creation. This must change our attitude to creation and to how we interact with it.

Each of the views expressed above can solicit a particular behavior and attitude towards creation. Those who view creation as having instrumental value, that is, creation has value only in as far as it serves human needs will tend to exploit creation for human good. We think this view or position stands in opposition to the teachings of scripture. The Bible offers a different perspective on the value of creation. In our view, the Bible affirms the intrinsic value of creation. Therefore, we support the view that sees creation having its own value independent of its usefulness to humanity. Creation's value is not dependent on its usefulness to meet human needs. The value of creation is divinely given. In the Genesis creation narratives, God proclaimed his entire creation—nonhuman creation as good, long

---

[20] Norman C. Habel & Peter Trudinger, eds. *Exploring Ecological Hermeneutics*. Atlanta: Society of Biblical Literature, 2008, 2.

[21] Ken Gnanakan, *Responsible Stewardship of God's Creation*. World Evangelical Alliance—Theological Commission, 2004, 31.

before human beings were created (Gen. 1 and 2). Creation has its own value because God declared it so!

The eco-justice proponents have formulated six eco-justice principles for creation care, which we believe, are helpful for our discussion. We will end this section with these six principles:[22]

- The principle of intrinsic worth: The universe, Earth and its components have intrinsic worth/value.
- The principle of interconnectedness: Earth is a community of interconnected living things that are mutually dependent on each other for life and survival.
- The principle of voice: Earth is a subject capable of raising its voice in celebration and against injustice.
- The principle of purpose: The universe, Earth and all its components are part of a dynamic cosmic design within which each piece has a place in the overall goal of that design.
- The principle of mutual custodianship: Earth is a balanced and diverse domain where responsible custodians can function as partners with, rather than rule over, Earth to sustain its balance and diverse Earth community
- The principle of resistance: Earth and its components not only suffer from human injustices but also actively resist them in the struggle for justice.

We must point out the significance of these eco-justice principles. These principles have roots in biblical teaching. More interestingly, we find a lot of commonality between the eco-justice principles and the ideas that undergird the African approach to creation care. These include the interconnectedness and solidarity of humanity with creation; with creation having its own life and purpose and the need to maintain the ecological balance and harmony between nature and humanity by respecting and acknowledging the awe, and wonder of creation. The idea that humanity depends on creation and that humanity's life and wellbeing is tied to that

---

22 Norman C. Habel and Peter Trudinger, eds., *Exploring Ecological Hermeneutics.* Atlanta, Society of Biblical Literature, 2008, 2.

of creation is important. Whatever affects creation affects human life, and what affects human life affects creation. Human life is intrinsically bound with creation. We need to recover the sacramental nature of creation. We need to encourage and recover these values and attitudes to nature that will instill some sense of awe and appreciation for God and his creation.

Creation has a higher purpose than just meeting human needs. Creation reveals God's power, wisdom, and glory. Creation serves as witness to God's goodness. After the flood in Genesis 9, we see God making a covenant with Noah, the earth, and every living creature in it. As we see, the earth was not created for human use. The earth was created by God for Himself. The book of Colossians speaking of the Creator says, all things were "created by him and for him" (Col. 1:15, 17). The earth is the Lord's!

Many see this as a new way of revering some traditional values which our western anthropological perspectives that placed humanity at the center of the universe and often misunderstood human "authority and dominion" over creation as a license for creation's exploitation. Through the eco-justice principles, humanity is forced to accept responsibility for creation care because it belongs to God and it is for God. Bergant suggests two traditional virtues that such a view of creation creates. The first is humility. Citing Job's discovery about his own limitations as human to understanding the wonder and mysteries of creation, Job discover the awesomeness of God's creation. He admitted the intrinsic value in creation. He greatly admired the wonderful truth he discovered about God's creation. He became humbled (Job 38–41).[23] The second value Bergant talks about is respect for creation. Humility will lead to respect for God's creation. The biblical writers show awe and respect for creation. This is mostly highlighted in the Psalms (Ps. 19:2–7, 89:6, 96:11–13; 148:1–13) by the psalmists.

In summary, from our discussions so far, we need to develop certain virtues and values that will help us address our ecological malaise. These values include the recognition of our interdependence and interconnectedness with creation. We must recognize creation's value and worth that should invoke awe and respect for creation.

---

23 Bergant, *The Earth is the Lord's*, 16–19.

How should Christians deal with the environmental and ecological crisis we find ourselves in today? Since the Bible is the source for our faith and practice, what are the biblical and theological foundations for our moral obligation to care for creation? I will explore each of this below.

Creation care: theological and biblical grounds

Theological grounds

The Triune God; Father, Son and Holy Spirit created the universe, heaven, earth and all that is in them (Gen. 1:1–2; John 1:1–3.). Creation testifies to God's power, wisdom, and glory (Ps. 19). The Scriptures attest to God's ownership of all creation. In Psalm 24:1, the Psalmist states clearly, "the earth is the LORD's, and everything in it. The world and all its people belong to him" (NLT). Similarly, Deuteronomy 10:14 reiterates the same idea: "The highest heavens and the earth and everything in it belong to the LORD your God" (NLT). These two scriptures and many more affirm that God is the creator and owner of the world. God is the owner of the earth because "he laid the earth's foundation on the seas and built it on the ocean depths" (Ps. 24:2, NLT).

Consequently, both human beings and the nonhuman creation belong to God because he created them. As Creator of all things, he rules overall and he desires our worship and adoration from all of his creation, those in heaven, and those on earth. There are two implications for this affirmation that that God is the sole owner of creation. First, Creation belongs to God. Second, if humans have any claims to creation, it is that God has given it to them as stewards to care for it. How do the implications of this affirmation shape our behavior and moral obligation to the care of creation? I will discuss the moral duty we have towards creation below.

We see in the Genesis 1 and 2 narratives about God's testimony about his creation. After creating the nonhuman creation and finally human beings, God declared his creation as very good. The goodness of creation reflects God's character and being as a good God. Creation, therefore, received an intrinsic goodness, worth and value which derives from God's own being, though creation is distinct from God. Anybody who "destroys or degrades the earth dirties its reflection of its Maker (because the earth is part of the creation that bears the mark of God's own goodness)."[24] We have insisted in this work that Christians must reflect the character and nature of God and our actions are derived from his own actions. God created a good world, so we cannot make it bad by destroying it. God values the creation and so must we!

If our actions are dependent on God's actions, we must ask the question: How is the triune God related to creation? In what ways has God cared for and sustained creation? The triune God's care for creation by sustaining, renewing and refreshing the face of the earth will become the foundation for our own ethical mandate to care and refresh the earth.

The creation narrative in Genesis 2:4–17 demonstrate God's care for creation. God cared for the earth by watering it with water from the ground. God also planted a garden and watered this garden, to care for it. He placed the human beings He created in his image in the garden with the charge to care and tend it. As he has cared for and tended the garden, He instructs the first human parent to tend and care for the garden (Gen. 2:15). We suggest that Genesis 1:27–28 (cf. Ps. 8:6–8) must be read together with Genesis 2:15. God sustains and loves his creation and he cares for it. He gives water and food to all creatures (Ps. 104, Acts 14:17). God expects humanity to take care of creation, nurture and tend it. That was the mandate he gave the first humans, because He is a good gardener who takes good care of his garden. He expects us to do well in taking care of creation just as He does!

In the creation account, we see God providing for humanity a good environment. God's creation in Genesis is described as very good. We know human sin affected this good creation and subjected it under a curse, and bondage (Gen. 3:17, Rom. 8:20–21). The harmony that existed between the human and nonhuman creation was destroyed. The earth and the nonhuman creation became hostile to human beings. However, through the death of Jesus Christ on the cross, God reconciled both his human and nonhuman creation to Himself (Rom. 5:10–11, 15–21; 2 Cor.

---

24 Chris Wright, *Old Testament Ethics*, 107.

5:17–21; Eph. 2:14–17, Col. 1:19–22; Rom. 8:19–23). Through the death of Christians on the cross with Christ, God has restored the harmony that existed between humanity and the nonhuman creation before sin entered the world. God required then from the first human creatures to be responsible stewards of the earth. Now, he requires the same responsible stewardship from humanity today towards creation and not wanton destruction of creation because he has restored and reconciled all things to himself.

The psalmist in Psalm 65:9–13, clearly says this of God as the creator and as the one who cares for creation and sustains the earth:

> You take care of the earth and water it, making it rich and fertile. The rivers of God will not run dry; they provide a bountiful harvest of grain, for you have ordered it so. You drench the plowed ground with rain, melting the clods and leveling the ridges. You soften the earth with showers and bless its abundant crops. You crown the year with a bountiful harvest; even the hard pathways overflow with abundance. The wilderness becomes a lush pasture, and the hillsides blossom with joy. The meadows are clothed with flocks of sheep, and the valleys are carpeted with grain. They all shout and sing for joy! (NLT)

The writer of Hebrews in the New Testament affirms Jesus Christ too, as the sustainer of all things by the power of his word (Heb. 1:1-3a). The New Testament writers linked Christ to creation as both creator and sustainer of the universe or world. Apostle Paul in Colossians asserts that Christ is co-creator and sustainer of creation with God and all of creation is for Him:

> Christ is the visible image of the invisible God. He existed before God made anything at all and is supreme over all creation. Christ is the one through whom God created everything in heaven and on earth. He made the things we can see and the things we cannot see—kings, kingdoms, rulers, and authorities. Everything has been *created through him* and

for him. He existed before everything else began, and he *holds all creation together* (Col. 1:15–17, NLT).[25]

Scripture teaches creation is the work of the Triune God. Like, the Father and the Son, the Spirit is also actively involved with creation and the preservation and renewal of the same. The Spirit of God gives life to the entire creation. The Psalmist attests to the Spirit's activity in creation. In Psalm 104:30, the Spirit is the agent of creation and the one who renews the face of the earth. All things are created through the Spirit. This reiterates the Spirit's involvement with creation in Genesis 1 and 2. The Spirit was the creative power behind all of creation.

We see from the above texts, God did not just create the earth and the heavens, he also sustains and upholds and cares for its wellbeing. God takes care of the earth so it can sustain and maintain human life and nonhuman creatures as well. We as human beings must have the same caring attitude toward the earth as God does.

Although God is above creation, because he is the creator, yet, he has always sustained and upheld creation by his word and power. He nurtures creation and provides for its wellbeing. He lovingly provides rain to water the earth; streams from mountains; provides and cares for nonliving creatures such as animals, birds, takes care of trees; pastures to grow and so many things he does to sustain his creation (Ps. 104:1–34). He cares for all his creation. He knows all his creatures (Ps. 36:6; 50:9–12). Our mandate to care for creation is based on God's own care for creation. God loves, cares, keeps, nurtures, and sustains human beings and his creation. We must also love, care, keep, nurture, and sustain creation. We will later suggest some practical ways of doing this. We should care for the land as God cares and watches over it (Deut. 11:11–12).

Creation proclaims God's love for the world. It proclaims God's glory and majesty. Creation's voice is heard throughout the earth (Ps. 19:1). God, the creator of heaven and earth cares for his entire creation consisting of human and non-human creation. We see this care in God's cosmic plan

---

25 The emphasis is mine.

of restoration and salvation that includes both human beings and non-human creation. Apostle Paul speaks of creations freedom and redemption from decay and groaning at the appearing of Christ (Rom. 8:21). Christ will restore the earth. God is the sustainer and reconciler of all things to himself—all of creation is restored to him through Christ. We must follow the triune God's example and actions. We must live in peace and harmony with all of creation.

Our ecological and moral mandate for creation care is grounded on the theological insights that God is the creator and owner of the world and that we are required to be faithful stewards of God's creation. This truth must engender humility and thoughtful care of God's creation. Bouma-Prediger is right is saying, "Authentic Christian faith requires ecological obedience. To care for the earth is integral to Christian faith."[26] We cannot claim to be children of God and not care about the things God cares about!

Biblical grounds for the theological affirmation

The second ground for creation care is based on the affirmation that creation is God's gift to humanity. Humans are stewards of this gift of creation that God has given to them. Psalm 115:16 says, "The heavens belong to the Lord, but he has given the earth to all humanity." Creation reveals God's goodness and loving kindness to humanity. This privilege of the earth given to humanity is grounded on the goodness of God, who is the maker of heaven and earth (Ps. 115:15). A steward is one who takes care of something on behalf of someone else. Since God is the owner of creation, we cannot use it as we wish. Jenkins is right to say, "Stewardship frames environmental problems within God's call to faithful relationship."[27] Humanity has the responsibility to keep, and faithfully care for the earth as God himself cares for it. Humanity's wellbeing is tied to the wellbeing of the earth.

---

26 Steven Bouma-Prediger, *For the beauty of the earth: a christian vision for creation care*. Grand Rapids, MI: Baker Academic, 2001, 14.
27 Willis Jenkins, *Ecologies of Grace: Environmental Ethics and Christian Theology*. New York: Oxford University Press, 2008, 153.

In Genesis 2, God gives humanity the responsibility to care for the garden he has planted. It can be said that this was God's intention for humanity to take care of creation. In the Torah, we find God reiterating his claim to the land as His, yet giving the responsibility to the people to care for it and preserve it for posterity. Humanity, created in the image of God, was given the privilege to be co-creators with God; to share responsibility with God in maintaining and preserving God's creation by caring for its wellbeing. Christians are stewards of God's creation. Christians in particular and humanity in general are to be good stewards of God's world. We cannot be complacent in our responsibility in caring for the environment. Unfortunately, often times it is Christians who pollute our environment rather than caring for creation and nurturing it.

Humanity was given the stewardship of creation and therefore, they must care for and preserve creation. "Dominion" theology of creation must be challenged. Rather, creation care and preservation of creation is Christ's mandate, He upholds all creation by his power and word. However, we share is this noble responsibility to do our part as we were mandated by God in Genesis 1:27–28 to care for creation. Christians cannot exploit creation for their selfish and greedy desires. We must respect the sacredness of nature and life. For human life is intrinsically bound to nature.

Some of the practical ways God provided for earth care is through the Sabbath laws. The Sabbath laws allowed the land to rest after seven years of continuous cultivation so it could replenish its fertility and potency. God gives instructions on environmental cleanliness concerning how we must dispose of human wastes. The question some may ask is whether such an approach of giving land a Sabbath is practical in our contemporary situation? The fact of the matter is whether we want to obey God's laws and trust that he is right in what he commands us to do. What is the fact? It is a fact that the current way in which we have overused the land has not been beneficial. The land is not producing the same amount of food it did produce, say, ten years ago. The reality is that each year's production from the land is much less that of the previous year. The land needs justice and rest. The law of God requires justice for land. We are to seek justice for all of creation. Human beings violate Justice for the earth.

In many African nations because of the scarcity of land, people farm on the same land for decades. The land is not yielding much food because its fertility is overstretched. The land is producing less and less each year even though we are using material such as fertilizer to boost production. These chemicals are becoming a health hazard. The land is damaged. African farmers need to learn from God and allow their lands to fallow so the land can regain its fertility and produce more food. Laws that respect the sanctity of creation—use of land, nurturing and caring for the environment, exploitation of natural resources—are based on wrong a theology of dominion. Our earth and the nonhuman creatures on it are crying for justice (Amos 4:13, 5:8–9, 9:5–6, Hosea 4:3, Amos 1:2, Jer. 12:10–11, Isa. 34).

Scripture does not sanction the exploitation and degradation of creation. Rather, Scripture holds a positive view of creation where God himself takes the role of caring for creation even in the new creation (Rev. 22:1–2). Jesus' teaching in the New Testament affirms God's care for all creation even the parts we think are insignificant. He cares for the sparrows and the lilies of the field (Matt. 6:26, 28, 29).

In ending this section, we would like to suggest McGrath's four basic principles from the creation narratives in Genesis as grounds for responsible stewardship of creation care.[28]

- The "Earth-keeping principle:" just as the Creator keeps and sustains humanity, so humanity must keep and sustain the creator's creation.
- The "Sabbath principle:" creation must be allowed to recover from human use of its resources.
- The Fruitfulness principle:" the fecundity of creation is to be enjoyed, not destroyed.
- The "fulfillment and limits principle:" there are limits set to humanity's role within creation, with boundaries set in place, which must be respected.

---

28 Alister E. McGrath, "The stewardship of creation: an evangelical affirmation" in *The Care of Creation: Focusing concern and action*, ed. R. J. Berry. Leicester: Inter-Varsity Press, 2000, 87.

Our stewardship responsibility to creation's care would be effective if we apply these four creation principles. Our care for creation and stewardship must pattern after God's own act of caring, sustaining, liberating, and redeeming all creatures. We must imitate the creative, redeeming, and reconciling God. As stewards, we must be faithful to the one who has entrusted the care of the earth to us, God.

Humans and creation restored and reconciled

We made the case that our current environmental crisis is a result of our sinfulness as human beings. If this is the case then, the solution to this problem is primarily a spiritual one. Humanity must overcome the estrangement sin brought between humanity and creation. The creator and redeemer, Jesus Christ, only make this possible. The Triune God, through the death of Jesus Christ has reconciled to himself all things: things in heaven, on earth and under the earth (Col. 1:19–20). God has restored our relationship with creation. Like humanity, creation is eagerly awaiting its complete restoration (Rom. 8:19–22). We should embrace creation and treat creation with love and respect.

If God is eager to redeem and reconcile creation, as he is eager to reconcile humanity to himself, then we as humans must have the same passion God has towards creation. Our ministry as reconcilers must include that of reconciling creation with humanity and human beings to God and to one another (2 Cor. 5:17–19). Christians who are in relationship with the creator and redeemer of the whole of creation must concern themselves with what God is concerned with, his work to reconcile the whole of creation to himself.

We must constantly remind ourselves that creation was not primarily made for human beings it was made for Christ.[29] God's purpose for creation is to redeem and restore creation—both human and nonhuman—so it can fulfill its purpose. Therefore, through Christ's death on the cross God

---

[29] Edward R. Brown, *Our Father's World: Mobilizing the Church to Care for Creation.* Downers Grove, IL: IVP Books, 46.

had reconciled creation to Himself; namely both human beings and non-human creation. At the coming of Christ, creation will be restored fully together with humanity so we can enjoy God's blessings forever.

The goal of creation is for it to glorify God and worship Him. God created the world for relationship, for both human and non-human creatures to honor and worship him. We see this in the book of Revelation where we have both humanity and the living creatures all surrounding the throne of God worshiping their creator and redeemer. (Rev. 4:6–11, 5:6–14, 7:9–12). In addition, in the New Creation, we see the earth playing a crucial role in enriching human wellbeing. The earth will continue to be the dwelling place of human beings with God being in the midst of them. Heaven will join with the earth. "'The 'river of the water of life' will flow from God's throne and 'the tree of life' will grow besides it, and the 'leaves of the tree are for the healing for the nations'" (Rev. 22:2).[30] Johnson makes an important observation. Nature will not be done away with. "Rather, it is restored into intimate relation with God and human beings through the river of the water of life and the tree of life."[31]

God created the earth and the heaven and humanity share the earth and the seas with other created beings. All creatures are therefore dependent on the earth and its resources for their wellbeing and survival. We must respect this interrelationship of creatures on the earth. God also made an everlasting and unconditional covenant with the whole of creation including human beings and his non-human creation after the flood (Gen. 6:9–17). Relationship is vital for our ecological vision. Both humans and the nonhuman creation of God are to bring worship and praise to God. The Psalmist shows how the whole of creation does this—the rivers, mountains; trees—all bring praise to God. We must celebrate this mutuality and interconnectedness with creation and foster this interdependence the well-being of both human beings and the nonhuman creation. We must give creation the opportunity to bring honor and praise to God's name by treating it right—that is by preserving its beauty and sacredness.

---

30 Carol Johnson, *And the Leaves of the Tree are for the Healing of the Nations: Biblical and Theological Foundations for Eco-Justice*, no date, no Publisher, 31.
31 Carol Johnson, *And the Leaves of the Tree are for the Healing of the Nations*, 31.

Creation care: Some practical principles

We all have some moral obligation to take care of creation because our very lives depend on how we treat creation. Therefore, our responsibility to care for creation is at three levels: individually, community and at the national level.

The individual level

- As an individual, I must intentionally take practical steps to ensure the environment where I live is clean. I must take interest in what goes on around me. Be aware of where I am or live. Know my surroundings well. Most Africans do not know their surroundings very well or rather we care little for our surroundings. We need to overcome this ecological illiteracy. We must develop ourselves to become ecologically literate. This involves, according to Orr, "knowing, caring, and practical competence."[32] Knowing our environment is not enough, we must care. Not only must we care, but we must also act responsibly based on the knowledge and passion we have. We must learn some practical skills to make our environment become more beautiful and habitable.
- I must develop sensibilities and values that enhance mutuality and my interdependence on creation and do all I can to enhance this interdependence. We can engage in practices that can restore some of our depleted resources by engaging in tree planting, cleaning our communities and other practical things we can do to create awareness for people to care for their environment. This can be both an individual and a community activity. Some practical things like recycling used bottles, cans, and paper can help build certain attitudes toward creation care.

---

32 See Bouma-Prediger, *For the beauty of the earth*, 22.

The community level
- Create awareness of the importance of caring for the earth and the danger of not doing so. Human survival is dependent on how we treat and care for creation. This creating of awareness must happen at the personal or individual level as well as at a corporate or community level. We must be aware and show concern for our living environment. Our environment will affect the quality of our lives. Therefore, at the community level we should seek to have a clean environment. We must take good care of our immediate environment wherever that may be. For example, where we have unclean neighborhoods, we can organize a community—cleaning day to clean our environment. We can plant trees in our neighborhoods and ensure a clean environment that is pleasing to the eye.

The national level
- We should have clear environmental policies and develop laws that deal with environment degradation and deal with those who despise creation and abuse it. Our governments should take serious interest in issues related to ecology and develop national policies that will protect the environment from the exploitation of those who seek to develop infrastructure and other facilities to ensure they do not contribute to the destruction of creation.
- We must examine some of the historical, political, economic, social, and religious forces that have shaped our world and the way we view the earth and our environment and change our attitudes and behavior toward creation bearing in mind some of the principles we have enlisted in this chapter. Some of these activities should include.
- Conservation or preservation—We care for what we love. What we love we try as much as possible to protect, preserve, and even will it to posterity. Based on our love for God and his creation, we must make firm commitments as Christians in particular and humanity in general, to preserve and conserve nature by caring

for it. This will involve the restoration of the forest we have destroyed, and cleaning the rivers and water resources we have by stopping the pollution of these resources. We must replenish our renewable resources such as forests. We must also change or renew our minds and attitude towards nature. Humanity's life and survival depends on how we preserve and care for our environment.

- We must respect animal rights, develop policies to conserve and protect our animal species from human exploitation, and from extinction; protect the rights of our future generation by bequeathing to them a good creation to sustain their lives and that of their children. We must also develop the use of land and land policies that are grounded on biblical principles and not on modern humanistic and utilitarian ethical values.
- Education is critical. We must teach people about conservation and preservation techniques that will help enhance and replenish the destructive tendencies of people concerning creation. For example, we must encourage and promote tree planting, cleaning of environment, water, rivers, etc., good sanitation by encouraging and ensuring the proper disposal of human and industrial wastes. We must have curriculum developed to teach environmental care in our schools and universities. In addition, we must make this environmental course foundational for all students.
- We must deal with greed and address our sinful nature of consumerism. Exploiting nature and the earth's resources to meet our insatiable desires can be detrimental to the life of the earth. Humanity is called to preserve and nurture life and not to destroy it. This attitude of greed is already having a toll on human life. We see it in the injustices that are rampant in all human societies in forms of economic exploitation and unfair and unjust social systems that have threatened the lives of many marginalized people.

- Avoid wasteful use of our natural resources. As we pointed out the world's resources are limited. Wanton use of these resources cannot be replenished. We must learn to use the resources of the earth responsibly.

Church and pastoral level

Edward Brown suggests five ways we can mobilized the Church to care for creation:[33]

- We need a form of worship that will help us to develop a sense of appreciation for the wonder, awe, and beauty of creation. Such worship must create or result in a passion and love to care for God's good creation. This can be facilitated by our liturgy. Our liturgy must emphasize the importance of creation in our worship. For example, water for baptism; oil for anointing and healing; bread and wine for the Eucharist or Holy Communion; the lights and colors, the voice and instruments, the smell of incense, wax and fire all of which are so much a part of liturgical celebration, and are also elements of creation.[34]
- Our teaching and preaching should build on the interconnectedness of humanity to creation and the comprehensive nature of God's redemption for the whole of creation and our part in this plan.
- We must determine to instill these values, the awe, wonder, respect and love of creation in our children's lives and point them to the God in whose creation they live.
- We must educate our communities about the importance of caring for the world in which we live to promote our wellbeing.
- We must make sure that our *missional outreach programs* incorporates creation-care teaching and earth-healing ministry within traditional church planting and evangelism.
- Appreciate creation as the source for your sustenance.

---

33 Edward R. Brown, *Our Father's World: Mobilizing the Church to Care for Creation.* Downers Grove, IL: IVP Books, 2006, 103.
34 Bergant, *The Earth is the Lord's*, 55.

- Stewardship—we must use resources with caution and modesty, restore and replenish the diminishing species and life forms, serve, keep and entrust the care of Creation to the next generation of humanity. We must prevent overuse and misuse of the earth's resources. Proper care must be taken to ensure we replenish those resources that can be replaced when used. We should encourage recycling of paper, bottles, plastics, etc.

Conclusion

Our moral responsibility and mandate to care for creation cannot be excluded from our Christian calling. The concern and care for creation must be a central feature of Christian discipleship. Care for creation is an integral part of what it means to be Jesus' disciple and to live in God's world. Caring for the earth is integral part of authentic discipleship. The Christian community must lead in this endeavor to preserve and care for creation. Our love for God must include his creation, which he loved and redeemed by His Son's death on the cross. We must take care of his world.

CHAPTER 13

Culture and Family

Introduction

In the first part of this book, we saw how the cultures and values of Africa, the west, and biblical values based on our relationship with God largely shape the moral lives of its peoples. Culture and the family are two important institutions that shape people's values and these values play a critical role in their moral lives. It is important therefore, for us to discuss the role of culture for morality. Our concern is not to discuss culture in its various facets, but to look at culture in the specific ways its values determine people's morality especially in relation family life. The family is a critical social system in every society. It has also been the primary moral institution. It has the responsibility to teach moral values to its members so they can live responsibly in society. How individual families turn out will affect the life of that society in a profound way. The story today about families is not very pleasant. There is a breakdown of families and family values.

Today, we see a lot of moral decay in all cultures in the world due to modernity's influence. These have effects on cultural and family values all over the world. Globalization of the world makes it possible for the spread of these new values through the media and other technological devices such as cell phones. Africa is struggling with some of these recent cultural and family values that pose a threat to its traditional cultural and family values. Because of the new cultural and family values, we are learning and practicing from other cultures of the world. As a result, African cultural and family values and some of the social institutions we hold dear as Africans are being eroded. Modernity is shaping our cultural and family values and our ethical behaviors. The family, which is the basic institution to teach morality, is under serious attack from forces that see such traditional, cultural, and family values as oppressive and outdated. How are we to respond to these cultural and family values that are threatening and destroying the moral fabric of our societies?

What can we learn from these traditional cultural, family, and biblical values that are necessary for family life? How can we augment and promote biblical values that will better help shape our moral and family life in society? I will attempt to deal with these questions.

Culture and its role in creating values and shaping morality

What is culture? According to Gyekye, "Culture encompasses the entire life of people; their morals, religious beliefs, social structures, political, and educational systems, forms of music and dance, and all other products of their creative spirit."[1] These elements of cultures induce certain ethical values that influence in a comprehensive way the thought and actions of people who share the particular culture. Put more pungently, cultures define for us most of the ethical words or language and values that become the basis for our behavior. For instance, ethical values such as truth, faithfulness, trust, honesty and probity, goodness, kindness, mercy, compassion, courage, loyalty, dependability, solidarity, responsibility and so forth all are ideas and values found in most cultures. Our understanding of these ethical terms primarily derives from our cultural contexts. It is also interesting to note that the Scripture affirms and encourages these values for our moral life as we have pointed out in this book. Culture, therefore, plays a critical role in helping to form our moral values in a profound way.

What is value? Value is simply anything that has worth. In other words, a thing has value if it has worth. When used in an ethical sense, we are

---

1 Kwame Gyekye, *African Cultural Values*, xiii.

referring to the moral principles and beliefs we consider as important and which influence the way we think and behave. Pilch and Malina define values as "the general quality and direction of life that human beings are expected to embody in their behavior." It refers to the quality ('of what sort?') and the goal or purpose (directionality) of human behavior in general or some aspect of human behavior."[2] They explain further, value is general, normative orientation of action in a social system. It is an emotionally anchored commitment to pursue and support certain directions or types of actions."[3] Therefore, values shape our morality. The values we acquire are very important if we want to lead an acceptable moral life.

Every culture has fundamental values that give shape to its people's moral ethos and give them their identity. For example, there are certain cultural values that shape the west's morality and give her, her identity. Such core values include value of the individual, materialism/wealth, equal opportunity, consumerism, freedom and liberty, individual rights, privacy, competition, self-confidence, self-reliance, marriage, entertainment and happiness. This list is not exhaustive. These values determine and motivate the way people think and behave. These values will inform family life and morality as well. For example, when it comes to moral issues relating to justice, freedom, and rights, the values the West shares on these matters become the basis for the moral discourse or engagement. The people in these cultures derive their moral, social, and personal judgments from these cultural values.[4] Some of the western cultural values mentioned above are shared in many of the nations of the non-western world, Asia, Africa and Latin America. This is the result of globalization, urbanization and the many technological advancements and revolutions taking place in these non-western worlds. We will later talk about how some of the cultural values in these cultures are specifically affecting Africa, particularly its family values.

---

2 John J. Pilch and Bruce J. Malina, eds. *Handbook of Biblical Social Values.* Peabody: Hendrickson Publishers, 2000, 13, xvi and 13.

3 Pilch, *Handbook,* xv.

4 Elliot Turiel, *The Culture of Morality: Social Development, Context, and Conflict.* Cambridge: Cambridge University Press, 2002, 71.

Like the west, there are certain fundamental cultural values that shape the way Africans think and behave. These values are considered important and give the bases for African morality. Some of these core cultural values include interdependence and collective responsibility, religion and spirituality, marriage, family, children, kinship, reciprocity, respect for the elderly, interconnectedness, brotherhood, sexual purity of young people and prosperity. Again, this list is not exhaustive.[5] All these values have moral implications for family life and behavior.

In my opinion, these cultural values and beliefs systems provide the motivational force, rationale, and impetus for individual, corporate, national and community behavior. For example, Africans' moral stance against homosexuality derives from their family values; at the core of this is biological reproduction to provide security and stability and continuation of the kinship system. Any marital arrangement that violates this important family value is not acceptable. Alternatively, the reason why abortion was less in traditional African societies was because they value children as a blessing from God. People who married then were encouraged to have as many children as they could, because children carried supreme value to Africans. They brought honor to the clan and the extended family or kinship. They did not worry about how these children would be catered for, because they believed the one (God) who had given them to their parents as gifts, would provide for their needs and would see to their wellbeing and prosperity.

This was not to shed the parents' moral responsibilities to their children and pass them on to someone else. Again, the African's values of interdependence, solidarity, and kinship ties played a critical role here. The African knows he/she is dependent on God for all of his/her needs and blessings. They believe, God will provide for those who do not have help. One African proverb says, "God drives away the flies on a tailless animal." God always comes to the aid of the helpless! In addition, they could count

---

5 See Kwame Gyekye, *African Cultural Value*. Gyekye discusses eleven broad African cultural values consisting of religious, human and brotherhood, communal and individualistic, moral, family, economic, chiefship and political, aesthetic, knowledge and wisdom, human rights and ancestors and tradition.

on the solidarity of the kinship ties where the well to do members of the family help those that are less fortunate.

In Africa, the principles governing family behavior are determined by the kinship system. The kinship system prescribes roles, and gives status to people. It determines the rules, duties, and obligations of the individual and group in all aspects of life within which the individual and the group interact. The moral and social obligation the individual had to the clan or relatives is that of reciprocity. The relatives take the responsibility to help the members to succeed in life. It is expected that this family member will remember and do the same for those who come behind him. Another African proverb says, "The one who looked after you to grow your teeth, you should look after them to lose their teeth." This underlines the African's ethic of responsibility and reciprocity.

However, modern ideologies are eroding traditional cultural and family values held by many nations around the world. Our moral obligations are no longer grounded upon these values but they are based on modern philosophical and humanistic ideologies. Modern ideologies such as humanism and secularism are attacking the traditional cultural values held by both western and African cultures such as family, religion, and respect for authority.

There has been a rise in secular values, which is based on "rationality," that advocates detachment from the beliefs, values, and practices of traditional religious ethos. Thus, religious values are eroded constantly and rationalism is becoming more and more accepted among modern minds. Kotze observes, "If churches lose their monopoly to define religious and moral norms, the whole moral system of society; or generally accepted norms and fundamental values, might break down."[6] The Church is losing its moral ground and conforming to the cultural values of society, setting aside biblical values on matters relating to the family. We will discuss the role of the Church in taking a critical role in shaping cultural and family moral values to ensure societies do not degenerate into moral malaise.

---

[6] Hennie Kotze, "The constant of Transformation: Eleven Years of Value Change in South Africa, 1990–2001" in *Changing Values, Persisting Cultures: Case Studies in value Change*, eds. Thorleif Pettersson and Yilmaz Esmer. Leiden: Brill, 2008, 350.

Social institutions enforce values more effectively. Institutions provide the general boundaries, qualities, and directions of living to take place. In this case, the family is the basic social institution that provides the space for nurturing values to enhance the quality of life and behavior of a person. In addition, these values are institutionalized by the culture as cultural values. So, when we talk of cultural values we are thinking about those values in a culture that shape people's moral behavior and practices. Our cultures shape our values and our values shape our morality. Two fundamental ways we acquire and learn values are through culture and family.

These values are very important to God and we must preserve their sanctity as Christians and as those who follow of God. These values are foundational for our moral lives! In addition, we are losing our value of solidarity and community. Africans are becoming more individualistic in our outlook. Such selfish and individualistic view of life is causing us to lose the value of social responsibility.

Evaluating our cultural values

As we have seen, there are useful values we can find in our cultures that we must promote. However, some have affected us negatively morally. How can we discern which values are helpful and which are not?

There are three ways we can evaluate culture based on Israel's experience and based on God's instructions to them regarding cultural practices. The first is total rejection of cultural practices and values that do not conform to biblical values. This means we must reject all the forms of cultural practices and values that are in opposition to God's word especially those that will make us lose our spirituality and devotion to God. We must reject secularism with is antireligious ethos and its rejection of authority. The second is the principle of qualified toleration. This might involve cultural values that are not contrary to God's word and scripture which can be tolerated. For example, such matters relating to polygamy and levirate marriage and divorce would fall into this category. We must accept situations and issues that are "less than God's ethical ideal but it is not classified as sin. Lastly is the principle of critical affirmation. Those values that are in line with biblical values must be affirmed and encouraged. For example, values such as hospitality, truth, community, solidarity, and integrity, to mention a few."[7]

We should reject cultural values and practices that do not conform to the moral teachings of the Bible. To mention a few of these values, I suggest we evaluate seriously our consumerism value. We have pointed out elsewhere in this book how this has driven us to moral catastrophe in terms of its focus on the self. This value has made us become greedy and egoistic people. Scripture teaches us to live modestly and humbly. Such cultural practices and values are detestable to God (Lev. 18:3). Some of these practices and values involve a variety of sexual perversions—homosexuality, cultic prostitution, rape, ritual killings, and incest. Incest in African society is a taboo. It is a detestable thing. Widow inheritance and ritual killings in Africa are some of the cultural practices that raise some moral concerns. God is concerned about sexual integrity and sexual ethics (Deut. 22:13–30, Lev. 18:6–18, 20:11–14, 19–21). This value is not appreciated in many of our modern cultures. Sex` is glorified in our societies and many younger people are practicing sex at very young age. The sexual perversions we see and the promiscuity we find in our societies is due to the culture of sexuality we are promoting. These behaviors and practices were very uncommon in traditional societies.

We must challenge cultural practices and values, social hierarchy, unhealthy relationship between husband (man) and wife (woman), relationships between parents and children, unfair or unjust cultural practices that have moral implications for the community's members that are incompatible with biblical ethics. We must repudiate such cultural practices. Throughout the Scriptures, we are exhorted to disengage ourselves from the things and practices that characterized our former ways of life that did not please God. These values should not determine our behavior any longer because the triune God has given us a higher cultural value that He has modeled for us.

---

[7] Wright, *Old Testament Ethics*, 349.

Social institutions enforce values more effectively. Institutions provide the general boundaries qualities and directions of living to take place. In this case, the family, which is the basic social institution, provides the space for nurturing values to enhance the quality of life and behavior of a person. In addition, these values are institutionalized by the culture as cultural values. So, when we talk of cultural values we are thinking about those values in a culture that shape people's moral behavior and practices. Our cultures shape our values and our values shape our morality. Two fundamental ways we acquire and learn values are through culture and family. We affirm some of the cultural values listed above as foundational for our moral behavior as individuals and our social life as family. We will look at the family and some of the values that have shaped its moral ideals.

The place and role of family in African cultures

What is family? The family is "a fundamental social group in society typically consisting of one or two parents and their children," or two or more people who share goals and values, have long term commitments to one another, and reside usually in the same dwelling place or a group of people sharing a common ancestry."[8] You can observe the broad nature of this definition. While this definition of family is acceptable to me, I would however, like to narrow this definition for the purposes of our chapter.

Traditionally, a man, woman, and children constitute the family. This is known by many as the nuclear family. As I mentioned earlier in this chapter, the African family is not just the nuclear family but it includes the extended family. The African family consists of the father, mother, children, plus the relatives of the parents and children—called the extended family. The extended family is made up of a large number of blood relatives who trace their ancestry to a common ancestor and who have social, economic responsibilities to each other. African communal values such as "hospitality, solidarity, mutual helpfulness, interdependence and concern for the

---

8 "Description of Family—American Heritage Dictionary," http://eduaction.yahoo.com/reference/dictionary/entry/family. Accessed May 6, 2011, "Family," http://www.thefreedictionary.com/family. Accessed May 6, 2011

well-being of every individual member of society, find their highest and most spontaneous expression in the institution of the family."[9]

Families are constituted through marriages. Again, marriages are between a man and a woman. The family is the only recognized social institution that establishes and maintains the family as well as for creating and sustaining kinship ties.[10] Kinship involving adult members who exercise authority over the young by assigning duties, obligations, and giving support to the younger folks. Marriage is vital in African societies and in kinship systems. There are reasons for this. Marriage "provides heirs (through procreation for the perpetuation of kinship" and "it helps in expanding the scopes of the lineage and kinship systems."[11] In Africa, marriage is a family, clan, and even a community affair. It is not left for the two persons marrying alone. The adults from the two families provide the moral and social support the couple needs to make their marriage succeed. The marriage ceremony is completed when the family and lineage of the bride receives the bride price or dowry from the man's family and clan. This bride price or dowry makes the marriage commitment between the couple binding. It was also meant to ensure marital stability and to guarantee good behavior.[12]

We pointed out that marriage is one of the cultural values Africa cherishes. It serves certain social and divine purposes. Socially, marriages sealed bonds with other family members and the community in which the marriage took place thus fostering unity. It harnesses support and interdependence of the couple on each other for their happiness and wellbeing that is expressed through their love for each other and the pleasure they derive from each other. Marriage also elevated the social status of the married person especially the young man. He is considered a responsible person who is

---

9 Kwame Gyekye, *African Cultural Values*, 75.

10 Kwame Gyekye, *African Cultural Values*, 76.

11 Ebebe John Ayah, "The Family as the Basic Structure of Society in Catholic Social Teaching and Communitarian Thought: An Assessment in Light of the Sociology of the Family." A Dissertation presented to the Faculty of Theology, Katholieke Universiteit Leuve for Doctor's Degree in Theology. Leuve, 2005, 14.

12 M. Aborampah, Family Structures in African Fertility Studies: Some conceptual and Methodological Issues," in *A Current Bibliography in African Affairs*, 1985–1986, Vol. 18, 130.

capable of caring for the material welfare of his wife and children. This earns him respect and honor in the community.

Furthermore, marriages have much value in African societies because through marriage the family name and honor is propagated. Therefore, procreation is foundational for marriages. This is the divine dimension or purpose of marriage. This was also God's intention for humanity, when he instituted the marriage institution. He wanted humanity "to be fruitful and fill the earth" (Gen. 1:28). Children carry important value in the family. Therefore, parents invest their lives in their children hoping one day they will grow up and take care of them when they are old. It also looks like in God's view man is incomplete without a woman and vice versa for the woman (Gen. 2:18). God's comment, "it is not good for man to be alone; I will make a helpmate suitable for him," is telling!

The family provides a basic unit of all human society. In fact, the family is the basic institution and key to the structure of society. Culture plays a critical role in how families function. The family's role is very critical for the proper functioning of society. Dysfunctional families in any society will result in that society becoming dysfunctional. It is in light of this that we have to discuss this important subject in our ethical discourse due to the incipient attacks against the family institution. As we pointed out in the section above, the family is one of the fundamental values in African cultures. It has both social and moral value.

Socially, the family serves as the basic unit for the primary socialization of children. In Africa, this is more than just the nuclear family but it includes the extended family. This extended family or kinship ties provide intricate networks of social ties. The kinship ties evoke strong bonds of relationships and moral responsibility towards members of the clan. Kinship is "a social relation derive[d] from consanguity (blood), relations, marriage, and adoption"[13] Socially; each member of the family is to ensure there is social cohesion between its members.

---

13 Nana Chief Azuma Ndagu Edward, "Rebuild Africa's Family Values." http://www.scribd.com/doc/12529432/Rebuild-Africas-Family-values-By-Chief-Azuma-Edward, 2. Accessed on May 6, 2011.

Morally, the family is the primary place to teach moral values to children. Family members have moral responsibility to each other to ensure they behave in a manner that will honor and not bring shame to the family. Families held certain values that guided and governed the way they lived and behaved towards each other and how they lived within the larger community. Parents taught their children these values. Some of these values include, love, respect for parents and the elderly, responsibility to parents, generosity, hospitality, truthfulness, loyalty, spirituality, creativity, industriousness, hard work and many others; the values listed here are not exhaustive. They simply include some of the core values that shaped African family ethics and behavior.

African family values under attack by western ideological, cultural, and moral values

African family values are under serious attack from western cultures. These attacks are on two fronts—modernity secularism on the one hand and ideological and technological advancement, on the other hand. Archbishop Tlhagale of Johannesburg points out pungently that "Africa's traditional cultural values 'are threatened by a new global ethic which aggressively seeks to persuade African governments and communities to accept new and different meanings of the concept of family, marriage and human sexuality.'" African families are struggling to be the "place of pardon, reconciliation, and peace" they have always been. This struggling is the result of the pressures posed by the "HIV-AIDS pandemic, globalization, the deterioration of the cultural value of marriage, political influence and the lack of role models."[14]

The moral fabrics of African family life are eroding due to several factors. Modernization, individualism, and urbanization are weakening the social strings that hold families together. Excessive individualization in modern society has led to the decline of traditional patriarchal family values. "There

---

14 http:/www.catholicnews.com/data/stories/cns/0904495.htm. Accessed May 9, 2011.

is increase in the number of unmarried couples, co-habitation, divorces, extra-marital births, dual income families, and smaller families. These trends are largely due to society's changing needs as more women enter the workforce, thereby challenging traditional gender roles and promoting women's societal liberation."[15] Work, economic, and the social pressures on families have put many families under stress. These pressures have threatened many marriages, which have ended in divorce because the social support from the extended family is crumbling.

In African societies, both young women and men were to be chaste before they marry. When young people violated their virginity, they brought shame and dishonor to themselves and to their families. Today this value is lost because of the global influence of western media on Africa where sexual engagements are idolized, pornographic materials are shown openly by media houses, and those involved with these acts are praised as celebrities.

Our modern cultural practices undermine family structures in favor of pursuit of individual pleasure and unbridled freedom. Culture and changing social circumstances, internal family dynamics are forcing new forms of family life on us. Some families have not offered positive role models for the children. Our children often have learned from us our bad behavior and practices. They learn to tell lies and cheat because they see us do that the same.

Traditional African family life is mostly communitarian. However with modernization and social, and economic factors facing many Africans there are significant changes taking place in family life. Families in urban cities are becoming nuclear in nature and losing the sense of community and the moral obligation they have previously had toward the extended family. The traditional support systems that gave support and stability to families are crumbling. Family values are being set aside. They are being eroded. Today it is common to find individuals living together in cities without being married.

---

15 Kotze, *Changing Values*, 351.

There are other sexual deviations like homosexuality and lesbianism entering our societies, our children have fallen victims to these, and other forms of sexual perversions. More recently, African Catholic bishops raised concerns on how African family values are being threatened by western ideology. In a story written by Sarah Delaney, published by the *Catholic News Service*, the bishops observed that violence; HIV/AIDS, and western ideas undermine the African family.[16] The bishops noted that the West's ideology of "biological gender identity, is not intrinsic to the person but is a social construct" contrary to African cultural and family values. Furthermore, this ideology "denies God's plan" in creating humanity male and female and this has created a negative impact on the centrality of traditional marriage and of motherhood and fatherhood.

Western cultural values such as gender equality and freedom of choice have given people power to "choose their sexual orientation, thus, "making homosexuality and lesbianism a culturally acceptable choice." Because of this, the West has influenced politics and has thus put "pressure on lawmakers to pass legislations favorable to contraceptives and abortive services as well as homosexuality."[17] The issue of homosexuality and lesbianism is a serious moral problem in Africa. The issue must not be seen as a matter of rights and choice but as a violation of moral values that African communities hold deeply.

Furthermore, we see many practices in our cultures that undermine respect for authority. Modernity resents any authority idea and sees it as violation of people's rights and infringement on their freedom. The role of parents to teach their children moral values and how to behave properly in society has been undermined by modernity's insistence on rights of individuals to do what they feel is good for them. Some who see it as abusive frown at parental discipline and violation of people's freedom of choice to do what they want. Parents are losing authority on their children. Children want their independence and reject any parental authority over them. We are seeing many of our youths engaging in all kinds of morally

---

16 Sarah Delaney, African Family values threatened by Western ideology." http:/www.catholicnews.com/data/stories/cns/0904495.htm. Accessed May 9, 2011.

17 http:/www.catholicnews.com/data/stories/cns/0904495.htm. Accessed May 9, 2011.

deprived activities such as drugs, alcohol abuse, engaging in pre-marital sex and many other negative choices that are destroying their lives. When confronted, they argue it is their life; they can live it any way they choose. Many parents find themselves helpless, because they cannot discipline their children by spanking. Such discipline is considered child abuse by western cultures. What must we do as Christians about this moral erosion-taking place in our societies? What can families do to restore these values again in our children? We will discuss these questions later on.

More recently, feminists who accuse these traditions as being patriarchal and bias towards male dominance have challenged some of the traditional roles of women. They have resisted these tendencies and they have opened the way for women to ensure their freedom and rights within the marriage relationship. They are concerned with the injustices that such cultural values bring against women. "Feminists' concerns for injustices and inequalities often have been voiced in the context of close interpersonal relationships within family."[18] We must take proper care as we deal with these issues especially where we see injustice committed against women, but we should not use this to undermine authority in the family.

Family as the primary place for building strong relationships and moral values

Why do we have to take seriously the family in our moral discourse? Two reasons: God is concerned about families and how we live in his world. Families have been given the primary responsibly to train their children morally so they can become good people who are concerned about the wellbeing of their fellow citizens.

The family has both social and ethical responsibility to train children to live morally in society. The wise counsel we find in Proverbs is key. "Teach your children to choose the right path, and when they are older, they will

---

18 Elliot Turiel, *The Culture of Morality: Social Development, Context, and Conflict*. Cambridge: Cambridge University Press, 2002, 71.

remain upon it." (Prov. 22:6, NLT; Deut. 6:1–4). The social collapse we find in some of our societies has its root in dysfunctional families and lack of maintaining moral discipline within the family. Teaching our children moral values that will help them make right decisions is our biblical mandate. Parents cannot sacrifice the important role God has given them.

Parental authority over children is God's model and plan for the family. God demands respect and honor for parents from children (Ex. 21:15–17, Deut. 27:15). This respect and honor involves children obeying the instructions and advice from their parents. The book of Proverbs emphasizes the importance of children obeying and following their parents' instructions so they will get wisdom, understanding what is right, just, and fair and be able to make right choices every time (Prov. 2:1–16). We must not sanction any cultural value that encourages rebellion of children to authority! Such attitudes will destroy our children. It will cut their lives short.

Likewise, parents have the responsibility to be fair to all children and show no favoritism or deprive the first born son within a polygamous family of his rights (Deut. 21:15–17). The African has a proverb that says, "When you support the plantain tree, prop up the banana tree also, for you do not know which of them will save you in time of famine." Opoku points out this proverb is "used as a warning to parents with many children to give them all equal attention, for no one knows which of them will provide support for the parents in their old age."[19] Parents must love all their children unconditionally, and treat them justly. When they discipline them, they must do that justly and with care and love.

It is important for parents to speak with one voice and teach what will improve their

Children's character—such that the children will pay attention to them (Prov. 1:8–9). Training must begin from early childhood (Prov. 22:6; 13:24), and is best if it combines both discipline (i.e. the rod, or punishment) and gentle but firm direction (Prov. 1:9; 13:4; 22:15).

---

19 Kofi Asare Opoku, *Hearing and keeping: Akan Proverbs*. Accra: Asempa Publishers, 1997, No 420, 84.

On their part, children are urged repeatedly to obey their parents and respect them (Prov. 1:8–9, 4:1), for such obedience is blessed with a long and prosperous life (Prov. 3:2). Family members and relatives should be helpful and loyal to each other (Prov. 17:17, 18:24). Even though children sometimes refuse to learn and are disobedient, and some parents also do not give the right training or set a good example, if parents and children follow the sage advice of the old, as presented in Proverbs, the quality of life in the modern world would be far better than it is now with all the violence, immorality, and lawlessness that abound.

Biblical foundations for family and its role in shaping the moral life

God instituted the idea of family. God created the first family by bringing together Adam and Eve. He blessed them and commanded them to "be fruitful and multiply." Therefore, the family must be modeled after God's design and purpose for its creation. It was God's intention that the family would become the basis and the environment where children are loved and nurtured to walk in the ways of the Lord. We see this truth in the desires of Adam's children to worship God through sacrifices. It is obvious that Adam's children learned to worship God from their parents. God's call of Abraham underlined this truth and intention of God as well. God said of Abraham, "I have singled him out so that he will direct his sons and their families to keep the way of the Lord and do what is right and just. Then I will do for him all that I have promised" (Gen. 18:17–19). This is God's plan and purpose for families so we can bring honor and praise to his name by following his instructions and living and doing what is right so society will do well. Therefore, the family is a vehicle for the worship of God, but also for moral life.

However, when we read the Scripture we see the many struggles that families encounter and go through. Some families do well by leading their family members to follow God. For example Joshua led his family to follow and serve the Lord (Josh. 24:15). Others do poorly by leading them away from following the ways of God. For example, Eli failed to train and restrain his sons from walking wickedly before the Lord and perverted justice and righteousness (1 Sam. 2:12–25). Their immoral behavior caused their death and that of their father. Wright accurately observes, "The material on the family (in the Bible) presents a series of paradoxes or ambiguities. This is inevitable because the family closely mirrors the ambiguity of human life itself. ...the human family shares the ambiguity inherent in every human being: made in the image of God and yet at the same time fallen and sinful."[20] Therefore, no family is perfect! However, God requires we do our best in training our children to be just. He requires us to be faithful in doing this. Once we have done our part, we can leave the rest to him. He will hold our children accountable for their own actions and deeds.

Notwithstanding the paradoxes and ambiguities, we find in Scripture numerous examples affirming families. The Bible sees the family as

> God's intended, creational context for human lives to begin, for them to be nurtured and shaped according to the values and standards that please God, to learn and express the social and relational skills essential to our humanity, to offer and receive support at many different levels of life and work, abundance and need.[21]

The family is the vehicle for human life to begin. It also serves as the context and place for human nurturing and training to occur. The family creates the space for children to learn life skills and competence, moral standards, discipline and to develop godly values that will shape their thinking and the moral life of family members to walk in God's ways.

The New Testament writers affirm the important role of families emphasizing the critical place of marriage; children and the responsibilities of parents to bring up their children in the Lord as well as children's duty to parents (Lk. 2:49–51, Mk. 10:2–12, 7:9–13, Matt. 5:31–32, 15:3–6,

---

20 Wright, *Old Testament Ethics*, 353.
21 Wright, *Old Testament Ethics*, 353.

19:1–9). Apostles Peter and Paul instruct the families and remind them of their duties to each other. They admonish husbands to love, honor, respect, and understand their wives. Wives are to submit to the authority, leadership of their husbands and be modest in their appearance. Children must obey and honor their parents while fathers are admonished not to make their children angry by the way, they treat them. They must "bring them up with the discipline and instruction approved by the Lord" (Eph. 5:21–31, 6:1–4, 1 Pt. 3:1–7).

Parents have the responsibility to model their own lives as moral examples for their children to follow. This is important because children learn best by imitating others who they see as role models. We are to nurture them in godly values such as faithfulness, kindness, compassion, justice, truth, impartiality, integrity, mercy, dependability and many other values the bible teaches. These values can best be inculcated in the lives of our children if they are modeled before their eyes by the way their parents live their lives in faithfulness, kindness, compassion, justice, telling the truth, impartiality, integrity, mercy, and dependability. When they see these values reflected in our lives, they will internalize them in their own lives.

It is important to mention here that parents are not responsible for how their children turn out as adults. We are all responsible before a righteous and just God who delights in our godly living. When we turn away from the "right way," that is, turn away from the ways of God and do what we want to please ourselves, God will hold us accountable for our own evil deeds. Those evil deeds we do will not be the responsibility of our parents to answer. It will be ours!

The prophet Ezekiel makes this clear in Ezekiel 18:10–22. God dealt with a wrong perception of the Israelites expressed by one of their proverbs: "'the parents have eaten sour grapes, but their children's mouths pucker at the taste?'" God says nobody will cite this proverb again. Rather, God says, "For all people are mine to judge-both parents and children alike. And this is my rule: The person who sins will be the one who dies" (Eze. 18:4, NLT). Parents will not be held responsible for their children's evil ways if they live righteous and just lives and children will not be held responsible for their parents' evil ways if they live righteous and just lives. The righteous will be rewarded for their goodness and the wicked people will be rewarded for their own wickedness. This must be comforting to parents so they do not feel shame when they find their children turning out to be rebellious against the ways of the Lord even though they brought them up in God's ways.

Creating godly and responsible families for society

The Old Testament Wisdom writers recognized the importance of the family as the basic unit of society. They spoke and stressed the need for its proper functioning for its stability and as the place for the good training of children. The NT writers pick up this theme as we have seen earlier on. God's purpose for families is for them to create space for worship, nurture, and training in righteousness. This is the goal for families.

This means families must know God's purpose for their existence. We must seek to build strong and stable families. We can only achieve this if we build our families on godly, biblical, values and principles. When families are strong and they are built on the solid foundation of the moral laws of God, there is the possibility that we will have a strong and morally credible society or nation. For a good family to be created, we must follow God's blue print for families described to us in the Bible. For a family to function and do well it will take all the members of the family to play their roles with commitment and dedication. God in his wisdom has provided certain roles for each member of the family to perform. What are the specific primary roles of fathers, mothers and children as well as the extended kinship?

First, the family must be well constituted through marriage. This can be traditional, civil, or ecclesiastical. In most African societies, these are the three recognized ways marriage is formalized. The Scriptures affirm monogamy as God's ideal for marriage and it is permanent. While divorce is becoming very common in many African societies—a trend that was uncommon before—we must intentionally address the problems leading to divorce which is often the result of western ideological stance on freedom and rights of individual to do what will make them happy, an unforgiving spirit and human sinfulness.

We also see many polygamous relationships in Africa. Polygamy is one of the customs and cultural practices tolerated in the Bible. Wright observes there are certain customs and cultural practices such as polygamy, divorce, and slavery that fall short of God's ideal or standards yet they received what he calls "qualified toleration." By this he means, these customs and practices were "regulated by legal safeguards in such a way as to soften or eliminate their worst effects."[22] Of course, we must mention that some of these deviations from God's standards are the result of human sinfulness. God hates divorce (Mal. 2:13–16). God's ideal for marriage is monogamy and permanence. Jesus' teaching on marriage affirms monogamous marriage as God's ideal for humanity. By his statement, "for this reason a man will leave his father and mother and be joined to his wife and the two will become one flesh." (Matt. 19:8, See Gen. 2:24). Divorce was given because of the "hardness of heart of the people" Jesus pointed that "from the beginning it was not so" (Deut. 22:28–29, 24:1–4, 21:14, Matt. 19:8).

Once the marriage is consummated, each of the partners is required to be faithful to each other. Adultery was prohibited by God in the Torah as well as in Wisdom literature and in the New Testament (Ex. 20:14, Prov. 2:16–22, 5:15–23, Matt. 5:27–30, 19:9, 18, Mk. 10:11, 12, 19, Lk. 16:18, 18:20, Rom. 13:9, Gal. 5:19, Jam. 2:11, 2 Pet. 2:14). Sexual sin within marriage is evil and dangerous. The marriage bed must be honored, it must be kept pure. Adultery leads to disgrace and even death (Prov. 5:21–23, 6:26–29, 32–35, Heb. 13:4). Both husband and wife must remain faithful to one another in marriage. In a marriage relationship a husband must love and be faithful to his wife (Pr. 5:15, 19), while a wife must be generous, good to her husband and contribute to his good standing in society (Prov. 31:10–28).

The parents' role is to provide a peaceful and loving environment for their children to grow. The parents must model their lives before their children, in speech and actions. They must become role models for them in spirituality, love, faithfulness, loyalty, respect, and industry. They must impact life skills, teaching about life, rules, and the consequences of breaking

---

22 Wright, *Old Testament Ethics*, 329–330.

them. They must create the space to develop creativity in the children, give them a sense of positive self-image, and teach moral standards and values based on God's word, social skills, and competence. Parents must teach, instruct, and train their children in the truth, righteousness, faithfulness so they grow up to become responsible adults in society (Prov. 22:6, Eph. 6:4).

One of the fundamental roles of the husband in a marriage is to leave his father and mother and cleave to his wife. (Gen. 2:24, Matt. 19:5–6, Eph. 5:31). It is important that the man leaves his father and mother's house where he has received support and nurture to his own house where he has been given the responsibility to support and care and nurture his own family. For a family to succeed in its function and purpose this leaving must take place. The reason for this is for the man to bond with his wife to become "one flesh." This is a metaphor for unity of purpose and of heart, mind, and soul.

Secondly, the husband must play his role of providing the basic needs of food, shelter, clothing and health, nurture and support for his family. The father or husband is the leader or the head of the family and he must play that role by giving leadership to his family. As a true leader he should not be domineering, arrogant and belittling" to his wife. Rather, he must follow the example of Jesus Christ who loved the church and gave himself for her. The husband must love his wife as Christ loves His Church. Christ gave his life for his church to "make her holy and clean, washed by baptism and God's word" (Eph. 5:26–27). Likewise, the husband must love his wife as they love their own bodies. The fathers' love for his family must be selfless and self-giving. Christ shows compassion, mercy, forgiveness, respect, and selflessness. These moral values are very critical for the proper functioning of any family (1 Tim 5:8, 1 Cor. 11:13, Eph. 5:23, Col. 3:18–19, 1 Pet. 3:7). He must do his best to meet the emotional, physical, sexual needs of his wife.

The wife's primary role is to provide care for the home. Like the Proverbs 31 woman. She must respect and submit herself to the authority and leadership of her husband. For this behavior of respect and submission to the husband is fitting for those who belong to the Lord (Col. 3:18, Eph. 5:21). The wives submission to the husband is grounded on Christ's relationship with his bride, the Church. The Church submits to Christ. In the same way, "wives must submit to their husbands in everything" (Eph. 6:24).

The children's role involves according the parents respect, honoring, obeying and accepting the discipline of their father or parents. This behavior of children honoring and respecting their parents is pleasing to God but it is also grounded on the fact of whose they are, they belong to God (Col. 3:20, Eph. 6:1–2). In a society that undermines authority, it is important that children are taught to understand the importance of this moral obligation within the family (Heb. 12:5–11, Prov. 13:24, 23:13, and 19:18). The bible teaches only fools despise wisdom, discipline, instruction, and training (Prov. 1:5, 17, 12:1). There is special value for children to obey, honor, and respect their parents. God promises such children long life and a life full of blessings (Eph. 6:3, Col. 3:20). Children who showed continuous disobedience and disrespect to their parents were punished severely by death (Deut. 21:18–21). This shows God's attitude to children who become rebellious and disrespect their parents who have done all they can to correct and discipline them, and they still choose to go their own way.

All the roles placed upon each member of the family must be exercised in the Lord. The Lord, is the foundation for this injunction to make sure that the family's wellbeing is taken seriously by all concerned and each member doing and taking the responsibility to ensure they perform their roles faithfully and diligently counting on the grace and power of God who enables us to do all things. These biblical family values must take priority in our effort to restore the family and fight against the insipient ideologies destroying the family in Africa. These roles and instructions from God's word must be taken seriously if we will restore the family to its God's intended purpose and function in society.

Modeling the Fatherhood of God in the family

The model family is the triune God. The triune God is family. In fact, one of the favorite names of God in the New Testament is Father, a name associated with the idea of family. He exists as Father, Son, and Holy Spirit; as family. Human families must be a reflection of God's essence as family. God is the father of all humankind. God is the source of all families. Paul affirms the fatherhood of God in his statement in Ephesians: "For this cause I bow my knees onto the Father, from whom every family in heaven and on earth is named…" (Eph. 3:14–15, NIV). Although most commentators of the NT see this as referring to the Church family—all Christians in heaven and on earth, as well as the faithful angels in heaven, I think this is a reference to God's fatherhood in general as the bonafide owner and creator of all human beings.

Besides being the natural father to all the families of the earth, the NT writers strongly emphasized the family motif by giving a spiritual dimension to the idea of family. The Church, which is described as the "body of Christ," is also called the family of God or the "household of God." It is within this spiritual community that all that takes place in the natural family also happens within the spiritual community—nurture, love, caring, support, meeting the needs of the members of the family all takes place.

Marriage is modeled after the love that exists between Christ and the Church, which is his body. We have asserted that marriage is foundational for family life. As participants of this body, we are to express God's character and nature in our family relationships. The Church is the family of God with God as the Father. The Church, then, serves as a model for human families. God as the head of the Church loves, nurtures, provides, disciplines, and cares for the needs of the Church. Human families exist to love, care, discipline, nurture, provide for the needs of the members of the family to promote their wellbeing.

Some practical suggestions and principles we need to apply to curb the incipient ideologies threatening family life in Africa

We must support parent's efforts to train their children by inculcating in them godly moral values, give serious attention to moral education of children, and resist the modern ideologies that diminish Christian family values. Families and communities must be made aware of this, since in Africa raising children is a community responsibility.

We must critically evaluate our cultural and family values that are in opposition to scriptures and can negatively affect the moral life of our societies. Values of rights and freedom can be used for evil purposes and we cannot accept them as morally good as they are defined and understood by our cultures and values. We need what Chris Wright refers to as critical affirmation of these values.

We must reject ideologies that are based on humanistic philosophies that accept certain practices and behavior as culturally appropriate or acceptable. This includes modern definitions of what family is and their insistence on people to learn to live and tolerate people who do not share the same moral values as theirs. While we agree to live in harmony with others, it does not mean they can impose their values on us by accepting what is morally wrong as right. We must uphold biblical values that reflect God's will and purpose for family life, marriage, and sexuality.

Family cohesion is possible if we create conditions that are "economically viable, socially credible and spiritual nourished."[23] We must address the economic, social, political pressures, and religious apathy militating against the family so we can sustain a functional society.

Sometimes the will of God and matters of the kingdom shifts Christian loyalty from family to the kingdom. While the scriptures want us to fulfill our family duties and obligations, we are called to give priority to matters of the kingdom. Sometimes such matters must be given higher priority than to human kinship obligations (Mk. 3:31–35, Lk. 9:59–60, 12:49–53, 14:25–26, Matt. 10:37, 19:16–30, Mk. 10:17–31).

Pastoral care before marriage and after marriage is the church's obligation and the church should help her members to live up to the challenges of Christian marriage against the socio-economic and cultural pressures marriages face in our societies today.

---

23 Wright, *Old Testament Ethics*, 353.

Conclusion

In this chapter, I set out to explore the role and place of culture in shaping family values. I discussed the different ways our cultural values have shaped our views on the family in our cultures. I have provided some biblical and theological foundations that challenge these cultural values and understanding of the family and provided a biblical and theological foundation for the family. I have looked at the respective roles each member of the family must play, and the biblical values we need to promote and develop to have a family that functions as God intends it. I underscore the importance of family as the place to nurture the moral values we need for life. The family is an important unit for society and we must give special attention to its wellbeing. Raising and building our families on biblical values will help us create a just and fair society where we care for each other's welfare and good.

CHAPTER 14

Biblical Law and African Legal Systems

"A social order which despises God's law places itself on death row: it is marked for judgment."[1]

Introduction

Law and order is one of the pillars that creates a peaceful and vibrate environment to promote human well being in every society. All throughout the history of humanity law has played a critical role in shaping and regulating the behavior of citizens so they can live in harmony with each other. Where there is lawlessness and impunity, confusion and chaos reign. It is important therefore for nations to enact and promulgate just and fair laws and create effective and efficient legal systems that are consistent with their cultural, moral and religious values, on the one hand and consistent with the moral laws of the creator who is the ultimate law giver on the other hand for the proper functioning of society.

One of Africa's problems is the administration of our legal systems and respect for the rule of law in our respective African countries. The problem in Africa is not that we do not have good laws. The problem is bad administration of the law and maintaining the rule of law. The modern African legal systems and its officers have been charged with abuse, dishonesty, corruption and often what has been termed as the "miscarriage of justice." Justice is perverted through corruption, bribery, long delays of

---

[1] Rushdoony, *The Institutes of Biblical Law*, USA: The Presbyterian and Reformed Publishing Company, 1973, 4.

trials, and bad investigations processes that eventually result in cases which are thrown out of the courts because the investigators did not conduct proper investigations.

My goal in this chapter is not to talk about law in general. This is the work of our law schools, lawyers, and those trained to do that. My concern about law relates to morality, particularly how law shapes our behavior and the moral problems we face in administering justice in a fair way. I am also concerned about our civil and moral responsibility as citizens to uphold and obey the laws of the land to ensure peace.

In this chapter, I would like to explore the moral, cultural, and religious values that are necessary for a just and fair administration of law in our African societies. I will look at both traditional African legal systems and biblical legal system and laws, focusing especially on how they administered the laws in their respective societies. I will suggest what we can learn from them and point out how this can help us in our modern societies to deal with some of the moral corruptions our legal system find itself in so we can have a just, fair judicial system that serves the wellbeing of humanity and promotes justice and peace in our countries. First, let us look at what law is.

The nature of law and order: Some definitions

Law may be defined as a body of rules derived from statutes or as "a rule of conduct or procedure established by custom, agreement, or authority." It comprises of a "body of rules and principles governing the affairs of a community and enforced by a political authority; a legal system; or the condition of social order and justice created by adherence to such a system" that orders their everyday lives. Law may comprise of legal institutions and procedures, legal values, legal concepts and ways of thinking and legal rule. It involves a legal process. It practically involves "legislating, adjudicating, administering, negotiating, and carrying on other legal activities."[2] In this study, law means a binding body of rules, customs or practices that govern

---

2 Harold J. Berman, *Law and Revolution: The Formation of Western Legal Tradition*. Cambridge, MA. Harvard University Press, 1983, 4–5.

the behavior and conduct of the members of society and are recognized by the community as binding and enforced by a controlling authority.

Order refers to a peaceful and tranquil environment necessary for human development and prosperity to take place. In relation to our topic, we will use order to mean a peaceful or harmonious condition of society that makes it possible for the proper administration of law to sustain the peace that society enjoys.

The rule of law

The rule of law is a legal maxim that says, "No person is above the law." The phrase rule of law is an ambiguous term, which means different things in different contexts. At least, there are three different ways to understand the term. First, the phrase can mean, "rule according to law." This requires and forces the government to exercise its power in "strict accordance with well-established and clearly defined laws and procedures." The second meaning is "rule under law." This means, "No branch of government is above the law and no public official may act arbitrarily or unilaterally outside of the law." Lastly, the term means, "rule according to a higher law." This ensures that "no law may be enforced by the government unless it conforms with certain universal principles (written or unwritten) of fairness, morality, and justice."[3]

In this chapter, we will use rule of law to mean no member of society is above the law and that the law must be exercised with fairness, morality, authenticity and reflect true justice. This means the law of the land is supreme over the acts of the government as well as private persons and the relationship between the state and the law of the land regulates the individual. We think the rule of law is necessary in any society for it will guarantee government accountability and protect the social rights of individuals. The existence of an independent and transparent judiciary is a fundamental aspect of the rule of law.[4]

---

3 http://www.answers.com/topic/rule-according-to-higher-law, "Rule according to higher law" West's Encyclopedia of American Law. Accessed, May 31, 2011.
4 http://definitions.uslegal.com/r/rule-of-law, accessed May 22, 2011.

Having defined the key terms, I would like to discuss general two critical issues that relate to law and which have generated debates for some time now. These concern the relationship between law and religion on the one hand and the relationship between morality and law on the other hand. I will examine these in order.

The relationship between law and religion

Liberal humanists have worked hard to remove religion from our contemporary legal systems. Most of the laws enacted or promulgated today are devoid of religion. We find this anti-religious attitude to law more profound in the west than in some other cultures of the world, although this attitude is becoming common in many developing countries due to western influence. Since most of western values are derived from secular and humanistic ideologies that are critical of religion, they tend to reject laws that have their basis rooted in religion to be intolerable and exclusive. Is religion vital for the creation of laws? If so, why is this frantic effort by humanists to rid law of any religious foundation? It is our contention that religion has a central role to play in the creation of any laws. This is because religion is a central feature in every society or culture; if we define religion broadly as anything that takes our devotion and loyalty and shape our values and the way we understand reality. In this sense, secularism is a form of religion.

Religion shapes our values, norms, goals, dispositions, and intensions that shape our view and response to the world around us. Laws reflect the values and norms of a community to enforce proper behavior that conforms to the kind of society the community wants to have. Most of these values on which the community's laws depend are derived from religious beliefs and practices. Therefore, religion provides values and these values become the source of our laws.

Rushdoony gives five reasons why law is intrinsically linked to religion. We will mention four of them that we think are relevant for our discussion:[5] First, he says law in every culture has its origin in religion. Rushdoony

---

5 Rushdoony, *The Institutes of Biblical Law*, 4–5.

asserts that law shapes human behavior in society and establishes the meaning of justice and righteousness. Second, law is in its essence religious, for it establishes the ultimate concerns of culture. In any culture "the source of law is the god of that society," this could be human reason, oligarchy, court, senate, ruler, and humanism. Third, he asserts that in many modern societies the source of law has moved from God to people or the state although biblical law and faith have been part of western legal systems in the past. Fourth, He thinks basically, a change in law in any culture will result in an explicit or implicit change in religion and that religion cannot be completely removed from any society; concluding, "since the foundations of law are inescapably religious, no society exists without a religious foundation or without a law-system which codifies the morality of its religion."[6]

If this is true, it is essential for all laws to be evaluated in light of God's laws to ensure they are just and reflect the will of God, the Creator and a just law giver. Secondly, it is important to recognize the central role religion might have on law. This is significant given the fact that the source of African traditional legal laws—traditions, customs, and taboos—and its administration has a religious dimension to it. God issued and made laws; ancestors are the custodians who exercised the legal laws with moral purity and fairness. This is understandable since religion is core to African life and practices and one of their central values. Therefore, there is nothing like secular laws in African traditional legal systems!

There will always be tension between the Church and State on the one hand, and what influence religion might have on state laws, on the other hand. The Scripture is clear on one thing. The State is God's servant to see to the wellbeing of humanity. Consequently, it must exercise justice according to God's laws and it has the power or authority from God to do so. If the State must administer justice, what do we consider just? Is it justice as God sees it, or is it justice as defined by our cultural values or humanistic philosophies? We think if God puts governments in their positions, they are responsible to God and they have the moral obligation

---

6 Rushdoony, *The Institutes of Biblical Law*, 5.

to follow and govern by the laws of God. The state cannot be God's servant and bypass God's laws. If God puts them there, then they must govern by God's laws! Not only must they govern by God's laws, but also all the laws they pass and enact must conform to God's moral laws.

The relationship between law and morality/ethics

The problem of the relationship between law and morality is universal; it is present in all cultures and societies.[7] That there is a close link between law and morality is clear. Morality is the way people behave and live their lives in community. These are based on the goals, values, and beliefs that guide their choices. Values have great influence on the choices people make. In other words, law shapes morality. Welch is right to say, "Law is a source for morality and morality a source for law."[8] The law "proscribes behavior and mandates others. The law reflects the values a community chooses to enhance, the rights it chooses to protect, and the goals it chooses to pursue."[9] The view that law is intrinsically linked to morality is not just significant for personal ethics, but it has moral implications for public policies as well and the manner in which the legal system works. We will discuss this later.

This is true with African moral laws. There is a close link between law and morality in traditional African societies. In African traditional legal systems, laws and morals are closely and necessarily related. The administrators of the law were people of high moral character. Given the situation in our courts and law enforcement agents and the observations we have made above, it seems to me that morality and the moral character of our judicial officers are not a central feature and criteria for appointing the people who administer justice in our modern African legal systems. This is evident in the lack of confidence many Africans have towards our current judiciary and legal systems and the call for judicial reforms going on in many African countries. There cannot be fair and just legal systems if the people who are

---

7 D. Don Welch, ed. *Law and Morality*. Philadelphia: Fortress Press, 1987, 2.
8 Welch, *Law and Morality*, 3.
9 Welch, *Law and Morality*, 3.

to bring justice become offenders themselves by violating the very laws they are supposed to uphold and ensure compliance.

Morality must be at the center of our legal system. The people who are entrusted to bring justice to the people must of necessity be people of integrity, just, and fair themselves otherwise justice will brutally be perverted. Those traditional moral qualities and values required for the elders to be justice bringers must hold for our judicial officers today. The moral character of our legal office is paramount if they will bring true justice that will build up authentic human relationships. There is need for integrity, honesty, humility, wisdom, courage, impartiality, and contentment.

We do not see this attitude extended to our legal system where officers who are found compromising their morality are removed from their positions. Therefore, through our silence, and non-action we have created a culture of moral impunity. People can live their lives anyway they choose and still hold on to their jobs and positions.

Ethics and character formation should form part of the curriculum for training our law enforcement officers such as the police, the prison wardens, lawyers and the judiciary. The moral integrity of our legal officers must be taken seriously if we will administer justice to our people so they live in peace. One way to ensure and enforce morality in our judicial system is to remove those who are found to compromise their moral character from their positions as was exemplified in former African societies where elders who were found to be corrupt were removed from the elders' council. In this way, we will not endorse moral impunity in our societies. We must hold on to our cultural and moral values that are founded on biblical values and not on the nature of the expediency of the law.

We pointed out earlier that our concern in this chapter is to explore the ways in which the laws were administered in both the African Traditional society and in the Bible and the values that were foundational for just and fair administration of the law in those contexts. We are now able to explore what we can learn from them in administering justice in our modern Africa. First, let us look at law and order in African traditional societies.

The role, function of law and order in traditional African societies

All societies have laws and regulations that control the behavior and lives of its citizens so they can live in peace and harmony with each other. Such laws are codified in their customs, traditions, mores, and taboos. These laws are oral laws; they are not written down. They are passed on from one generation to the other. Children are taught these traditions, customs, taboos and more as they grow up through proverbs, rituals, songs, stories, and so forth. The laws regulated the life and behavior of the people, how they should go about their activities for the interest of the community and the individual. The purpose and role of the law was to build harmonious social relationships and to have a strong community which lived in peace and harmony.

Secondly, the law served an educational function. It provided and set boundaries for human behavior—what they could do and what they could not do as members of the community. There were sanctions that were imposed on those who broke the law. This was meant to be a lesson for the lawbreaker and served as a lesson or deterrent for the one who might want to commit the same crime. The laws served the purpose of creating the right attitude of mind and heart in the community to live and conform to the right way of living in a society.[10]

The chiefs and the elders' council ran these legal institutions. Elders are respected in Africa due to the experience and wisdom that comes with age. In Africa, a person's usefulness does not diminish simply because he or she becomes old and economically unproductive. However, respect for the elderly is not automatic. Elderly people must conduct themselves in a particular way that is becoming of elders. When this is not done, they may lose the respect they deserve. To be an elder therefore, carries a lot of responsibility.

However, not all elders served on the elder's council to administer justice. The administration of justice was the privilege of people who had proven

---

10 David Daube, *Law and Wisdom in the Bible*. Edited and compiled by Calum Carmichael. West Conshohocken, PA: Templeton Press, 2010, 56–59.

themselves as honorable and worthy in the community by showing and demonstrating a high level of integrity. The elders who were charged with the responsibility to administer justice to the people were men of repute; people with proven character. The moral caliber of the "legal officials" was men and women of integrity, honest, respectable and with impeccable character, full of wisdom, fair, courageous to speak the truth at all cost, and impartial. They were responsible for maintaining law and order to ensure that the traditions, mores, customs, and taboos were adhered to without any violations to ensure the peace and well-being of the community.

Elders who compromised their integrity by bad conduct were removed from the elder's council so they could not tarnish the honor and integrity of the elder's court. This ensured that the officers continued to live upright and blameless lives.

The elders' role was to be fair and just in the judgments so continuous harmony existed in the community. Restoring mutual and cordial relationships was the goal of all their judgments. They were to maintain harmony in the community and anyone who failed to take this seriously and violated the harmony could face one of the harshest punishments, banishment from the community. As Okafo asserts "The native African …understands and construes "control," "justice," and "law" themes as instruments for general societal cohesion, rather than agents for advancing individual or factional group interests."[11] Community is central. Maintaining and building community is central in the African administration of justice.

Restoration and reconciliation as a goal of the African justice systems

One of the African judicial system's goals was restoration of the offender to community. The process involved restoration which may include fines, reparation, or restitutions, sanctioned by the elders for the offender to pay.

---

11 Nonso Okafo. "Relevance of African Traditional Jurisprudence on Control, Justice, and Law: A Critique of the Igbo Experience" in *African Journal of Criminology & Justice Studies: AJCJS, Volume 2, No. 1, June 2006*, 38. Accessed at www. PDF version.

This fine or restitution was not seen as retributive but as distributive justice. It was all aimed at restoring the offender to the life of the community. Thus, the African justice system was not primarily a retributive justice, but restorative justice, the goal was reconciliation. Fines were not punitive but restorative, to bring the aggrieved parties together after the case or dispute is settled. This is often celebrated with a meal. The ultimate goal being restoring relationships.

Community is a central African value. Therefore, our laws were to enhance this value. In contrast, our modern legal systems are vindictive and retributive. It is grounded on a cultural value that is individualistic and based on the rights of the individual and his happiness. They tend to create tension and disharmony. Court rulings always create tension and enmity between people. There is need to review some of the foreign value systems found in our laws that are not helping us to maintain peace and order in our society because they ignore fundamental values important to the community or the society.

African justice systems serve a particular function and goal. The goal is to foster peace and harmony within the living community. Okafo makes this observation about the African legal systems:

> The mechanisms of justice are aimed primarily at peacemaking. The Native African systems are designed with the understanding that the quest for peace in a society necessarily begins with peaceful coexistence between individual members of the society. Peace between individual members and smaller groups will add up to a peaceful society. Thus, peacemaking is the main thrust of the Native African systems of control, justice, and law.[12]

He continues, "Thus the Native African systems are designed to redress wrongs, fine-tune claims, preserve norms, and prevent the break-up of

---

12 Nonso Okafo. "Relevance of African Traditional Jurisprudence on Control, Justice, and Law: A Critique of the Igbo Experience" 44.

interpersonal and group relationships."[13] Law and order are important in enhancing the proper functioning of every human society. The purpose for this order is to build strong human relationships. Such cordial relationships cement human cohesiveness. People must feel safe where they know they are respected and their neighbors respect their fundamental rights to hold property. This is key to peace and harmonious living. Law and order will be effective if there is a just legal system that is administered justly by people of integrity who respect the rule of law. The present legal system is not serving us well because it ignores certain fundamental cultural values. Relational justice is not at the center of our modern legal systems. This is very critical. True justice must ensure reconciliation. This is essential and important for an effective legal system in Africa based on our cultural, moral, and religious values.

The African modern legal systems: Its problems

At the ideological level, secular and humanistic ideologies and rationality has influenced the promulgation of laws that serves certain human interests and reflects the cultural and moral values of these ideologies but these laws are in gross violation of our cultural, moral, and religious values. Some of these include laws such as reproductive health, same sex orientation that are framed as human right issues, but that are also against African cultural, moral, and religious values. In the same way, the administration of justice is rooted on the same cultural and moral values that are foundations of these laws. They are rooted in rationality and the logic of the law. They tend to advance the interest of the individual and have very little room for community interests.

In addition, the administration of the law is rooted deeply in western materialist values, wealth, and prosperity. Legal officers charge such high legal fees with many bureaucratic red tapes that make most legal services unaffordable for the majority of people in the society. The legal system

---

13 Ikenna Nzimiro, *Studies in Ibo Political Systems: Chieftaincy and Politics in Four Niger States*, Berkeley, California, USA: University of California Press, 1972. Okafo, 44.

is only favorable for the rich; they are the ones who can really afford legal services.

This materialistic value has combined with some African cultural values to give more import to this behavior. There are certain cultural values and practices that have undermined the modern African legal systems. The one significant problem affecting law enforcement in Africa by legal officers is corruption. Corruption has infested and corrupted our legal system. Justice is only achieved by the rich and powerful. The poor are denied justice because they cannot afford the cost.

This attitude might be traced to our cultural value. Traditional cultures once allowed the "use public office or authority for private advantage and gain."[14] Bribery, which is enforced by traditional cultural value of gift giving and reciprocity, may have contributed to the breakdown of the proper functioning of the legal system. Our law enforcement officers have been sucked into the culture of materialism. Money has become everything; people are indulging in all forms of dishonest activities to make money. One of the quickest ways for people to make money is through bribing. By taking bribes, many have been blinded and have perverted justice in the process. This is in contrast to the people who executed justice in traditional African cultures. Material gain and riches did not influence them. They pursued the truth and ensured that justice was served and those who sought justice got it!

Poor investigating skills, dismissing cases on technical grounds, bureaucratic red tapes, long pending cases in our courts, are all part of the failure of our legal systems. We need to restore credibility and the integrity of our legal system.

We will now turn to the Bible. What was the role and function of biblical law in the lives of the people of God? How was justice administered in the Bible to ensure that it was fair and just? What biblical values were foundational for the administration of justice?

---

14 David C. Buxbaum, ed., *Traditional and Modern Legal Institutions in Asia and Africa*. Leiden; Brill, 1967, 3.

The role, function, and purpose of the biblical law in society

The role of biblical laws in society

Does biblical law have any meaning and place for society today? We believe it does. We agree with Rushdoony "It is a modern heresy that holds that the law of God has no meaning or any binding force for man today. It is an aspect of the influence of humanistic and evolutionary thought on the church, and it posits an evolving, developing god."[15] Biblical law contains certain fundamental laws that are necessary for governing society, not forgetting that the world and its peoples belong to God and therefore are primarily under the rule of God.

We pointed out in our previous section that law is a common feature in every society. This is because laws provide the mechanism to regulate the behavior of society so they can live in harmony and peace with one another. In other words, the law helps in regulating human relationships. This is true with biblical laws. Biblical law was God's way of providing the moral mechanisms and boundaries, reflecting the divine will as to how humanity is to behave in society. Thus, biblical law encompasses every aspect of human life—religious, social, civil, economics, and criminal.

God gave Israel laws to regulate their relationships and behavior towards Him, towards one another and towards his nonhuman creation. The laws God gave Israel were to help create a godly and just society that would advance human development and wellbeing. All of biblical law is relational law. The purpose of biblical law was to build and maintain good relationships between neighbors and society in general. God demands law and order in his creation so there will be no anarchy and confusion in his restored creation. This we pointed out was also the goal of African traditional laws. Biblical and traditional laws have one thing in common building social relationships for the good and wellbeing of society to live peaceably with each other.

---

15 Rousas John Rushdoony, *The Institutes of Biblical Law*, 2.

All laws have their source in a divine being. Biblical laws have their source and origin in God. God is the Great Law Giver. Biblical laws are divine laws. They give guidance and direction for human life and behavior. Chris Wright astutely points out that the *Torah*, which refers to the whole of Old Testament Laws, simply means "guidance,' "instructions" and not just law. The *Torah* functioned as guidance and instructions in moral behavior and showed how Israel ought to live within a community. Biblical laws shaped the social and religious behavior of Israel. It outlined for them their legal responsibilities and set the boundaries that gave form to their behavior in society and regulated their relationship with God. The *Torah* expresses God's will for how human societies should live with Him and with one another (Ex. 20:2–17, Deut. 5:6–21).[16]

More importantly, biblical law was a way of life and not just a mechanism to promote law and order in the social life of the people of God.[17] Biblical law was relational. It shaped and directed their responsibility within the community. The laws concerned with the wellbeing of the people in their relationship with God, and their relationship with their fellow human beings. The laws served to protect and advance human well being.

The laws regulated Israel's social relations by placing on her certain moral responsibilities towards her fellow human beings especially in dealing with matters involving dispute over property damage, assault, negligence, family matters, sexual issues, economic disputes, and many others.[18] It also outlined some of the social responsibilities the community must have towards the weaker members of society (Ex. 22:21–27), regulations concerning judicial procedure (Ex. 23:14–19). We also see God gave them practical instructions concerning family life and sexual behavior (Lev. 18, 20), as well as laws governing their social life and behavior (Lev. 19:1–19).

Biblical law follows a certain format. Biblical law first asserts principles (Ex. 20:15, Deut. 25:4), second it cites cases to develop the implications of those principles (1 Cor. 9:9, 10, 14, 1 Tim. 5:18, Lev. 19:13, Deut. 24:14,

---

16 Wright, *Old Testament Ethics*, 284–5.
17 Elliot N. Dorff and Arthur Rosett. *A Living Tree: The Roots and Growth of Jewish Law*. New York: State University of New York Press, 1988, 94.
18 Wright, *Old Testament Ethics*, 285.

Lk. 10:7) and third, its goal is to enhance and restore God's fundamental order in society (Lk. 19:2–9, Matt. 5:23–26, Eph. 4:28).[19] This is very important for the administrators of the law to be able to interpret and administer the law justly. Where the cases was very difficult to judge they consulted and sought God's counsel and wisdom on the matter.

The functions and purposes of biblical laws

Biblical laws have specific functions and serve certain purposes within the community of God's people. They function to foster peace, justice, and liberty. The law is a means to protect the righteous but more importantly for the wicked to show them the way they are to live their lives so they can avoid doing what is wrong (1 Tim 1:9, 10). The law is only a means and not an end in itself. It helps to restrain the wicked from their evil behavior so the righteous will live in safety and peace (Ps. 125:3, Prov. 12:21). The law serves the following functions and purpose:

Law as a means for keeping peace and order

The law is to promote human harmony in a given society. The law was a mechanism put in place to deal with conflicts that might result in revenge because of the wrong or injury caused to another person. It was to prevent fighting and feuds. The law promoted justice, peace, freedom, and the happiness and wellbeing of the citizens of a nation or community. Our modern laws must promote peace and order. When any law fails in this primary task, that law must be discarded. Such law might lead to anarchy.

Law as an instrument of justice

What relations are there between justice and law? Often there is the tendency for one to think that laws always bring about justice. This is not true and Clarks is helpful in helping us to understand this relationship. He points out "justice and law, as words, have no necessary connection, nor is the law a necessary an instrument by which justice is attained."[20] This is

---

19 Rushdoony, *The Institutes of Biblical Law*, 12.
20 Harold Clark, *Biblical Law: Being a Text of the Statutes, Ordinances, and Judgments Established in the Holy Bible—with many Allusions to Secular Laws: Ancient, medieval and*

very important because often times the law is used to perpetuate injustice in societies where we have authoritarian rule and there is no respect for the rule of law by government. Such governments use law, and the whole legal system to commit injustices against the citizens knowing very well that they control the legal system of the nation and so they can run away with their evil ways and deeds without the arms of the law catching them.

The goal of the law is to bring justice. The judges' desires and passions must be to bring justice to those who come to them with cases to judge (2 Sam. 15:4). The law is meant to bring justice among humanity. Justice is the "constant, perpetual disposition to render" to every person his/her due. Because certain cultural, political, economic and social forces, can influence the meaning of the concept of justice it is important for this to be understood in light of God's word.[21]

Law as basis for liberty and freedom

The law defines Christian liberty or freedom. (Ps. 119:5). The Law was a schoolmaster. According to Apostle Paul (Gal. 3:24), the law functioned as a teacher of proper conduct. David saw the law as light and fountain of life" (Prov. 6:23, 13:14). Paul taught the law is holy, and the commandments are holy, just, and good (Rom. 7:12, 22). The law is needed to promote right behavior. This requires that the laws must be just and good. However, we know that good laws and just laws may be misused by some dishonest people who lack integrity and are not interested in seeking out the truth. The law must be applied rightly and justly if it is going to have any significant impact on human behavior so that it will influence life (1 Tim 1:18). We must never use the law as an "instrument of tyranny" or as a "weapon of offence by the law breakers."[22] The law of liberty or of rights is not a license to continue in our evil ways and do whatever we like. True liberty and freedom come as we submit ourselves to the laws of God and walk in his ways (James1:25, Ps. 119:44–45). True freedom comes by submitting

---

Modern—Documented to the Scriptures, Judicial Decisions and legal Literature. Portland, OR: Binfords & Mort, 1944Clark, 19.

21 Clark, *Biblical Law*, 20–21
22 Clark, *Biblical Law*, 17.

ourselves to the Spirit of God, for he is the one who gives true freedom (1 Cor. 3:17).

The scope and extent of biblical laws

Biblical law covers all areas of human life. Biblical writers categorized biblical laws into four broad areas. For example, Wright gives this classification as criminal law, case law, family law, cultic law, compassionate law and the administration of justice.[23] Even though Clarks' work is outdated, I find his classification interesting and worth citing here. His classification includes political law, civil law, economics and welfare laws, general laws, penal law that deals with crimes and punishments, and administration of law that deals with the procedure of law.[24] I think biblical law covers most of the fundamentals of our modern laws and expresses some of the basic values of traditional African laws that could help us in the way we formulate and administer these laws so they can serve the good of our societies today.

Our concern here is not to evaluate how comprehensive our modern laws are. Our interest is to address the moral decay in our legal systems and the constant pressure from outside partners who are pushing our legal systems to enact and promulgate laws that are against our cultural values. What can we learn from our traditional legal systems and biblical law to address these pertinent concerns? What principles can we draw from scriptures to help us deal with these moral problems of corruption and abuse of the African legal systems so the rule of law will be promoted in Africa?

There are two broad principles I think are very critical for us to deal with these problems. First, biblical law lays down broad and basic principles, which are fundamental for any just and fair laws. These principles include the dignity of human life, the sanctity of life, basic rights—individual, property, family laws, and so forth that must govern human lives and relationship in order to bring about shalom and blessings for humanity.

---

[23] Wright, *Old Testament Ethics*, 288–301.
[24] Harold Clark, *Biblical* Law, See the Table of Contents xii-xx.

We must ensure the religious values the Bible promotes and that underline these fundamental rights are taken very seriously.

The second sets of principles we can learn from biblical laws is in the area of the administration of the laws or of justice. Our current processes for administering justice and maintaining law and order are bedeviled with corruption, brutality, and bureaucratic red tapes and many other problems so that many see the legal system advancing injustice instead of promoting justice in the society. Many people do not have confidence in the legal systems in many African countries and many question the integrity of legal processes. One can have good laws but if they are not administered with integrity, honesty, and fairness, the entire legal system can crumble. Such systems often create regimes of impunity and anarchy. People lose respect for the law. We think both biblical administration of law and order with the traditional African way of administering justice will help us with our current dilemma. We will discuss this in detail in our next section.

Perhaps, the problems we are facing with the African legal systems are not because we have bad laws. It seems to me that the problems have more to do with the administration of justice. How justice is served to the people, who seek it is flouted by corruption and bribery. The rich seem to have the law on their side. The integrity of judicial offices and those legal officials who are entrusted with such a huge and sober responsibility to ensure justice is given to all who seek it, have compromised their character and values. They never follow the African values of honesty, integrity, seeking the truth and being fair. The Bible critically affirms these values when it comes to the administration of justice. Citizens have the right to fair trial and speedy justice. Most cases in African law courts have gone on for years and some even over a decade and there is no indication that the cases will be resolved soon. As the saying goes: "Justice delayed is justice denied." What moral principles and values can we learn from Scripture on the administration of justice?

The administration of justice and the moral character of its officers

As we have also stated in this book, God is the foundation of every justice system. He is just and fair in his judgments. Moreover, because of His character as a fair and just God, He demands that all who have the authority to administer justice follow his footsteps.

The Bible is concerned about proper and effective administration of justice. The Bible gives clear procedural guidelines for the administration of justice. To ensure quick and prompt handling of legal cases brought to the leaders in the community, local elders and judges were appointed within the community to handle the legal matters.

The need for local/traditional courts

To speed up justice, different cases were handled differently and by different people within the local community in the Bible. For instance, the victim's next-of-kin who has to avenge the blood of the family member killed handled the issue dealing with murder. In African traditional societies when someone kills a person accidentally, the community knew what to do and how to resolve the matter peacefully between the parties concerned. There are ways the traditional courts dealt with murder, which was effective and brought reconciliation, justice to the dead person's family and restoration of the offender. In this way, reconciliation was achieved in a more effective manner.

Criminal offences such as idolatry, kidnapping, disrespect for parents were public cases that demanded a capital punishment; there were other crimes as well. Judges also handled civil cases. There is a need to institutionalize traditional and family courts to deal with some of the legal matters relating to family and marriage. In the biblical legal system, local elders and special judges were appointed in the communities to administer justice to the people. (Num. 25:5 Deut. 16:18, 17:8–13, 25:1–3). This helped to expedite legal cases so that justice would be given promptly. The volume of cases pending in our centralized legal systems for many years has rendered the whole legal system ineffective.

There is a need to legislate and pass laws to empower and establish local courts/traditional courts to deal with some of the simple and not complicated legal matters to local elders to handle while the more complicated legal issues be assigned to the state courts. These local and community courts can handle most of the petty legal cases in an appropriate cultural manner. We must put a legal framework in place to sanction the decisions of these community courts as binding. It will ease our crowded prisons and save the government money in providing food and other social services to those detained in our prisons as they wait for their cases to be determined. We must affirm and empower local traditional courts with the elders as judges to deal with accidental murder cases while the state deals with the violent ones such as armed robbery and intentional killing.

The character of law enforcement agents

God warned the administrators of justice to carry out that responsibility diligently and apply the law with fairness. God warned also the judges against taking bribes and showing favoritism and therefore corrupting justice. Exodus 23:1–9 outlines the duties and responsibilities of the parties involved with litigation. Witnesses must "act with integrity, honesty, and independence."[25] Although people swear under oath to tell the truth, we see in practice many lies are told in the witness box and often time justice is denied for those who desperately need it. Witnesses should not give false reports or collude with evil people to tell lies in the witness box. One must persistently defend the truth. Following public opinion by going against the truth is not acceptable. The witness must not change his or her testimony to favor the poor nor the rich. He must be honest (Ex. 20:16, 23:1–3, 6, Mk. 10:19, Lk. 18:20)! False swearing, giving false testimony, or witness is against the law. Such witnesses violate the law and they could face capital punishment if found guilty in the Scriptures. Telling lies against another person was a serious criminal offence. Though a court can charge a witness for giving false information in our legal system, we are yet to see that happen.

---

25 Wright, *Old Testament Ethics*, 303.

In African societies when the elders see the offender is telling lies, they make them take an oath and a curse is administered with the oath. If the offender were guilty, because he gave false witness or lied, whatever the curse was would happen to the guilty person. This was also the case in the administration of justice in the Bible (Judg. 17:2). This was to ensure that justice is not denied a person because someone told a lie about the person. Truth finding was central to giving justice to people and so all forms of falsehood was treated with the contempt it deserves. Exodus 23:4–5, affirms the idea that the goal of the administration of justice or the law is to promote and restore good relationship between members of the community. There is the tendency for relationships to become strained if there is litigation against a member of the community. Such strained relationships could be extended to the family members or the property of the other party. The Bible warns the parties in a dispute not to "neglect the requirements of brotherly obligation even though they are engaged in legal conflict."[26]

Lastly, the judges must discharge their duties with integrity and fairness. They must be impartial and not corrupt. God warned them not to twist justice against someone because of his status, nor charge anybody falsely with evil or put an innocent person to death. They must not take bribes for bribes have a tendency to blind and cause one to pervert justice thus, causing harm to the one who is right. Judges must treat the aliens who appear before them with respect and understanding and compassion because they know what it means to be an alien (Ex. 23:6–9, Lev. 19:15). The survival of the people in the land will depend on how their judges administer true justice in the land (Deut. 16:18–20).

One of the fundamental reasons why judges must judge with fairness is because God is a just judge. King Jehoshaphat made this fact clear when he appointed judges in his kingdom to administer justice. He said to them,

> Always think carefully before pronouncing judgment. Remember that you do not judge to please people but to please

---

26 Wright, *Old Testament Ethics*, 304.

the Lord. He will be with you when you render the verdict in each case that comes before you. Fear the Lord and judge with care, for the Lord our God does not tolerate perverted justice, partiality, or the taking of bribes.... You must always act in the fear of the Lord, with integrity and undivided hearts (2 Chron. 20:6–7, 9, NLT).

God demands that the legal processes we follow in administering justice are fair and just. Anything short of this goal is unacceptable to Him and he takes these matters of justice seriously because it is the essence of who He is. Wright is correct in pointing out that

> There is growing awareness in our own day that people, especially, the powerless, the poor, the illiterate, the immigrant, the asylum seeker are as often hurt by the cumbersome and complicated process of the law, even good law, as they are victims of bad law or deliberate injustice. Legal processes that are delayed, demeaning, and discriminatory, or simply unaffordable by the poor, are as bad as active injustice and oppression.[27]

How can we ensure that our legal systems are just and that they promote the social wellbeing of our societies? What should the Church's role be in this? We think the Church's fundamental role is to ensure that the laws of our country are just, they promote the wellbeing of our people, and that all citizens follow these laws.

Creating just and righteous legal systems

For any society to have a legal system that is just and fair, we must acknowledge that God is good, righteous, and just. God is the great lawgiver

---

27 Wright, *Old Testament Ethics*, 304.

and the great judge. He is the model for justice. He is righteous in all his ways and he judges righteously and justly.

Most of the rules of biblical law are rules of universal jurisprudence, which are essential to the existence of any organized society. They can serve as a paradigm for our quest to develop and promulgate laws that are just and fair. They cover some of the basic issues that affect human relationship and existence; family, religion, property, value of human life, and basic rights for the vulnerable in society—the poor, aliens, slaves, widows, and many others. The Church must cooperate with legal institutions that formulate our laws to raise some of these concerns, and encourage them to take the biblical values we have outline in this chapter seriously, as they make laws and administer those laws.

The goal of the biblical justice and judicial system is to bring restorative justice to the community so the community will live in peace and prosperity. Proper administration of law should bring God's shalom to humanity. This must be the goal for our legal systems in Africa. For us to achieve this goal, we must look critically at our judicial and legal systems in Africa and evaluate the results we have had in our justice systems to determine if they have brought about restoration or not. If not, we need to work on this. It might mean that we need to focus on our legal training and formulations of laws to give serious attention to this aim and purpose of biblical law.

The laws of any society must reflect justice and compassion. We cannot transform society by laws alone. There is the need for solid and good moral foundation built in humanity to be able to use the law in the right way so transformation can take place.

If people do not have a good moral foundation, good and just laws may be used unjustly or simply ignored (Amos 2:6, Neh. 5:1–13).[28] Nehemiah castigated the landowners and moneylenders who were using the land laws, violating the loan laws to redeem land from their impoverished relatives, and taking exorbitant interests on loans for their own greed. Nehemiah appealed to their consciences, pointing out what they were doing was not

---

28 Wright, *Old Testament Ethics*, 324.

right, and appealed to them to "walk in the fear of the Lord" and to do what was right.

The powerful and those with affluence can make unjust laws to their own advantage. Oppression can be given legal backing through dubious legislation. This is true with many African laws and decrees that have legitimated oppression and autocratic rule. Isaiah warns such people:

> Destruction is certain for the unjust judges, for those who issue unfair laws. They deprive the poor, the widows, and the orphans of justice. Yes, they rob widows and fatherless children! (Isa. 10:1–2 NLT)

Humanity will always twist the laws for their own selfish interests because of the wickedness of the human heart. In our society where we have entrenched evil and injustice into our legal systems, we need God's power to break this evil power over our legal systems. It is important that people experience God's grace, which comes through salvation and restoration if we will establish, maintain, and restore genuine social justice.[29] Wright is right to point out that "The law by itself cannot achieve those ends. Justice flows from the knowledge of *God*, not merely from the knowledge of the *law*."[30]

Given the fact that true justice is restorative, there are certain laws in our legal system that we must deal with. This has to do with capital punishment. I think in our traditional judicial systems capital punishment was not common unless the crime was one that brought calamity to the entire community or it was committed against the gods and they were no other means of rectifying the problem. There are many who have been condemned to be hanged, and they have been kept in condemned cells for many years and still have not been executed. The psychological pain and torture they go through every day not knowing when they will be executed is disturbing. In trying to pursue justice, injustice is done to these people.

---

29 Wright, *Old Testament Ethics*, 325.
30 Wright, *Old Testament Ethics*, 325

I think we must expunge the death penalty from our laws in Africa. Jesus rescinds the death penalty law as we see expressed by his attitude toward the woman who was brought before him caught in adultery (John 8:1–11). Jesus showed compassion and mercy towards her. If the goal of justice is to restore people then when we see genuine repentance, we can temper justice with mercy. This is the nature and character of God. There must be room in our legal systems for people to seek forgiveness and see it provided when genuine repentance has taken place and is evident in the life of the offender so he or she can be restored to the community.

The necessity to uphold law and order in society

Christians must be law-abiding citizens and not lawbreakers! Salvation restores us to a position of law keeping.[31] Without law and obedience to that law, society would collapse into anarchy and fall into the hands of hoodlums. In essence, the law helps to keep the wicked and lawless in check through the sanctions it provides and at the same time bring life to the righteous and good person to experience shalom and blessings. What are some of the principles we can learn from the Bible in terms of keeping law and order in our societies so we can live peacefully with all human beings?

God's purpose for Israel to keep the law is to maintain its social relationship and life. This is paradigmatic for us today. It is important to recognize that keeping the laws of God and of the land was mandatory for the people of Israel. Their very life and survival depended on it. Concerning the law, Israel was commanded to pay careful attention to the law to do it (Deut. 10:12–13, Ps. 119).

Upholding law and order is our moral responsibility as citizens of the nation. We owe this moral responsibility to the nation. This is God's requirement for us. It is God's will that we live in peace with all human beings. Any behavior that will jeopardize a peaceful coexistence must be avoided. We must seek peace and justice in a way that will enhance human dignity and wellbeing.

---

31 Rushdoony, *The Institutes of Biblical Law*, 3.

The necessity to uphold the law must go beyond the threat of punishment or sanctions that will be given against those who violate the law. Rather we must obey the laws because they are critical to our survival, as a nation and that; we are participants in the democratic process of making these laws through our representatives to govern our lives and affairs. We owe society a moral duty to maintain and uphold the peace and tranquility we enjoy as citizens. Therefore, obeying the laws of a land is a necessary precondition for a peaceful human community. Following the law enhanced social relationships thus fostering good neighborliness and seeking to promote the wellbeing of the community. Therefore, in the legal codes there are laws set up to relate harmonious social relations. Where there are breaches, compensations and restitutions are paid to restore relationships.

Besides the social reasons for upholding, the law there is a theological reason for obedience to the law in the Bible. The law was a sort of Covenant between God and humanity. By ratifying, the covenant with God, Israel was under moral obligation to uphold the laws of God.

How can we obey God's laws and the laws of our land? Love is the foundation for biblical law. God who is love and just gives us his just laws and he desires that His people live to reflect his holiness, justice, and peace. The motivation for being law-abiding citizens is rooted in our love for God. God is our highest ethical motivation. Both the OT writes and Jesus emphasized the importance of putting God first in all we do. Wright makes this important observation:

> No moral imperative ranks higher than the command to love God with the totality of one's whole being. This fundamental principle is enshrined in the Shema…, is further established in the order of the Ten Commandments, which begins with the prohibition of worshipping any other god before… the Lord. It is given even more stringent social clout in the sharp and uncompromising instructions in Deuteronomy 13.[32]

---

32 Wright, *Old Testament Ethics*, 306.

Jesus reiterated the same idea when he told his disciples that if they truly love him they will keep his commandments (Jn. 14:15). Loving God is fundamental to our obedience to his commands, which is to do justice, show mercy and walk humbly before him.

Lastly, the final reason why we should obey the laws of the land is that we are commanded by the Lord to respect the rule of Law. At the core of many biblical exhortations to obey the law is in compliance with God's command and the threat of severe punishment for those who disobey those laws and rewards and blessings for those who obey them (Lev. 26:3–46). Biblical law was the national law of Israel. It was binding on all Israelites, as well as on the aliens who lived among them (Deut. 31:12). There is value in keeping the laws of the land. Doing so will enhance our lives. Disobeying the laws of the land will deprive us of life (Ezek. 20:13, 21, 25).

The laws of the land are binding on all citizens, aliens, whether they are temporary or permanent residents or mere travelers. As long as one lives in this place, the laws of the land are binding on the individual.

Breaking the law of the land through for example, stealing, corruption, bribery, adultery, murder, coveting another person's property or land is a crime against God since God is the lawgiver and every person and everything in his creation belongs to Him. Therefore, an offence against the law is an offence against God (Ps. 51:4). I would like to suggest some principles to deal with the problem of the administration of justice.

Some basic biblical principles and values we need to apply to improve our African legal systems

- There are many ways that justice was administered in the Bible. It was not always through a centralized courthouse where all cases are heard and decided. There were at least two structures that aided this process of administration of justice. There are those that related to the family. Chris Wright calls this family-focused justice. This is not about legal matters that related to family laws. Rather, provisions were made in the laws for family members to have legal duties to the wider community to take legal responsibility rather than a public authority such as the state or public prosecutor to do so. In this case, some of the traditional institutions can be mandated and empowered to administer justice to free the courts and ease the congestion of cases in the courts.

- There is need for proper education in matters related to the laws of the land. This is very important. In a continent where we have high rates of illiteracy, it is easy for people to be ignorant of the laws and they can easily become prey to manipulations and exploitations by the rich and powerful. One of the basic biblical values is the need for children to be taught the Torah from the home. We must be able to simplify the laws of the land so people can learn them and live as responsible members of society. To do this the laws must be published and the government must take the responsibility to ensure citizens get to know what the laws say and understand the implications of not obeying the laws of the land. Since we say, ignorance is not an excuse to break the law; we must ensure that citizens are not ignorant of the law. This was a biblical mandate! In traditional African societies, the laws—customs and traditions were taught to children in their homes. They grew up knowing what these customs and traditions were. They knew how to live and how to avoid breaking the customs, which they understood carry certain consequences. To be law-abiding citizens, people must know what the laws are. Civic education is critical and we must encourage and support efforts in this area by civil society groups working in this area.

- We should perhaps make good use of the African traditional courts that were run by the elders of the community. It would be good if the legal institutions in African can explore ways in which they can incorporate this important institution in the administration of justice in Africa. These institutions are more trusted and they are not corrupted by the pollution that exists in our modern court systems. The elders who run these institutions are people who have proven character, trustworthy, just, and fair. They are not given to bribery and corruption because they know they sit in the place of the ancestors and they are to be faithful and true to the laws of the land and ensure they are followed. If they break this trust not only does it bring shame and dishonor to their name, but the ancestors can also judge them, in whose seat they sit to make decisions for the living.

- In administering justice, one must have the fear of God and determine to walk in his ways. This is one of the foundations for wisdom. The fear of the Lord is the beginning of wisdom. Since judges' work involves having great wisdom to make decisions, it is important they draw from the source of all wisdom, God. Moral values such as integrity, honesty, pursuing the truth, wisdom, incorruptibility, impartiality, understanding, and compassion set out in the Bible for judges which we also see demonstrated by the elders in Africa who are involved with judicial matters must be taken very seriously if we will have a just legal system. Judges and judicial officers must do justice, love mercy and walk humbly before God (Micah 6:8). This is what God's character is. Judges must reflect the character of the one who has called them to this task of bringing justice to those who need it. When they fail in giving justice, they fail the God who has appointed them and they will be answerable to Him.
- The law we enact in Africa must reflect our religious ethos. Since God and religion is central to the African life, our laws must reflect the will of God. We owe it to ourselves to develop laws that reflect our religious and moral values. There is the tendency by humanistic ideologies of today to promote humanistic ethics by relegating religion to the background. If this happens, it will be a disaster for us. Already we see in many African countries the pressure from other secular cultures to enact laws that give room for tolerance and to accept certain cultural values and practices that go against our own values and ethics by embracing rationality and tolerance. We should not shy away from our

religious values. If God is the center of African religiosity, then he must be center in our laws and ethics as well.

- To ensure true justice, legal penalties must be specific, appropriate, and proportionate, supervised and subject to maximum limits. The dignity and human rights of convicted offenders must also be recognized and affirmed and accorded the offenders in the administration of justice (Deut. 25:2–3). This is because the Bible holds the view that these offenders are still our brothers. Therefore, in spite of the offense, we must treat them as our brothers and not as enemies. We must respect those we call criminals.[33]
- In light of the above bullet, I would like to raise one critical issue here concerning our prisons. The whole prison system in Africa must be looked at as a critical part of our justice system. There was no room for imprisonment prescribed in the Old Testament legal laws. Biblical law did not endorse prisons. There were no prisons in the African judicial systems either. We need to think about our prisons and evaluate their effectiveness in restoring people to community. This is very important and significant. In African traditional system, offenders were dealt with and they were quickly restored to life in the communities. The current prisons are different. Our modern prisons, which are associated with our legal systems is bringing a lot of strain on African governments' budgets. Thousands of people are incarcerated in our prisons and living in horrible human conditions with many violations of human rights. They are isolated from the community. In fact, when they are released from prison and they come back to the community they are rejected by the community. The prisons are not meeting the goal of biblical and African traditional justice, which is restoration to community. Our prisons are not reforming and restoring offenders to the community. Are there ways that our legal systems will see justice

---

33 Wright, *Old Testament Ethics*, 313.

as relational justice whereby they deal with offenders, so the purpose of the punishment given is to restore relationship with the aggrieved party and not to make them enemies? In this way, we can build strong and vital relationships with offenders so that they can transform their behavior and contribute to the building of that community.

- The Bible will help as we formulate laws on "needs" verses "rights." Biblical laws prioritize human needs over strict legal rights and claims. This important principle is very vital in societies where people's rights take precedent over people's urgent needs. Before God, people matter more than things. Even better yet, some people's needs and circumstances matter more than other people's legitimate claims.[34] For example, the need of a refugee slave, a female prisoner, a debtor and landless person were more important against the claims of his owner, the rights of a soldier, the legal claims of a creditor and against the legal property of a landowner respectively (Deut. 23:15–16, 21:10–14, 24:10–13, 24:19–22).[35] The principle is this according to Wrights, "The law inculcates an ethos in which even the law itself, and the rights, and claims it gives to people, must yield to the realities of human need."[36] In fact, just laws must serve human needs and priority must be given to those needs than the legal rights and process. This principle will help us to put human needs at the center rather than just interest in the rights the laws provides for us, as individuals that neglect the urgent human needs around us that we have to meet.

---

34 Wright, *Old Testament Ethics*, 312.
35 Wright, *Old Testament Ethics*, 314.
36 Wright, *Old Testament Ethics*, 314.

Conclusion

In this chapter, I explored biblical law and showed its relevance for our task in the administration of justice in Africa. I pointed out biblical law and justice is based on the character of God as just and righteous. God requires all who are in positions to administer justice and the law to do so reflecting his character of fairness to all who seek the services of the justice system. This requires officers who have proven qualities of integrity, fear God, and seek his wisdom as they administer the law and justice in our societies.

Bibliography

Aborampah, M. Family Structures in African Fertility Studies: Some conceptual and Methodological Issues," in *A Current Bibliography in African Affairs*, 1985–1986, Vol. 18.

Ackah, C. A. *Akan Ethics: A study of the Moral ideas and the Moral behavior of the Akan Tribes of Ghana*. Accra: Ghana University Press, 1988.

Arieli, Yehoshua. "Individualism: A European Concept Crosses the Atlantic" in Donald Capps and Richard Fenn, eds. *Individualism Reconsidered Readings Bearing on the Endangered Self in Modern Society*. New Jersey, Princeton Theological Seminary: Center for Religion, Self and Society, 1992.

Asare Opoku, Kofi. *Hearing and keeping: Akan Proverbs*. Accra: Asempa Publishers, 1997.

Augsburger, David. *Conflict Mediation across Cultures: Pathways and Patterns*. Louisville, Westminster/John Knox, 1992.

Ayah, Ebebe John. "The Family as the Basic Structure of Society in Catholic Social Teaching and Communitarian Thought: An Assessment in Light of the Sociology of the Family." A Dissertation presented to the Faculty of Theology, Katholieke Universiteit Leuve for Doctor's Degree in Theology. Leuve, 2005.

Banks, Robert. *God the Worker*. Australia: Albatross Book, 1992.

Barclay, John M.B. *Obey the Truth: Paul's Ethics in Galatians*. Minneapolis: Fortress Press, 1988.

Barnette, Henlee H. *The Church and the Ecological Crisis*. Grand Rapids, MI: William B. Eerdmans Publishing Company, 1972.

Bediako, Kwame "De-Sacralization and Democratization:" Some Theological Reflections on the Role of Christianity in Nation-Building in Modern Africa," in *Transformation*, 12 (1995): 8.

Beker, J.C. "Paul's Theology: Consistent or Inconsistent?" *New Testament Studies* 34/3 (1988).

Beker, J. C. *Paul the Apostle: The Triumph of God in Life and Thought.* Edinburgh: T&T Clark, 1980.

Bergant, Dianne. *The Earth is the Lord's: The Bible, Ecology, and Worship.* Collegeville, MN: The Liturgical Press, 1998.

Bergmann, Sigurd. *Creation Set Free: The Spirit as Liberator of Nature.* Trans. by Douglas Stott. Grand Rapids, MI: William B. Eerdmans Publishing Company, 2005.

Berman, Harold J. *Law and Revolution: The Formation of Western Legal Tradition.* Cambridge, MA. Harvard University Press, 1983.

Birch, Charles, William Eakin and Jay B. McDaniel, eds., *Liberating Life.* Maryknoll: Orbis Books, 1990.

Block, Peter. *Stewardship: Choosing Service over Self-Interest.* San Francisco, CA: Berrett-Koehler Publishers, 1993.

Brandon, Guy. *Free to Live: Expressing the Love of Christ in an Age of Debt.* London: SPCK, 2010.

Brendan, B.S.J. "Living Out the Righteousness of God: The Contribution of Rom 6:1–8, 13 to an Understanding of Paul's Ethical Presupposition," *The Catholic Biblical Quarterly* 43:4 (1981), 565–567.

Brown, Colin. *Philosophy and the Christian Faith: A Historical Sketch from the Middle Ages to the Present Day.* Dowers Grove, IL: InterVarsity Press, 1968.

Brown, Edward R. *Our Father's World: Mobilizing the Church to Care for Creation.* Downers Grove, IL: InterVarsity Press Books.

Brueggemann, Walter. *The Prophetic Imagination.* Philadelphia: Fortress, 1978.

Brunner, Emil. *The Divine Imperative,* Trans. by Olive Wyon. Philadelphia: The Westminster Press 1937.

Bujo, Benezet. *The Ethical Dimension of Community: The African Model and the Dialogue Between North and South.* Nairobi: Paulines Publications, 1998.

Buckle, Stephen. "Natural Law" in *A Companion to Ethics* by Peter Singer, ed. Oxford, Blackwell Publishers, 1993.

Burch, M. "Justice" in A. Elwell, ed. *Evangelical Dictionary of Theology,* 2nd ed. Grand Rapids: Baker Academic, 2001.

Busia, K. A. *Africa in Search of Democracy.* London: Routledge & Kengan Paul, 1967.

Bouma-Prediger, Steven. *For the beauty of the earth: a christian vision for creation care.* Grand Rapids, MI: Baker Academic, 2001.

Burnside, J. P. et al. *Religion and Rehabilitation.* Cullompton: Willan Publishing, 2004.

Buxbaum, David C. Ed., *Traditional and Modern Legal Institutions in Asia and Africa*. Leiden: Brill, 1967.

Carmody, John. *Ecology and Religion: Towards a New Christian Theology of Nature*. New York: Paulist Press, 1983.

Clark, Harold. *Biblical Law: Being a Text of the Statutes, Ordinances, and Judgments Established in the Holy Bible—with many Allusions to Secular Laws: Ancient, medieval and Modern—Documented to the Scriptures, Judicial Decisions and legal Literature*. Portland, OR: Binfords & Mort, 1944.

Coady, C. A. J. "Politics and the Problem of Dirty Hands," in *A Companion to Ethics*, ed. Peter Singer. Cambridge, MA: Basil Blackwell, 1991.

Cole, Graham. "Christianity as a Relational Religion," in Michael Schluter and John Ashcroft, eds. *Jubilee Manifesto: A Framework, Agenda and Strategy for Christian Social Reform*. Leicester: InterVarsity Press, 2005.

Collste, Göran "Moral Justification for Power," in Stewardship: *Management, Ethics and Ecclesiology*, ed. Sven-Erik Brodd. Uppsala, Sweden: Church of Sweden Research Department, 1993.

Cosden, D. *A Theology of Work: Work and the New Creation*. Milton Keynes, UK: Paternoster, 2004.

Cranfield, C.E.B. "St. Paul and the Law" *SJT* 17 (1964), 43–68.

Cranefield, C. E. B. *A Critical and Exegetical Commentary on the Epistle to the Romans*. 2 Vols. Edinburgh: T&T Clark, 1975.

Danquah, J.B. *Akan Doctrine of God*. London: Frank Cass, 1968.

Daube, David. *Law and Wisdom in the Bible*. Edited and compiled by Calum Carmichael. West Conshohocken, PA: Templeton Press, 2010.

Deidun, T.J. *New Covenant Morality in Paul*. Rome: Biblical Institute Press, 1981.

Delaney, Sarah. "African Family values threatened by Western ideology." http:/www.catholicnews.com/data/stories/cns/0904495.htm. Accessed May 9, 2011.

Dennison, William D. "Indicative and Imperative: the Basic Structure of Pauline Ethics," *Calvin Theological Journal* (1979).

"Description of Family—American Heritage Dictionary," http://eduaction.yahoo.com/reference/dictionary/entry/family. Accessed May 6, 2011.

Dodd, C.H. Indicative and Imperative: the Basic Structure of Pauline Ethics", *Calvin Theological Journal* (1979).

Donahue, John R. S.J., "Biblical Perspectives on Justice" in *The Faith That Does Justice: Examining the Christian Sources of Social Change,* ed. John C. Haughey, S.J. New York: Paulist Press, 1977.

Dorff, Elliot N. and Arthur Rosett. *A Living Tree: The Roots and Growth of Jewish Law*. New York: State University of New York Press, 1988.

Dunn, J. D. G. *Romans* (WBC) I. Dallas, Texas: Word Books Publisher, 1988.

Dunn, J. D. G. "Works of the Law and the Curse of the Law, Gal 3:10–14" *NTS* 31 (1985).

Dyrness, William A. *How Does America Hear the Gospel?* Grand Rapids, Michigan: Wm. B. Eerdmans Publishing Company, 1989.

Epzstein, Leone. *Social Justice in the Ancient Near East and the People of the Bible.* London: SMC Press, 1983.

Erikson, T. H. *Ethnicity and Nationalism: Anthropological Perspectives*, 2nd ed. London: Pluto Press, 2002.

"Family," http://www.thefreedictionary.com/family. Accessed May 6, 2011.

Farley, Wendy. *Tragic Vision and Divine Compassion*. Louisville, KY: Westminster Press, 1990.

Fee, Gordon. "Toward a Theology of 1 Corinthians." Atlanta: SBL, 1990.

Fortes, M. & Evans-Pritchard (eds.), *African Political Systems*. London: KPI, 1987.

Fuller, D.P. *Gospel and Law: Contrast or Continuum?* Grand Rapids: Eerdmans, 1980.

Furnish, V.P. "Belonging to Christ: A Paradigm for Ethics in First Corinthians" *Interpretation* 44/2 (April 1990).

Gbadegesin, Segun. *African Philosophy: Traditional Yoruba Metaphysics and Contemporary African Realities*. New York: Peter Lang, 1991.

Gifford, Paul. *African Christianity: Its Public Role* (Bloomington and Indianapolis: Indiana University Press, 1998).

Gifford, Paul. *Christianity and Politics in Doe's Liberia*. Cambridge, U.K.: Cambridge University Press, 1993.

Gill, Robin. *A Textbook of Christian Ethics*. Edinburgh: T. & T. Clark, 1985.

Gnanakan, Ken. *Responsible Stewardship of God's Creation*. World Evangelical Alliance—Theological Commission, 2004.

Grenz, Stanley. *The Moral Quest. Foundations of Christian Ethics*. Downers Grove, IL: InterVarsity Press, 1997.

de Gruchy, John W. "The Dialectic of Reconciliation: Church and the Transition to Democracy in South Africa" in *The Reconciliation of Peoples: Challenge to the Churches.* Eds. Gregory Baum and Harold Wells Maryknoll, N.Y.: Orbis Books, 1997.

Gyekye, Kwame. *African Cultural Value: An Introduction*. Accra: Ghana: Sankofa Publishing Company, 1996.

Haan, Roelf. *The Economics of Honour: Biblical reflections on money and property*. Translated by Nancy Forest-Flier, Geneva: WCC Publications, 1988.

Habel, Norman C., & Peter Trudinger, eds. *Exploring Ecological Hermeneutics*. Atlanta: Society of Biblical Literature, 2008.

Haldane, John. "Medieval and Renaissance Ethics", in *A Companion to Ethics* by Peter Singer, ed. Oxford, Blackwell Publishers, 1993.

Hamilton, Neil Q. "The Holy Spirit and Eschatology in Paul." Edinburgh: Oliver and Boyd Ltd, 1957.

Hauerwas, Stanley. *Character and the Christian Life: A Study in theological Ethics*. San Antonio: Trinity University Press, 1985.

Hauerwas, Stanley. *A Community of Character: Towards a Constructive Christian Social Ethics*. Notre Dame: University of Notre Dame Press, 1981.

Hays, Richard B. "The Problem of Method in New Testament Ethics," *Interpretation* 44/1 (January 1990).

Hays, Richard B. *The Moral Vision of the New Testament: Community, Cross, New Creation, a Contemporary Introduction to New Testament Ethics*. San Francisco: HarperSanFrancsco, 1996.

Hazelton, Roger. "Humanistic Ethics" in *A New Dictionary of Christian Ethics*, eds. J. Macquarrie and J. Childress. London: SCM Press, 1986.

Helm, P. "Idealism" in *New Dictionary of Theology*, eds. S.B. Ferguson and D.F. Wright. Leicester: InterVarsity Press, 1988.

Henry, Carl F.H. *Christian Personal Ethics*. Grand Rapids: Baker Book House, 1977.

Hodge, Charles. *Commentary on the Epistle to the Romans*. Grand Rapids: Wm. B. Eerdmans, 1947.

http://definitions.uslegal.com/r/rule-of-law, Accessed May 22, 2011.

http:// en.wikipedia.org/wiki/human_nature. Accessed January 20, 2011.

http://en.wikipedia.org/wiki/Ecology. Accessed April 19, 2011.

http://en.wikipedia.org/wiki/Politics. Accessed January 2011.

http://en.wikipedia.org/wiki/Politics. Accessed January 2011.

http://en.wikipedia.org/wiki/Stewardship, Accessed February 2011.

http://www.ascensionhealth.org/index.php?option=com_content&view=article&id=90: principle-of-stewardship&Itemid-171. Accessed February 2011.

http://www.answers.com/topic/rule-of-law, "Rule of Law" West's Encyclopedia of American Law." Accessed, May 31, 2011.

http:/www.catholicnews.com/data/stories/cns/0904495.htm. Accessed May 9, 2011.

http://www.oed.com/view/Entry/80307?redirectedFrom=governance#. Accessed February 2011.

http://www.oed.com/view/Entry/237575?redirectedFrom=politics#. Accessed February 2011

http://www.unescap.org/pdd/prs/ProjectActivities/ongiong/gg/Goverance.asp. Accessed January 2011.

Hutchinson, John & Anthony D. Smith, eds. *Ethnicity*. Oxford: Oxford University Press, 1996.

Idowu, B. *Oludumare, God in Yoruba Belief.* London: Longmans, 1963.

Idowu, B.E. *African Traditional Religion: A Definition*. London: SCM Press, 1973.

Jenkins, Richard. *Rethinking Ethnicity: Arguments and Explorations*. London: Sage Publications 1997.

Jenkins, Willis. *Ecologies of Grace: Environmental Ethics and Christian Theology*. New York: Oxford University Press, 2008.

Johnson, Carol. *And the Leaves of the Tree are for the Healing of the Nations: Biblical and Theological Foundations for Eco-Justice*, no date, no Publisher, no date.

Johnson, Elizabeth. *She Who Is: The Mystery of God in Feminist Theological Discourse*. New York: Crossroad, 2002.

Justice: West Encyclopedia of America Law, American Heritage Dictionary. Accessed February 25, 2011.

Justice-Wikipedia, http://en.wikipedia.or/wiki/Justice, Accessed February 2011).

Kaiser, Walter C. Jr. *Toward Old Testament Ethics*. Grand Rapids, MI: Academie Books, 1983.

Kant, Emmanuel. *Religion within the Limits of Reason Alone*, Trans. by T. M. Greene and H. T. Hudson Harper Touch Books, 1960.

Klyne Snodgrass, "Spheres of Influence: A Possible Solution to the Problem of Paul and the Law" *JSNT* 39 (1988), 93–113.

Kudadjie, J.N. "Does Religion determine Morality in African Society? A View Point" in *Religion in a Pluralistic Society* ed. J.S. Pobee, Leiden: E.J. Brill, 1976.

Lartey, E. *Pastoral Counseling in Intercultural Perspective: A Study of Some African (Ghanaian) and Anglo-American View on Human Existence and Counseling.* New York: Peter Lang, 1987.

Lewis, Jim. *A Theology of Work*, www.thewitness.org, 2003.

Lohfink, Gerherd. *Jesus and Community: The Social Dimension of Christian Faith.* Philadelphia: Fortress Press, 1984.

Lukes, Steven *Key Concepts in the Social Sciences: Individualism.* Basil: Blackwell, 1973.

Malchow, Bruce V. *Social Justice in the Hebrew Bible.* Collegeville, Minnesota: Liturgical Press, 1996.

MacGaffey, Wyatt. "Aesthetics and Politics of Violence in Central Africa," *Journal of African Cultural Studies* 13:1, In Honour of Professor Terence Ranger (June 2000): 63–75.

MacIntyre, Alasdair. *After Virtue*, Notre Dame: University of Notre Dame Press, 1981.

Mallešević, Siniša. *The Sociology of Ethnicity.* London: Sage Publications, 2004.

Marshall, L.H. *The Challenge of New Testament Ethics.* London: Macmillan, 1950.

Martin, Kingsley. *Objections to Humanism*, ed. H.J. Blackham. London: Constable, 1963.

Mbiti, John. *African Religions and Philosophy.* New York: Doubleday, 1970.

McFague, Sallie. *Models of God: Theology for the Ecological Nuclear Age.* Philadelphia: Fortress press, 1987.

McGrath, Alister E. "The stewardship of creation: an evangelical affirmation" in *The Care of Creation: Focusing concern and action*, ed. R. J. Berry. Leicester: InterVarsity Press, 2000.

McKenna, David. *Love your Work!* USA: Victor Books, 1990.

Mills, Paul. "The Economy," in *Jubilee Manifesto: A framework, agenda, & strategy for christian social reform.* Ed. Michael Schluter & John Ashcroft. Leicester: InterVarsity Press, 2005.

Meeks, M. Douglas. *God the Economist: The Doctrine of God and Political Economy.* Minneapolis: Fortress, 1989.

Meeks, Wayne. "A Hermeneutics of Social Embodiement" *Harvard Theological Review* 79 (1986).

Mein, Andrew. "Psalm 101 and the Ethics of Kingship," in *Ethical and Unethical in the Old Testament*, ed. Katharine Dell. New York, T & T Clark, 2010.

Mehl, Roger *Catholic Ethics and Protestants Ethics*, Trans. by James H. Fartey. Philadelphia: The Westminster Press, 1971.

Moo, D. J. "Law, Works of the Law, and Legalism in Paul," *Wesley Theological Journal* (WTJ) 45 (1983).

Moo, D. J. "Exegetical Note: Romans 6:1–14" *Trinity Journal* 3.2 (1982).

Mott, Stephen C. *Biblical Ethics and Social Change*. Oxford: Oxford University Press, 1982.

Murray, John. *The Imputation of Adam's Sin*. Phillipsburg: Presbyterian and Reformed Publishing Co. 1959.

Theissen, H. C. *Lectures in Systematic Theology* rev. ed. by V. D. Doerksen. Grand Rapids: Wm. B. Eerdmans, 1979.

Nana Chief Azuma Ndagu Edward, "Rebuild Africa's Family Values." http://www.scribd.com/doc/12529432/Rebuild-Africas-Family-values-By-Chief-Azuma-Edward. Accessed on May 6, 2011.

Niebuhr, Reinhold. *The Nature and Destiny of Man: A Christian Interpretation*, Vol. I. London: Nisbet and Co. Ltd, 1941.

Nygren, Anders. *Romans*. Philadelphia: Fortress Press, 1975.

Nzimiro, Ikenna. *Studies in Ibo Political Systems: Chieftaincy and Politics in Four Niger States*, Berkeley, California, USA: University of California Press, 1972.

Obeng, Emmanuel Adow. "Healing the Groaning Creation in Africa," in *Theology of Reconstruction: Exploratory Essays* 2nd ed. Eds. Mary N. Getui and Emmanuel A. Obeng. Nairobi, Acton Publishers, 2003.

Okafo, Nonso. "Relevance of African Traditional Jurisprudence on Control, Justice, and Law: A Critique of the Igbo Experience" in *African Journal of Criminology & Justice Studies: AJCJS Volume 2, No. 1, June 2006*. Accessed at www. PDF version.

O'Neill. Onora. "Kantian Ethics," in *A Companion to Ethics* by Peter Singer, ed. Oxford, Blackwell Publishers, 1993.

Opoku, Kofi Asare. *Hearing and Keeping: Akan Proverbs, African Proverbs Series*, Vol. 2. Ed. John S. Mbiti. Accra, Ghana: Asempa Publishers, 1997.

Pilch, John J. and Bruce J. Malina, eds. *Handbook of Biblical Social Values*. Peabody: Hendrickson Publishers, 2000.

"Power" in *Webster's New World Dictionary*. London: Pocket Books, 2003.

Preece, G. "Work, Theology of" in *Global Dictionary of Theology*, eds. William Dyrness and Matti-Veli Karkkainen. Downers Grove: InterVarsity Press, 2008.

von Rad, Gerhard. *Old Testament Theology Vol. 1*. New York: Harper & Row, 1962, 1965.

Rahner Karl and Herber Vorgrimler. *Dictionary of Theology*, 2nd ed. New York: Crossroad, 1981Rasmussen, Larry L. *Earth Community, Earth Ethics*. Maryknoll, NY: Orbis Books, 1996.

Reid, W.S. "Work" in *Evangelical Dictionary of Theology*, ed. Walter E. Elwell. Grand Rapids: Baker Books, 1984.

Reimer, David J. "Sdq" in *New International Dictionary of the Old Testament Theology and Exegesis*, ed. Willem A. VanGemeren, vol.3. Grand Rapids, Michigan: Zondervan, 1997.

Ridderbos, H. "When the Time Had Fully Come" *Studies in New Testament Theology*. Grand Rapids: Wm. B. Eerdmans, 1957.

Ridderbos, Herman. *Paul: An Outline of His Theology* trans. J.R. DeWitt. Grand Rapids: Wm. B. Eerdmans, 1975.

Rushdoony, Rousas John. *The Institutes of Biblical Law*. USA: The Presbyterian and Reformed Publishing Company, 1973.

Sandel, Michael J. *Justice*. New York; Farrar, Straus and Giroux, 2009.

Schluter, Michael. "Welfare," in *Jubilee Manifesto: A framework, agenda, & strategy for christian social reform.* Ed. Michael Schluter & John Ashcroft. Leicester: InterVarsity Press, 2005.

Schreiter, Robert J. *Reconciliation: Mission and Ministry in a Changing Social Order*. Maryknoll, N.Y.: Orbis Books, 1992.

Schrenk, "Righteousness" vol. II *TDNT* ed. Gerhard Kittel.

Schubert, Paul. "Paul and the NT Ethic in the Thought of John Knox," *Christian History and Interpretation*, eds. W.R. Farmer et al. Cambridge: CUP, 1967.

Seitz, Lane R. "Stewardship: Managing God's resources for the Growth of the Kingdom." Unpublished Doctor of Ministry Dissertation. Pasadena: Fuller Theological Seminary, 1991.

Sempebwa, Joshua W. *African Traditional Moral Norms and Their Implication for Christianity* St. Augustine: Stelyter Verlag, 1983.

Sider, Ronald J. *Rich Christians in an Age of Hunger*. Dallas, TX: Word Publishing 1990.

Sindima, Harvey. "Community of Life: Ecological Theology in African Perspective," in *Liberating Life: Contemporary Approaches to Ecological*

Theology, eds. Charles Birch, William Eaken, and Jay B. McDaniel. Maryknoll: Orbis Books, 1990.

Singer, Peter. Ed. *A Companion to Ethics*. Oxford: Blackwell Publishers, 1993.

Smith, Edwin W. *African Beliefs and Christian Faith*. London: Lutherworth Press, 1936.

Smith, John E. "Autonomy of Ethics" in *A New Dictionary of Christian Ethics*, eds. J. Macquarrie and James Childress. London: S C M Press, 1967.

Tannehill, R. C. *Dying and Rising with Christ*. Berlin: Verlag Alfred Topelmann, 1967.

Taylor, Justin. *Working out a Theology of God*, Boundless.org, 2008.

Taylor, Paul. Ed. *Problems of Moral Philosophy*, 2nd ed. Belmont, CA: Dickenson, 1972.

Tienou, Tite. "The Samaritans: A biblical theological mirror for understanding racial, ethnic, and religious identity?" in *This side of heaven: race, ethnicity, and Christian faith*. Eds. Robert J. Priest and Alvaro L. Nieves. New York: Oxford University Press, 2009.

Thielicke, Helmut. *Theological Ethic: Foundations* Vol. 1. Grand Rapids: Wm. B. Eerdmans, 1979.

Thiroux, Jacques P. *Ethics: Theories and Practice*. Encino, CA: Glencoe Publishing Co. Inc., 1977.

Tonkin, Elizabeth et al, "History of Ethnicity" in Hutchison and Smith eds. *Ethnicity*. Oxford: oxford University Press, 1996.

Turiel, Elliot. *The Culture of Morality: Social Development, Context, and Conflict*. Cambridge: Cambridge University Press, 2002.

Volf, Miroslav. *Exclusion and Embrace: A Theological Exploration of Identity and Otherness, and Reconciliation*. Nashville: Abingdon Press, 1996.

Volf, Miroslav. "Materiality of Salvation: An Investigation in the Soteriologies of Liberation and Pentecostal Theologies," in *Journal of Ecumenical Studies* 26 (Summer 1989), 447–467.

Vos, Geerhadus. "The Eschatological Aspect of the Pauline Conception of the Spirit," *Biblical and Theological Studies*. New York: Charles Scribner's Sons, 1912.

Weinfeld, Moshe. *Social Justice in Ancient Israel and in the Ancient Near East*. Jerusalem: The MagnesPress, the Hebrew University, 1994.

Weiss, Paul. *Man's Freedom*. New Haven: Yale University Press, 1950.

Welch, D. Don. Ed. *Law and Morality*. Philadelphia: Fortress Press, 1987.

Wells, Harold. "Theology for Reconciliation: Biblical Perspective on Forgiveness and Grace" in Gregory Baum and Harold Wells. Eds. *The Reconciliation of Peoples: Challenge to the Churches*. Maryknoll, New York: Orbis Books, 1997.

Williams, Ritva H. *Stewards, Prophets, Keepers of the Word in the Early Church*. Peabody: MA, Hendrickson Publishers, 2006.

Williamson, B.G. *Akan Religion and the Christian Faith*. Accra: Ghana Universities Press, 1955.

Winter, D. "Motivation in Christian Behavior" in *Law, Morality and the Bible: A Symposium*, Eds. Bruce Kaye and Gordon Wenham. Leicester: InterVarsity Press, 1978.

Wiredu, Kwesi. *Philosophy and an African Culture*. Cambridge: Cambridge University Press, 1980.

Wright, Christopher J.H. *An Eye for An Eye: The Place of Old Testament Ethics for Today*. Downers Grove, IL: InterVarsity Press, 1983.

Wright, Christopher J. H. *Old Testament Ethics for the People of God*. Downers Grove, IL: InterVarsity Press, 2004.

Wrong, Michela "The Emperor Mobutu," *Transition*, No. 81/82 (2000), 92–112.

Zeisler, J. A. "The Meaning of Righteousness in Paul: A Linguistic and Theological Enquiry" (*SNTSMS* 20:1972), 23–32.

Ziesler, J. A. *The Meaning of Righteousness in Paul: A Linguistic and Theological Enquiry*. Cambridge: Cambridge University Press, 1972.

www.ingramcontent.com/pod-product-compliance
Lightning Source LLC
Chambersburg PA
CBHW052010290426
44112CB00014B/2192